THE COLLECTED PLAYS
OF W. B. YEATS

W. B. YEATS

The

COLLECTED PLAYS

of

W. B. YEATS

NEW EDITION

With Five Additional Plays

THE MACMILLAN COMPANY

New York

PREFACE

1934

THE plays in this book are intended for hearers and for readers; all have been played at the Abbey Theatre, Dublin, except *Calvary*, which has not yet been played anywhere. The dates in the list of Contents, and under the title of each play, refer to the year of their publication. Those who think of producing any particular play should seek for it in *Plays and Controversies, Plays*, and *Wheels and Butterflies*. The Note on *The Countess Cathleen*, for instance, in *Plays and Controversies* contains a simplified version of the last scene, and when I have known of appropriate music for some play I have given it in Note or Appendix. The version of *The Hour-Glass* in the present book has been but once played at the Abbey Theatre and once elsewhere, whereas the prose version in *Plays* has been played a great many times; speakers of verse are rare. I do not include in the present book *Fighting the Waves,* a prose version of *The Only Jealousy of Emer* so arranged as to admit of many dancers and to be immediately intelligible to an average theatrical audience; it can be found in *Wheels and Butterflies*. In *Plays* and *Plays and Controversies* I have explained my indebtedness to Lady Gregory. If I could have persuaded her, she would have signed *The Unicorn from the Stars,* her share in it is so great. She had generally some part wherever there is dialect, and often where there is not.

W. B. Y.

CONTENTS

THE COUNTESS CATHLEEN

1892

'The sorrowful are dumb for thee'

Lament of Morian Shehone
for Miss Mary Bourke

TO
MAUD GONNE

THE COUNTESS CATHLEEN

PERSONS IN THE PLAY

Shemus Rua, *a Peasant* Aleel, *a Poet*
Mary, *his wife* The Countess Cathleen
Teigue, *his son* Oona, *her foster-mother*
Two Demons disguised as Merchants
Peasants, Servants, Angelical Beings

The Scene is laid in Ireland and in old times

SCENE I

*A room with lighted fire, and a door into the open air, through which
one sees, perhaps, the trees of a wood, and these trees should be painted
in flat colour upon a gold or diapered sky. The walls are of one colour.
The scene should have the effect of missal painting. Mary, a woman of
forty years or so, is grinding a quern.*

Mary. What can have made the grey hen flutter so?
    [*Teigue, a boy of fourteen, is coming in with turf, which he lays
        beside the hearth.*
Teigue. They say that now the land is famine-struck
  The graves are walking.
Mary.   What can the hen have heard?
Teigue. And that is not the worst; at Tubber-vanach
  A woman met a man with ears spread out,
  And they moved up and down like a bat's wing.
Mary. What can have kept your father all this while?
Teigue. Two nights ago, at Carrick-orus churchyard,
  A herdsman met a man who had no mouth,
  Nor eyes, nor ears; his face a wall of flesh;
  He saw him plainly by the light of the moon.
Mary. Look out, and tell me if your father's coming.
                                [*Teigue goes to door*.

Teigue. Mother!
Mary.   What is it?

Teigue.   In the bush beyond,
 There are two birds—if you can call them birds—
 I could not see them rightly for the leaves—
 But they've the shape and colour of horned owls,
 And I'm half certain they've a human face.
Mary. Mother of God, defend us!
Teigue.   They're looking at me.
 What is the good of praying? father says.
 God and the Mother of God have dropped asleep.
 What do they care, he says, though the whole land
 Squeal like a rabbit under a weasel's tooth?
Mary. You'll bring misfortune with your blasphemies
 Upon your father, or yourself, or me.
 Would God that he were home—ah, there he is.

            [Shemus comes in.

 What was it kept you in the wood? You know
 I cannot get all sorts of accidents
 Out of my mind till you are home again.
Shemus. I'm in no mood to listen to your clatter.
 Although I tramped the woods for half a day,
 I've taken nothing, for the very rats,
 Badgers, and hedgehogs seem to have died of drought,
 And there was scarce a wind in the parched leaves.
Teigue. Then you have brought no dinner.
Shemus.   After that
 I sat among the beggars at the cross-roads,
 And held a hollow hand among the others.
Mary. What, did you beg?
Shemus.   I had no chance to beg,
 For when the beggars saw me they cried out
 They would not have another share their alms,
 And hunted me away with sticks and stones.
Teigue. You said that you would bring us food or money.
Shemus. What's in the house?
Teigue.   A bit of mouldy bread.
Mary. There's flour enough to make another loaf.
Teigue. And when that's gone?
Mary.   There is the hen in the coop.
Shemus. My curse upon the beggars, my curse upon them!
Teigue. And the last penny gone.
Shemus.   When the hen's gone,
 What can we do but live on sorrel and dock,
 And dandelion, till our mouths are green?

Mary. God, that to this hour has found bit and sup,
  Will cater for us still.
Shemus.   His kitchen's bare.
  There were five doors that I looked through this day
  And saw the dead and not a soul to wake them.
Mary. Maybe He'd have us die because He knows,
  When the ear is stopped and when the eye is stopped,
  That every wicked sight is hid from the eye,
  And all fool talk from the ear!   [*A stringed instrument without.*
Shemus.   Who's passing there?
  And mocking us with music?
Teigue.   A young man plays it.
  There's an old woman and a lady with him.
Shemus. What is the trouble of the poor to her?
  Nothing at all or a harsh radishy sauce
  For the day's meat.
Mary.   God's pity on the rich!
  Had we been through as many doors, and seen
  The dishes standing on the polished wood
  In the wax candle light, we'd be as hard,
  And there's the needle's eye at the end of all.
Shemus. My curse upon the rich!
Teigue.   They're coming here.
Shemus. Then down upon that stool, down quick, I say,
  And call up a whey face and a whining voice,
  And let your head be bowed upon your knees.
Mary. Had I but time to put the place to rights!
            Cathleen, Oona, and Aleel enter
Cathleen. God save all here. There is a certain house,
  An old grey castle with a kitchen garden,
  A cider orchard and plot for flowers,
  Somewhere among these woods.
Mary.   We know it, lady.
  A place that's set among impassable walls
  As though world's trouble could not find it out.
Cathleen. It may be that we are that trouble, for we—
  Although we've wandered in the wood this hour—
  Have lost it too, yet I should know my way,
  For I lived all my childhood in that house.
Mary. Then you are Countess Cathleen?
Cathleen.   And this woman,
  Oona, my nurse, should have remembered it,
  For we were happy for a long time there.

Oona. The paths are overgrown with thickets now,
Or else some change has come upon my sight.
Cathleen. And this young man, that should have known the woods—
Because we met him on their border but now,
Wandering and singing like a wave of the sea—
Is so wrapped up in dreams of terrors to come
That he can give no help.
Mary.   You have still some way,
But I can put you on the trodden path
Your servants take when they are marketing.
But first sit down and rest yourself awhile,
For my old fathers served your fathers, lady,
Longer than books can tell—and it were strange
If you and yours should not be welcome here.
Cathleen. And it were stranger still were I ungrateful
For such kind welcome—but I must be gone,
For the night's gathering in.
Shemus.   It is a long while
Since I've set eyes on bread or on what buys it.
Cathleen. So you are starving even in this wood,
Where I had thought I would find nothing changed.
But that's a dream, for the old worm o' the world
Can eat its way into what place it pleases.   [*She gives money.*
Teigue. Beautiful lady, give me something too;
I fell but now, being weak with hunger and thirst,
And lay upon the threshold like a log.
Cathleen. I gave for all and that was all I had.
But look, my purse is empty. I have passed
But starving men and women all this day,
And they have had the rest; but take the purse,
The silver clasps on't may be worth a trifle.
And if you'll come to-morrow to my house
You shall have twice the sum.   [*Aleel begins to play.*
Shemus [*muttering*].   What, music, music!
Cathleen. Ah, do not blame the finger on the string;
The doctors bid me fly the unlucky times
And find distraction for my thoughts, or else
Pine to my grave.
Shemus.   I have said nothing, lady.
Why should the like of us complain?
Oona.   Have done.
Sorrows that she's but read of in a book
Weigh on her mind as if they had been her own.

*[Oona, Mary, and Cathleen go out. Aleel looks defiantly at
Shemus.*

Aleel [*singing*]. Were I but crazy for love's sake
    I know who'd measure out his length,
    I know the heads that I should break,
    For crazy men have double strength.
    I know—all's out to leave or take,
    Who mocks at music mocks at love;
    Were I but crazy for love's sake,
    No need to pick and choose.

               [Snapping his fingers in Shemus' face.
               Enough!
    I know the heads that I should break.

      [He takes a step towards the door and then turns again.
Shut to the door before the night has fallen,
For who can say what walks, or in what shape
Some devilish creature flies in the air; but now
Two grey horned owls hooted above our heads.

    *[He goes out, his singing dies away. Mary comes in. Shemus has
    been counting the money.*

Shemus. So that fool's gone.
Teigue.   He's seen the horned owls too.
    There's no good luck in owls, but it may be
    That the ill luck's to fall upon his head.
Mary. You never thanked her ladyship.
Shemus.   Thank her
    For seven halfpence and a silver bit?
Teigue. But for this empty purse?
Shemus.   What's that for thanks,
    Or what's the double of it that she promised,
    With bread and flesh and every sort of food
    Up to a price no man has heard the like of
    And rising every day?
Mary.   We have all she had;
    She emptied out the purse before our eyes.
Shemus [*to Mary, who has gone to close the door*]. Leave that door
    open.
Mary.   When those that have read books,
    And seen the seven wonders of the world,
    Fear what's above or what's below the ground,
    It's time that poverty should bolt the door.
Shemus. I'll have no bolts, for there is not a thing
    That walks above the ground or under it

I had not rather welcome to this house
Than any more of mankind, rich or poor.
Teigue. So that they brought us money.
Shemus.   I heard say
There's something that appears like a white bird,
A pigeon or a seagull or the like,
But if you hit it with a stone or a stick
It clangs as though it had been made of brass,
And that if you dig down where it was scratching
You'll find a crock of gold.
Teigue.   But dream of gold
For three nights running, and there's always gold.
Shemus. You might be starved before you've dug it out.
Teigue. But maybe if you called, something would come.
They have been seen of late.
Mary.   Is it call devils?
Call devils from the wood, call them in here?
Shemus. So you'd stand up against me, and you'd say
Who or what I am to welcome here.   [*He hits her.*
That is to show who's master.
Teigue.   Call them in.
Mary. God help us all!
Shemus.   Pray, if you have a mind to.
It's little that the sleepy ears above
Care for your words; but I'll call what I please.
Teigue. There is many a one, they say, had money from them.
Shemus [*at door*]. Whatever you are that walk the woods at night,
So be it that you have not shouldered up
Out of a grave—for I'll have nothing human—
And have free hands, a friendly trick of speech,
I welcome you. Come, sit beside the fire.
What matter if your head's below your arms
Or you've a horse's tail to whip your flank,
Feathers instead of hair, that's all but nothing.
Come, share what bread and meat is in the house,
And stretch your heels and warm them in the ashes.
And after that, let's share and share alike
And curse all men and women. Come in, come in.
What, is there no one there?   [*Turning from door.*
                     And yet they say
They are as common as the grass, and ride
Even upon the book in the priest's hand.
    [*Teigue lifts one arm slowly and points towards the door and*

*begins moving backward. Shemus turns, he also sees something
and begins moving backward. Mary does the same. A man
dressed as an Eastern merchant comes in carrying a small carpet.
He unrolls it and sits crosslegged at one end of it. Another man
dressed in the same way follows, and sits at the other end. This
is done slowly and deliberately. When they are seated they take
money out of embroidered purses at their girdles and begin arranging it on the carpet.*

Teigue. You speak to them.

Shemus.   No, you.

Teigue.   'Twas you that called them.

Shemus [*coming nearer*]. I'd make so bold, if you would pardon it,
  To ask if there's a thing you'd have of us.
  Although we are but poor people, if there is,
  Why, if there is——

First Merchant.   We've travelled a long road,
  For we are merchants that must tramp the world,
  And now we look for supper and a fire
  And a safe corner to count money in.

Shemus. I thought you were . . . but that's no matter now—
  There had been words between my wife and me
  Because I said I would be master here,
  And ask in what I pleased or who I pleased,
  And so . . . but that is nothing to the point,
  Because it's certain that you are but merchants.

First Merchant. We travel for the Master of all merchants.

Shemus. Yet if you were that I had thought but now
  I'd welcome you no less. Be what you please
  And you'll have supper at the market rate.
  That means that what was sold for but a penny
  Is now worth fifty.

First Merchant [*arranging money*]. Our Master bids us pay
  So good a price that all who deal with us
    Shall eat, drink, and be merry.

Shemus [*to Mary*].   Bestir yourself,
  Go kill and draw the fowl, while Teigue and I
  Lay out the plates and make a better fire.

Mary. I will not cook for you.

Shemus.   Not cook! not cook!
  Do not be angry. She wants to pay me back
  Because I struck her in that argument.
  But she'll get sense again. Since the dearth came

We rattle one on another as though we were
Knives thrown into a basket to be cleaned.

Mary. I will not cook for you, because I know
In what unlucky shape you sat but now
Outside this door.

Teigue.　　　　　　It's this, your honours:
Because of some wild words my father said
She thinks you are not of those who cast a shadow.

Shemus. I said I'd make the devils of the wood
Welcome, if they'd a mind to eat and drink;
But it is certain that you are men like us.

First Merchant. It's strange that she should think we cast no shadow,
For there is nothing on the ridge of the world
That's more substantial than the merchants are
That buy and sell you.

Mary.　　　　　　If you are not demons,
And seeing what great wealth is spread out there,
Give food or money to the starving poor.

First Merchant. If we knew how to find deserving poor
We'd do our share.

Mary.　　　　　　But seek them patiently.

First Merchant. We know the evils of mere charity.

Mary. Those scruples may befit a common time.
I had thought there was a pushing to and fro,
At times like this, that overset the scale
And trampled measure down.

First Merchant.　　　　　　But if already
We'd thought of a more prudent way than that?

Second Merchant. If each one brings a bit of merchandise,
We'll give him such a price he never dreamt of.

Mary. Where shall the starving come at merchandise?

First Merchant. We will ask nothing but what all men have.

Mary. Their swine and cattle, fields and implements
Are sold and gone.

First Merchant.　　　　　　They have not sold all yet.
For there's a vaporous thing—that may be nothing,
But that's the buyer's risk—a second self,
They call immortal for a story's sake.

Shemus. They come to buy our souls?

Teigue.　　　　　　I'll barter mine.
Why should we starve for what may be but nothing?

Mary. Teigue and Shemus——

Shemus.   What can it be but nothing?
  What has God poured out of His bag but famine?
  Satan gives money.
Teigue.   Yet no thunder stirs.
First Merchant. There is a heap for each.
                              [*Shemus goes to take money.*
                                      But, no, not yet,
  For there's a work I have to set you to.
Shemus. So, then, you're as deceitful as the rest,
  And all that talk of buying what's but a vapour
  Is fancy bread. I might have known as much,
  Because that's how the trick-o'-the-loop man talks.
First Merchant. That's for the work, each has its separate price;
  But neither price is paid till the work's done.
Teigue. The same for me.
Mary.   O God, why are You still?
First Merchant. You've but to cry aloud at every crossroad,
  At every house door, that we buy men's souls
  And give so good a price that all may live
  In mirth and comfort till the famine's done,
  Because we are Christian men.
Shemus.   Come, let's away.
Teigue. I shall keep running till I've earned the price.
Second Merchant [*who has risen and gone towards fire*]. Stop; you
      must have proof behind the words,
  So here's your entertainment on the road.
                    [*He throws a bag of money on the ground.*
  Live as you please; our Master's generous.
      [*Teigue and Shemus have stopped. Teigue takes the money.*
      They go out.
Mary. Destroyers of souls, God will destroy you quickly.
  You shall at last dry like dry leaves and hang
  Nailed like dead vermin to the doors of God.
Second Merchant. Curse to your fill, for saints will have their dreams.
First Merchant. Though we're but vermin that our Master sent
  To overrun the world, he at the end
  Shall pull apart the pale ribs of the moon
  And quench the stars in the ancestral night.
Mary. God is all-powerful.
Second Merchant.   Pray, you shall need Him.
  You shall eat dock and grass, and dandelion,
  Till that low threshold there becomes a wall,
  And when your hands can scarcely drag your body

We shall be near you.   [*Mary faints.*
   [*The First Merchant takes up the carpet, spreads it before the fire
     and stands in front of it warming his hands.*
First Merchant.   Our faces go unscratched.
  Wring the neck o' that fowl, scatter the flour,
  And look if there is bread upon the shelves.
  We'll turn the fowl upon the spit and roast it,
  And eat the supper we were bidden to,
  Now that the house is quiet, praise our Master,
  And stretch and warm our heels among the ashes.

SCENE II

FRONT SCENE.—*A wood with perhaps distant view of turreted house at
one side, but all in flat colour, without light and shade and against a
diapered or gold background.*

     *Countess Cathleen comes in leaning upon Aleel's arm.
           Oona follows them.*

Cathleen [*stopping*]. Surely this leafy corner, where one smells
  The wild bee's honey, has a story too?
Oona. There is the house at last.
Aleel.   A man, they say,
  Loved Maeve the Queen of all the invisible host,
  And died of his love nine centuries ago.
  And now, when the moon's riding at the full,
  She leaves her dancers lonely and lies there
  Upon that level place, and for three days
  Stretches and sighs and wets her long pale cheeks.
Cathleen. So she loves truly.
Aleel.   No, but wets her cheeks,
  Lady, because she has forgot his name.
Cathleen. She'd sleep that trouble away—though it must be
  A heavy trouble to forget his name—
  If she had better sense.
Oona.   Your own house, lady.
Aleel. She sleeps high up on wintry Knocknarea
  In an old cairn of stones; while her poor women
  Must lie and jog in the wave if they would sleep—

Being water-born—yet if she cry their names
They run up on the land and dance in the moon
Till they are giddy and would love as men do,
And be as patient and as pitiful.
But there is nothing that will stop in their heads,
They've such poor memories, though they weep for it.
O yes, they weep; that's when the moon is full.

Cathleen. Is it because they have short memories
They live so long?

Aleel.   What's memory but the ash
That chokes our fires that have begun to sink?
And they've a dizzy, everlasting fire.

Oona. There is your own house, lady.

Cathleen.   Why, that's true,
And we'd have passed it without noticing.

Aleel. A curse upon it for a meddlesome house!
Had it but stayed away I would have known
What Queen Maeve thinks on when the moon is pinched;
And whether now—as in the old days—the dancers
Set their brief love on men.

Oona.   Rest on my arm.
These are no thoughts for any Christian ear.

Aleel. I am younger, she would be too heavy for you.

[*He begins taking his lute out of the bag. Cathleen, who has turned
   towards Oona, turns back to him.*

This hollow box remembers every foot
That danced upon the level grass of the world,
And will tell secrets if I whisper to it.

[*Sings*]

Lift up the white knee;
Hear what they sing,
Those young dancers
That in a ring
Raved but now
Of the hearts that broke
Long, long ago
For their sake.

Oona. New friends are sweet.

Aleel.   But the dance changes,
Lift up the gown,
All that sorrow
Is trodden down.

Oona. The empty rattle-pate! Lean on this arm,

That I can tell you is a christened arm,
And not like some, if we are to judge by speech.
But as you please. It is time I was forgot.
Maybe it is not on this arm you slumbered
When you were as helpless as a worm.

Aleel. Stay with me till we come to your own house.

Cathleen [*sitting down*]. When I am rested I will need no help.

Aleel. I thought to have kept her from remembering
The evil of the times for full ten minutes;
But now when seven are out you come between.

Oona. Talk on; what does it matter what you say,
For you have not been christened?

Aleel.   Old woman, old woman,
You robbed her of three minutes' peace of mind,
And though you live unto a hundred years,
And wash the feet of beggars and give alms,
And climb Cro-Patrick, you shall not be pardoned.

Oona. How does a man who never was baptized
Know what Heaven pardons?

Aleel.   You are a sinful woman.

Oona. I care no more than if a pig had grunted.

Enter Cathleen's steward

Steward. I am not to blame, for I had locked the gate.
The forester's to blame. The men climbed in
At the east corner where the elm-tree is.

Cathleen. I do not understand you. Who has climbed?

Steward. Then God be thanked, I am the first to tell you.
I was afraid some other of the servants—
Though I've been on the watch—had been the first,
And mixed up truth and lies, your ladyship.

Cathleen [*rising*]. Has some misfortune happened?

Steward.   Yes, indeed.
The forester that let the branches lie
Against the wall's to blame for everything,
For that is how the rogues got into the garden.

Cathleen. I thought to have escaped misfortune here.
Has any one been killed?

Steward.   O no, not killed.
They have stolen half a cart-load of green cabbage.

Cathleen. But maybe they were starving.

Steward.   That is certain.
To rob or starve, that was the choice they had.

Cathleen. A learned theologian has laid down

That starving men may take what's necessary,
And yet be sinless.
Oona.   Sinless and a thief!
There should be broken bottles on the wall.
Cathleen. And if it be a sin, while faith's unbroken
God cannot help but pardon. There is no soul
But it's unlike all others in the world,
Nor one but lifts a strangeness to God's love
Till that's grown infinite, and therefore none
Whose loss were less than irremediable
Although it were the wickedest in the world.

Enter Teigue and Shemus

Steward. What are you running for? Pull off your cap.
Do you not see who's there?
Shemus.   I cannot wait.
I am running to the world with the best news
That has been brought it for a thousand years.
Steward. Then get your breath and speak.
Shemus.   If you'd my news
You'd run as fast and be as out of breath.
Teigue. Such news, we shall be carried on men's shoulders.
Shemus. There's something every man has carried with him
And thought no more about than if it were
A mouthful of the wind; and now it's grown
A marketable thing!
Teigue.   And yet it seemed
As useless as the paring of one's nails.
Shemus. What sets me laughing when I think of it,
Is that a rogue who's lain in lousy straw,
If he but sell it, may set up his coach.
Teigue [*laughing*]. There are two gentlemen who buy men's souls.
Cathleen. O God!
Teigue.   And maybe there's no soul at all.
Steward. They're drunk or mad.
Teigue.   Look at the price they give. [*Showing money.*
Shemus [*tossing up money*]. 'Go cry it all about the world', they said.
  ' "Money for souls, good money for a soul." '
Cathleen. Give twice and thrice and twenty times their money,
And get your souls again. I will pay all.
Shemus. Not we! not we! For souls—if there are souls—
But keep the flesh out of its merriment.
I shall be drunk and merry.

Teigue.   Come, let's away.   [*He goes.*
Cathleen. But there's a world to come.
Shemus.   And if there is,
　I'd rather trust myself into the hands
　That can pay money down than to the hands
　That have but shaken famine from the bag. [*He goes out* R. *lilting.*
　'There's money for a soul, sweet yellow money.
　There's money for men's souls, good money, money.'
Cathleen [*to Aleel*]. Go call them here again, bring them by force,
　Beseech them, bribe, do anything you like;   [*Aleel goes.*
　And you too follow, add your prayers to his.
                              [*Oona, who has been praying, goes out.*
　Steward, you know the secrets of my house.
　How much have I?
Steward.   A hundred kegs of gold.
Cathleen. How much have I in castles?
Steward.   As much more.
Cathleen. How much have I in pasture?
Steward.   As much more.
Cathleen. How much have I in forests?
Steward.   As much more.
Cathleen. Keeping this house alone, sell all I have,
　Go barter where you please, but come again
　With herds of cattle and with ships of meal.
Steward. God's blessing light upon your ladyship.
　You will have saved the land.
Cathleen.   Make no delay.   [*He goes* L.
                    Aleel and Oona return
Cathleen. They have not come; speak quickly.
Aleel.   One drew his knife
　And said that he would kill the man or woman
　That stopped his way; and when I would have stopped him
　He made this stroke at me; but it is nothing.
Cathleen. You shall be tended. From this day for ever
　I'll have no joy or sorrow of my own.
Oona. Their eyes shone like the eyes of birds of prey.
Cathleen. Come, follow me, for the earth burns my feet
　Till I have changed my house to such a refuge
　That the old and ailing, and all weak of heart,
　May escape from beak and claw; all, all, shall come
　Till the walls burst and the roof fall on us.
　From this day out I have nothing of my own.   [*She goes.*

Oona [*taking Aleel by the arm and as she speaks bandaging his wound*]
　She has found something now to put her hand to,
　And you and I are of no more account
　Than flies upon a window-pane in the winter.   [*They go out.*

SCENE III

Hall in the house of Countess Cathleen. At the left an oratory with steps leading up to it. At the right a tapestried wall, more or less repeating the form of the oratory, and a great chair with its back against the wall. In the centre are two or more arches through which one can see dimly the trees of the garden. Cathleen is kneeling in front of the altar in the oratory; there is a hanging lighted lamp over the altar. Aleel enters.

Aleel. I have come to bid you leave this castle and fly
　Out of these woods.
　　　　　　[*Cathleen rises from the altar and comes into the hall.*
Cathleen.　　　　　　What evil is there here
　That is not everywhere from this to the sea?
Aleel. They who have sent me walk invisible.
Cathleen. So it is true what I have heard men say,
　That you have seen and heard what others cannot.
Aleel. I was asleep in my bed, and while I slept
　My dream became a fire; and in the fire
　One walked and he had birds about his head.
Cathleen. I have heard that one of the old gods walked so.
Aleel. It may be that he is angelical;
　And, lady, he bids me call you from these woods.
　And you must bring but your old foster-mother,
　And some few serving-men, and live in the hills,
　Among the sounds of music and the light
　Of waters, till the evil days are done.
　For here some terrible death is waiting you,
　Some unimagined evil, some great darkness
　That fable has not dreamt of, nor sun nor moon
　Scattered.
Cathleen.　　No, not angelical.
Aleel.　　　　　　　　　This house
　You are to leave with some old trusty man,
　And bid him shelter all that starve or wander
　While there is food and house-room.

Cathleen. He bids me go
Where none of mortal creatures but the swan
Dabbles, and there you would pluck the harp, when the trees
Had made a heavy shadow about our door,
And talk among the rustling of the reeds,
When night hunted the foolish sun away
With stillness and pale tapers. No—no—no!
I cannot. Although I weep, I do not weep
Because that life would be most happy, and here
I find no way, no end. Nor do I weep
Because I had longed to look upon your face,
But that a night of prayer has made me weary.
Aleel [*prostrating himself before her*]. Let Him that made mankind,
the angels and devils
And dearth and plenty, mend what He has made,
For when we labour in vain and eye still sees,
Heart breaks in vain.
Cathleen. How would that quiet end?
Aleel. How but in healing?
Cathleen. You have seen my tears,
And I can see your hand shake on the floor.
Aleel [*faltering*]. I thought but of healing. He was angelical.
Cathleen [*turning away from him*]. No, not angelical, but of the old
gods,
Who wander about the world to waken the heart—
The passionate, proud heart—that all the angels,
Leaving nine heavens empty, would rock to sleep.
   [*She goes to the oratory door; Aleel holds his clasped hands to-
   wards her for a moment hesitatingly, and then lets them fall
   beside him.*
Cathleen. Do not hold out to me beseeching hands.
This heart shall never waken on earth. I have sworn,
By her whose heart the seven sorrows have pierced,
To pray before this altar until my heart
Has grown to Heaven like a tree, and there
Rustled its leaves, till Heaven has saved my people.
Aleel [*who has risen*]. When one so great has spoken of love to one
So little as I, though to deny him love,
What can he but hold out beseeching hands,
Then let them fall beside him, knowing how greatly
They have overdared?
   [*He goes towards the door of the hall. The Countess Cathleen
   takes a few steps towards him.*

Cathleen.   If the old tales are true,
   Queens have wed shepherds and kings beggar-maids;
   God's procreant waters flowing about your mind
   Have made you more than kings or queens; and not you
   But I am the empty pitcher.
Aleel.   Being silent,
   I have said all, yet let me stay beside you.
Cathleen. No, no, not while my heart is shaken. No,
   But you shall hear wind cry and water cry,
   And curlew cry, and have the peace I longed for.
Aleel. Give me your hand to kiss.
Cathleen.   I kiss your forehead.
   And yet I send you from me. Do not speak;
   There have been women that bid men to rob
   Crowns from the Country-under-Wave or apples
   Upon a dragon-guarded hill, and all
   That they might sift the hearts and wills of men,
   And trembled as they bid it, as I tremble
   That lay a hard task on you, that you go,
   And silently, and do not turn your head.
   Good-bye; but do not turn your head and look;   [*Aleel goes.*
   Above all else, I would not have you look.
   I never spoke to him of his wounded hand,
   And now he is gone. [*She looks out.*]
   I cannot see him, for all is dark outside.
   Would my imagination and my heart
   Were as little shaken as this holy flame!
     [*She goes slowly into the oratory. The distant sound of an alarm
      bell. The two Merchants enter hurriedly.*
Second Merchant. They are ringing the alarm, and in a moment
   They'll be upon us.
First Merchant [*going to a door at the side*]. Here is the Treasury.
   You'd my commands to put them all to sleep.
Second Merchant. Some angel or else her prayers protected them.
     [*Goes into the Treasury and returns with bags of treasure. First
      Merchant has been listening at the oratory door.*
First Merchant. She has fallen asleep.
     [*Second Merchant goes out through one of the arches at the back
      and stands listening. The bags are at his feet.*
Second Merchant.   We've all the treasure now,
   So let's away before they've tracked us out.
First Merchant. I have a plan to win her.
Second Merchant.   You have time enough

If you would kill her and bear off her soul
Before they are upon us with their prayers;
They search the Western Tower.
First Merchant.   That may not be.
We cannot face the heavenly host in arms.
Her soul must come to us of its own will;
But being of the ninth and mightiest Hell,
Where all are kings, I have a plan to win it.
Lady, we've news that's crying out for speech.
                    [*Cathleen wakes and comes to door of oratory.*
Cathleen. Who calls?
First Merchant.   Lady, we have brought news.
Cathleen.   What are you?
First Merchant. We are merchants, and we know the book of the world
Because we have walked upon its leaves; and there
Have read of late matters that much concern you;
And noticing the castle door stand open,
Come in to find an ear.
Cathleen.   The door stands open
That no one who is famished or afraid
Despair of help or of a welcome with it.
But you have news, you say.
First Merchant.   We saw a man
Heavy with sickness in the bog of Allen,
Whom you had bid buy cattle. Near Fair Head
We saw your grain ships lying all becalmed
In the dark night; and not less still than they,
Burned all their mirrored lanthorns in the sea.
Cathleen. Thanks be to God there's money in the house
That can buy grain from those who have stored it up
To prosper on the hunger of the poor.
But you've been far and know the signs of things,
When will this famine end?
First Merchant.   Day copies day,
And there's no sign of change, nor can it change,
With the wheat withered and the cattle dead.
Cathleen. And heard you of the demons who buy souls?
First Merchant. There are some men who hold they have wolves' heads,
And say their limbs—dried by the infinite flame—
Have all the speed of storms; others, again,
Say they are gross and little; while a few
Will have it they seem much as mortals are,
But tall and brown and travelled—like us, lady—

Yet all agree a power is in their looks
That makes men bow, and flings a casting-net
About their souls, and that all men would go
And barter those poor vapours, were it not
You bribe them with the safety of your gold.

Cathleen. Praise God that I am wealthy! Why do they sell?

First Merchant. As we came in at the great door we saw
Your porter sleeping in his niche—a soul
Too little to be worth a hundred pence,
And yet they buy it for a hundred crowns.
But for a soul like yours, I heard them say,
They would give five hundred thousand crowns and more.

Cathleen. How can a heap of crowns pay for a soul?
Is the green grave so terrible a thing?

First Merchant. Some sell because the money gleams, and some
Because they are in terror of the grave,
And some because their neighbours sold before,
And some because there is a kind of joy
In casting hope away, in losing joy,
In ceasing all resistance, in at last
Opening one's arms to the eternal flames,
In casting all sails out upon the wind;
To this—full of the gaiety of the lost—
Would all folk hurry if your gold were gone.

Cathleen. There is a something, Merchant, in your voice
That makes me fear. When you were telling how
A man may lose his soul and lose his God
Your eyes were lighted up, and when you told
How my poor money serves the people, both—
Merchants, forgive me—seemed to smile.

First Merchant.   I laugh
To think that all these people should be swung
As on a lady's shoe-string,—under them
The glowing leagues of never-ending flame.

Cathleen. There is a something in you that I fear;
A something not of us; were you not born
In some most distant corner of the world?

[*The Second Merchant, who has been listening at the door, comes
forward, and as he comes a sound of voices and feet is heard.*

Second Merchant. Away now—they are in the passage—hurry,
For they will know us, and freeze up our hearts
With Ave Marys, and burn all our skin
With holy water.

First Merchant.   Farewell; for we must ride
  Many a mile before the morning come;
  Our horses beat the ground impatiently.
                    [*They go out. A number of Peasants enter by other door.*
First Peasant. Forgive us, lady, but we heard a noise.
Second Peasant. We sat by the fireside telling vanities.
First Peasant. We heard a noise, but though we have searched the
    house
  We have found nobody.
Cathleen.   You are too timid,
  For now you are safe from all the evil times,
  There is no evil that can find you here.
Oona [*entering hurriedly*]. Ochone! The treasure-room is broken in.
  The door stands open, and the gold is gone.
                              [*Peasants raise a lamentable cry.*
Cathleen. Be silent. [*The cry ceases.*] Have you seen nobody?
Oona.   Ochone!
  That my good mistress should lose all this money!
Cathleen. Let those among you not too old to ride
  Get horses and search all the country round.
  I'll give a farm to him who finds the thieves.
      [*A man with keys at his girdle has come in while she speaks. There
      is a general murmur of 'The porter! the porter!'*
Porter. Demons were here. I sat beside the door
  In my stone niche, and two owls passed me by,
  Whispering with human voices.
Old Peasant.   God forsakes us.
Cathleen. Old man, old man, He never closed a door
  Unless one opened. I am desolate
  Because of a strange thought that's in my heart;
  But I have still my faith; therefore be silent;
  For surely He does not forsake the world,
  But stands before it modelling in the clay
  And moulding there His image. Age by age
  The clay wars with His fingers and pleads hard
  For its old, heavy, dull and shapeless ease;
  But sometimes—though His hand is on it still—
  It moves awry and demon hordes are born.
                              [*Peasants cross themselves.*
  Yet leave me now, for I am desolate.
  I hear a whisper from beyond the thunder.
                              [*She comes from the oratory door.*
  Yet stay an instant. When we meet again

I may have grown forgetful. Oona, take
These two—the larder and the dairy keys.
                    [*To the Porter.*]
But take you this. It opens the small room
Of herbs for medicine, every kind of herb.
The book of cures is on the upper shelf.
Porter. Why do you do this, lady; did you see
  Your coffin in a dream?
Cathleen.   Ah, no, not that.
  But I have come to a strange thought. I have heard
  A sound of wailing in unnumbered hovels,
  And I must go down, down—I know not where—
  Pray for all men and women mad from famine;
  Pray, you good neighbours.
    [*The Peasants all kneel. Countess Cathleen ascends the steps to
    the door of the oratory, and turning round stands there mo-
    tionless for a little, and then cries in a loud voice:*
                    Mary, Queen of angels,
And all you clouds on clouds of saints, farewell!

SCENE IV

FRONT SCENE.—*A wood near the Castle, as in Scene II.
A group of Peasants pass.*

First Peasant. I have seen silver and copper, but not gold.
Second Peasant. It's yellow and it shines.
First Peasant.   It's beautiful.
  The most beautiful thing under the sun,
  That's what I've heard.
Third Peasant.   I have seen gold enough.
Fourth Peasant. I would not say that it's so beautiful.
First Peasant. But doesn't a gold piece glitter like the sun?
  That's what my father, who'd seen better days,
  Told me when I was but a little boy—
  So high—so high, it's shining like the sun,
  Round and shining, that is what he said.
Second Peasant. There's nothing in the world it cannot buy.
First Peasant. They've bags and bags of it.
    [*They go out. The two Merchants follow silently. Then Aleel
    passes over the stage singing.*

Aleel.   Impetuous heart be still, be still,
    Your sorrowful love can never be told,
    Cover it up with a lonely tune.
    He who could bend all things to His Will
    Has covered the door of the infinite fold
    With the pale stars and the wandering moon.

SCENE V

*The house of Shemus Rua. There is an alcove at the back with curtains;
in it a bed, and on the bed is the body of Mary with candles round it.
The two Merchants while they speak put a large book upon a table,
arrange money, and so on.*

First Merchant. Thanks to that lie I told about her ships
    And that about the herdsman lying sick,
    We shall be too much thronged with souls to-morrow.
Second Merchant. What has she in her coffers now but mice?
First Merchant. When the night fell and I had shaped myself
    Into the image of the man-headed owl,
    I hurried to the cliffs of Donegal,
    And saw with all their canvas full of wind
    And rushing through the parti-coloured sea
    Those ships that bring the woman grain and meal.
    They're but three days from us.
Second Merchant.   When the dew rose
    I hurried in like feathers to the east,
    And saw nine hundred oxen driven through Meath
    With goads of iron. They're but three days from us.
First Mechant. Three days for traffic.
        [*Peasants crowd in with Teigue and Shemus.*
Shemus.   Come in, come in, you are welcome.
    That is my wife. She mocked at my great masters,
    And would not deal with them. Now there she is;
    She does not even know she was a fool,
    So great a fool she was.
Teigue.   She would not eat
    One crumb of bread bought with our masters' money,
    But lived on nettles, dock, and dandelion.
Shemus. There's nobody could put into her head
    That death is the worst thing can happen us,
    Though that sounds simple, for her tongue grew rank

With all the lies that she had heard in chapel.
Draw to the curtain. [*Teigue draws it.*] You'll not play the fool
While these good gentlemen are there to save you.
Second Merchant. Since the drought came they drift about in a throng,
Like autumn leaves blown by the dreary winds.
Come, deal—come, deal.
First Merchant.   Who will come deal with us?
Shemus. They are out of spirit, sir, with lack of food,
Save four or five. Here, sir, is one of these;
The others will gain courage in good time.
Middle-aged Man. I come to deal—if you give honest price.
First Merchant [*reading in a book*]. 'John Maher, a man of substance,
with dull mind,
And quiet senses and unventurous heart.
The angels think him safe.' Two hundred crowns,
All for a soul, a little breath of wind.
Middle-aged Man. I ask three hundred crowns. You have read there
That no mere lapse of days can make me yours.
First Merchant. There is something more writ here—'Often at night
He is wakeful from a dread of growing poor,
And thereon wonders if there's any man
That he could rob in safety.'
A Peasant.   Who'd have thought it?
And I was once alone with him at midnight.
Another Peasant. I will not trust my mother after this.
First Merchant. There is this crack in you—two hundred crowns.
A Peasant. That's plenty for a rogue.
Another Peasant.   I'd give him nothing.
Shemus. You'll get no more—so take what's offered you.

[*A general murmur, during which the Middle-aged Man takes*
money, and slips into background, where he sinks on to a seat.

First Merchant. Has no one got a better soul than that?
If only for the credit of your parishes,
Traffic with us.
A Woman.   What will you give for mine?
First Merchant [*reading in book*]. 'Soft, handsome, and still young'—
not much, I think.
'It's certain that the man she's married to
Knows nothing of what's hidden in the jar
Between the hour-glass and the pepper pot.'
The Woman. The scandalous book!
First Merchant.   'Nor how when he's away

At the horse-fair the hand that wrote what's hid
Will tap three times upon the window-pane.'
The Woman. And if there is a letter, that is no reason
Why I should have less money than the others.
First Merchant. You're almost safe. I give you fifty crowns.

[She turns to go.

A hundred, then.
Shemus.   Woman, have sense—come, come.
Is this a time to haggle at the price?
There, take it up. There, take it up. That's right.

[She takes them and goes into the crowd.

First Merchant. Come, deal, deal, deal. It is but for charity
We buy such souls at all; a thousand sins
Made them our Master's long before we came.

Aleel enters

Aleel. Here, take my soul, for I am tired of it.
I do not ask a price.
Shemus.   Not ask a price?
How can you sell your soul without a price?
I would not listen to his broken wits.
His love for Countess Cathleen has so crazed him
He hardly understands what he is saying.
Aleel. The trouble that has come on Countess Cathleen,
The sorrow that is in her wasted face,
The burden in her eyes, have broke my wits,
And yet I know I'd have you take my soul.
First Merchant. We cannot take your soul, for it is hers.
Aleel. No, but you must. Seeing it cannot help her
I have grown tired of it.
First Merchant.   Begone from me,
I may not touch it.
Aleel.   Is your power so small?
And must I bear it with me all my days?
May you be scorned and mocked!
First Merchant.   Drag him away.
He troubles me.   [*Teigue and Shemus lead Aleel into the crowd.*
Second Merchant.   His gaze has filled me, brother,
With shaking and a dreadful fear.
First Merchant.   Lean forward
And kiss the circlet where my Master's lips
Were pressed upon it when he sent us hither;
You shall have peace once more.

[*Second Merchant kisses the gold circlet that is about the head of
the First Merchant.*

                                            I, too, grow weary,
But there is something moving in my heart
Whereby I know that what we seek the most
Is drawing near—our labour will soon end.
Come, deal, deal, deal, deal, deal; are you all dumb?
What, will you keep me from our ancient home,
And from the eternal revelry?
Second Merchant.   Deal, deal.
Shemus. They say you beat the woman down too low.
First Merchant. I offer this great price: a thousand crowns
    For an old woman who was always ugly.
        [*An old Peasant Woman comes forward, and he takes up a book
        and reads:*
    There is but little set down here against her.
    'She has stolen eggs and fowl when times were bad,
    But when the times grew better has confessed it;
    She never missed her chapel of a Sunday
    And when she could, paid dues.' Take up your money.
Old Woman. God bless you, sir. [*She screams.*] O, sir, a pain went
        through me!
First Merchant. That name is like a fire to all damned souls.
        [*Murmur among the Peasants, who shrink back from her as she
        goes out.*
A Peasant. How she screamed out!
Second Peasant.   And maybe we shall scream so.
Third Peasant. I tell you there is no such place as Hell.
First Merchant. Can such a trifle turn you from your profit?
    Come, deal; come, deal.
Middle-aged Man.   Master, I am afraid.
First Merchant. I bought your soul, and there's no sense in fear
    Now the soul's gone.
Middle-aged Man.   Give me my soul again.
Woman [*going on her knees and clinging to Merchant*]. And take this
        money too, and give me mine.
Second Merchant. Bear bastards, drink or follow some wild fancy;
    For cryings out and sighs are the soul's work,
    And you have none.   [*Throws the Woman off.*
Peasant.   Come, let's away.
Another Peasant.   Yes, yes.
Another Peasant. Come quickly; if that woman had not screamed
    I would have lost my soul.

Another Peasant.   Come, come away.
  [*They turn to door, but are stopped by shouts of* 'Countess Cathleen! Countess Cathleen!'
Cathleen [*entering*]. And so you trade once more?
First Merchant.   In spite of you.
  What brings you here, saint with the sapphire eyes?
Cathleen. I come to barter a soul for a great price.
Second Merchant. What matter, if the soul be worth the price?
Cathleen. The people starve, therefore the people go
  Thronging to you. I hear a cry come from them
  And it is in my ears by night and day,
  And I would have five hundred thousand crowns
  That I may feed them till the dearth go by.
First Merchant. It may be the soul's worth it.
Cathleen.   There is more:
  The souls that you have bought must be set free.
First Merchant. We know of but one soul that's worth the price.
Cathleen. Being my own it seems a priceless thing.
Second Merchant. You offer us——
Cathleen.   I offer my own soul.
A Peasant. Do not, do not, for souls the like of ours
  Are not precious to God as your soul is.
  O, what would Heaven do without you, lady?
Another Peasant. Look how their claws clutch in their leathern gloves.
First Merchant. Five hundred thousand crowns; we give the price.
  The gold is here; the souls even while you speak
  Have slipped out of our bond, because your face
  Has shed a light on them and filled their hearts.
  But you must sign, for we omit no form
  In buying a soul like yours.
Second Merchant.   Sign with this quill.
  It was a feather growing on the cock
  That crowed when Peter dared deny his Master,
  And all who use it have great honour in Hell.
                    [*Cathleen leans forward to sign.*
Aleel [*rushing forward and snatching the pen from her*]. Leave all
    things to the Builder of the Heavens.
Cathleen. I have no thoughts; I hear a cry—a cry.
Aleel [*casting the pen on the ground*]. I have seen a vision under a
    green hedge,
  A hedge of hips and haws—men yet shall hear
  The archangels rolling Satan's empty skull
  Over the mountain-tops.

First Merchant.   Take him away.

[*Teigue and Shemus drag him roughly away so that he falls upon
    the floor among the Peasants. Cathleen picks up the parchment
    and signs, then turns towards the Peasants.*

Cathleen. Take up the money, and now come with me;
    When we are far from this polluted place
    I will give everybody money enough.

[*She goes out, the Peasants crowding round her and kissing her
    dress. Aleel and the two Merchants are left alone.*

Second Merchant. We must away and wait until she dies,
    Sitting above her tower as two grey owls,
    Waiting as many years as may be, guarding
    Our precious jewel; waiting to seize her soul.

First Merchant. We need but hover over her head in the air,
    For she has only minutes. When she signed
    Her heart began to break. Hush, hush, I hear
    The brazen door of Hell move on its hinges,
    And the eternal revelry float hither
    To hearten us.

Second Merchant. Leap feathered on the air
    And meet them with her soul caught in your claws.

[*They rush out. Aleel crawls into the middle of the room. The
    twilight has fallen and gradually darkens as the scene goes on.
    There is a distant muttering of thunder and a sound of rising
    storm.*

Aleel. The brazen door stands wide, and Balor comes
    Borne in his heavy car, and demons have lifted
    The age-weary eyelids from the eyes that of old
    Turned gods to stone; Barach, the traitor, comes
    And the lascivious race, Cailitin,
    That cast a Druid weakness and decay
    Over Sualtim's and old Dectora's child;
    And that great king Hell first took hold upon
    When he killed Naoise and broke Deirdre's heart:
    And all their heads are twisted to one side,
    For when they lived they warred on beauty and peace
    With obstinate, crafty, sidelong bitterness.

Oona enters

    Crouch down, old heron, out of the blind storm.

Oona. Where is the Countess Cathleen? All this day
    Her eyes were full of tears, and when for a moment
    Her hand was laid upon my hand it trembled,
    And now I do not know where she is gone.

Aleel. Cathleen has chosen other friends than us,
And they are rising through the hollow world.
Demons are out, old heron.

Oona. God guard her soul!

Aleel. She's bartered it away this very hour,
As though we two were never in the world.

[*He points downward.*

First, Orchil, her pale, beautiful head alive,
Her body shadowy as vapour drifting
Under the dawn, for she who awoke desire
Has but a heart of blood when others die;
About her in a vapoury multitude
Of women alluring devils with soft laughter;
Behind her a host heat of the blood made sin,
But all the little pink-white nails have grown
To be great talons.

[*He seizes Oona and drags her into the middle of the room and
points downward with vehement gestures. The wind roars.*

They begin a song
And there is still some music on their tongues.

Oona [*casting herself face downwards on the floor*]. O Maker of all,
protect her from the demons,
And if a soul must needs be lost, take mine.

[*Aleel kneels beside her, but does not seem to hear her words. The
Peasants return. They carry the Countess Cathleen and lay her
upon the ground before Oona and Aleel. She lies there as if dead.*

Oona. O that so many pitchers of rough clay
Should prosper and the porcelain break in two!

[*She kisses the hands of Cathleen.*

A Peasant. We were under the tree where the path turns,
When she grew pale as death and fainted away.
And while we bore her hither cloudy gusts
Blackened the world and shook us on our feet.
Draw the great bolt, for no man has beheld
So black, bitter, blinding, and sudden a storm.

[*One who is near the door draws the bolt.*

Cathleen. O, hold me, and hold me tightly, for the storm
Is dragging me away.

[*Oona takes her in her arms. A woman begins to wail.*

Peasants. Hush!

Other Peasants. Hush!

Peasant Women. Hush!

Other Peasant Women. Hush!

Cathleen [*half rising*]. Lay all the bags of money in a heap,
　　And when I am gone, old Oona, share them out
　　To every man and woman: judge, and give
　　According to their needs.
A Peasant Woman.　　　　　And will she give
　　Enough to keep my children through the dearth?
Another Peasant Woman. O Queen of Heaven, and all you blessed
　　saints,
　　Let us and ours be lost so she be shriven.
Cathleen. Bend down your faces, Oona and Aleel;
　　I gaze upon them as the swallow gazes
　　Upon the nest under the eave, before
　　She wander the loud waters. Do not weep
　　Too great a while, for there is many a candle
　　On the High Altar though one fall. Aleel,
　　Who sang about the dancers of the woods
　　That know not the hard burden of the world,
　　Having but breath in their kind bodies, farewell!
　　And farewell, Oona, you who played with me,
　　And bore me in your arms about the house
　　When I was but a child and therefore happy,
　　Therefore happy, even like those that dance.
　　The storm is in my hair and I must go.　　　　　[*She dies.*
Oona. Bring me the looking-glass.
　　　[*A woman brings it to her out of the inner room. Oona holds it
　　　over the lips of Cathleen. All is silent for a moment. And then
　　　she speaks in a half scream;*
　　　　　　　　　　　　O, she is dead!
A Peasant. She was the great white lily of the world.
Another Peasant. She was more beautiful than the pale stars.
An Old Peasant Woman. The little plant I loved is broken in two.
　　　[*Aleel takes looking-glass from Oona and flings it upon the floor
　　　so that it is broken in many pieces.*
Aleel. I shatter you in fragments, for the face
　　That brimmed you up with beauty is no more:
　　And die, dull heart, for she whose mournful words
　　Made you a living spirit has passed away
　　And left you but a ball of passionate dust.
　　And you, proud earth and plumy sea, fade out!
　　For you may hear no more her faltering feet,
　　But are left lonely amid the clamorous war
　　Of angels upon devils.

[He stands up; almost every one is kneeling, but it has grown so dark that only confused forms can be seen.

                And I who weep
Call curses on you, Time and Fate and Change,
And have no excellent hope but the great hour
When you shall plunge headlong through bottomless space.

      [A flash of lightning followed immediately by thunder.

A Peasant Woman. Pull him upon his knees before his curses
Have plucked thunder and lightning on our heads.
Aleel. Angels and devils clash in the middle air,
And brazen swords clang upon brazen helms.

      [A flash of lightning followed immediately by thunder.

Yonder a bright spear, cast out of a sling,
Has torn through Balor's eye, and the dark clans
Fly screaming as they fled Moytura of old.

      [Everything is lost in darkness.

An Old Man. The Almighty wrath at our great weakness and sin
Has blotted out the world and we must die.

    [The darkness is broken by a visionary light. The Peasants seem to be kneeling upon the rocky slope of a mountain, and vapour full of storm and ever-changing light is sweeping above them and behind them. Half in the light, half in the shadow, stand armed angels. Their armour is old and worn, and their drawn swords dim and dinted. They stand as if upon the air in formation of battle and look downward with stern faces. The Peasants cast themselves on the ground.

Aleel. Look no more on the half-closed gates of Hell,
But speak to me, whose mind is smitten of God,
That it may be no more with mortal things,
And tell of her who lies there.   *[He seizes one of the angels.*
                  Till you speak
You shall not drift into eternity.
The Angel. The light beats down; the gates of pearl are wide;
And she is passing to the floor of peace,
And Mary of the seven times wounded heart
Has kissed her lips, and the long blessed hair
Has fallen on her face; The Light of Lights
Looks always on the motive, not the deed,
The Shadow of Shadows on the deed alone.

      [Aleel releases the Angel and kneels.

Oona. Tell them who walk upon the floor of peace
That I would die and go to her I love;

The years like great black oxen tread the world,
And God the herdsman goads them on behind,
And I am broken by their passing feet.
    [*A sound of far-off horns seems to come from the heart of the light.
    The vision melts away, and the forms of the kneeling Peasants
    appear faintly in the darkness.*

THE END

THE LAND OF HEART'S DESIRE
1894

'O Rose, thou art sick'
William Blake

TO
FLORENCE FARR

THE LAND OF HEART'S DESIRE

PERSONS IN THE PLAY

Maurteen Bruin   Mary Bruin
Bridget Bruin   Father Hart
Shawn Bruin   A Faery Child

*The Scene is laid in the Barony of Kilmacowen, in the
County of Sligo, and at a remote time*

*A room with a hearth on the floor in the middle of a deep alcove to the
right. There are benches in the alcove and a table; and a crucifix on the
wall. The alcove is full of a glow of light from the fire. There is an open
door facing the audience to the left, and to the left of this a bench.
Through the door one can see the forest. It is night, but the moon or
a late sunset glimmers through the trees and carries the eye far off
into a vague, mysterious world. Maurteen Bruin, Shawn Bruin, and
Bridget Bruin sit in the alcove at the table or about the fire. They are
dressed in the costume of some remote time, and near them sits an old
priest, Father Hart. He may be dressed as a friar. There is food and
drink upon the table. Mary Bruin stands by the door reading a book. If
she looks up she can see through the door into the wood.*

Bridget. Because I bid her clean the pots for supper
    She took that old book down out of the thatch;
    She has been doubled over it ever since.
    We should be deafened by her groans and moans
    Had she to work as some do, Father Hart;
    Get up at dawn like me and mend and scour
    Or ride abroad in the boisterous night like you,
    The pyx and blessed bread under your arm.
Shawn. Mother, you are too cross.
Bridget.   You've married her,
    And fear to vex her and so take her part.
Maurteen [*to Father Hart*]. It is but right that youth should side with
       youth;

34

She quarrels with my wife a bit at times,
And is too deep just now in the old book!
But do not blame her greatly: (she will grow
As quiet as a puff-ball in a tree
When but the moons of marriage dawn and die
For half a score of times.) [1]

Father Hart.   Their hearts are wild,
  As be the hearts of birds, till children come.

Bridget. She would not mind the kettle, milk the cow,
  Or even lay the knives and spread the cloth.

Shawn. Mother, if only——

Maurteen.   Shawn, this is half empty;
  Go, bring up the best bottle that we have.

Father Hart. I never saw her read a book before,
  What can it be?

Maurteen [*to Shawn*]. What are you waiting for?
  You must not shake it when you draw the cork;
  It's precious wine, so take your time about it.   [*Shawn goes.*
  [*To Father Hart.*] (There was a Spaniard wrecked at Ocris Head,
  When I was young, and I have still some bottles.)
  He cannot bear to hear her blamed; the book
  Has lain up in the thatch these fifty years;
  My father told me my grandfather wrote it,
  And killed a heifer for the binding of it—
  (But supper's spread, and we can talk and eat.)
  It was little good he got out of the book,
  Because it filled his house with rambling fiddlers,
  And rambling ballad-makers and the like.
  (The griddle-bread is there in front of you.)
  Colleen, what is the wonder in that book,
  That you must leave the bread to cool? Had I
  Or had my father read or written books
  There were no stocking stuffed with yellow guineas
  To come when I am dead to Shawn and you.

Father Hart. You should not fill your head with foolish dreams.
  What are you reading?

Mary.   How a Princess Edain,
  A daughter of a King of Ireland, heard
  A voice singing on a May Eve like this,
  And followed, half awake and half asleep,
  Until she came into the Land of Faery,

[1] Amateurs perform this more often than any other play of mine, and I urge
them to omit all lines that I have enclosed in heavy round brackets ( ).—W.B.Y.

Where nobody gets old and godly and grave,
Where nobody gets old and crafty and wise,
Where nobody gets old and bitter of tongue.
And she is still there, busied with a dance
Deep in the dewy shadow of a wood,
(Or where stars walk upon a mountain-top.)

Maurteen. Persuade the colleen to put down the book;
My grandfather would mutter just such things,
And he was no judge of a dog or a horse,
And any idle boy could blarney him;
Just speak your mind.

Father Hart.   Put it away, my colleen;
(God spreads the heavens above us like great wings
And gives a little round of deeds and days,
And then come the wrecked angels and set snares,
And bait them with light hopes and heavy dreams,
Until the heart is puffed with pride and goes
Half shuddering and half joyous from God's peace;)
For it was some wrecked angel, blind with tears,
Who flattered Edain's heart with merry words.
My colleen, I have seen some other girls
Restless and ill at ease, but years went by
And they grew like their neighbours and were glad
In minding children, working at the churn,
And gossiping of weddings and of wakes;
(For life moves out of a red flare of dreams
Into a common light of common hours,
Until old age bring the red flare again.)

Maurteen. That's true—but she's too young to know it's true.

Bridget. She's old enough to know that it is wrong
To mope and idle.

Maurteen.   I've little blame for her;
She's dull when my big son is in the fields,
And that and maybe this good woman's tongue
Have driven her to hide among her dreams
Like children from the dark under the bedclothes.

Bridget. She'd never do a turn if I were silent.

Maurteen. And maybe it is natural upon May Eve
To dream of the Good People. But tell me, girl,
If you've the branch of blessed quicken wood
That women hang upon the post of the door
That they may send good luck into the house?
Remember they may steal new-married brides

After the fall of twilight on May Eve,
Or what old women mutter at the fire
Is but a pack of lies.
Father Hart.   It may be truth.
We do not know the limit of those powers
God has permitted to the evil spirits
For some mysterious end. You have done right [*to Mary*];
It's well to keep old innocent customs up.
        [*Mary Bruin has taken a bough of quicken wood from a seat and
        hung it on a nail in the door-post. A girl child strangely dressed,
        perhaps in faery green, comes out of the wood and takes it
        away.*
Mary. I had no sooner hung it on the nail
Before a child ran up out of the wind;
She has caught it in her hand and fondled it.
(Her face is pale as water before dawn.)
Father Hart. Whose child can this be?
Maurteen.   No one's child at all.
She often dreams that some one has gone by,
When there was nothing but a puff of wind.
Mary. They have taken away the blessed quicken wood,
They will not bring good luck into the house;
Yet I am glad that I was courteous to them,
For are not they, likewise, children of God?
Father Hart. Colleen, they are the children of the Fiend,
And they have power until the end of time,
When God shall fight with them a great pitched battle
And hack them into pieces.
Mary.   He will smile,
Father, perhaps, and open His great door.
Father Hart. Did but the lawless angels see that door
They would fall, slain by everlasting peace;
And when such angels knock upon our doors,
Who goes with them must drive through the same storm.
        [*An arm comes round the door-post and knocks and beckons. It is
        clearly seen in the silvery light. Mary Bruin goes to door and
        stands in it for a moment. Maurteen Bruin is busy filling Father
        Hart's plate. Bridget Bruin stirs the fire.*
Mary [*coming to table*]. There's somebody out there that beckoned me
And raised her hand as though it held a cup,
And she was drinking from it, so it may be
That she is thirsty.
            [*She takes milk from the table and carries it to the door.*

Father Hart.   That will be the child
  That you would have it was no child at all.
Bridget. (And maybe, Father, what he said was true;
  For there is not another night in the year
  So wicked as to-night.
Maurteen.   Nothing can harm us
  While the good Father's underneath our roof.
Mary. A little queer old woman dressed in green.
Bridget. The Good People beg for milk and fire
  Upon May Eve—woe to the house that gives,
  For they have power upon it for a year.
Maurteen. Hush, woman, hush!
Bridget.   She's given milk away.
  I knew she would bring evil on the house.
Maurteen. Who was it?
Mary.   Both the tongue and face were strange.
Maurteen. Some strangers came last week to Clover Hill;
  She must be one of them.)
Bridget.   I am afraid.
Father Hart. The Cross will keep all evil from the house
  While it hangs there.
Maurteen.   Come, sit beside me, colleen,
  And put away your dreams of discontent,
  For I would have you light up my last days,
  Like the good glow of the turf; and when I die
  You'll be the wealthiest hereabout, for, colleen,
  I have a stocking full of yellow guineas
  Hidden away where nobody can find it.
Bridget. You are the fool of every pretty face,
  And I must spare and pinch that my son's wife
  May have all kinds of ribbons for her head.
Maurteen. Do not be cross; she is a right good girl!
  (The butter is by your elbow, Father Hart.
  My colleen, have not Fate and Time and Change
  Done well for me and for old Bridget there?)
  We have a hundred acres of good land,
  And sit beside each other at the fire.
  I have this reverend Father for my friend,
  I look upon your face and my son's face—
  We've put his plate by yours—and here he comes,
  And brings with him the only thing we have lacked,
  Abundance of good wine. [*Shawn comes in.*] Stir up the fire,
  And put new turf upon it till it blaze;

To watch the turf-smoke coiling from the fire,
And feel content and wisdom in your heart,
This is the best of life; (when we are young
We long to tread a way none trod before,
But find the excellent old way through love,
And through the care of children, to the hour
For bidding Fate and Time and Change good-bye.)

[*Mary stands for a moment in the door (and then takes a sod
    of turf from the fire and goes out through the door. Shawn
    follows her and meets her coming in.*)

Shawn. What is it draws you to the chill o' the wood?
    There is a light among the stems of the trees
    That makes one shiver.
Mary.   A little queer old man
    Made me a sign to show he wanted fire
    To light his pipe.
Bridget.   You've given milk and fire
    Upon the unluckiest night of the year and brought,
    For all you know, evil upon the house.
    Before you married you were idle and fine
    And went about with ribbons on your head;
    And now—no, Father, I will speak my mind—
    She is not a fitting wife for any man——
Shawn. Be quiet, mother!
Maurteen.   You are much too cross.
Mary. What do I care if I have given this house,
    Where I must hear all day a bitter tongue,
    Into the power of faeries!
Bridget.   You know well
    How calling the Good People by that name,
    Or talking of them over-much at all,
    May bring all kinds of evil on the house.
Mary. Come, faeries, take me out of this dull house!
    Let me have all the freedom I have lost;
    Work when I will and idle when I will!
    Faeries, come take me out of this dull world,
    For I would ride with you upon the wind,
    (Run on the top of the dishevelled tide,)
    And dance upon the mountains like a flame.
Father Hart. You cannot know the meaning of your words.
Mary. Father, I am right weary of four tongues:
    A tongue that is too crafty and too wise,
    A tongue that is too godly and too grave,

A tongue that is more bitter than the tide,
And a kind tongue too full of drowsy love,
Of drowsy love and my captivity.

[*Shawn Bruin leads her to a seat at the left of the door.*

Shawn. Do not blame me; I often lie awake
Thinking that all things trouble your bright head.
How beautiful it is—your broad pale forehead
Under a cloudy blossoming of hair!
Sit down beside me here—these are too old,
And have forgotten they were ever young.

Mary. O, you are the great door-post of this house,
And I the branch of blessed quicken wood,
And if I could I'd hang upon the post
Till I had brought good luck into the house.

[*She would put her arms about him, but looks shyly at the priest
and lets her arms fall.*

Father Hart. My daughter, take his hand—by love alone
God binds us to Himself and to the hearth,
That shuts us from the waste beyond His peace,
From maddening freedom and bewildering light.

Shawn. Would that the world were mine to give it you,
And not its quiet hearths alone, but even
All that bewilderment of light and freedom,
If you would have it.

Mary.   I would take the world
And break it into pieces in my hands
To see you smile watching it crumble away.

Shawn. Then I would mould a world of fire and dew,
With no one bitter, grave or over-wise,
And nothing marred or old to do you wrong,
And crowd the enraptured quiet of the sky
With candles burning to your lonely face.

Mary. Your looks are all the candles that I need.

Shawn. Once a fly dancing in a beam of the sun,
Or the light wind blowing out of the dawn,
Could fill your heart with dreams none other knew,
But now the indissoluble sacrament
Has mixed your heart that was most proud and cold
With my warm heart for ever; the sun and moon
Must fade and heaven be rolled up like a scroll,
But your white spirit still walk by my spirit.

[*A Voice singing in the wood.*

Maurteen. There's some one singing. Why, it's but a child.
  It sang, 'The lonely of heart is withered away.'
  A strange song for a child, but she sings sweetly.
  Listen, listen!   *[Goes to door.*
Mary.   O, cling close to me,
  Because I have said wicked things to-night.
The Voice. The wind blows out of the gates of the day,
  The wind blows over the lonely of heart,
  And the lonely of heart is withered away.
  While the faeries dance in a place apart,
  Shaking their milk-white feet in a ring,
  Tossing their milk-white arms in the air;
  For they hear the wind laugh and murmur and sing
  Of a land where even the old are fair,
  And even the wise are merry of tongue;
  But I heard a reed of Coolaney say,
  'When the wind has laughed and murmured and sung
  The lonely of heart is withered away!'
Maurteen. Being happy, I would have all others happy,
  So I will bring her in out of the cold.

                [He brings in the Faery Child.
The Child. (I tire of winds and waters and pale lights.
Maurteen. And that's no wonder, for when night has fallen)
  The wood's a cold and a bewildering place,
  But you are welcome here.
The Child.   I am welcome here.
  (But when I tire of this warm little house)
  There is one here that must away, away.
Maurteen. O, listen to her dreamy and strange talk.
  Are you not cold?
The Child.   I will crouch down beside you,
  For I have run a long, long way this night.
Bridget. You have a comely shape.
Maurteen.   Your hair is wet.
Bridget. I'll warm your chilly feet.
Maurteen.   You have come indeed
  A long, long way—for I have never seen
  Your pretty face—and must be tired and hungry.
  Here is some bread and wine.
The Child.   The wine is bitter.
  Old mother, have you no sweet food for me?
Bridget. I have some honey.   *[She goes into the next room.*

Maurteen.   You have coaxing ways.
   The mother was quite cross before you came.
        [*Bridget returns with the honey and fills a porringer with milk.*
Bridget. She is the child of gentle people; look
   At her white hands and at her pretty dress.
   I've brought you some new milk, but wait a while
   And I will put it to the fire to warm,
   For things well fitted for poor folk like us
   Would never please a high-born child like you.
The Child. From dawn, when you must blow the fire ablaze,
   You work your fingers to the bone, old mother.
   The young may lie in bed and dream and hope,
   But you must work your fingers to the bone
   Because your heart is old.
Bridget.   The young are idle.
The Child. Your memories have made you wise, old father;
   The young must sigh through many a dream and hope,
   But you are wise because your heart is old.
                    [*Bridget gives her more bread and honey.*
Maurteen. O, who would think to find so young a girl
   Loving old age and wisdom?
The Child.   No more, mother.
Maurteen. What a small bite! The milk is ready now.
                              [*Hands it to her.*

   What a small sip!
The Child.   Put on my shoes, old mother.
   For I would like to dance now I have eaten.
   The reeds are dancing by Coolaney lake,
   And I would like to dance until the reeds
   And the white waves have danced themselves asleep.
        [*Bridget puts on the shoes, and the Child is about to dance, but
        suddenly sees the crucifix and shrieks and covers her eyes.*
   What is that ugly thing on the black cross?
Father Hart. You cannot know how naughty your words are!
   That is our Blessed Lord.
The Child.   Hide it away!
Bridget. I have begun to be afraid again.
The Child. Hide it away!
Maurteen.   That would be wickedness!
Bridget. That would be sacrilege!
The Child.   The tortured thing!
   Hide it away!
Maurteen.   Her parents are to blame.

Father Hart. That is the image of the Son of God.

The Child [*caressing him*]. Hide it away, hide it away!

Maurteen.   No, no.

Father Hart. Because you are so young and like a bird,
    That must take fright at every stir of the leaves,
    I will go take it down.

The Child.   Hide it away!
    And cover it out of sight and out of mind!
        [*Father Hart takes crucifix from wall and carries it towards inner
            room.*

Father Hart. Since you have come into this barony,
    I will instruct you in our blessed Faith;
    And being so keen-witted you'll soon learn.   [*To the others.*]
    We must be tender to all budding things.
    Our Maker let no thought of Calvary
    Trouble the morning stars in their first song.
                                        [*Puts crucifix in inner room.*

The Child. Here is level ground for dancing; I will dance.
                        [*Sings*]
                The wind blows out of the gates of the day,
                The wind blows over the lonely of heart,
                And the lonely of heart is withered away.   [*She dances.*

Mary [*to Shawn*]. Just now when she came near I thought I heard
    Other small steps beating upon the floor,
    And a faint music blowing in the wind,
    Invisible pipes giving her feet the tune.

Shawn. I heard no steps but hers.

Mary.   I hear them now.
    The unholy powers are dancing in the house.

Maurteen. Come over here, and if you promise me
    Not to talk wickedly of holy things
    I will give you something.

The Child.   Bring it me, old father.

Maurteen. Here are some ribbons that I bought in the town
    For my son's wife—but she will let me give them
    To tie up that wild hair the winds have tumbled.

The Child. Come, tell me, do you love me?

Maurteen.   Yes, I love you.

The Child. Ah, but you love this fireside. Do you love me?

Father Hart. When the Almighty puts so great a share
    Of His own ageless youth into a creature,
    To look is but to love.

The Child.   But you love Him?

Bridget. She is blaspheming.

The Child. And do you love me too?

Mary. I do not know.

The Child. You love that young man there,
    Yet I could make you ride upon the winds,
    (Run on the top of the dishevelled tide,)
    And dance upon the mountains like a flame.

Mary. O Queen of Angels and kind saints defend us!
    Some dreadful thing will happen. A while ago
    She took away the blessed quicken wood.

Father Hart. You fear because of her unmeasured prattle;
    She knows no better. Child, how old are you?

The Child. When winter sleep is abroad my hair grows thin,
    My feet unsteady. When the leaves awaken
    My mother carries me in her golden arms.
    I'll soon put on my womanhood and marry
    The spirits of wood and water, but who can tell
    When I was born for the first time? I think
    I am much older than the eagle-cock
    (That blinks and blinks on Ballygawley Hill,)
    And he is the oldest thing under the moon.

Father Hart. O, she is of the faery people.

The Child. One called.
    I sent my messengers for milk and fire;
    She called again and after that I came.

    [*All except Shawn and Mary Bruin gather behind the priest for
        protection.*

Shawn [*rising*]. Though you have made all these obedient,
    You have not charmed my sight and won from me
    A wish or gift to make you powerful;
    I'll turn you from the house.

Father Hart. No, I will face her.

The Child. Because you took away the crucifix
    I am so mighty that there's none can pass,
    Unless I will it, where my feet have danced
    Or where I've whirled my finger-tips.

    [*Shawn tries to approach her and cannot.*

Maurteen. Look, look!
    There something stops him—look how he moves his hands
    As though he rubbed them on a wall of glass!

Father Hart. I will confront this mighty spirit alone;
    Put fear away; the Father is with us,
    (The Holy Martyrs and the Innocents,

The adoring Magi in their coats ot mail,)
And He who died and rose on the third day,
(And all the nine angelic hierarchies.)
    [The Child kneels upon the settle beside Mary and puts her arms
      about her.
Cry, daughter, to the Angels and the Saints.
The Child. You shall go with me, newly-married bride,
  And gaze upon a merrier multitude.
  (White-armed Nuala, Aengus of the Birds,
  Fiachra of the hurtling foam, and him
  Who is the ruler of the Western Host,
  Finvara, and their Land of Heart's Desire.)
  Where beauty has no ebb, decay no flood,
  But joy is wisdom, time an endless song.
  I kiss you and the world begins to fade.
Shawn. Awake out of that trance—and cover up
  Your eyes and ears.
Father Hart.   She must both look and listen,
  For only the soul's choice can save her now.
  Come over to me, daughter; stand beside me;
  Think of this house and of your duties in it.
The Child. Stay and come with me, newly-married bride,
  For if you hear him you grow like the rest;
  Bear children, cook, and bend above the churn,
  And wrangle over butter, fowl, and eggs,
  Until at last, grown old and bitter of tongue,
  You're crouching there and shivering at the grave.
Father Hart. Daughter, I point you out the way to Heaven.
The Child. But I can lead you, newly-married bride,
  Where nobody gets old and crafty and wise,
  Where nobody gets old and godly and grave,
  Where nobody gets old and bitter of tongue,
  And where kind tongues bring no captivity;
  For we are but obedient to the thoughts
  That drift into the mind at a wink of the eye.
Father Hart. By the dear Name of the One crucified,
  I bid you, Mary Bruin, come to me.
The Child. I keep you in the name of your own heart.
Father Hart. It is because I put away the crucifix
  That I am nothing, and my power is nothing.
  I'll bring it here again.
Maurteen [*clinging to him*]. No.
Bridget.   Do not leave us.

Father Hart. O, let me go before it is too late;
   It is my sin alone that brought it all.   *[Singing outside.*
The Child. I hear them sing, 'Come, newly-married bride,
   Come to the woods and waters and pale lights.'
Mary. I will go with you.
Father Hart.   She is lost, alas!
The Child [*standing by the door*]. But clinging mortal hope must fall
      from you,
   For we who ride the winds, run on the waves,
   And dance upon the mountains are more light
   Than dewdrops on the banner of the dawn.
Mary. O, take me with you.
Shawn.   Beloved, I will keep you.
   I've more than words, I have these arms to hold you,
   Nor all the faery host, do what they please,
   Shall ever make me loose you from these arms.
Mary. Dear face! Dear voice!
The Child.   Come, newly-married bride.
Mary. I always loved her world—and yet—and yet——
The Child. White bird, white bird, come with me, little bird.
Mary. She calls me!
The Child.   Come, come with me, little bird.
          [Distant dancing figures appear in the wood.
Mary. I can hear songs and dancing.
Shawn.   Stay with me.
Mary. I think that I would stay—and yet—and yet——
The Child. Come, little bird with crest of gold.
Mary [*very softly*].   And yet——
The Child. Come, little bird with silver feet!
        [Mary Bruin dies, and the Child goes.
Shawn.   She is dead!
Bridget. Come from that image; body and soul are gone.
   You have thrown your arms about a drift of leaves,
   Or bole of an ash-tree changed into her image.
Father Hart. Thus do the spirits of evil snatch their prey
   Almost out of the very hand of God;
   And day by day their power is more and more,
   And men and women leave old paths, for pride
   Comes knocking with thin knuckles on the heart.
[*Outside there are dancing figures and it may be a white bird, and
    many voices singing:*
        The wind blows out of the gates of the day,
        The wind blows over the lonely of heart,

And the lonely of heart is withered away;
(While the faeries dance in a place apart,
Shaking their milk-white feet in a ring,
Tossing their milk-white arms in the air;
For they hear the wind laugh, and murmur and sing
Of a land where even the old are fair,
And even the wise are merry of tongue;
But I heard a reed of Coolaney say—
'When the wind has laughed and murmured and sung,
The lonely of heart is withered away.')

THE END

CATHLEEN NI HOULIHAN

1902

CATHLEEN NI HOULIHAN

PERSONS IN THE PLAY

Peter Gillane

Michael Gillane, *his son, going to be married*

Patrick Gillane, *a lad of twelve, Michael's brother*

Bridget Gillane, *Peter's wife*

Delia Cahel, *engaged to Michael*

The Poor Old Woman

Neighbours

Interior of a cottage close to Killala, in 1798. Bridget is standing at a table undoing a parcel. Peter is sitting at one side of the fire, Patrick at the other.

Peter. What is the sound I hear?

Patrick. I don't hear anything. [*He listens.*] I hear it now. It's like cheering. [*He goes to the window and looks out.*] I wonder what they are cheering about. I don't see anybody.

Peter. It might be a hurling.

Patrick. There's no hurling to-day. It must be down in the town the cheering is.

Bridget. I suppose the boys must be having some sport of their own. Come over here, Peter, and look at Michael's wedding clothes.

Peter [*shifts his chair to table*]. Those are grand clothes, indeed.

Bridget. You hadn't clothes like that when you married me, and no coat to put on of a Sunday more than any other day.

Peter. That is true, indeed. We never thought a son of our own would be wearing a suit of that sort for his wedding, or have so good a place to bring a wife to.

Patrick [*who is still at the window*]. There's an old woman coming down the road. I don't know is it here she is coming.

Bridget. It will be a neighbour coming to hear about Michael's wedding. Can you see who it is?

Patrick. I think it is a stranger, but she's not coming to the house. She's turned into the gap that goes down where Maurteen and his sons are shearing sheep. [*He turns towards Bridget.*] Do you remember what Winny of the Cross-Roads was saying the other night about the strange woman that goes through the country whatever time there's war or trouble coming?

Bridget. Don't be bothering us about Winny's talk, but go and open the door for your brother. I hear him coming up the path.

Peter. I hope he has brought Delia's fortune with him safe, for fear the people might go back on the bargain and I after making it. Trouble enough I had making it.

[*Patrick opens the door and Michael comes in.*

Bridget. What kept you, Michael? We were looking out for you this long time.

Michael. I went round by the priest's house to bid him be ready to marry us to-morrow.

Bridget. Did he say anything?

Michael. He said it was a very nice match, and that he was never better pleased to marry any two in his parish than myself and Delia Cahel.

Peter. Have you got the fortune, Michael?

Michael. Here it is.

[*Michael puts bag on table and goes over and leans against chimney-jamb. Bridget, who has been all this time examining the clothes, pulling the seams and trying the lining of the pockets, etc., puts the clothes on the dresser.*

Peter [*getting up and taking the bag in his hand and turning out the money*]. Yes, I made the bargain well for you, Michael. Old John Cahel would sooner have kept a share of this a while longer. 'Let me keep the half of it until the first boy is born,' says he. 'You will not,' says I. 'Whether there is or is not a boy, the whole hundred pounds must be in Michael's hands before he brings your daughter to the house.' The wife spoke to him then, and he gave in at the end.

Bridget. You seem well pleased to be handling the money, Peter.

Peter. Indeed, I wish I had had the luck to get a hundred pounds, or twenty pounds itself, with the wife I married.

Bridget. Well, if I didn't bring much I didn't get much. What had you the day I married you but a flock of hens and you feeding them, and a few lambs and you driving them to the market at Ballina? [*She is vexed and bangs a jug on the dresser.*] If I brought no fortune I worked it out in my bones, laying down the baby, Michael that is standing there now, on a stook of straw, while I dug the potatoes, and never asking big dresses or anything but to be working.

Peter. That is true, indeed. [*He pats her arm.*

Bridget. Leave me alone now till I ready the house for the woman that is to come into it.

Peter. You are the best woman in Ireland, but money is good, too. [*He begins handling the money again and sits down.*] I never thought to see so much money within my four walls. We can do great things now we have it. We can take the ten acres of land we have the chance

of since Jamsie Dempsey died, and stock it. We will go to the fair
at Ballina to buy the stock. Did Delia ask any of the money for her
own use, Michael?

Michael. She did not, indeed. She did not seem to take much notice of
it, or to look at it at all.

Bridget. That's no wonder. Why would she look at it when she had
yourself to look at, a fine, strong young man? It is proud she must
be to get you; a good steady boy that will make use of the money,
and not be running through it or spending it on drink like another.

Peter. It's likely Michael himself was not thinking much of the fortune
either, but of what sort the girl was to look at.

Michael [*coming over towards the table*]. Well, you would like a nice
comely girl to be beside you, and to go walking with you. The fortune only lasts for a while, but the woman will be there always.

Patrick [*turning round from the window*]. They are cheering again
down in the town. Maybe they are landing horses from Enniscrone.
They do be cheering when the horses take the water well.

Michael. There are no horses in it. Where would they be going and no
fair at hand? Go down to the town, Patrick, and see what is going on.

Patrick [*opens the door to go out, but stops for a moment on the threshold*]. Will Delia remember, do you think, to bring the greyhound
pup she promised me when she would be coming to the house?

Michael. She will surely.   [*Patrick goes out, leaving the door open.*

Peter. It will be Patrick's turn next to be looking for a fortune, but he
won't find it so easy to get it and he with no place of his own.

Bridget. I do be thinking sometimes, now things are going so well with
us, and the Cahels such a good back to us in the district, and Delia's
own uncle a priest, we might be put in the way of making Patrick a
priest some day, and he so good at his books.

Peter. Time enough, time enough. You have always your head full of
plans, Bridget.

Bridget. We will be well able to give him learning, and not to send him
tramping the country like a poor scholar that lives on charity.

Michael. They're not done cheering yet.

> [*He goes over to the door and stands there for a moment, putting
> up his hand to shade his eyes.*

Bridget. Do you see anything?

Michael. I see an old woman coming up the path.

Bridget. Who is it, I wonder? It must be the strange woman Patrick
saw a while ago.

Michael. I don't think it's one of the neighbours anyway, but she has
her cloak over her face.

Bridget. It might be some poor woman heard we were making ready for the wedding and came to look for her share.

Peter. I may as well put the money out of sight. There is no use leaving it out for every stranger to look at.

[*He goes over to a large box in the corner, opens it and puts the bag in and fumbles at the lock.*

Michael. There she is, father! [*An Old Woman passes the window slowly. She looks at Michael as she passes.*] I'd sooner a stranger not to come to the house the night before my wedding.

Bridget. Open the door, Michael; don't keep the poor woman waiting.

[*The Old Woman comes in. Michael stands aside to make way for her.*

Old Woman. God save all here!

Peter. God save you kindly!

Old Woman. You have good shelter here.

Peter. You are welcome to whatever shelter we have.

Bridget. Sit down there by the fire and welcome.

Old Woman [*warming her hands*]. There is a hard wind outside.

[*Michael watches her curiously from the door. Peter comes over to the table.*

Peter. Have you travelled far to-day?

Old Woman. I have travelled far, very far; there are few have travelled so far as myself, and there's many a one that doesn't make me welcome. There was one that had strong sons I thought were friends of mine, but they were shearing their sheep, and they wouldn't listen to me.

Peter. It's a pity indeed for any person to have no place of their own.

Old Woman. That's true for you indeed, and it's long I'm on the roads since I first went wandering.

Bridget. It is a wonder you are not worn out with so much wandering.

Old Woman. Sometimes my feet are tired and my hands are quiet, but there is no quiet in my heart. When the people see me quiet, they think old age has come on me and that all the stir has gone out of me. But when the trouble is on me I must be talking to my friends.

Bridget. What was it put you wandering?

Old Woman. Too many strangers in the house.

Bridget. Indeed you look as if you'd had your share of trouble.

Old Woman. I have had trouble indeed.

Bridget. What was it put the trouble on you?

Old Woman. My land that was taken from me.

Peter. Was it much land they took from you?

Old Woman. My four beautiful green fields.

Peter [*aside to Bridget*]. Do you think could she be the widow Casey that was put out of her holding at Kilglass a while ago?

Bridget. She is not. I saw the widow Casey one time at the market in Ballina, a stout fresh woman.

Peter [*to Old Woman*]. Did you hear a noise of cheering, and you coming up the hill?

Old Woman. I thought I heard the noise I used to hear when my friends came to visit me.

[*She begins singing half to herself.*

> I will go cry with the woman,
> For yellow-haired Donough is dead,
> With a hempen rope for a neckcloth,
> And a white cloth on his head,——

Michael [*coming from the door*]. What is it that you are singing, ma'am?

Old Woman. Singing I am about a man I knew one time, yellow-haired Donough that was hanged in Galway.

[*She goes on singing, much louder.*

> I am come to cry with you, woman,
> My hair is unwound and unbound;
> I remember him ploughing his field,
> Turning up the red side of the ground,
> And building his barn on the hill
> With the good mortared stone;
> O! we'd have pulled down the gallows
> Had it happened in Enniscrone!

Michael. What was it brought him to his death?

Old Woman. He died for love of me: many a man has died for love of me.

Peter [*aside to Bridget*]. Her trouble has put her wits astray.

Michael. Is it long since that song was made? Is it long since he got his death?

Old Woman. Not long, not long. But there were others that died for love of me a long time ago.

Michael. Were they neighbours of your own, ma'am?

Old Woman. Come here beside me and I'll tell you about them. [*Michael sits down beside her on the hearth.*] There was a red man of the O'Donnells from the north, and a man of the O'Sullivans from the south, and there was one Brian that lost his life at Clontarf by the sea, and there were a great many in the west, some that died hundreds of years ago, and there are some that will die to-morrow.

Michael. Is it in the west that men will die to-morrow?

Old Woman. Come nearer, nearer to me.

Bridget. Is she right, do you think? Or is she a woman from beyond the world?

Peter. She doesn't know well what she's talking about, with the want and the trouble she has gone through.

Bridget. The poor thing, we should treat her well.

Peter. Give her a drink of milk and a bit of the oaten cake.

Bridget. Maybe we should give her something along with that, to bring her on her way. A few pence or a shilling itself, and we with so much money in the house.

Peter. Indeed I'd not begrudge it to her if we had it to spare, but if we go running through what we have, we'll soon have to break the hundred pounds, and that would be a pity.

Bridget. Shame on you, Peter. Give her the shilling and your blessing with it, or our own luck will go from us.

[*Peter goes to the box and takes out a shilling.*

Bridget [*to the Old Woman*]. Will you have a drink of milk, ma'am?

Old Woman. It is not food or drink that I want.

Peter [*offering the shilling*]. Here is something for you.

Old Woman. This is not what I want. It is not silver I want.

Peter. What is it you would be asking for?

Old Woman. If anyone would give me help he must give me himself, he must give me all.

[*Peter goes over to the table staring at the shilling in his hand in a bewildered way, and stands whispering to Bridget.*

Michael. Have you no one to care you in your age, ma'am?

Old Woman. I have not. With all the lovers that brought me their love I never set out the bed for any.

Michael. Are you lonely going the roads, ma'am?

Old Woman. I have my thoughts and I have my hopes.

Michael. What hopes have you to hold to?

Old Woman. The hope of getting my beautiful fields back again; the hope of putting the strangers out of my house.

Michael. What way will you do that, ma'am?

Old Woman. I have good friends that will help me. They are gathering to help me now. I am not afraid. If they are put down to-day they will get the upper hand to-morrow. [*She gets up.*] I must be going to meet my friends. They are coming to help me and I must be there to welcome them. I must call the neighbours together to welcome them.

Michael. I will go with you.

Bridget. It is not her friends you have to go and welcome, Michael; it is the girl coming into the house you have to welcome. You have plenty to do; it is food and drink you have to bring to the house. The woman that is coming home is not coming with empty hands; you would not have an empty house before her. [*To the Old Woman.*] Maybe you don't know, ma'am, that my son is going to be married to-morrow.

Old Woman. It is not a man going to his marriage that I look to for help.

Peter [*to Bridget*]. Who is she, do you think, at all?

Bridget. You did not tell us your name yet, ma'am.

Old Woman. Some call me the Poor Old Woman, and there are some that call me Cathleen, the daughter of Houlihan.

Peter. I think I knew some one of that name, once. Who was it, I wonder? It must have been some one I knew when I was a boy. No, no; I remember, I heard it in a song.

Old Woman [*who is standing in the doorway*]. They are wondering that there were songs made for me; there have been many songs made for me. I heard one on the wind this morning.

[*Sings*]

> Do not make a great keening
> When the graves have been dug to-morrow.
> Do not call the white-scarfed riders
> To the burying that shall be to-morrow.
> Do not spread food to call strangers
> To the wakes that shall be to-morrow;
> Do not give money for prayers
> For the dead that shall die to-morrow. . . .

They will have no need of prayers, they will have no need of prayers.

Michael. I do not know what that song means, but tell me something I can do for you.

Peter. Come over to me, Michael.

Michael. Hush, father, listen to her.

Old Woman. It is a hard service they take that help me. Many that are red-cheeked now will be pale-cheeked; many that have been free to walk the hills and the bogs and the rushes will be sent to walk hard streets in far countries; many a good plan will be broken; many that have gathered money will not stay to spend it; many a child will be born and there will be no father at its christening to give it a name. They that have red cheeks will have pale cheeks for my sake, and for all that, they will think they are well paid.

[*She goes out; her voice is heard outside singing.*

> They shall be remembered for ever,
> They shall be alive for ever,
> They shall be speaking for ever,
> The people shall hear them for ever.

Bridget [*to Peter*]. Look at him, Peter; he has the look of a man that has got the touch. [*Raising her voice.*] Look here, Michael, at the wedding clothes. Such grand clothes as these are! You have a right to fit them on now; it would be a pity to-morrow if they did not fit. The boys would be laughing at you. Take them, Michael, and go into the room and fit them on. [*She puts them on his arm.*

Michael. What wedding are you talking of? What clothes will I be wearing to-morrow?

Bridget. These are the clothes you are going to wear when you marry Delia Cahel to-morrow.

Michael. I had forgotten that.

[*He looks at the clothes and turns towards the inner room, but stops at the sound of cheering outside.*

Peter. There is the shouting come to our own door. What is it has happened?

[*Neighbours come crowding in, Patrick and Delia with them.*

Patrick. There are ships in the Bay; the French are landing at Killala!

[*Peter takes his pipe from his mouth and his hat off, and stands up. The clothes slip from Michael's arm.*

Delia. Michael! [*He takes no notice.*] Michael! [*He turns towards her.*] Why do you look at me like a stranger?

[*She drops his arm. Bridget goes over towards her.*

Patrick. The boys are all hurrying down the hillside to join the French.

Delia. Michael won't be going to join the French.

Bridget [*to Peter*]. Tell him not to go, Peter.

Peter. It's no use. He doesn't hear a word we're saying.

Bridget. Try and coax him over to the fire.

Delia. Michael, Michael! You won't leave me! You won't join the French, and we going to be married!

[*She puts her arms about him, he turns towards her as if about to yield.*

Old Woman's voice outside.
They shall be speaking for ever,
The people shall hear them for ever.

[*Michael breaks away from Delia, stands for a second at the door, then rushes out, following the Old Woman's voice. Bridget takes Delia, who is crying silently, into her arms.*

Peter [*to Patrick, laying a hand on his arm*]. Did you see an old woman going down the path?

Patrick. I did not, but I saw a young girl, and she had the walk of a queen.

THE END

THE POT OF BROTH

1904

THE POT OF BROTH

PERSONS IN THE PLAY

John Coneely, *an elderly man*
Sibby Coneely, *a young or middle-aged woman*
A Tramp

A cottage kitchen. Fire on the hearth; table with cabbage, onions, a plate of meal, etc. Half-open door. A Tramp enters, looks about.

Tramp. What sort are the people of this house, I wonder? Was it a good place for me to come to look for my dinner, I wonder? What's in that big pot? [*Lifts cover.*] Nothing at all! What's in the little pot? [*Lifts cover.*] Nothing at all! What's in that bottle, I wonder? [*Takes it up excitedly and tastes.*] Milk! milk in a bottle! I wonder they wouldn't afford a tin can to milk the cow into! Not much chance for a poor man to make a living here. What's in that chest? [*Kneels and tries to lift cover.*] Locked! [*Smells at the keyhole.*] There's a good smell—there must be a still not far off.

> [*Gets up and sits on chest. A noise heard outside, shouts, footsteps, and loud frightened cackling.*

Tramp. What in the earthly world is going on outside? Any one would think it was the Fiannta-h-Eireann at their hunting!

Sibby's voice. Stop the gap, let you stop the gap, John. Stop that old schemer of a hen flying up on the thatch like as if she was an eagle!

John's voice. What can I do, Sibby? I all to had my hand upon her when she flew away!

Sibby's voice. She's out into the garden! Follow after her! She has the wide world before her now.

Tramp. Sibby he called her. I wonder is it Sibby Coneely's house I am in? If that's so it's a bad chance I have of going out heavier than I came in. I often heard of her, a regular slave-driver that would starve the rats. A niggard with her eyes on kippeens, that would skin a flea for its hide! It was the bad luck of the world brought me here, and not a house or a village between this and Tubber. And it isn't much I have left to bring me on there. [*Begins emptying out his pockets on the chest.*] There's my pipe and not a grain to fill it with! There's my handkerchief I got at the coronation dinner! There's my knife and nothing left of it but the handle. [*Shakes his pocket out.*] And there's a crust of the last dinner I got, and the last I'm likely to get till to-morrow. That's all I have in the world unless the stone I picked up to pelt at that yelping dog a while ago. [*Takes stone out of pocket and tosses it up and down.*] In the time long ago I usen't to have much trouble to find a dinner, getting over the old women and getting round the young ones! I remember the time I met the old minister on the path and sold him his own flock of turkeys. My wits used to fill my stomach then, but I'm afraid they're going from me now with all the hardship I went through.   [*Cackling heard again and cries.*

Sibby's voice. Catch her, she's round the bush! Put your hands in the nettles, don't be daunted!

[*A choked cackle and prolonged screech.*

Tramp. There's a dinner for somebody anyway. That it may be for myself! How will I come round her, I wonder? There is no more pity in her heart than there's a soul in a dog. If all the saints were standing barefoot before her she'd bid them to call another day. It's myself I have to trust to now, and my share of talk. [*Looks at the stone.*] I know what I'll do, I know what the tinker did with a stone, and I'm as good a man as he is anyway. [*He jumps up and waves the stone over his head.*] Now, Sibby! If I don't do it one way I'll do it another. My wits against the world!

There's broth in the pot for you, old man,
There's broth in the pot for you, old man,
     There's cabbage for me
     And broth for you,
And beef for Jack the journeyman.

I wish you were dead, my gay old man,
I wish you were dead, my gay old man,
     I wish you were dead
     And a stone at your head,
So as I'd marry poor Jack the journeyman.

John's voice [*outside*]. Bring it in, bring it in, Sibby. You'll be late with the priest's dinner.

Sibby's voice. Can't you wait a minute till I'll draw it?

Enter John

John. I didn't know there was any one in the house.

Tramp. It's only this minute I came in, tired with the length of the road I am, and fasting since morning.

John [*begins groping among the pots and pans*]. I'll see can I find any-

thing here for you . . . I don't see much . . . Maybe there's something in the chest.

[*He takes key from a hiding-place at back of hearth, opens chest,
takes out bottle, takes out a ham-bone and is cutting a bit from
it when Sibby enters, carrying chicken by the neck. John drops
the ham-bone on a bench.*]

Sibby. Hurry now, John, after all the time you have wasted. Why didn't
you steal up on the old hen that time she was scratching in the dust?

John. Sure I thought one of the chickens would be the tenderest.

Sibby. Cock you up with tenderness! All the expense I'm put to! My
grand hen I've been feeding these five years! Wouldn't that have
been enough to part with? Indeed I wouldn't have thought of parting with her itself, but she had got tired of laying since Easter.

John. Well, I thought we ought to give his Reverence something that
would have a little good in it.

Sibby. What does the age of it matter? A hen's a hen when it's on the
table. [*Sitting down to pluck chicken.*] Why couldn't the Kernans
have given the priest his dinner the way they always do? What did
it matter their mother's brother to have died? It is an excuse they had
made up to put the expense of the dinner on me.

John. Well, I hope you have a good bit of bacon to put in the pot along
with the chicken.

Sibby. Let me alone. The taste of meat on the knife is all that high-up
people like the clergy care for, nice genteel people, no way greedy
like potato-diggers or harvest men.

John. Well, I never saw the man, gentle or simple, wouldn't be glad of
his fill of bacon and he hungry.

Sibby. Let me alone, I'll show the Kernans what I can do. I have what
is better than bacon, a nice bit of a ham I am keeping in the chest
this good while, thinking we might want it for company. [*She catches
sight of Tramp and calls out.*] Who is there? A beggarman, is it?
Then you may quit this house if you please. We have nothing for
you. [*She gets up and opens the door.*]

Tramp [*comes forward*]. It is a mistake you are making, ma'am, it is
not asking anything I am. It is giving I am more used to. I was never
in a house yet but there would be a welcome for me in it again.

Sibby. Well, you have the appearance of a beggar, and if it isn't begging
you are, what way do you make your living?

Tramp. If I was a beggar, ma'am, it is to common people I would be
going and not to a nice grand woman like yourself, that is only used
to be talking with high-up noble people.

Sibby. Well, what is it you are asking? If it's a bit to eat you want, I can't give it to you, for I have company coming that will clear all before them.

Tramp. Is it me ask anything to eat? [*Holds up stone.*] I have here what is better than beef and mutton, and currant cakes and sacks of flour.

Sibby. What is it at all?

Tramp [*mysteriously*]. Those that gave it to me wouldn't like me to tell that.

Sibby [*to John*]. Do you think is he a man that has friends among the Sidhe?

John. Your mind is always running on the Sidhe since the time they made John Molloy find buried gold on the bridge of Limerick. I see nothing in it but a stone.

Tramp. What can you see in it, you that never saw what it can do?

John. What is it it can do?

Tramp. It can do many things, and what it's going to do now is to make me a drop of broth for my dinner.

Sibby. I'd like to have a stone that could make broth.

Tramp. No one in the world but myself has one, ma'am, and no other stone in the world has the same power, for it has enchantment on it. All I'll ask of you now, ma'am, is the loan of a pot with a drop of boiling water in it.

Sibby. You're welcome to that much. John, fill the small pot with water.
[*John fills the pot from a kettle.*

Tramp [*putting in stone*]. There now, that's all I have to do but to put it on the fire to boil, and it's a grand pot of broth will be before me then.

Sibby. And is that all you have to put in it?

Tramp. Nothing at all but that—only, maybe, a bit of an herb for fear the enchantment might slip away from it. You wouldn't have a bit of Slanlus in the house, ma'am, that was cut with a black-handled knife?

Sibby. No, indeed, I have none of that in the house.

Tramp. Or a bit of the Fearavan that was picked when the wind was from the north?

Sibby. No, indeed, I'm sorry there's none.

Tramp. Or a sprig of the Athair-talav, the father of herbs?

John. There's plenty of it by the hedge. I'll go out and get it for you.

Tramp. O, don't mind taking so much trouble; those leaves beside me will do well enough. [*He takes a couple of good handfuls of the cabbage and onions and puts them in.*]

Sibby. But where at all did you get the stone?

Tramp. Well, this is how it happened. I was out one time, and a grand greyhound with me, and it followed a hare, and I went after it. And

I came up at last to the edge of a gravel pit where there were a few withered furzy bushes, and there was my fine hound sitting up, and it shivering, and a little old man sitting before it, and he taking off a hareskin coat. [*Looking round at the ham-bone.*] Give me the loan of a kippeen to stir the pot with. . . . [*He takes the ham-bone and puts it into the pot.*]

John. Oh! the ham-bone!

Tramp. I didn't say a ham-bone, I said a hareskin coat.

Sibby. Hold your tongue, John, if it's deaf you are getting.

Tramp [*stirring the pot with the ham-bone*]. Well, as I was telling you, he was sitting up, and one time I thought he was as small as a nut, and the next minute I thought his head to be in the stars. Frightened I was.

Sibby. No wonder, no wonder at all in that.

Tramp. He took the little stone then—that stone I have with me—out of the side pocket of his coat, and he showed it to me. 'Call off your dog', says he, 'and I'll give you that stone, and if ever you want a good drop of broth or a bit of stirabout, or a drop of poteen itself, all you have to do is to put it down in a pot with a drop of water and stir it awhile, and you'll have the thing you were wanting ready before you.'

Sibby. Poteen! Would it make that?

Tramp. It would, ma'am; and wine, the same as the Clare Militia uses.

Sibby. Let me see what does it look like now. [*Is bending forward.*]

Tramp. Don't look at it for your life, ma'am. It might bring bad luck on any one that would look at it, and it boiling. I must put a cover on the pot, or I must colour the water some way. Give me a handful of that meal.

[*Sibby holds out a plate of meal and he puts in a handful or two.*

John. Well, he is a gifted man!

Sibby. It would be a great comfort to have a stone like that. [*She has finished plucking the chicken which lies in her lap.*]

Tramp. And there's another thing it does, ma'am, since it came into Catholic hands. If you put it into a pot of a Friday with a bit of the whitest meat in Ireland in it, it would turn it as black as black.

Sibby. That is no less than a miracle. I must tell Father John about that.

Tramp. But to put a bit of meat with it any other day of the week, it would do it no harm at all, but good. Look here now, ma'am, I'll put that nice little hen you have in your lap in the pot for a minute till you'll see. [*Takes it and puts it in.*]

John [*sarcastically*]. It's a good job this is not a Friday!

Sibby. Keep yourself quiet, John, and don't be interrupting the talk or you'll get a knock on the head like the King of Lochlann's grand-mother.

John. Go on, go on, I'll say no more.

Tramp. If I'm passing this way some time of a Friday, I'll bring a nice bit of mutton, or the breast of a turkey, and you'll see how it will be no better in two minutes than a fistful of bog mould.

Sibby [*getting up*]. Let me take the chicken out now.

Tramp. Stop till I'll help you, ma'am, you might scald your hand. I'll show it to you in a minute as white as your own skin, where the lily and the rose are fighting for mastery. Did you ever hear what the boys in your own parish were singing after you being married from them—such of them that had any voice at all and not choked with crying, or senseless with the drop of drink they took to comfort them and to keep their wits from going, with the loss of you?

[*Sibby sits down again complacently.*

Sibby. Did they do that indeed?

Tramp. They did, ma'am, this is what they used to be singing:
>   Philomel, I've listened oft
>   To thy lay, near weeping willow—

No, that's not it—it's a queer thing the memory is—
>   'Twas at the dance at Dermody's that first I caught a sight
>   of her.

No, that's not it either—ah, now I have it.
>   My Paistin Finn is my sole desire,
>   And I am shrunken to skin and bone.

Sibby. Why would they call me Paistin?

Tramp. And why wouldn't they? Would you wish them to put your right name in a song, and your man ready to knock the brains of any man will as much as look your side of the road?

Sibby. Well, maybe so.

Tramp. I was standing by the man that made the song, and he writing it with an old bit of a carpenter's pencil, and the tears running down—
>   My Paistin Finn is my sole desire,
>   And I am shrunken to skin and bone,
>   For all my heart has had for its hire
>   Is what I can whistle alone and alone.
>   *Oro, oro!*
>   *To-morrow night I will break down the door.*

[*Sibby takes a fork and rises to take out the chicken. Tramp puts his hand to stop her and goes on:*
>   What is the good of a man and he

Alone and alone with a speckled shin?
I would that I drank with my love on my knee,
Between two barrels at the inn.
  Oro, oro!
To-morrow night I will break down the door.
[*Sibby half rises again. Tramp puts his hand upon her hand.*
Tramp. Wait now till you hear the end [*sings*]:
Alone and alone nine nights I lay
Between two bushes under the rain;
I thought to have whistled her down that way,
I whistled and whistled and whistled in vain.
  Oro, oro!
To-morrow night I will break down the door.
[*He repeats the verse, Sibby singing too and beating time with fork.*
Sibby [*to John*]. I always knew I was too good for you! [*She goes on humming.*]
John. Well, he has the poor woman bewitched.
Sibby [*suddenly coming to her wits*]. Did you take the chicken out yet?
Tramp [*taking it out and giving it a good squeeze into the pot*]. I did, ma'am. Look at it there.   [*He takes it and lays it on table.*
John. How is the broth getting on?
Tramp [*tasting it with a spoon*]. It's grand. It's always grand.
Sibby. Give me a taste of it.
Tramp [*takes the pot off and slips the ham-bone behind him*]. Give me some vessel till I'll give this sky-woman a taste of it.
  [*John gives him an egg-cup which he fills and gives to Sibby. John gives him a mug, and he fills this for himself, pouring it back and forward from the mug to a bowl that is on the table, and drinking gulps now and again. Sibby blows at hers and smells it.*
Sibby. There's a good smell on it anyway. [*Tasting.*] It's lovely. O, I'd give the world and all to have the stone that made that!
Tramp. The world and all wouldn't buy it, ma'am. If I was inclined to sell it the Lord Lieutenant would have given me Dublin Castle and all that's in it long ago.
Sibby. O, couldn't we coax it out of you any way at all?
Tramp [*drinking more soup*]. The whole world wouldn't coax it out of me except maybe for one thing . . . [*looks depressed*]. Now I think of it, there's only one reason I might think of parting with it at all.
Sibby [*eagerly*]. What reason is that?
Tramp. It's a misfortune that overtakes me, ma'am, every time I make an attempt to keep a pot of my own to boil it in, and I don't like to be always under a compliment to the neighbours, asking the loan

of one. But whatever way it is, I never can keep a pot with me. I had a right to ask one of the little man that gave me the stone. The last one I bought got the bottom burned out of it one night I was giving a hand to a friend that keeps a still, and the one before that I hid under a bush one time I was going into Ennis for the night, and some boys in the town dreamed about it and went looking for treasure in it, and they found nothing but eggshells, but they brought it away for all that. And another one . . .

Sibby. Give me the loan of the stone itself, and I'll engage I'll keep a pot for it. . . . Wait now till I'll make some offer to you. . . .

Tramp [*aside*]. I'd best not be stopping to bargain, the priest might be coming in on me. [*Gets up.*] Well, ma'am, I'm sorry I can't oblige you. [*Goes to door, shades his eyes and looks out, turns suddenly.*] I have no time to lose, ma'am, I'm off. [*Comes to table and takes his hat.*] Well, ma'am, what offer will you make?

John. You might as well leave it for a day on trial first.

Tramp [*to John*]. I think it likely I'll not be passing this way again. [*To Sibby.*] Well, now, ma'am, as you were so kind, and for the sake of the good treatment you gave me, I'll ask nothing at all for it. Here it is for you and welcome, and that you may live long to use it! But I'll just take a little bit in my bag that'll do for my supper, for fear I mightn't be in Tubber before night. [*He takes up the chicken.*] And you won't begrudge me a drop of whisky when you can make plenty for yourself from this out. [*Takes the bottle.*]

John. You deserve it, you deserve it indeed. You are a very gifted man. Don't forget the kippeen!

Tramp. It's here! [*Slaps his pocket and exit. John follows him.*]

Sibby [*looking at the stone in her hand*]. Broth of the best, stirabout, poteen, wine itself, he said! And the people that will be coming to see the miracle! I'll be as rich as Biddy Early before I die!

[*John comes back.*

Sibby. Where were you, John?

John. I just went out to shake him by the hand. He's a very gifted man.

Sibby. He is so indeed.

John. And the priest's at the top of the boreen coming for his dinner. Maybe you'd best put the stone in the pot again.

THE END

THE KING'S THRESHOLD

1904

THE KING'S THRESHOLD

PERSONS IN THE PLAY

King Guaire
Seanchan (*pronounced* Shanahan)
His Pupils
The Mayor of Kinvara
Two Cripples
Brian, *an old servant*

The Lord High Chamberlain
A Soldier
A Monk
Court Ladies
Two Princesses
Fedelm

Steps before the Palace of King Guaire at Gort. A table or litter in front of steps at one side, with food on it, and a bench. Seanchan lying on steps. Pupils before steps. King on the upper step before a curtained door.

King. I welcome you that have the mastery
  Of the two kinds of Music: the one kind
  Being like a woman, the other like a man.
  Both you that understand stringed instruments,
  And how to mingle words and notes together
  So artfully that all the Art's but Speech
  Delighted with its own music; and you that carry
  The twisted horn, and understand the notes
  That lacking words escape Time's chariot;
  For the high angels that drive the horse of Time—
  The golden one by day, by night the silver—
  Are not more welcome to one that loves the world
  For some fair woman's sake.
                              I have called you hither
  To save the life of your great master, Seanchan,
  For all day long it has flamed up or flickered
  To the fast-cooling hearth.
Oldest Pupil.   When did he sicken?
  Is it a fever that is wasting him?
King. No fever or sickness. He has chosen death:
  Refusing to eat or drink, that he may bring
  Disgrace upon me; for there is a custom,
  An old and foolish custom, that if a man
  Be wronged, or think that he is wronged, and starve

70

Upon another's threshold till he die,
The common people, for all time to come,
Will raise a heavy cry against that threshold,
Even though it be the King's.

Oldest Pupil.   My head whirls round;
I do not know what I am to think or say.
I owe you all obedience, and yet
How can I give it, when the man I have loved
More than all others, thinks that he is wronged
So bitterly that he will starve and die
Rather than bear it? Is there any man
Will throw his life away for a light issue?

King. It is but fitting that you take his side
Until you understand how light an issue
Has put us by the ears. Three days ago
I yielded to the outcry of my courtiers—
Bishops, Soldiers, and Makers of the Law—
Who long had thought it against their dignity
For a mere man of words to sit amongst them
At the great council of the State and share
In their authority. I bade him go,
Though at the first with kind and courteous words,
But when he pleaded for the poets' right,
Established at the establishment of the world,
I said that I was King, and that all rights
Had their original fountain in some king,
And that it was the men who ruled the world,
And not the men who sang to it, who should sit
Where there was the most honour. My courtiers—
Bishops, Soldiers, and Makers of the Law—
Shouted approval; and amid that noise
Seanchan went out, and from that hour to this,
Although there is good food and drink beside him,
Has eaten nothing.

Oldest Pupil.   I can breathe again.
You have taken a great burden from my mind,
For that old custom's not worth dying for.

King. Persuade him to eat or drink. Till yesterday
I thought that hunger and weakness had been enough;
But finding them too trifling and too light
To hold his mouth from biting at the grave,
I called you hither, and all my hope's in you,
And certain of his neighbours and good friends

That I have sent for. While he is lying there,
Perishing there, my good name in the world
Is perishing also. I cannot give way,
Because I am King; because, if I give way,
My nobles would call me a weakling, and, it may be,
The very throne be shaken.

Oldest Pupil.   I will persuade him.
Your words had been enough persuasion, King;
But being lost in sleep or reverie,
He cannot hear them.

King.   Make him eat or drink.
Nor is it all because of my good name
I'd have him do it, for he is a man
That might well hit the fancy of a king,
Banished out of his country, or a woman's
Or any other's that can judge a man
For what he is. But I that sit a throne,
And take my measure from the needs of the State,
Call his wild thought that overruns the measure,
Making words more than deeds, and his proud will
That would unsettle all, most mischievous,
And he himself a most mischievous man.
                    [*He turns to go, and then returns again.*
Promise a house with grass and tillage land,
An annual payment, jewels and silken wear,
Or anything but that old right of the poets.   [*He goes into palace.*

Oldest Pupil. The King did wrong to abrogate our right;
But Seanchan, who talks of dying for it,
Talks foolishly. Look at us, Seanchan;
Waken out of your dream and look at us,
Who had ridden under the moon and all the day,
Until the moon has all but come again,
That we might be beside you.

Seanchan [*half turning round, leaning on his elbow, and speaking as
      if in a dream*].   I was but now
In Almhuin, in a great high-raftered house,
With Finn and Osgar. Odours of roast flesh
Rose round me, and I saw the roasting spits;
And then the dream was broken, and I saw
Grania dividing salmon by a stream.

Oldest Pupil. Hunger has made you dream of roasting flesh;
And though I all but weep to think of it,
The hunger of the crane, that starves himself

At the full moon because he is afraid
Of his own shadow and the glittering water,
Seems to me little more fantastical
Than this of yours.

Seanchan.   Why, that's the very truth.
It is as though the moon changed everything—
Myself and all that I can hear and see;
For when the heavy body has grown weak,
There's nothing that can tether the wild mind
That, being moonstruck and fantastical,
Goes where it fancies. I have even thought
I knew your voice and face, but now the words
Are so unlikely that I needs must ask
Who is it that bids me put my hunger by.

Oldest Pupil. I am your oldest pupil, Seanchan;
The one that has been with you many years—
So many that you said at Candlemas
I had almost done with school, and all but knew
Every thing that's known of poetry.

Seanchan. My oldest pupil? No, that cannot be,
For it is some one of the courtly crowds
That have been round about me from sunrise,
And I am tricked by dreams; but I'll refute them.
At Candlemas I bid that pupil tell me
Why poetry is honoured, wishing to know
If he had any weighty argument
For distant countries and strange, churlish kings.
What did he answer?

Oldest Pupil.   I said the poets hung
Images of the life that was in Eden
About the child-bed of the world, that it,
Looking upon those images, might bear
Triumphant children. But why must I stand here,
Repeating an old lesson, while you starve?

Seanchan. Tell on, for I begin to know the voice.
What evil thing will come upon the world
If the Arts perish?

Oldest Pupil.   If the Arts should perish,
The world that lacked them would be like a woman
That, looking on the cloven lips of a hare,
Brings forth a hare-lipped child.

Seanchan.   But that's not all:
For when I asked you how a man should guard

Those images, you had an answer also,
If you're the man that you have claimed to be,
Comparing them to venerable things
God gave to men before He gave them wheat.

Oldest Pupil. I answered—and the word was half your own—
That he should guard them as the Men of Dea
Guard their four treasures, as the Grail King guards
His holy cup, or the pale, righteous horse
The jewel that is underneath his horn,
Pouring out life for it as one pours out
Sweet heady wine. . . . But now I understand;
You would refute me out of my own mouth;
And yet a place at council, near the King,
Is nothing of great moment, Seanchan.
How does so light a thing touch poetry?

[*Seanchan is now sitting up. He still looks dreamily in front of him.*

Seanchan. At Candlemas you called this poetry
One of the fragile, mighty things of God,
That die at an insult.

Oldest Pupil [*to other Pupils*]. Give me some true answer,
Upon that day he spoke about the Court
And called it the first comely child of the world,
And said that all that was insulted there
The world insulted, for the Courtly life
Is the world's model. How shall I answer him?
Can you not give me some true argument?
I will not tempt him with a lying one.

Youngest Pupil. O, tell him that the lovers of his music
Have need of him.

Seanchan.   But I am labouring
For some that shall be born in the nick o' time,
And find sweet nurture, that they may have voices,
Even in anger, like the strings of harps;
And how could they be born to majesty
If I had never made the golden cradle?

Youngest Pupil [*throwing himself at Seanchan's feet*]. Why did you
          take me from my father's fields?
If you would leave me now, what shall I love?
Where shall I go? What shall I set my hand to?
And why have you put music in my ears,
If you would send me to the clattering houses?
I will throw down the trumpet and the harp,
For how could I sing verses or make music

With none to praise me, and a broken heart?
Seanchan. What was it that the poets promised you,
   If it was not their sorrow? Do not speak.
   Have I not opened school on these bare steps,
   And are you not the youngest of my scholars?
   And I would have all know that when all falls
   In ruin, poetry calls out in joy,
   Being the scattering hand, the bursting pod,
   The victim's joy among the holy flame,
   God's laughter at the shattering of the world.
   And now that joy laughs out, and weeps and burns
   On these bare steps.
Youngest Pupil.   O master, do not die!
Oldest Pupil. Trouble him with no useless argument.
   Be silent! There is nothing we can do
   Except find out the King and kneel to him,
   And beg our ancient right. For here are some
   To say whatever we could say and more,
   And fare as badly. Come, boy, that is no use.
                                    [*Raises Youngest Pupil.*
   If it seem well that we beseech the King,
   Lay down your harps and trumpets on the stones
   In silence, and come with me silently.
   Come with slow footfalls, and bow all your heads,
   For a bowed head becomes a mourner best.
      [*They lay harps and trumpets down one by one, and then go out
      very solemnly and slowly, following one another. Enter Mayor,
      two Cripples, and Brian, an old servant. The Mayor, who has
      been heard, before he came upon the stage, muttering 'Chief
      Poet', Ireland', etc., crosses in front of Seanchan to the other
      side of the steps. Brian takes food out of basket. The Cripples are
      watching the basket. The Mayor has an Ogham stick in his hand.*
Mayor [*as he crosses*]. 'Chief poet, Ireland, townsman, grazing land',
   those are the words I have to keep in mind, 'Chief poet, Ireland,
   townsman, grazing land'. I have got them all right now, they are
   all here cut upon the Ogham stick, 'Chief poet, Ireland, townsman,
   grazing land', and that's the right order. [*He keeps muttering over
   his speech during what follows.*]
First Cripple. It would serve the King right if Seanchan drove away
   his luck. What's there about a king that's in the world from birth
   to burial like another man, that he should change old customs that
   were in it as long as the world has been a world?
Second Cripple. If I were the King I wouldn't meddle with him;

there is something queer about a man that makes rhymes. I knew a man that would be making rhymes year in year out under a thorn at the crossing of three roads, and he was no sooner dead than every thorn-tree from Inchy to Kiltartan withered, and he a ragged man like ourselves.

First Cripple. Those that make rhymes have a power from beyond the world.

Mayor. I am getting ready.

First Cripple. Was it he that told you about the blessed well? And the little holy fish?

Mayor. Hush! Hush!

Second Cripple. It was he surely.

First Cripple. And it rising up out of the blessed well to cure the crippled.

Second Cripple. Rising up every seventh year.

Mayor. I'm half ready now.

Brian. There's not a mischief I begrudge the King, if it were any other man but my master——

Mayor. Hush, I am ready.

Brian. That died to bring it upon him. There, I have set out the food, and if my master won't eat it, I'll home and get provision for his wake, for that's no great way off.

Mayor. It's my turn.

Brian. Have your say, but don't be long about it.

Mayor [*going close to Seanchan*]. Chief poet of Ireland, I am the Mayor of your own town, Kinvara. I am come to tell you that the news of this great trouble between you and the King of Gort has plunged us into sorrow, part for you our honoured townsman, and part for our good town. [*Begins to hesitate, scratching his head.*] But what comes after that? Something about the King.

Brian. Get on, the food is all set out, and maybe when you are done he'll eat a bit.

Mayor. Don't hurry me.

First Cripple. Give me a taste of it, he'll not begrudge it.

Second Cripple. Let them that have their limbs starve if they like, we have to keep in mind the stomach God has left to us.

Mayor. Hush! I have it. The King was said to be most friendly, and we had good reason for thinking that he was about to give us those grazing lands we so much need, being so pinched that our mowers mow with knives between the stones. We asked nothing but what was reasonable. We ask you for the sake of the town to do what the King wants and then maybe he'll do what we want; we ask nothing but what's reasonable.

Seanchan. Reason, O reason in plenty. Yet you have yellowy white hair and not too many teeth. How comes it that you have been so long in the world and not found reason out? [*While saying this he has turned half round; he hardly looks at the Mayor.*]

Brian [*trying to pull the Mayor away*]. What's the good in saying all that, haven't they been reasoning with him all day long? No wonder he is tired of it. I have set the food before him ready.

Mayor [*shoving Brian away*]. Don't hurry me. It's small respect you are showing to the town. Get further off. [*To Seanchan.*] We would not have you think, weighty as these considerations are, that they have been as weighty in our minds as our desire that one we take so much pride in, a man that is an honour to our town, should live and prosper. Therefore we beseech you to give way in what is after all a matter of no importance, a matter of mere sentiment, that we may always keep our pride in you. [*He finishes this speech with a pompous air, motions to Brian to bring the food, and sits on seat.*]

Brian. Master, eat this, it's not king's food that's cooked for everybody and nobody. Here's barleybread out of your father's oven and dulse from Duras. Here is the dulse, your honour, it is wholesome, it has the good taste of the sea. [*Takes dulse in one hand and bread in the other and presses them into Seanchan's hand. Seanchan shows by his movements his different feeling to Brian.*]

First Cripple. He has taken it and there will be nothing left.

Second Cripple. He wanted his own sort. What's honey to a cat, corn to a dog, or a green apple to a ghost in a churchyard?

Seanchan [*pressing food back into Brian's hands*]. Eat it yourself, old man, you have come a long journey and, it may be, ate nothing on the road.

Brian. How could I eat it and your honour starving? It is your father that sends it. He cried because the stiffness that is in his bones prevented him coming, and he bade me tell you that he is old and has need of you, that the people will be pointing at him, that he will not be able to lift up his head if you turn the King's favour away, that he cared you well and you in your young age, and that it's right you should care him now.

Seanchan. What did my mother say?

Brian. Your mother gave no message, for when they told her that you had it in mind to starve or get again the ancient right of the poets, she said, 'No message will do any good. We cannot change him,' and she went indoors, lay down upon the bed and turned her face out of the light. [*A pause.*] Here's pigeons' eggs from Duras, and these were laid by your own hens.

Seanchan. She sent no message. Our mothers know us, they knew us before birth, and that is why they know us even better than sweethearts upon whose breasts we have lain. Tell them that my mother was in the right, go tell them that, go tell them that she knew me.

Mayor. What is he saying? I never understood a poet's talk more than the baa of a sheep. [*Comes over from seat. Seanchan turns away.*] You have not heard, it may be, having been so much away, how many cattle died last winter from lacking grass, how much sickness there was because the poor had nothing but salt fish to live on through the winter.

Brian. Get away and leave the place to me, for your sack's empty.

Mayor. Is it get away? Is that the way I'm to be spoken to? Am I not the Mayor? Am I not in authority? Am I not in the King's place? Answer me that.

Brian. Then show the people what a king is like; root up old customs, old habits, old rights.

Mayor. Holy Saint Colman!

First Cripple. That's what the King does, and that's what you'd like to do.

Second Cripple. Foul the holy well.

First Cripple. Roast the lucky fish.

Second Cripple. Put it into your own stomach, and it meant to cure cripples.

Mayor. How dare you take his name into your mouth, how dare you lift up your voice against the King?

Brian. How dare you praise him? I will have nobody praise him or any other king that robs my master.

Mayor. And hadn't he the right to? And hadn't he the right to strike your master's head off, being the King? Or your head, or my head! I say, Long live the King! because he didn't take our heads from us. Call out long life for him.

Brian. Is it cry out for him?

    [*The five following speeches should be spoken in a rhythmical chant, or should rise into song.*]

    There's nobody 'll call out for him,
    But smiths will turn their anvils,
    The millers turn their wheels,
    The farmers turn their churns,
    The witches turn their thumbs,
    Till he be broken and splintered into pieces.

Mayor. He might, if he'd a mind to it,
    Be digging out our tongues,
    Or dragging out our hair,
    Or bleaching us like calves,

Or weaning us like lambs,
But for the kindness and the softness that is in him.
First Cripple. The curse of the poor be upon him,
  The curse of the widows upon him,
  The curse of the children upon him,
  The curse of the bishops upon him,
  Until he be as rotten as an old mushroom!
Second Cripple. The curse of wrinkles be upon him!
  Wrinkles where his eyes are,
  Wrinkles where his nose is,
  Wrinkles where his mouth is,
  And a little old devil looking out of every wrinkle!
Brian. And nobody will sing for him,
  And nobody will hunt for him,
  And nobody will fish for him,
  And nobody will pray for him,
  But ever and always curse him and abuse him.
Mayor. I say, Long live the King.   [*Brian seizes the Mayor.*
  Help! Help!
Brian.   That's how I shout for the King.
Mayor. Help! Help! Am I not in the King's place, am I not in authority?
Brian. So you are—so you are. That's why I've got a hold of you.
First Cripple. We're teaching the King to be kind to the poor.
Mayor. Help! Help! Wait till we're in Kinvara!
First Cripple [*beating the Mayor on the legs with his crutch*]. I'll beat
  the royalty out of his legs.
    [*The Chamberlain comes down steps shouting,* 'Silence! silence!
    silence!'
Chamberlain. How dare you make this uproar at the doors,
  Deafening the very greatest in the land,
  As if the farmyards and the rookeries
  Had all been emptied!
First Cripple.   It is the Chamberlain.   [*Cripples go out.*
Chamberlain. Pick up the litter there, and get you gone!
  Be quick about it! Have you no respect
  For this worn stair, this all but sacred door,
  Where suppliants and tributary kings
  Have passed, and the world's glory knelt in silence?
  Have you no reverence for what all other men
  Hold honourable?
Brian.   If I might speak my mind,
  I'd say the King would have his luck again

If he would let my master have his rights.

Chamberlain. Pick up your litter! Take your noise away!

Make haste, and get the clapper from the bell!

Brian [*putting last of food into basket*]. What do the great and power-
ful care for rights

That have no armies?

> [*Chamberlain begins shoving them out with his staff.*

Mayor. My lord, I am not to blame.

I'm the King's man, and they attacked me for it.

Brian. We have our prayers, our curses and our prayers,

And we can give a great name or a bad one.

> [*Mayor is shoving Brian out before him with one hand. He keeps
> his face to Chamberlain, and keeps bowing. The Chamberlain
> shoves him with his staff.*

Mayor. We could not make the poet eat, my lord.

> [*Chamberlain shoves him with his staff.*

Much honoured [*is shoved again*]—honoured to speak with you,
my lord;

But I'll go find the girl that he's to marry.

She's coming, but I'll hurry her, my lord.

Between ourselves, my lord [*is shoved again*], she is a great coaxer.

Much honoured, my lord. O, she's the girl to do it;

For when the intellect is out, my lord,

Nobody but a woman's any good. [*Is shoved again.*

Much honoured, my lord [*is shoved again*], much honoured, much
honoured! [*Is shoved out, shoving Brian out before him.*

> [*All through this scene, from the outset of the quarrel, Seanchan
> has kept his face turned away, or hidden in his cloak. While the
> Chamberlain has been speaking, the Soldier and the Monk have
> come out of the palace. The Monk stands on top of steps at one
> side, Soldier a little down steps at the other side. Court Ladies
> are seen at opening in the palace curtain behind Soldier. Cham-
> berlain is in the centre.*

Chamberlain [*to Seanchan*]. Well, you must be contented, for your
work

Has roused the common sort against the King,

And stolen his authority. The State

Is like some orderly and reverend house

Wherein, the master being dead of a sudden,

The servants quarrel where they have a mind to,

And pilfer here and there.

> [*Pause, finding that Seanchan does not answer
> How many days

Will you keep up this quarrel with the King,
And the King's nobles, and myself, and all,
Who'd gladly be your friends, if you would let them?

[*Going near to Monk.*

If you would try, you might persuade him, father.
I cannot make him answer me, and yet,
If fitting hands would offer him the food,
He might accept it.

Monk. Certainly I will not.
I've made too many homilies, wherein
The wanton imagination of the poets
Has been condemned, to be his flatterer.
If pride and disobedience are unpunished
Who will obey?

Chamberlain [*going to other side towards Soldier*]. If you would speak
    to him,
You might not find persuasion difficult,
With all the devils of hunger helping you.

Soldier. I will not interfere, and if he starve
For being obstinate and stiff in the neck,
'Tis but good riddance.

Chamberlain. One of us must do it.
It might be, if you'd reason with him, ladies,
He would eat something, for I have a notion
That if he brought misfortune on the King,
Or the King's house, we'd be as little thought of
As summer linen when the winter's come.

First Girl. But it would be the greater compliment
If Peter 'd do it.

Second Girl. Reason with him, Peter.
Persuade him to eat; he's such a bag of bones!

Soldier. I'll never trust a woman's word again!
There's nobody that was so loud against him
When he was at the council; now the wind's changed,
And you that could not bear his speech or his silence
Would have him there in his old place again;
I do believe you would, but I won't help you.

Second Girl. Why will you be so hard upon us, Peter?
You know we have turned the common sort against us,
And he looks miserable.

First Girl. We cannot dance,
Because no harper will pluck a string for us.

Second Girl. I cannot sleep with thinking of his face.

First Girl. And I love dancing more than anything.
Second Girl. Do not be hard on us; but yesterday
  A woman in the road threw stones at me.
  You would not have me stoned?
First Girl.   May I not dance?
Soldier. I will do nothing. You have put him out,
  And now that he is out—well, leave him out.
First Girl. Do it for my sake, Peter.
Second Girl.   And for mine.
      [*Each girl as she speaks takes Peter's hand with her right hand,
        stroking down his arm with her left. While Second Girl is strok-
        ing his arm, First Girl leaves go and gives him the dish.*
Soldier. Well, well; but not your way.   [*To Seanchan.*]
                              Here's meat for you.
  It has been carried from too good a table
  For men like you, and I am offering it
  Because these women have made a fool of me.   [*A pause.*
  You mean to starve? You will have none of it?
  I'll leave it there, where you can sniff the savour.
  Snuff it, old hedgehog, and unroll yourself!
  But if I were the King, I'd make you do it
  With wisps of lighted straw.
Seanchan.   You have rightly named me.
  I lie rolled up under the ragged thorns
  That are upon the edge of those great waters
  Where all things vanish away, and I have heard
  Murmurs that are the ending of all sound.
  I am out of life; I am rolled up, and yet,
  Hedgehog although I am, I'll not unroll
  For you, King's dog! Go to the King, your master.
  Crouch down and wag your tail, for it may be
  He has nothing now against you, and I think
  The stripes of your last beating are all healed.
          [*The Soldier has drawn his sword.*
Chamberlain [*striking up sword*]. Put up your sword, sir; put it up,
      I say!
  The common sort would tear you into pieces
  If you but touched him.
Soldier.   If he's to be flattered,
  Petted, cajoled, and dandled into humour,
  We might as well have left him at the table.
                  [*Goes to one side sheathing sword.*
Seanchan. You must needs keep your patience yet awhile,

For I have some few mouthfuls of sweet air
To swallow before I have grown to be as civil
As any other dust.
Chamberlain.   You wrong us, Seanchan.
There is none here but holds you in respect;
And if you'd only eat out of this dish,
The King would show how much he honours you.

[Bowing and smiling.

Who could imagine you'd so take to heart
Being driven from the council? I am certain
That you, if you will only think it over,
Will understand that it is men of law,
Leaders of the King's armies, and the like,
That should sit there.
Seanchan.   Somebody has deceived you,
Or maybe it was your own eyes that lied,
In making it appear that I was driven
From the great council. You have driven away
The images of them that weave a dance
By the four rivers in the mountain garden.
Chamberlain. You mean we have driven poetry away.
But that's not altogether true, for I,
As you should know, have written poetry.
And often when the table has been cleared,
And candles lighted, the King calls for me,
And I repeat it him. My poetry
Is not to be compared with yours; but still,
Where I am honoured, poetry, in some measure,
Is honoured too.
Seanchan.   Well, if you are a poet,
Cry out that the King's money would not buy,
Nor the high circle consecrate his head,
If poets had never christened gold, and even
The moon's poor daughter, that most whey-faced metal,
Precious; cry out that not a man alive
Would ride among the arrows with high heart,
Or scatter with an open hand, had not
Our heady craft commended wasteful virtues.
And when that story's finished, shake your coat
Where little jewels gleam on it, and say,
A herdsman, sitting where the pigs had trampled,
Made up a song about enchanted kings,
Who were so finely dressed one fancied them

All fiery, and women by the churn
And children by the hearth caught up the song
And murmured it, until the tailors heard it.

Chamberlain. If you would but eat something, you'd find out
That you have had these thoughts from lack of food,
For hunger makes us feverish.

Seanchan. Cry aloud
That when we are driven out we come again
Like a great wind that runs out of the waste
To blow the tables flat; and thereupon
Lie down upon the threshold till the King
Restore to us the ancient right of the poets.

Monk. You cannot shake him. I will to the King,
And offer him consolation in his trouble,
For that man there has set his teeth to die.
He is a man that hates obedience,
Discipline, and orderliness of life;
I cannot mourn him.

First Girl. 'Twas you that stirred it up.
You stirred it up that you might spoil our dancing.
Why shouldn't we have dancing? We're not in Lent.
Yet nobody will pipe or play to us;
And they will never do it if he die.
And that is why you are going.

Monk. What folly's this?

First Girl. Well, if you did not do it, speak to him—
Use your authority; make him obey you.
What harm is there in dancing?

Monk. Hush! begone!
Go to the fields and watch the hurley players,
Or any other place you have a mind to.
This is not woman's work.

First Girl. Come! let's away!
We can do nothing here.

Monk. The pride of the poets!
Dancing, hurling, the country full of noise,
And King and Church neglected. Seanchan,
I'll take my leave, for you are perishing
Like all that let the wanton imagination
Carry them where it will, and it's not likely
I'll look upon your living face again.

Seanchan. Come nearer, nearer!

Monk. Have you some last wish?

Seanchan. Stoop down, for I would whisper it in your ear.
　Has that wild God of yours, that was so wild
　When you'd but lately taken the King's pay,
　Grown any tamer? He gave you all much trouble.
Monk. Let go my habit!
Seanchan.　　　　　　Have you persuaded him
　To chirp between two dishes when the King
　Sits down to table?
Monk.　　　　　　Let go my habit, sir! [*Crosses to centre of stage.*
Seanchan. And maybe he has learned to sing quite softly
　Because loud singing would disturb the King,
　Who is sitting drowsily among his friends
　After the table has been cleared. Not yet!
　　[*Seanchan has been dragged some feet clinging to the Monk's
　　habit.*
　You did not think that hands so full of hunger
　Could hold you tightly. They are not civil yet.
　I'd know if you have taught him to eat bread
　From the King's hand, and perch upon his finger.
　I think he perches on the King's strong hand,
　But it may be that he is still too wild.
　You must not weary in your work; a king
　Is often weary, and he needs a God
　To be a comfort to him.
　　[*The Monk plucks his habit away and goes into palace. Seanchan
　　holds up his hand as if a bird perched upon it. He pretends to
　　stroke the bird.*
　　　　　　　　A little God,
　With comfortable feathers, and bright eyes.
First Girl. There will be no more dancing in our time.
　For nobody will play the harp or the fiddle.
　Let us away, for we cannot amend it,
　And watch the hurley.
Second Girl.　　　　　Hush! he is looking at us.
Seanchan. Yes, yes, go to the hurley, go to the hurley,
　Go to the hurley! Gather up your skirts—
　Run quickly! You can remember many love songs;
　I know it by the light that's in your eyes—
　But you'll forget them. You're fair to look upon.
　Your feet delight in dancing, and your mouths
　In the slow smiling that awakens love.
　The mothers that have borne you mated rightly.
　They'd little ears as thirsty as your ears

For many love songs. Go to the young men.
Are not the ruddy flesh and the thin flanks
And the broad shoulders worthy of desire?
Go from me! Here is nothing for your eyes.
But it is I that am singing you away—
Singing you to the young men.

> [*The two young Princesses come out of palace. While he has been
> speaking the Girls have shrunk back holding each other's hands.*

First Girl.   Be quiet!
Look who it is has come out of the house.
Princesses, we are for the hurling field.
Will you go there?
First Princess.   We will go with you, Aileen.
But we must have some words with Seanchan,
For we have come to make him eat and drink.
Chamberlain. I will hold out the dish and cup for him
While you are speaking to him of his folly,
If you desire it, Princess.   [*He has taken dish and cup.*
First Princess.   No, Finula
Will carry him the dish and I the cup.
We'll offer them ourselves.   [*They take cup and dish.*
First Girl.   They are so gracious;
The dear little Princesses are so gracious.

> [*Princess holds out her hand for Seanchan to kiss it. He does not
> move.*

Although she is holding out her hand to him,
He will not kiss it.
First Princess.   My father bids us say
That, though he cannot have you at his table,
You may ask any other thing you like
And he will give it you. We carry you
With our own hands a dish and cup of wine.
First Girl. O, look! he has taken it! He has taken it!
The dear Princesses! I have always said
That nobody could refuse them anything.

> [*Seanchan takes the cup in one hand. In the other he holds for a
> moment the hand of the Princess.*

Seanchan. O, long, soft fingers and pale finger-tips,
Well worthy to be laid in a king's hand!
O, you have fair white hands, for it is certain
There is uncommon whiteness in these hands.
But there is something comes into my mind,
Princess. A little while before your birth,

I saw your mother sitting by the road
In a high chair; and when a leper passed,
She pointed him the way into the town.
He lifted up his hand and blessed her hand—
I saw it with my own eyes. Hold out your hands;
I will find out if they are contaminated,
For it has come into my thoughts that maybe
The King has sent me food and drink by hands
That are contaminated. I would see all your hands.
You've eyes of dancers; but hold out your hands,
For it may be there are none sound among you.

      [*The Princesses have shrunk back in terror.*

First Princess. He has called us lepers. [*Soldier draws sword.*
Chamberlain.   He's out of his mind,
 And does not know the meaning of what he said.
Seanchan [*standing up*]. There's no sound hand among you—no sound
  hand.
 Away with you! away with all of you!
 You are all lepers! There is leprosy
 Among the plates and dishes that you have carried.
 And wherefore have you brought me leper's wine?

    [*He flings the contents of the cup in their faces.*

 There, there! I have given it to you again. And now
 Begone, or I will give my curse to you.
 You have the leper's blessing, but you think
 Maybe the bread will something lack in savour
 Unless you mix my curse into the dough.

  [*They go out hurriedly in all directions. Seanchan is staggering in
   the middle of the stage.*

 Where did I say the leprosy had come from?
 I said it came out of a leper's hand,

        Enter Cripples

 And that he walked the highway. But that's folly,
 For he was walking up there in the sky.
 And there he is even now, with his white hand
 Thrust out of the blue air, and blessing them
 With leprosy.
First Cripple. He's pointing at the moon
 That's coming out up yonder, and he calls it
 Leprous, because the daylight whitens it.
Seanchan. He's holding up his hand above them all—
 King, noblemen, princesses—blessing all.
 Who could imagine he'd have so much patience?

First Cripple [*clutching the other Cripple*]. Come out of this!
Second Cripple [*pointing to food*]. If you don't need it, sir,
    May we not carry some of it away?
            [*They cross towards food and pass in front of Seanchan*
Seanchan. Who's speaking? Who are you?
First Cripple.   Come out of this!
Second Cripple. Have pity on us, that must beg our bread
    From table to table throughout the entire world,
    And yet be hungry.
Seanchan.   But why were you born crooked?
    What bad poet did your mothers listen to
    That you were born so crooked?
First Cripple.   Come away!
    Maybe he's cursed the food, and it might kill us.
Second Cripple. Yes, better come away.   [*They go out.*
Seanchan [*staggering and speaking wearily*].
                    He has great strength
    And great patience to hold his right hand there,
    Uplifted, and not wavering about.
    He is much stronger than I am, much stronger.
        [*Sinks down on steps. Mayor and Fedelm have entered.*
Mayor. He is delirious now.
Fedelm.   Before I speak
    Of food or drink I'll take him out of this.
    For while he is on this threshold and can hear,
    It may be, the voices that made mock of him,
    He would not listen.
Mayor.   No, speak to him at once.
    Press food upon him while delirious
    And he may eat not knowing what he does.   [*Mayor goes out.*
Fedelm. Seanchan! Seanchan!   [*He remains looking into the sky.*
               Can you not hear me, Seanchan?
    It is myself.
        [*He looks at her, dreamily at first, then takes her hand.*
Seanchan.   Is this your hand, Fedelm?
    I have been looking at another hand
    That is up yonder.
Fedelm.   I have come for you.
Seanchan. Fedelm, I did not know that you were here.
Fedelm. And can you not remember that I promised
    That I would come and take you home with me
    When I'd the harvest in? And now I've come,

And you must come away, and come on the instant.
Seanchan. Yes, I will come. But is the harvest in?
This air has got a summer taste in it.
Fedelm. But is not the wild middle of the summer
A better time to marry? Come with me now!
Seanchan [*seizing her by both wrists*]. Who taught you that? For it's
a certainty,
Although I never knew it till last night,
That marriage, because it is the height of life,
Can only be accomplished to the full
In the high days of the year. I lay awake:
There had come a frenzy into the light of the stars,
And they were coming nearer, and I knew
All in a minute they were about to marry
Clods out upon the ploughlands, to beget
A mightier race than any that has been.
But some that are within there made a noise,
And frighted them away.
Fedelm.   Come with me now!
We have far to go, and daylight's running out.
Seanchan. The stars had come so near me that I caught
Their singing. It was praise of that great race
That would be haughty, mirthful, and white-bodied,
With a high head, and open hand, and how,
Laughing, it would take the mastery of the world.
Fedelm. But you will tell me all about their songs
When we're at home. You have need of rest and care,
And I can give them you when we're at home.
And therefore let us hurry, and get us home.
Seanchan. It's certain that there is some trouble here,
Although it's gone out of my memory.
And I would get away from it. Give me your help.   [*Trying to rise.*
But why are not my pupils here to help me?
Go, call my pupils, for I need their help.
Fedelm. Come with me now, and I will send for them,
For I have a great room that's full of beds
I can make ready; and there is a smooth lawn
Where they can play at hurley and sing poems
Under an apple-tree.
Seanchan.   I know that place:
An apple-tree, and a smooth level lawn
Where the young men can sway their hurley sticks.

[*Sings*]
The four rivers that run there,
 Through well-mown level ground,
Have come out of a blessed well
That is all bound and wound
By the great roots of an apple
And all the fowls of the air
Have gathered in the wide branches
And keep singing there.

[*Fedelm, troubled, has covered her eyes with her hands.*

Fedelm. No, there are not four rivers, and those rhymes
  Praise Adam's paradise.

Seanchan.   I can remember now,
  It's out of a poem I made long ago
  About the Garden in the East of the World,
  And how spirits in the images of birds
  Crowd in the branches of old Adam's crab-tree.
  They come before me now, and dig in the fruit
  With so much gluttony, and are so drunk
  With that harsh wholesome savour, that their feathers
  Are clinging one to another with the juice.
  But you would lead me to some friendly place,
  And I would go there quickly.

Fedelm [*helping him to rise*].   Come with me.

        [*He walks slowly, supported by her, till he comes to table.*

Seanchan. But why am I so weak? Have I been ill?
  Sweetheart, why is it that I am so weak?   [*Sinks on to seat.*

Fedelm [*goes to table*]. I'll dip this piece of bread into the wine,
  For that will make you stronger for the journey.

Seanchan. Yes, give me bread and wine; that's what I want,
  For it is hunger that is gnawing me.

    [*He takes bread from Fedelm, hesitates, and then thrusts it back
    into her hand.*

  But no; I must not eat it.

Fedelm.   Eat, Seanchan,
  For if you do not eat it you will die.

Seanchan. Why did you give me food? Why did you come?
  For had I not enough to fight against
  Without your coming?

Fedelm.   Eat this little crust,
  Seanchan, if you have any love for me.

Seanchan. I must not eat it—but that's beyond your wit.

Child! child! I must not eat it, though I die.

Fedelm [*passionately*]. You do not know what love is; for if you loved,
    You would put every other thought away.
    But you have never loved me.

Seanchan [*seizing her by wrist*].   You, a child,
    Who had but seen a man out of the window,
    Tell me that I know nothing about love,
    And that I do not love you? Did I not say
    There was a frenzy in the light of the stars
    All through the livelong night, and that the night
    Was full of marriages? But that fight's over
    And all that's done with, and I have to die.

Fedelm [*throwing her arms about him*]. I will not be put from you,
        although I think
    I had not grudged it you if some great lady,
    If the King's daughter, had set out your bed.
    I will not give you up to death; no, no!
    And are not these white arms and this soft neck
    Better than the brown earth?

Seanchan [*struggling to disengage himself*]. Begone from me!
    There's treachery in those arms and in that voice.
    They're all against me. Why do you linger there?
    How long must I endure the sight of you?

Fedelm. O, Seanchan! Seanchan!

Seanchan [*rising*].   Go where you will,
    So it be out of sight and out of mind.
    I cast you from me like an old torn cap,
    A broken shoe, a glove without a finger,
    A crooked penny; whatever is most worthless.

Fedelm [*bursts into tears*]. O, do not drive me from you!

Seanchan [*takes her in his arms*].   What did I say,
    My dove of the woods? I was about to curse you.
    It was a frenzy. I'll unsay it all.
    But you must go away.

Fedelm.   Let me be near you.
    I will obey like any married wife.
    Let me but lie before your feet.

Seanchan.   Come nearer.   [*Kisses her.*
    If I had eaten when you bid me, sweetheart,
    The kiss of multitudes in times to come
    Had been the poorer.

             [*Enter King from palace, followed by the two Princesses.*

King [*to Fedelm*].   Has he eaten yet?

Fedelm. No, King, and will not till you have restored
  The right of the poets.

King [*coming down and standing before Seanchan*]. Seanchan, you
  have refused
  Everybody I have sent, and now
  I come to you myself.

Fedelm.   Come nearer, King.
  He is now so weak he cannot hear your voice.

King. Seanchan, put away your pride as I
  Have put my pride away. I had your love
  Not a great while ago, and now you have planned
  To put a voice by every cottage fire,
  And in the night when no one sees who cries,
  To cry against me till my throne has crumbled.
  And yet if I give way I must offend
  My courtiers and nobles till they, too,
  Strike at the crown. What would you have of me?

Seanchan. When did the poets promise safety, King?

King. Seanchan, I bring you bread in my own hands,
  And bid you eat because of all these reasons,
  And for this further reason, that I love you.

            [*Seanchan pushes bread away, with Fedelm's hand.*
  You have refused, Seanchan?

Seanchan.   We have refused it.

King. I have been patient, though I am a king,
  And have the means to force you. But that's ended,
  And I am but a king, and you a subject.
  Nobles and courtiers, bring the poets hither;

      *Enter Court Ladies, Monk, Soldiers, Chamberlain, and
      Courtiers with Pupils, who have halters round their necks*

  For you can have your way. I that was man,
  With a man's heart, am now all king again.
  Speak to your master; beg your lives of him;
  Show him the halter that is round your necks.
  If his heart's set upon it, he may die;
  But you shall all die with him.   [*Goes up steps.*
            Beg your lives!
  Begin, for you have little time to lose.
  Begin it, you that are the oldest pupil.

Oldest Pupil. Die, Seanchan, and proclaim the right of the poets,

King. Silence! you are as crazy as your master.
  But that young boy, that seems the youngest of you,

I'd have him speak. Kneel down before him, boy;
Hold up your hands to him that you may pluck
That milky-coloured neck out of the noose.
Youngest Pupil. Die, Seanchan, and proclaim the right of the poets.
Seanchan. Come nearer me that I may know how face
  Differs from face and touch you with my hands.
  O more than kin, O more than children could be,
  For children are but born out of our blood
  And share our frailty. O my chicks, my chicks!
  That I have nourished underneath my wings
  And fed upon my soul.   *[He rises and walks down steps.*
                    I need no help.
  He needs no help that joy has lifted up
  Like some miraculous beast out of Ezekiel.
  The man that dies has the chief part in the story,
  And I will mock and mock that image yonder,
  That evil picture in the sky—no, no!
  I have all my strength again, I will outface it.
  O, look upon the moon that's standing there
  In the blue daylight—take note of the complexion,
  Because it is the white of leprosy
  And the contagion that afflicts mankind
  Falls from the moon. When I and these are dead
  We should be carried to some windy hill
  To lie there with uncovered face awhile
  That mankind and that leper there may know
  Dead faces laugh.   *[He falls and then half rises.*
        King! King! Dead faces laugh.   *[He dies.*
Oldest Pupil. King, he is dead; some strange triumphant thought
  So filled his heart with joy that it has burst,
  Being grown too mighty for our frailty,
  And we who gaze grow like him and abhor
  The moments that come between us and that death
  You promised us.
King.   Take up his body.
  Go where you please and lay it where you please,
  So that I cannot see his face or any
  That cried him towards his death.
Youngest Pupil.   Dead faces laugh!
  The ancient right is gone, the new remains,
  And that is death.
        [They go towards the King holding out their halters.
      We are impatient men,

So gather up the halters in your hands.

King. Drive them away.

> [*He goes into the palace. The Soldiers block the way before the Pupils.*

Soldier.   Here is no place for you,
For he and his pretensions now are finished.
Begone before the men-at-arms are bidden
To beat you from the door.

Oldest Pupil.   Take up his body
And cry that, driven from the populous door,
He seeks high waters and the mountain birds
To claim a portion of their solitude.

> [*They make a litter with cloak and staffs or use one discovered, heaped with food, at the opening of the play.*

Youngest Pupil. And cry that when they took his ancient right
They took all common sleep; therefore he claims
The mountain for his mattress and his pillow.

Oldest Pupil. And there he can sleep on, not noticing,
Although the world be changed from worse to worse,
Amid the changeless clamour of the curlew.

> [*They raise the litter on their shoulders and move a few steps.*

Youngest Pupil [*motioning to them to stop*]. Yet make triumphant
     music; sing aloud,
For coming times will bless what he has blessed
And curse what he has cursed.

Oldest Pupil.   No, no, be still,
Or pluck a solemn music from the strings.
You wrong his greatness speaking so of triumph.

Youngest Pupil. O silver trumpets, be you lifted up
And cry to the great race that is to come.
Long-throated swans upon the waves of time,
Sing loudly, for beyond the wall of the world
That race may hear our music and awake.

Oldest Pupil [*motioning the musicians to lower their trumpets*].
Not what it leaves behind it in the light
But what it carries with it to the dark
Exalts the soul; nor song nor trumpet-blast
Can call up races from the worsening world
To mend the wrong and mar the solitude
Of the great shade we follow to the tomb.

> [*Fedelm and the Pupils go out carrying the litter. Some play a mournful music.*

THE END

THE SHADOWY WATERS

(Acting Version)

1911

THE SHADOWY WATERS

(Acting Version)

PERSONS IN THE PLAY

Forgael	Sailors
Aibric	Dectora

A mast and a great sail, a large tiller, a poop rising several feet above the stage, and from the overhanging stern a lanthorn hangs. The sea or sky is represented by a semicircular cloth of which nothing can be seen except a dark abyss. The persons move but little. Some sailors are discovered crouching by the sail. Forgael is asleep and Aibric standing by the tiller on the raised poop.

First Sailor. It is long enough, and too long, Forgael has been bringing us through the waste places of the great sea.

Second Sailor. We did not meet with a ship to make a prey of these eight weeks, or any shore or island to plunder or to harry. It is a hard thing, age to be coming on me, and I not to get the chance of doing a robbery that would enable me to live quiet and honest to the end of my lifetime.

First Sailor. We are out since the new moon. What is worse again, it is the way we are in a ship, the barrels empty and my throat shrivelled with drought, and nothing to quench it but water only.

Forgael [*in his sleep*]. Yes; there, there; that hair that is the colour of burning.

First Sailor. Listen to him now, calling out in his sleep.

Forgael [*in his sleep*]. That pale forehead, that hair the colour of burning.

First Sailor. Some crazy dream he is in, and believe me it is no crazier than the thought he has waking. He is not the first that has had the wits drawn out from him through shadows and fantasies.

Second Sailor. That is what ails him. I have been thinking it this good while.

First Sailor. Do you remember that galley we sank at the time of the full moon?

Second Sailor. I do. We were becalmed the same night, and he sat up there playing that old harp of his until the moon had set.

First Sailor. I was sleeping up there by the bulwark, and when I woke in the sound of the harp a change came over my eyes, and I could see very strange things. The dead were floating upon the sea yet, and it seemed as if the life that went out of every one of them had turned to the shape of a man-headed bird—grey they were, and they rose up of a sudden and called out with voices like our own, and flew away singing to the west. Words like this they were singing: 'Happiness beyond measure, happiness where the sun dies'.

Second Sailor. I understand well what they are doing. My mother used to be talking of birds of the sort. They are sent by the lasting watchers to lead men away from this world and its women to some place of shining women that cast no shadow, having lived before the making of the earth. But I have no mind to go following him to that place.

First Sailor. Let us creep up to him and kill him in his sleep.

Second Sailor. I would have made an end of him long ago, but that I was in dread of his harp. It is said that when he plays upon it he has power over all the listeners, with or without the body, seen or unseen, and any man that listens grows to be as mad as himself.

First Sailor. What way can he play it, being in his sleep?

Second Sailor. But who would be our captain then to make out a course from the Bear and the Polestar, and to bring us back home?

First Sailor. I have that thought out. We must have Aibric with us. He knows the constellations as well as Forgael. He is a good hand with the sword. Join with us; be our captain, Aibric. We are agreed to put an end to Forgael, before he wakes. There is no man but will be glad of it when it is done. Join with us, and you will have the captain's share and profit.

Aibric. Silence! for you have taken Forgael's pay.

First Sailor. Little pay we have had this twelvemonth. We would never have turned against him if he had brought us, as he promised, into seas that would be thick with ships. That was the bargain. What is the use of knocking about and fighting as we do unless we get the chance to drink more wine and kiss more women than lasting peaceable men through their long lifetime? You will be as good a leader as ever he was himself, if you will but join us.

Aibric. And do you think that I will join myself
To men like you, and murder him who has been
My master from my earliest childhood up?
No! nor to a world of men like you
When Forgael's in the other scale. Come! come!

I'll answer to more purpose when you have drawn
That sword out of its scabbard.

First Sailor.   You have awaked him.
We had best go, for we have missed this chance.   [*Sailors go out.*

Forgael. Have the birds passed us? I could hear your voice,
But there were others.

Aibric.   I have seen nothing pass.

Forgael. You are certain of it? I never wake from sleep
But that I am afraid they may have passed;
For they're my only pilots. I have not seen them
For many days, and yet there must be many
Dying at every moment in the world.

Aibric. They have all but driven you crazy, and already
The sailors have been plotting for your death;
Whatever has been cried into your ears
Has lured you on to death.

Forgael.   No; but they promised—

Aibric. I know their promises. You have told me all.
They are to bring you to unheard-of passion,
To some strange love the world knows nothing of,
Some Ever-living woman as you think,
One that can cast no shadow, being unearthly.
But that's all folly. Turn the ship about,
Sail home again, be some fair woman's friend;
Be satisfied to live like other men,
And drive impossible dreams away. The world
Has beautiful women to please every man.

Forgael. But he that gets their love after the fashion
Loves in brief longing and deceiving hope
And bodily tenderness, and finds that even
The bed of love, that in the imagination
Had seemed to be the giver of all peace,
Is no more than a wine-cup in the tasting,
And as soon finished.

Aibric.   All that ever loved
Have loved that way—there is no other way.

Forgael. Yet never have two lovers kissed but they
Believed there was some other near at hand,
And almost wept because they could not find it.

Aibric. When they have twenty years; in middle life
They take a kiss for what a kiss is worth,
And let the dream go by.

Forgael.   It's not a dream,

But the reality that makes our passion
As a lamp shadow—no—no lamp, the sun.
What the world's million lips are thirsting for
Must be substantial somewhere.
Aibric.   I have heard the Druids
Mutter such things as they awake from trance.
It may be that the dead have lit upon it,
Or those that never lived; no mortal can.
Forgael. I only of all living men shall find it.
Aibric. Then seek it in the habitable world,
Or leap into that sea and end a journey
That has no other end.
Forgael.   I cannot answer.
I can see nothing plain; all's mystery.
Yet sometimes there's a torch inside my head
That makes all clear, but when the light is gone
I have but images, analogies,
The mystic bread, the sacramental wine,
The red rose where the two shafts of the cross,
Body and soul, waking and sleep, death, life,
Whatever meaning ancient allegorists
Have settled on, are mixed into one joy.
For what's the rose but that? miraculous cries,
Old stories about mystic marriages,
Impossible truths? But when the torch is lit
All that is impossible is certain,
I plunge in the abyss.   [*Sailors come in.*
First Sailor. Look there! there in the mist! A ship of spices!
Second Sailor. We would not have noticed her but for the sweet smell
   through the air. Ambergris and sandalwood, and all the herbs the
   witches bring from the sunrise.
First Sailor. No; but opoponax and cinnamon.
Forgael [*taking the tiller from Aibric*]. The Ever-living have kept my
   bargain; they have paid you on the nail.
Aibric. Take up that rope to make her fast while we are plundering her.
First Sailor. There is a king on her deck and a queen. Where there is
   one woman it is certain there will be others.
Aibric. Speak lower or they'll hear.
First Sailor. They cannot hear; they are too much taken up with one
   another. Look! he has stooped down and kissed her on the lips.
Second Sailor. When she finds out we have as good men aboard she
   may not be too sorry in the end.
First Sailor. She will be as dangerous as a wild cat. These queens think

more of the riches and the great name they get by marriage than
of a ready hand and a strong body.

Second Sailor. There is nobody is natural but a robber. That is the
reason the whole world goes tottering about upon its bandy legs.

Aibric. Run upon them now, and overpower the crew while yet asleep.

[*Sailors and Aibric go out. The clashing of swords and confused
voices are heard from the other ship, which cannot be seen because of the sail.*

Forgael [*who has remained at the tiller*]. There! there! They come!
    Gull, gannet, or diver,
But with a man's head, or a fair woman's.
They hover over the masthead awhile
To wait their friends, but when their friends have come
They'll fly upon that secret way of theirs,
One—and one—a couple—five together.
And now they all wheel suddenly and fly
To the other side, and higher in the air,
They've gone up thither, friend's run up by friend;
They've gone to their beloved ones in the air,
In the waste of the high air, that they may wander
Among the windy meadows of the dawn.
But why are they still waiting? Why are they
Circling and circling over the masthead?
Ah! now they all look down—they'll speak of me
What the Ever-living put into their minds,
And of that shadowless unearthly woman
At the world's end. I hear the message now,
But it's all mystery. There's one that cries,
'From love and hate'. Before the sentence ends
Another breaks upon it with a cry,
'From love and death and out of sleep and waking'.
And with the cry another cry is mixed,
'What can we do, being shadows?' All mystery,
And I am drunken with a dizzy light.
But why do they still hover overhead?
Why are you circling there? Why do you linger?
Why do you not run to your desire,
Now that you have happy winged bodies?
Being too busy in the air, and the high air,
They cannot hear my voice. But why that circling?

                    [*The Sailors have returned. Dectora is with them.*

[*Turning and seeing her.*] Why are you standing with your eyes
    upon me?

You are not the world's core. O no, no, no!
That cannot be the meaning of the birds.
You are not its core. My teeth are in the world,
But have not bitten yet.
Dectora.   I am a queen,
   And ask for satisfaction upon these
   Who have slain my husband and laid hands upon me.
Forgael. I'd set my hopes on one that had no shadow:—
   Where do you come from? who brought you to this place?
   Why do you cast a shadow? Answer me that.
Dectora. Would that the storm that overthrew my ships,
   And drowned the treasures of nine conquered nations,
   And blew me hither to my lasting sorrow,
   Had drowned me also. But, being yet alive,
   I ask a fitting punishment for all
   That raised their hands against him.
Forgael.   There are some
   That weigh and measure all in these waste seas—
   They that have all the wisdom that's in life,
   And all that prophesying images
   Made of dim gold rave out in secret tombs;
   They have it that the plans of kings and queens
   Are dust on the moth's wing; that nothing matters
   But laughter and tears—laughter, laughter and tears—
   That every man should carry his own soul
   Upon his shoulders.
Dectora.   You've nothing but wild words,
   And I would know if you would give me vengeance.
Forgael. When she finds out that I'll not let her go—
   When she knows that.
Dectora.   What is that you are muttering?
   That you'll not let me go? I am a queen.
Forgael. Although you are more beautiful than any,
   I almost long that it were possible;
   But if I were to put you on that ship,
   With sailors that were sworn to do your will,
   And you had spread a sail for home, a wind
   Would rise of a sudden, or a wave so huge
   It had washed among the stars and put them out,
   And beat the bulwark of your ship on mine,
   Until you stood before me on the deck—
   As now.
Dectora.   Has wandering in these desolate seas

And listening to the cry of wind and wave
Driven you mad?

Forgael.　　　　　But, queen, I am not mad.

Dectora. And yet you say the water and the wind
Would rise against me.

Forgael.　　　　　No, I am not mad—
If it be not that hearing messages
From lasting watchers that outlive the moon
At the most quiet midnight is to be stricken.

Dectora. And did those watchers bid you take me captive?

Forgael. Both you and I are taken in the net.
It was their hands that plucked the winds awake
And blew you hither; and their mouths have promised
I shall have love in their immortal fashion.
They gave me that old harp of the nine spells
That is more mighty than the sun and moon,
Or than the shivering casting-net of the stars,
That none might take you from me.

Dectora [*first trembling back from the mast where the harp is, and then
　　laughing*].　　　　　For a moment
Your raving of a message and a harp
More mighty than the stars half troubled me.
But all that's raving. Who is there can compel
The daughter and granddaughter of a king
To be his bedfellow?

Forgael.　　　　　Until your lips
Have called me their beloved, I'll not kiss them.

Dectora. My husband and my king died at my feet,
And yet you talk of love.

Forgael.　　　　　The movement of time
Is shaken in these seas, and what one does
One moment has no might upon the moment
That follows after.

Dectora.　　　　　I understand you now.
You have a Druid craft of wicked music,
Wrung from the cold women of the sea—
A magic that can call a demon up,
Until my body give you kiss for kiss.

Forgael. Your soul shall give the kiss.

Dectora.　　　　　I am not afraid
While there's a rope to run into a noose
Or wave to drown. But I have done with words,

And I would have you look into my face
And know that it is fearless.

Forgael.   Do what you will,
For neither I nor you can break a mesh
Of the great golden net that is about us.

Dectora. There's nothing in the world that's worth a fear.

[*She passes Forgael and stands for a moment looking into his face.*
I have good reason for that thought.

[*She runs suddenly on to the raised part of the poop.*
And now
I can put fear away as a queen should.

[*She mounts on the bulwark, and turns towards Forgael.*
Fool, fool! Although you have looked into my face
You did not see my purpose. I shall have gone
Before a hand can touch me.

Forgael [*folding his arms*].   My hands are still;
The Ever-living hold us. Do what you will,
You cannot leap out of the golden net.

First Sailor. There is no need for you to drown. Give us our pardon
and we will bring you home on your own ship, and make an end of
this man that is leading us to death.

Dectora. I promise it.

Aibric.   I stand upon his side.
I'd strike a blow for him to give him time
To cast his dreams away.

First Sailor. He has put a sudden darkness over the moon.

Dectora. Nine swords with handles of rhinoceros horn
To him that strikes him first!

First Sailor. I will strike him first. No! for that music of his might put
a beast's head upon my shoulders, or it may be two heads and they
devouring one another.

Dectora. I'll give a golden galley full of fruit
That has the heady flavour of new wine
To him that wounds him to the death.

First Sailor. I'll strike at him. His spells, when he dies, will die with him
and vanish away.

Second Sailor. I'll strike at him.

The Others.   And I! And I! And I!

[*Forgael plays upon the harp.*

First Sailor [*falling into a dream*]. It is what they are saying, there is
some person dead in the other ship; we have to go and wake him.
They did not say what way he came to his end, but it was sudden.

Second Sailor. You are right, you are right. We have to go to that wake.

Dectora. He has flung a Druid spell upon the air,
  And set you dreaming.

Second Sailor. What way can we raise a keen, not knowing what name to call him by?

First Sailor. Come on to his ship. His name will come to mind in a moment. All I know is he died a thousand years ago, and was never yet waked.

Second Sailor. How can we wake him having no ale?

First Sailor. I saw a skin of ale aboard her—a pigskin of brown ale.

Third Sailor. Come to the ale, a pigskin of brown ale, a goatskin of yellow!

First Sailor [*singing*]. Brown ale and yellow; yellow and brown ale; a goatskin of yellow!

All [*singing*]. Brown ale and yellow; yellow and brown ale!

> [*Sailors go out.*

Dectora. Protect me now, gods that my people swear by!

  [*Aibric has risen from the ground where he had fallen. He has begun looking for his sword as if in a dream.*

Aibric. Where is my sword that fell out of my hand
  When I first heard the news? Ah, there it is!

  [*He goes dreamily towards the sword, but Dectora runs at it and takes it up before he can reach it.*

  [*Sleepily.*] Queen, give it me.

Dectora.   No, I have need of it.

Aibric. Why do you need a sword? But you may keep it.
  Now that he's dead I have no need of it,
  For everything is gone.

A Sailor [*calling from the other ship*]. Come hither, Aibric,
  And tell me who it is that we are waking.

Aibric [*half to Dectora, half to himself*]. What name had that dead king? Arthur of Britain?
  No, no—not Arthur. I remember now.
  It was golden-armed Iollan, and he died
  Broken-hearted, having lost his queen
  Through wicked spells. That is not all the tale,
  For he was killed. O! O! O! O! O! O!
  For golden-armed Iollan has been killed.

  [*He goes out. While he has been speaking, and through part of what follows, one hears the singing of the Sailors from the other ship. Dectora stands with the sword lifted in front of Forgael. He changes the tune.*

Dectora. I will end all your magic on the instant.

[Her voice becomes dreamy, and she lowers the sword slowly, and finally lets it fall. She spreads out her hair. She takes off her crown and lays it upon the deck.

The sword is to lie beside him in the grave.
It was in all his battles. I will spread my hair,
And wring my hands, and wail him bitterly,
For I have heard that he was proud and laughing,
Blue-eyed, and a quick runner on bare feet,
And that he died a thousand years ago.
O! O! O! O!

[Forgael changes the tune]
But no, that is not it.
I knew him well, and while I heard him laughing
They killed him at my feet. O! O! O! O!
For golden-armed Iollan that I loved.
But what is it that made him say I loved him?
It was that harper put it in my thoughts,
But it is true. Why did they run upon him,
And beat the golden helmet with their swords?

Forgael. Do you not know me, lady? I am he
That you are weeping for.

Dectora.   No, for he is dead.
O! O! O! O! for golden-armed Iollan.

Forgael. It was so given out, but I will prove
That the grave-diggers in a dreamy frenzy
Have buried nothing but my golden arms.
Listen to that low-laughing string of the moon
And you will recollect my face and voice,
For you have listened to me playing it
These thousand years.

[He starts up, listening to the birds. The harp slips from his hands, and remains leaning against the bulwarks behind him.
What are the birds at there?
Why are they all a-flutter of a sudden?
What are you calling out above the mast?
If railing and reproach and mockery
Because I have awakened her to love
By magic strings, I'll make this answer to it:
Being driven on by voices and by dreams
That were clear messages from the Ever-living,
I have done right. What could I but obey?
And yet you make a clamour of reproach.

Dectora [laughing]. Why, it's a wonder out of reckoning

That I should keen him from the full of the moon
To the horn, and he be hale and hearty.
Forgael. How have I wronged her now that she is merry?
But no, no, no! your cry is not against me.
You know the councils of the Ever-living,
And all the tossing of your wings is joy,
And all that murmuring's but a marriage song;
But if it be reproach, I answer this:
There is not one among you that made love
By any other means. You call it passion,
Consideration, generosity;
But it was all deceit, and flattery
To win a woman in her own despite,
For love is war, and there is hatred in it;
And if you say that she came willingly—
Dectora. Why do you turn away and hide your face
That I would look upon for ever?
Forgael.   My grief!
Dectora. Have I not loved you for a thousand years?
Forgael. I never have been golden-armed Iollan.
Dectora. I do not understand. I know your face
Better than my own hands.
Forgael.   I have deceived you
Out of all reckoning.
Dectora.   Is it not true
That you were born a thousand years ago,
In islands where the children of Aengus wind
In happy dances under a windy moon,
And that you'll bring me there?
Forgael.   I have deceived you;
I have deceived you utterly.
Dectora.   How can that be?
Is it that though your eyes are full of love
Some other woman has a claim on you,
And I've but half?
Forgael.   O no!
Dectora.   And if there is,
If there be half a hundred more, what matter?
I'll never give another thought to it;
No, no, nor half a thought; but do not speak.
Women are hard and proud and stubborn-hearted,
Their heads being turned with praise and flattery;

And that is why their lovers are afraid
To tell them a plain story.

Forgael.   That's not the story;
But I have done so great a wrong against you,
There is no measure that it would not burst.
I will confess it all.

Dectora.   What do I care,
Now that my body has begun to dream,
And you have grown to be a burning coal
In the imagination and intellect?
If something that's most fabulous were true—
If you had taken me by magic spells,
And killed a lover or husband at my feet—
I would not let you speak, for I would know
That it was yesterday and not to-day
I loved him; I would cover up my ears,
As I am doing now. [*A pause.*] Why do you weep?

Forgael. I weep because I've nothing for your eyes
But desolate waters and a battered ship.

Dectora. O, why do you not lift your eyes to mine?

Forgael. I weep—I weep because bare night's above,
And not a roof of ivory and gold.

Dectora. I would grow jealous of the ivory roof,
And strike the golden pillars with my hands.
I would that there was nothing in the world
But my beloved—that night and day had perished,
And all that is and all that is to be,
And all that is not the meeting of our lips.

Forgael. Why do you turn your eyes upon bare night?
Am I to fear the waves, or is the moon
My enemy?

*Dector*a.   I looked upon the moon,
Longing to knead and pull it into shape
That I might lay it on your head as a crown.
But now it is your thoughts that wander away,
For you are looking at the sea. Do you not know
How great a wrong it is to let one's thought
Wander a moment when one is in love?

   [*He has moved away. She follows him. He is looking out over the
      sea, shading his eyes.*
Why are you looking at the sea?

Forgael.   Look there!

There where the cloud creeps up upon the moon.
Dectora. What is there but a troop of ash-grey birds
    That fly into the west?
        [The scene darkens, but there is a ray of light upon the figures.
Forgael.   But listen, listen!
Dectora. What is there but the crying of the birds?
Forgael. If you'll but listen closely to that crying
    You'll hear them calling out to one another
    With human voices.
Dectora.   Clouds have hid the moon.
    The birds cry out, what can I do but tremble?
Forgael. They have been circling over our heads in the air,
    But now that they have taken to the road
    We have to follow, for they are our pilots,
    They're crying out. Can you not hear their cry?—
    'There is a country at the end of the world
    Where no child's born but to outlive the moon.'
        [The Sailors come in with Aibric. They carry torches.
Aibric. We have lit upon a treasure that's so great
    Imagination cannot reckon it.
    The hold is full—boxes of precious spice,
    Ivory images with amethyst eyes,
    Dragons with eyes of ruby. The whole ship
    Flashes as if it were a net of herrings.
    Let us return to our own country, Forgael,
    And spend it there. Have you not found this queen?
    What more have you to look for on the seas?
Forgael. I cannot—I am going on to the end.
    As for this woman, I think she is coming with me.
Aibric. Speak to him, lady, and bid him turn the ship.
    He knows that he is taking you to death;
    He cannot contradict me.
Dectora.   Is that true?
Forgael. I do not know for certain.
Dectora.   Carry me
    To some sure country, some familiar place.
    Have we not everything that life can give
    In having one another?
Forgael.   How could I rest
    If I refused the messengers and pilots
    With all those sights and all that crying out?
Dectora. I am a woman, I die at every breath.
Aibric [*to the Sailors*]. To the other ship, for there's no help in words.

And I will follow you and cut the rope
When I have said farewell to this man here,
For neither I nor any living man
Will look upon his face again.

    [*Sailors go out, leaving one torch perhaps in a torchholder on the
      bulwark.*

Forgael [*to Dectora*].   Go with him,
  For he will shelter you and bring you home.

Aibric [*taking Forgael's hand*]. I'll do it for his sake.

Dectora.   No. Take this sword
  And cut the rope, for I go on with Forgael.

Aibric. Farewell! Farewell!   [*He goes out. The light grows stronger.*

Dectora.   The sword is in the rope—
  The rope's in two—it falls into the sea,
  It whirls into the foam. O ancient worm,
  Dragon that loved the world and held us to it,
  You are broken, you are broken. The world drifts away,
  And I am left alone with my beloved,
  Who cannot put me from his sight for ever.
  We are alone for ever, and I laugh,
  Forgael, because you cannot put me from you.
  The mist has covered the heavens, and you and I
  Shall be alone for ever. We two—this crown—
  I half remember. It has been in my dreams.
  Bend lower, O king, that I may crown you with it.
  O flower of the branch, O bird among the leaves,
  O silver fish that my two hands have taken
  Out of the running stream, O morning star,
  Trembling in the blue heavens like a white fawn
  Upon the misty border of the wood,
  Bend lower, that I may cover you with my hair,
  For we will gaze upon this world no longer.

                    [*The harp begins to burn as with fire.*

Forgael [*gathering Dectora's hair about him*]. Beloved, having dragged
      the net about us,
  And knitted mesh to mesh, we grow immortal;
  And that old harp awakens of itself
  To cry aloud to the grey birds, and dreams,
  That have had dreams for father, live in us.

THE END

DEIRDRE

1907

TO

MRS. PATRICK CAMPBELL

who in the generosity of her genius has played my
Deirdre in Dublin and London with the Abbey
Company, as well as with her own people, and

IN MEMORY OF

ROBERT GREGORY

who designed the beautiful scene she played it in.

DEIRDRE

PERSONS IN THE PLAY

Musician.

Fergus, *an old man*

Naoise (*pronounced Neesh-e*), *a young king*

Deirdre, *his queen*

A Dark-faced Messenger

Conchubar (*pronounced* Conohar), *the old King of Uladh, who is still strong and vigorous*

A Dark-faced Executioner

A Guest-house in a wood. It is a rough house of timber; through the doors and some of the windows one can see the great spaces of the wood, the sky dimming, night closing in. But a window to the left shows the thick leaves of a coppice; the landscape suggests silence and loneliness. There is a door to right and left, and through the side windows one can see anybody who approaches either door, a moment before he enters. In the centre, a part of the house is curtained off; the curtains are drawn. There are unlighted torches in brackets on the walls. There is, at one side, a small table with a chessboard and chessmen upon it. At the other side of the room there is a brazier with a fire; two women, with musical instruments beside them, crouch about the brazier: they are comely women of about forty. Another woman, who carries a stringed instrument, enters hurriedly; she speaks, at first standing in the doorway.

First Musician. I have a story right, my wanderers,
    That has so mixed with fable in our songs
    That all seemed fabulous. We are come, by chance,
    Into King Conchubar's country, and this house
    Is an old guest-house built for travellers
    From the seashore to Conchubar's royal house,
    And there are certain hills among these woods
    And there Queen Deirdre grew.
Second Musician.   That famous queen
    Who has been wandering with her lover Naoise
    Somewhere beyond the edges of the world?
First Musician [*going nearer to the brazier*]. Some dozen years ago,
        King Conchubar found
    A house upon a hillside in this wood,

And there a child with an old witch to nurse her,
And nobody to say if she were human,
Or of the gods, or anything at all
Of who she was or why she was hidden there,
But that she'd too much beauty for good luck.
He went up thither daily, till at last
She put on womanhood, and he lost peace,
And Deirdre's tale began. The King was old.
A month or so before the marriage-day,
A young man, in the laughing scorn of his youth,
Naoise, the son of Usna, climbed up there,
And having wooed, or, as some say, been wooed,
Carried her off.

Second Musician.   The tale were well enough
Had it a finish.

First Musician.   Hush! I have more to tell;
But gather close about that I may whisper
The secrets of a king.

Second Musician.   There's none to hear!

First Musician. I have been to Conchubar's house and followed up
A crowd of servants going out and in
With loads upon their heads: embroideries
To hang upon the walls, or new-mown rushes
To strew upon the floors, and came at length
To a great room.

Second Musician.   Be silent; there are steps!

> *Enter Fergus, an old man, who moves about from door to*
> *window excitedly through what follows*

Fergus. I thought to find a message from the King.
You are musicians by these instruments,
And if as seems—for you are comely women—
You can praise love, you'll have the best of luck,
For there'll be two, before the night is in,
That bargained for their love, and paid for it
All that men value. You have but the time
To weigh a happy music with a sad,
To find what is most pleasing to a lover,
Before the son of Usna and his queen
Have passed this threshold.

First Musician.   Deirdre and her man!

Fergus. I was to have found a message in this house,
And ran to meet it. Is there no messenger
From Conchubar to Fergus, son of Rogh?

First Musician. Are Deirdre and her lover tired of life?
Fergus. You are not of this country, or you'd know
  That they are in my charge and all forgiven.
First Musician. We have no country but the roads of the world.
Fergus. Then you should know that all things change in the world,
  And hatred turns to love and love to hate,
  And even kings forgive.
First Musician.   An old man's love
  Who casts no second line is hard to cure;
  His jealousy is like his love.
Fergus.   And that's but true.
  You have learned something in your wanderings.
  He was so hard to cure that the whole court,
  But I alone, thought it impossible;
  Yet after I had urged it at all seasons,
  I had my way, and all's forgiven now;
  And you shall speak the welcome and the joy
  That I lack tongue for.
First Musician.   Yet old men are jealous.
Fergus [*going to door*]. I am Conchubar's near friend, and that
      weighed somewhat,
  And it was policy to pardon them.
  The need of some young, famous, popular man
  To lead the troops, the murmur of the crowd,
  And his own natural impulse, urged him to it.
  They have been wandering half a dozen years.
First Musician. And yet old men are jealous.
Fergus [*coming from door*].   Sing the more sweetly
  Because, though age is arid as a bone,
  This man has flowered. I've need of music, too;
  If this grey head would suffer no reproach,
  I'd dance and sing—
      [*Dark-faced men with strange, barbaric dress and arms begin to
      pass by the doors and windows. They pass one by one and in
      silence.*
                         and dance till the hour ran out,
  Because I have accomplished this good deed.
First Musician. Look there—there at the window, those dark men,
  With murderous and outlandish-looking arms—
  They've been about the house all day.
Fergus [*looking after them*].   What are you?
  Where do you come from, who is it sent you here?
First Musician. They will not answer you.

Fergus.   They do not hear.
First Musician. Forgive my open speech, but to these eyes
  That have seen many lands they are such men
  As kings will gather for a murderous task
  That neither bribes, commands, nor promises
  Can bring their people to.
Fergus.   And that is why
  You harped upon an old man's jealousy.
  A trifle sets you quaking. Conchubar's fame
  Brings merchandise on every wind that blows.
  They may have brought him Libyan dragon-skin,
  Or the ivory of the fierce unicorn.
First Musician. If these be merchants, I have seen the goods
  They have brought to Conchubar, and understood
  His murderous purpose.
Fergus.   Murderous, you say?
  Why, what new gossip of the roads is this?
  But I'll not hear.
First Musician.   It may be life or death.
  There is a room in Conchubar's house, and there——
Fergus. Be silent, or I'll drive you from the door.
  There's many a one that would do more than that,
  And make it prison, or death, or banishment
  To slander the High King.
                    [*Suddenly restraining himself and speaking gently.*
                            He is my friend;
  I have his oath, and I am well content.
  I have known his mind as if it were my own
  These many years, and there is none alive
  Shall buzz against him, and I there to stop it.
  I know myself, and him, and your wild thought
  Fed on extravagant poetry, and lit
  By such a dazzle of old fabulous tales
  That common things are lost, and all that's strange
  Is true because 'twere pity if it were not. [*Going to the door again.*
  Quick! quick! your instruments! they are coming now.
  I hear the hoofs a-clatter. Begin that song!
  But what is it to be? I'd have them hear
  A music foaming up out of the house
  Like wine out of a cup. Come now, a verse
  Of some old time not worth remembering,
  And all the lovelier because a bubble.
  Begin, begin, of some old king and queen,

Of Lugaidh Redstripe or another; no, not him,
He and his lady perished wretchedly.

First Musician [singing]
'Why is it', Queen Edain said,
    'If I do but climb the stair . . .

Fergus. Ah! that is better. . . . They are alighted now.
Shake all your cockscombs, children; these are lovers.

[Fergus goes out.

First Musician
'Why is it', Queen Edain said,
    'If I do but climb the stair
To the tower overhead,
    When the winds are calling there,
Or the gannets calling out
    In waste places of the sky,
There's so much to think about
    That I cry, that I cry?'

Second Musician
But her goodman answered her:
    'Love would be a thing of naught
Had not all his limbs a stir
    Born out of immoderate thought;
Were he anything by half,
    Were his measure running dry.
Lovers, if they may not laugh,
    Have to cry, have to cry.'

*[Deirdre, Naoise, and Fergus have been seen for a moment through
the windows, but now they have entered.*

The Three Musicians [together]
But is Edain worth a song
    Now the hunt begins anew?
Praise the beautiful and strong;
    Praise the redness of the yew;
Praise the blossoming apple-stem.
    But our silence had been wise.
What is all our praise to them
    That have one another's eyes?

Deirdre. Silence your music, though I thank you for it;
But the wind's blown upon my hair, and I
Must set the jewels on my neck and head
For one that's coming.

Naoise.   Your colour has all gone
 As 'twere with fear, and there's no cause for that.
Deirdre. These women have the raddle that they use
 To make them brave and confident, although
 Dread, toil, or cold may chill the blood o' their cheeks.
 You'll help me, women. It is my husband's will
 I show my trust in one that may be here
 Before the mind can call the colour up.
 My husband took these rubies from a king
 Of Surracha that was so murderous
 He seemed all glittering dragon. Now wearing them
 Myself wars on myself, for I myself—
 That do my husband's will, yet fear to do it—
 Grow dragonish to myself.

 [*The women have gathered about her. Naoise has stood looking
 at her, but Fergus brings him to the chess-table.*

Naoise.   No messenger!
 It's strange that there is none to welcome us.
Fergus. King Conchubar has sent no messenger
 That he may come himself.
Naoise.   And being himself,
 Being High King, he cannot break his faith.
 I have his word and I must take that word,
 Or prove myself unworthy of my nurture
 Under a great man's roof.
Fergus.   We'll play at chess
 Till the King comes. It is but natural
 That she should doubt him, for her house has been
 The hole of the badger and the den of the fox.
Naoise. If I had not King Conchubar's word I'd think
 That chess-board ominous.
Fergus.   How can a board
 That has been lying there these many years
 Be lucky or unlucky?
Naoise.   It is the board
 Where Lugaidh Redstripe and that wife of his,
 Who had a seamew's body half the year,
 Played at the chess upon the night they died.
Fergus. I can remember now, a tale of treachery,
 A broken promise and a journey's end—
 But it were best forgot.

 [*Deirdre has been standing with the women about her. They have
 been helping her to put on her jewels and to put the pigment on*

*her cheeks and arrange her hair. She has gradually grown atten-
tive to what Fergus is saying.*

Naoise.　　　　　　　　If the tale's true,
  When it was plain that they had been betrayed,
  They moved the men and waited for the end
  As it were bedtime, and had so quiet minds
  They hardly winked their eyes when the sword flashed.
Fergus. She never could have played so, being a woman,
  If she had not the cold sea's blood in her.
Deirdre. The gods turn clouds and casual accidents
  Into omens.
Naoise.　　　　　It would but ill become us,
  Now that King Conchubar has pledged his word,
  Should we be startled by a cloud or a shadow.
Deirdre. There's none to welcome us.
Naoise.　　　　　　　　　　Being his guest,
  Words that would wrong him can but wrong ourselves.
Deirdre. An empty house upon the journey's end!
  Is that the way a king that means no mischief
  Honours a guest?
Fergus.　　　　　　He is but making ready
  A welcome in his house, arranging where
  The moorhen and the mallard go, and where
  The speckled heathcock on a golden dish.
Deirdre. Had he no messenger?
Naoise.　　　　　　　　Such words and fears
  Wrong this old man who's pledged his word to us.
  We must not speak or think as women do,
  That when the house is all abed sit up
  Marking among the ashes with a stick
  Till they are terrified.—Being what we are
  We must meet all things with an equal mind.
  [*To Fergus.*] Come, let us look if there's a messenger
  From Conchubar. We cannot see from this
  Because we are blinded by the leaves and twigs,
  But it may be the wood will thin again.
  It is but kind that when the lips we love
  Speak words that are unfitting for kings' ears
  Our ears be deaf.
Fergus.　　　　　　But now I had to threaten
  These wanderers because they would have weighed
  Some crazy fantasy of their own brain
  Or gossip of the road with Conchubar's word.

If I had thought so little of mankind
I never could have moved him to this pardon.
I have believed the best of every man,
And find that to believe it is enough
To make a bad man show him at his best,
Or even a good man swing his lantern higher.

> [*Naoise and Fergus go out. The last words are spoken as they
> go through the door. One can see them through part of
> what follows, either through door or window. They move
> about, talking or looking along the road towards Conchubar's
> house.*

First Musician. If anything lies heavy on your heart,
Speak freely of it, knowing it is certain
That you will never see my face again.

Deirdre. You've been in love?

First Musician.   If you would speak of love,
Speak freely. There is nothing in the world
That has been friendly to us but the kisses
That were upon our lips, and when we are old
Their memory will be all the life we have.

Deirdre. There was a man that loved me. He was old;
I could not love him. Now I can but fear.
He has made promises, and brought me home;
But though I turn it over in my thoughts,
I cannot tell if they are sound and wholesome,
Or hackles on the hook.

First Musician.   I have heard he loved you
As some old miser loves the dragon-stone
He hides among the cobwebs near the roof.

Deirdre. You mean that when a man who has loved like that
Is after crossed, love drowns in its own flood,
And that love drowned and floating is but hate;
And that a king who hates sleeps ill at night
Till he has killed; and that, though the day laughs,
We shall be dead at cock-crow.

First Musician.   You've not my thought.
When I lost one I loved distractedly,
I blamed my crafty rival and not him,
And fancied, till my passion had run out,
That could I carry him away with me,
And tell him all my love, I'd keep him yet.

Deirdre. Ah! now I catch your meaning, that this king
Will murder Naoise, and keep me alive.

First Musician. 'Tis you that put that meaning upon words
  Spoken at random.

Deirdre.   Wanderers like you,
  Who have their wit alone to keep their lives,
  Speak nothing that is bitter to the ear
  At random; if they hint at it at all
  Their eyes and ears have gathered it so lately
  That it is crying out in them for speech.

First Musician. We have little that is certain.

Deirdre.   Certain or not,
  Speak it out quickly, I beseech you to it;
  I never have met any of your kind
  But that I gave them money, food, and fire.

First Musician. There are strange, miracle-working, wicked stones,
  Men tear out of the heart and the hot brain
  Of Libyan dragons.

Deirdre.   The hot Istain stone,
  And the cold stone of Fanes, that have power
  To stir even those at enmity to love.

First Musician. They have so great an influence, if but sewn
  In the embroideries that curtain in
  The bridal bed.

Deirdre.   O Mover of the stars
  That made this delicate house of ivory,
  And made my soul its mistress, keep it safe!

First Musician. I have seen a bridal bed, so curtained in,
  So decked for miracle in Conchubar's house,
  And learned that a bride's coming.

Deirdre.   And I the bride?
  Here is worse treachery than the seamew suffered,
  For she but died and mixed into the dust
  Of her dear comrade, but I am to live
  And lie in the one bed with him I hate.
  Where is Naoise? I was not alone like this
  When Conchubar first chose me for his wife;
  I cried in sleeping or waking and he came,
  But now there is worse need.

Naoise [*entering with Fergus*].   Why have you called?
  I was but standing there, without the door.

Deirdre. I have heard terrible mysterious things,
  Magical horrors and the spells of wizards.

Fergus. Why, that's no wonder. You have been listening

To singers of the roads that gather up
The stories of the world.

Deirdre. But I have one
To make the stories of the world but nothing.

Naoise. Be silent if it is against the King
Whose guest you are.

Fergus. No, let her speak it out.
I know the High King's heart as it were my own,
And can refute a slander, but already
I have warned these women that it may be death.

Naoise. I will not weigh the gossip of the roads
With the King's word. I ask your pardon for her:
She has the heart of the wild birds that fear
The net of the fowler or the wicker cage.

Deirdre. Am I to see the fowler and the cage
And speak no word at all?

Naoise. You would have known,
Had they not bred you in that mountainous place,
That when we give a word and take a word
Sorrow is put away, past wrong forgotten.

Deirdre. Though death may come of it?

Naoise. Though death may come.

Deirdre. When first we came into this empty house
You had foreknowledge of our death, and even
When speaking of the paleness of my cheek
Your own cheek blanched.

Naoise. Listen to this old man.
He can remember all the promises
We trusted to.

Deirdre. You speak from the lips out,
And I am pleading for your life and mine.

Naoise. Listen to this old man, for many think
He has a golden tongue.

Deirdre. Then I will say
What it were best to carry to the grave.
Look at my face where the leaf raddled it
And at these rubies on my hair and breast.
It was for him, to stir him to desire,
I put on beauty; yes, for Conchubar.

Naoise. What frenzy put these words into your mouth?

Deirdre. No frenzy, for what need is there for frenzy
To change what shifts with every change of the wind,

Or else there is no truth in men's old sayings?
Was I not born a woman?
Naoise.   You're mocking me.
Deirdre. And is there mockery in this face and eyes,
Or in this body, in these limbs that brought
So many mischiefs? Look at me and say
If that that shakes my limbs be mockery.
Naoise. What woman is there that a man can trust
But at the moment when he kisses her
At the first midnight?
Deirdre.   Were it not most strange
That women should put evil in men's hearts
And lack it in themselves? And yet I think
That being half good I might change round again
Were we aboard our ship and on the sea.
Naoise. We'll to the horses and take ship again.
Fergus. Fool, she but seeks to rouse your jealousy
With crafty words.
Deirdre.   Were we not born to wander?
These jewels have been reaped by the innocent sword
Upon a mountain, and a mountain bred me;
But who can tell what change can come to love
Among the valleys? I speak no falsehood now.
Away to windy summits, and there mock
The night-jar and the valley-keeping bird!
Fergus. Men blamed you that you stirred a quarrel up
That has brought death to many. I have made peace,
Poured water on the fire, but if you fly
King Conchubar may think that he is mocked
And the house blaze again: and in what quarter,
If Conchubar were the treacherous man you think,
Would you find safety now that you have come
Into the very middle of his power,
Under his very eyes?
Deirdre.   Under his eyes
And in the very middle of his power!
Then there is but one way to make all safe:
I'll spoil this beauty that brought misery
And houseless wandering on the man I loved.
These wanderers will show me how to do it;
To clip this hair to baldness, blacken my skin
With walnut juice, and tear my face with briars.

O that the creatures of the woods had torn
  My body with their claws!

Fergus.   What, wilder yet!

Deirdre [*to Naoise*]. Whatever were to happen to my face
  I'd be myself, and there's not any way
  But this to bring all trouble to an end.

Naoise. Leave the gods' handiwork unblotched, and wait
  For their decision, our decision is past.

          [*A Dark-faced Messenger comes to the threshold.*

Fergus. Peace, peace; the messenger is at the door;
  He stands upon the threshold; he stands there;
  He stands, King Conchubar's purpose on his lips.

Messenger. Supper is on the table. Conchubar
  Is waiting for his guests.

Fergus.   All's well again!
  All's well! All's well! You cried your doubts so loud
  That I had almost doubted.

Naoise.   We doubted him,
  And he the while but busy in his house
  For the more welcome.

Deirdre.   The message is not finished.

Fergus. Come quickly. Conchubar will laugh, that I——
  Although I held out boldly in my speech—
  That I, even I——

Deirdre.   Wait, wait! He is not done.

Messenger. Deirdre and Fergus, son of Rogh, are summoned;
  But not the traitor that bore off the Queen.
  It is enough that the King pardon her,
  And call her to his table and his bed.

Naoise. So, then, it's treachery.

Fergus.   I'll not believe it.

Naoise. Lead on and I will follow at your heels
  That I may challenge him before his court
  To match me there, or match me in some place
  Where none can come between us but our swords,
  For I have found no truth on any tongue
  That's not of iron.

Messenger.   I am Conchubar's man,
  I am content to serve an iron tongue:
  That Tongue commands that Fergus, son of Rogh,
  And Deirdre come this night into his house,
  And none but they.   [*He goes, followed by Naoise.*

Fergus.   Some rogue, some enemy,
  Has bribed him to embroil us with the King;
  I know that he has lied because I know
  King Conchubar's mind as if it were my own,
  But I'll find out the truth.
                         [*He is about to follow Naoise, but Deirdre stops him.*
Deirdre.   No, no, old man.
  You thought the best, and the worst came of it;
  We listened to the counsel of the wise,
  And so turned fools. But ride and bring your friends.
  Go, and go quickly. Conchubar has not seen me;
  It may be that his passion is asleep,
  And that we may escape.
Fergus.   But I'll go first,
  And follow up that Libyan heel, and send
  Such words to Conchubar that he may know
  At how great peril he lays hands upon you.
                         Naoise enters
Naoise. The Libyan, knowing that a servant's life
  Is safe from hands like mine, but turned and mocked.
Fergus. I'll call my friends, and call the reaping-hooks,
  And carry you in safety to the ships.
  My name has still some power. I will protect,
  Or, if that is impossible, revenge.   [*Goes out by other door.*
Naoise [*who is calm, like a man who has passed beyond life*].
  The crib has fallen and the birds are in it;
  There is not one of the great oaks about us
  But shades a hundred men.
Deirdre.   Let's out and die,
  Or break away, if the chance favour us.
Naoise. They would but drag you from me, stained with blood.
  Their barbarous weapons would but mar that beauty,
  And I would have you die as a queen should—
  In a death-chamber. You are in my charge.
  We will wait here, and when they come upon us,
  I'll hold them from the doors, and when that's over,
  Give you a cleanly death with this grey edge.
Deirdre. I will stay here; but you go out and fight.
  Our way of life has brought no friends to us,
  And if we do not buy them leaving it,
  We shall be ever friendless.
Naoise.   What do they say?
  That Lugaidh Redstripe and that wife of his

Sat at this chess-board, waiting for their end.
They knew that there was nothing that could save them,
And so played chess as they had any night
For years, and waited for the stroke of sword.
I never heard a death so out of reach
Of common hearts, a high and comely end.
What need have I, that gave up all for love,
To die like an old king out of a fable,
Fighting and passionate? What need is there
For all that ostentation at my setting?
I have loved truly and betrayed no man.
I need no lightning at the end, no beating
In a vain fury at the cage's door.
[*To Musicians.*] Had you been here when that man and his queen
Played at so high a game, could you have found
An ancient poem for the praise of it?
It should have set out plainly that those two,
Because no man and woman have loved better,
Might sit on there contentedly, and weigh
The joy comes after. I have heard the seamew
Sat there, with all the colour in her cheeks,
As though she'd say: 'There's nothing happening
But that a king and queen are playing chess.'
Deirdre. He's in the right, though I have not been born
    Of the cold, heighty waves, my veins being hot,
    And though I have loved better than that queen,
    I'll have as quiet fingers on the board.
    O, singing women, set it down in a book,
    That love is all we need, even though it is
    But the last drops we gather up like this;
    And though the drops are all we have known of life,
    For we have been most friendless—praise us for it,
    And praise the double sunset, for naught's lacking
    But a good end to the long, cloudy day.
Naoise. Light torches there and drive the shadows out,
    For day's grey end comes up.
        [*A Musician lights a torch in the fire and then crosses before the
        chess-players, and slowly lights the torches in the sconces. The
        light is almost gone from the wood, but there is a clear evening
        light in the sky, increasing the sense of solitude and loneliness.*
Deirdre.   Make no sad music.
    What is it but a king and queen at chess?
    They need a music that can mix itself

Into imagination, but not break
The steady thinking that the hard game needs.

    [During the chess, the Musicians sing this song]

        Love is an immoderate thing
          And can never be content
        Till it dip an ageing wing
          Where some laughing element
        Leaps and Time's old lanthorn dims.
          What's the merit in love-play,
        In the tumult of the limbs
          That dies out before 'tis day,
        Heart on heart, or mouth on mouth,
          All that mingling of our breath,
        When love-longing is but drouth
          For the things come after death?

    [During the last verses Deirdre rises from the board and kneels
      at Naoise's feet.

Deirdre. I cannot go on playing like that woman
    That had but the cold blood of the sea in her veins.

Naoise. It is your move. Take up your man again.

Deirdre. Do you remember that first night in the woods
    We lay all night on leaves, and looking up,
    When the first grey of the dawn awoke the birds,
    Saw leaves above us? You thought that I still slept,
    And bending down to kiss me on the eyes,
    Found they were open. Bend and kiss me now,
    For it may be the last before our death.
    And when that's over, we'll be different;
    Imperishable things, a cloud or a fire.
    And I know nothing but this body, nothing
    But that old vehement, bewildering kiss.

                 [Conchubar comes to the door.

First Musician. Children, beware!

Naoise [*laughing*].   He has taken up my challenge;
    Whether I am a ghost or living man
    When day has broken, I'll forget the rest,
    And say that there is kingly stuff in him.

      [Turns to fetch spear and shield, and then sees that Conchubar
      has gone.

First Musician. He came to spy upon you, not to fight.

Naoise. A prudent hunter, therefore, but no king.
    He'd find if what has fallen in the pit
    Were worth the hunting, but has come too near,

And I turn hunter. You're not man, but beast.
Go scurry in the bushes, now, beast, beast,
For now it's topsy-turvy, I upon you.

[*He rushes out after Conchubar.*

Deirdre. You have a knife there, thrust into your girdle.
  I'd have you give it me.
First Musician.   No, but I dare not.
Deirdre. No, but you must.
First Musician.   If harm should come to you,
  They'd know I gave it.
Deirdre [*snatching knife*]. There is no mark on this
  To make it different from any other
  Out of a common forge.   [*Goes to the door and looks out.*
First Musician.   You have taken it,
  I did not give it you; but there are times
  When such a thing is all the friend one has.
Deirdre. The leaves hide all, and there's no way to find
  What path to follow. Why is there no sound?

[*She goes from door to window.*

First Musician. Where would you go?
Deirdre.   To strike a blow for Naoise,
  If Conchubar call the Libyans to his aid.
  But why is there no clash? They have met by this!
First Musician. Listen. I am called wise. If Conchubar win,
  You have a woman's wile that can do much,
  Even with men in pride of victory.
  He is in love and old. What were one knife
  Among a hundred?
Deirdre [*going towards them*]. Women, if I die,
  If Naoise die this night, how will you praise?
  What words seek out? for that will stand to you;
  For being but dead we shall have many friends.
  All through your wanderings, the doors of kings
  Shall be thrown wider open, the poor man's hearth
  Heaped with new turf, because you are wearing this

[*Gives Musician a bracelet.*

  To show that you have Deirdre's story right.
First Musician. Have you not been paid servants in love's house
  To sweep the ashes out and keep the doors?
  And though you have suffered all for mere love's sake
  You'd live your lives again.
Deirdre.   Even this last hour.

Conchubar enters with dark-faced men

Conchubar. One woman and two men; that is the quarrel
   That knows no mending. Bring in the man she chose
   Because of his beauty and the strength of his youth.
           [*The dark-faced men drag in Naoise entangled in a net.*
Naoise. I have been taken like a bird or a fish.
Conchubar. He cried 'Beast, beast!' and in a blind-beast rage
   He ran at me and fell into the nets,
   But we were careful for your sake, and took him
   With all the comeliness that woke desire
   Unbroken in him. I being old and lenient,
   I would not hurt a hair upon his head.
Deirdre. What do you say? Have you forgiven him?
Naoise. He is but mocking us. What's left to say
   Now that the seven years' hunt is at an end?
Deirdre. He never doubted you until I made him,
   And therefore all the blame for what he says
   Should fall on me.
Conchubar.   But his young blood is hot,
   And if we're of one mind, he shall go free,
   And I ask nothing for it, or, if something,
   Nothing I could not take. There is no king
   In the wide world that, being so greatly wronged,
   Could copy me, and give all vengeance up.
   Although her marriage-day had all but come,
   You carried her away; but I'll show mercy.
   Because you had the insolent strength of youth
   You carried her away; but I've had time
   To think it out through all these seven years.
   I will show mercy.
Naoise.   You have many words.
Conchubar. I will not make a bargain; I but ask
   What is already mine.
     [*Deirdre moves slowly towards Conchubar while he is speaking,*
      her eyes fixed upon him.
               You may go free
   If Deirdre will but walk into my house
   Before the people's eyes, that they may know,
   When I have put the crown upon her head,
   I have not taken her by force and guile.
   The doors are open, and the floors are strewed
   And in the bridal chamber curtains sewn
   With all enchantments that give happiness
   By races that are germane to the sun.

And nearest him, and have no blood in their veins—
For when they're wounded the wound drips with wine—
Nor speech but singing. At the bridal door
Two fair king's daughters carry in their hands
The crown and robe.

Deirdre.   O no! Not that, not that!
Ask any other thing but that one thing,
Leave me with Naoise. We will go away
Into some country at the ends of the earth.
We'll trouble you no more; and there is no one
That will not praise you if you pardon us.
'He is good, he is good', they'll say to one another;
'There's nobody like him, for he forgave
Deirdre and Naoise.'

Conchubar.   Do you think that I
Shall let you go again, after seven years
Of longing, and of planning here and there,
And trafficking with merchants for the stones
That make all sure, and watching my own face
That none might read it?

Deirdre [*to Naoise*].   It's better to go with him.
Why should you die when one can bear it all?
My life is over; it's better to obey.
Why should you die? I will not live long, Naoise.
I'd not have you believe I'd long stay living;
O no, no, no! You will go far away.
You will forget me. Speak, speak, Naoise, speak,
And say that it is better that I go.
I will not ask it. Do not speak a word,
For I will take it all upon myself.
Conchubar, I will go.

Naoise.   And do you think
That, were I given life at such a price,
I would not cast it from me? O my eagle!
Why do you beat vain wings upon the rock
When hollow night's above?

Deirdre.   It's better, Naoise.
It may be hard for you, but you'll forget.
For what am I, to be remembered always?
And there are other women. There was one,
The daughter of the King of Leodas;
I could not sleep because of her. Speak to him;
Tell it out plain, and make him understand.

And if it be he thinks I shall stay living,
Say that I will not.

Naoise.   Would I had lost life
Among those Scottish kings that sought it of me
Because you were my wife, or that the worst
Had taken you before this bargaining!
O eagle! If you were to do this thing,
And buy my life of Conchubar with your body,
Love's law being broken, I would stand alone
Upon the eternal summits, and call out,
And you could never come there, being banished.

Deirdre [*kneeling to Conchubar*]. I would obey, but cannot. Pardon us.
I know that you are good. I have heard you praised
For giving gifts; and you will pardon us,
Although I cannot go into your house.
It was my fault. I only should be punished.

                              [*Unseen by Deirdre, Naoise is gagged.*

The very moment these eyes fell on him,
I told him; I held out my hands to him;
How could he refuse? At first he would not—
I am not lying—he remembered you.
What do I say? My hands?—No, no, my lips—
For I had pressed my lips upon his lips—
I swear it is not false—my breast to his;

        [*Conchubar motions; Naoise, unseen by Deirdre, is taken behind
            the curtain.*

Until I woke the passion that's in all,
And how could he resist? I had my beauty.
You may have need of him, a brave, strong man,
Who is not foolish at the council-board,
Nor does he quarrel by the candle-light
And give hard blows to dogs. A cup of wine
Moves him to mirth, not madness.   [*She stands up.*
                              What am I saying?
You may have need of him, for you have none
Who is so good a sword, or so well loved
Among the common people. You may need him,
And what king knows when the hour of need may come?
You dream that you have men enough. You laugh.
Yes; you are laughing to yourself. You say,
'I am Conchubar—I have no need of him.'
You will cry out for him some day and say,

'If Naoise were but living'——[*she misses Naoise*]. Where is he?
Where have you sent him? Where is the son of Usna?
Where is he, O, where is he?

> [*She staggers over to the Musicians. The Executioner has come
> out with a sword on which there is blood; Conchubar points to
> it. The Musicians give a wail.*

Conchubar. The traitor who has carried off my wife
   No longer lives. Come to my house now, Deirdre,
   For he that called himself your husband's dead.
Deirdre. O, do not touch me. Let me go to him.   [*Pause.*
   King Conchubar is right. My husband's dead.
   A single woman is of no account,
   Lacking array of servants, linen cupboards,
   The bacon hanging—and King Conchubar's house
   All ready, too—I'll to King Conchubar's house.
   It is but wisdom to do willingly
   What has to be.
Conchubar.   But why are you so calm?
   I thought that you would curse me and cry out,
   And fall upon the ground and tear your hair.
Deirdre [*laughing*]. You know too much of women to think so;
   Though, if I were less worthy of desire,
   I would pretend as much; but, being myself,
   It is enough that you were master here.
   Although we are so delicately made,
   There's something brutal in us, and we are won
   By those who can shed blood. It was some woman
   That taught you how to woo: but do not touch me:
   I shall do all you bid me, but not yet,
   Because I have to do what's customary.
   We lay the dead out, folding up the hands,
   Closing the eyes, and stretching out the feet,
   And push a pillow underneath the head,
   Till all's in order; and all this I'll do
   For Naoise, son of Usna.
Conchubar.   It is not fitting.
   You are not now a wanderer, but a queen,
   And there are plenty that can do these things.
Deirdre [*motioning Conchubar away*]. No, no. Not yet. I cannot be
       your queen
   Till the past's finished, and its debts are paid.
   When a man dies, and there are debts unpaid,

He wanders by the debtor's bed and cries,
'There's so much owing.'
Conchubar.   You are deceiving me.
  You long to look upon his face again.
  Why should I give you now to a dead man
  That took you from a living?   [*He makes a step towards her.*
Deirdre.   In good time.
  You'll stir me to more passion than he could,
  And yet, if you are wise, you'll grant me this:
  That I go look upon him that was once
  So strong and comely and held his head so high
  That women envied me. For I will see him
  All blood-bedabbled and his beauty gone.
  It's better, when you're beside me in your strength,
  That the mind's eye should call up the soiled body,
  And not the shape I loved. Look at him, women.
  He heard me pleading to be given up,
  Although my lover was still living, and yet
  He doubts my purpose. I will have you tell him
  How changeable all women are; how soon
  Even the best of lovers is forgot
  When his day's finished.
Conchubar.   No; but I will trust
  The strength that you have praised, and not your purpose.
Deirdre [*almost with a caress*]. It is so small a gift and you will grant it
  Because it is the first that I have asked.
  He has refused. There is no sap in him;
  Nothing but empty veins. I thought as much.
  He has refused me the first thing I have asked—
  Me, me, his wife. I understand him now;
  I know the sort of life I'll have with him;
  But he must drag me to his house by force.
  If he refuses [*she laughs*], he shall be mocked of all.
  They'll say to one another, 'Look at him
  That is so jealous that he lured a man
  From over sea, and murdered him, and yet
  He trembled at the thought of a dead face!'
                    [*She has her hand upon the curtain.*
Conchubar. How do I know that you have not some knife,
  And go to die upon his body?
Deirdre.   Have me searched,
  If you would make so little of your queen.

It may be that I have a knife hid here
Under my dress. Bid one of these dark slaves
To search me for it.   [*Pause.*
Conchubar.   Go to your farewells, Queen.
Deirdre. Now strike the wire, and sing to it a while,
   Knowing that all is happy, and that you know
   Within what bride-bed I shall lie this night,
   And by what man, and lie close up to him,
   For the bed's narrow, and there outsleep the cockcrow.
                         [*She goes behind the curtain.*
First Musician. They are gone, they are gone. The proud may lie by the
      proud.
Second Musician. Though we were bidden to sing, cry nothing loud.
First Musician. They are gone, they are gone.
Second Musician.   Whispering were enough.
First Musician. Into the secret wilderness of their love.
Second Musician. A high, grey cairn. What more is to be said?
First Musician. Eagles have gone into their cloudy bed.
      [*Shouting outside. Fergus enters. Many men with scythes and
      sickles and torches gather about the doors. The house is lit with
      the glare of their torches.*
Fergus. Where's Naoise, son of Usna, and his queen?
   I and a thousand reaping-hooks and scythes
   Demand him of you.
Conchubar.   You have come too late.
   I have accomplished all. Deirdre is mine;
   She is my queen, and no man can rob me.
   I had to climb the topmost bough, and pull
   This apple among the winds. Open the curtain
   That Fergus learn my triumph from her lips.
      [*The curtain is drawn back. The Musicians begin to keen with
      low voices.*
   No, no; I'll not believe it. She is not dead—
   She cannot have escaped a second time!
Fergus. King, she is dead; but lay no hand upon her.
   What's this but empty cage and tangled wire,
   Now the bird's gone? But I'll not have you touch it.
Conchubar. You are all traitors, all against me—all.
   And she has deceived me for a second time;
   And every common man can keep his wife,
   But not the King.
      [*Loud shouting outside:* 'Death to Conchubar!' 'Where is Naoise?'

etc. *The dark-faced men gather round Conchubar and draw*
their swords; but he motions them away.

I have no need of weapons,
There's not a traitor that dare stop my way.
Howl, if you will; but I, being King, did right
In choosing her most fitting to be Queen,
And letting no boy lover take the sway.

THE END

AT THE HAWK'S WELL

1917

AT THE HAWK'S WELL

PERSONS IN THE PLAY

Three Musicians (*their faces made up to resemble masks*)
The Guardian of the Well (*with face made up to resemble a mask*)
An Old Man (*wearing a mask*)
A Young Man (*wearing a mask*)

Time—the Irish Heroic Age

*The stage is any bare space before a wall against which stands a pat-
terned screen. A drum and a gong and a zither have been laid close to
the screen before the play begins. If necessary, they can be carried in,
after the audience is seated, by the First Musician, who also can attend
to the lights if there is any special lighting. We had two lanterns upon
posts—designed by Mr. Dulac—at the outer corners of the stage, but
they did not give enough light, and we found it better to play by the
light of a large chandelier. Indeed, I think, so far as my present experi-
ence goes, that the most effective lighting is the lighting we are most
accustomed to in our rooms. These masked players seem stranger when
there is no mechanical means of separating them from us. The First
Musician carries with him a folded black cloth and goes to the centre
of the stage towards the front and stands motionless, the folded cloth
hanging from between his hands. The two other Musicians enter and,
after standing a moment at either side of the stage, go towards him and
slowly unfold the cloth, singing as they do so:*

> I call to the eye of the mind
> A well long choked up and dry
> And boughs long stripped by the wind,
> And I call to the mind's eye
> Pallor of an ivory face,
> Its lofty dissolute air,
> A man climbing up to a place
> The salt sea wind has swept bare.

*As they unfold the cloth, they go backward a little so that the
stretched cloth and the wall make a triangle with the First Musician
at the apex supporting the centre of the cloth. On the black cloth is a*

136

gold pattern suggesting a hawk. The Second and Third Musicians now slowly fold up the cloth again, pacing with a rhythmic movement of the arms towards the First Musician and singing:

What were his life soon done!
Would he lose by that or win?
A mother that saw her son
Doubled over a speckled shin,
Cross-grained with ninety years,
Would cry, 'How little worth
Were all my hopes and fears
And the hard pain of his birth!'

The words 'a speckled shin' are familiar to readers of Irish legendary stories in descriptions of old men bent double over the fire. While the cloth has been spread out, the Guardian of the Well has entered and is now crouching upon the ground. She is entirely covered by a black cloak; beside her lies a square blue cloth to represent a well. The three Musicians have taken their places against the wall beside their instruments of music; they will accompany the movements of the players with gong or drum or zither.

First Musician [*singing*].
        The boughs of the hazel shake,
        The sun goes down in the west.
Second Musician [*singing*].
        The heart would be always awake,
        The heart would turn to its rest.
        [*They now go to one side of the stage rolling up the cloth.*
First Musician [*speaking*]. Night falls;
        The mountain-side grows dark;
        The withered leaves of the hazel
        Half choke the dry bed of the well;
        The guardian of the well is sitting
        Upon the old grey stone at its side,
        Worn out from raking its dry bed,
        Worn out from gathering up the leaves.
        Her heavy eyes
        Know nothing, or but look upon stone.
        The wind that blows out of the sea
        Turns over the heaped-up leaves at her side;
        They rustle and diminish.
Second Musician. I am afraid of this place.
Both Musicians [*singing*].

'Why should I sleep?' the heart cries,
'For the wind, the salt wind, the sea wind,
Is beating a cloud through the skies;
I would wander always like the wind.'
An Old Man enters through the audience

First Musician [*speaking*]. That old man climbs up hither,
  Who has been watching by his well
  These fifty years.
  He is all doubled up with age;
  The old thorn-trees are doubled so
  Among the rocks where he is climbing.

  [*The Old Man stands for a moment motionless by the side of the
  stage with bowed head. He lifts his head at the sound of a drum-
  top. He goes towards the front of the stage moving to the taps
  of the drum. He crouches and moves his hands as if making a
  fire. His movements, like those of the other persons of the play,
  suggest a marionette.*

First Musician [*speaking*]. He has made a little heap of leaves;
  He lays the dry sticks on the leaves
  And, shivering with cold, he has taken up
  The fire-stick and socket from its hole.
  He whirls it round to get a flame;
  And now the dry sticks take the fire,
  And now the fire leaps up and shines
  Upon the hazels and the empty well.

Musicians [*singing*].
                'O wind, O salt wind, O sea wind!'
                Cries the heart, 'it is time to sleep;
                Why wander and nothing to find?
                Better grow old and sleep.'

Old Man [*speaking*]. Why don't you speak to me? Why don't you say:
  'Are you not weary gathering those sticks?
  Are not your fingers cold?' You have not one word,
  While yesterday you spoke three times. You said:
  'The well is full of hazel leaves.' You said:
  'The wind is from the west.' And after that:
  'If there is rain it's likely there'll be mud.'
  To-day you are as stupid as a fish,
  No, worse, worse, being less lively and as dumb.   [*He goes nearer.*
  Your eyes are dazed and heavy. If the Sidhe
  Must have a guardian to clean out the well
  And drive the cattle off, they might choose somebody
  That can be pleasant and companionable

Once in the day. Why do you stare like that?
You had that glassy look about the eyes
Last time it happened. Do you know anything?
It is enough to drive an old man crazy
To look all day upon these broken rocks,
And ragged thorns, and that one stupid face,
And speak and get no answer.

Young Man [*who has entered through the audience during the last
speech*].   Then speak to me,
For youth is not more patient than old age;
And though I have trod the rocks for half a day
I cannot find what I am looking for.

Old Man.   Who speaks?
Who comes so suddenly into this place
Where nothing thrives? If I may judge by the gold
On head and feet and glittering in your coat,
You are not of those who hate the living world.

Young Man. I am named Cuchulain, I am Sualtim's son.

Old Man. I have never heard that name.

Young Man.   It is not unknown.
I have an ancient house beyond the sea.

Old Man. What mischief brings you hither?—you are like those
Who are crazy for the shedding of men's blood,
And for the love of women.

Young Man.   A rumour has led me,
A story told over the wine towards dawn.
I rose from table, found a boat, spread sail,
And with a lucky wind under the sail
Crossed waves that have seemed charmed, and found this shore.

Old Man. There is no house to sack among these hills
Nor beautiful woman to be carried off.

Young Man. You should be native here, for that rough tongue
Matches the barbarous spot. You can, it may be,
Lead me to what I seek, a well wherein
Three hazels drop their nuts and withered leaves,
And where a solitary girl keeps watch
Among grey boulders. He who drinks, they say,
Of that miraculous water lives for ever.

Old Man. And are there not before your eyes at the instant
Grey boulders and a solitary girl
And three stripped hazels?

Young Man.   But there is no well.

Old Man. Can you see nothing yonder?

Young Man.   I but see
   A hollow among stones half-full of leaves.
Old Man. And do you think so great a gift is found
   By no more toil than spreading out a sail,
   And climbing a steep hill? O, folly of youth,
   Why should that hollow place fill up for you,
   That will not fill for me? I have lain in wait
   For more than fifty years, to find it empty,
   Or but to find the stupid wind of the sea
   Drive round the perishable leaves.
Young Man.   So it seems
   There is some moment when the water fills it.
Old Man. A secret moment that the holy shades
   That dance upon the desolate mountain know,
   And not a living man, and when it comes
   The water has scarce plashed before it is gone.
Young Man. I will stand here and wait. Why should the luck
   Of Sualtim's son desert him now? For never
   Have I had long to wait for anything.
Old Man. No! Go from this accursed place! This place
   Belongs to me, that girl there, and those others,
   Deceivers of men.
Young Man.   And who are you who rail
   Upon those dancers that all others bless?
Old Man. One whom the dancers cheat. I came like you
   When young in body and in mind, and blown
   By what had seemed to me a lucky sail.
   The well was dry, I sat upon its edge,
   I waited the miraculous flood, I waited
   While the years passed and withered me away.
   I have snared the birds for food and eaten grass
   And drunk the rain, and neither in dark nor shine
   Wandered too far away to have heard the plash,
   And yet the dancers have deceived me. Thrice
   I have awakened from a sudden sleep
   To find the stones were wet.
Young Man.   My luck is strong,
   It will not leave me waiting, nor will they
   That dance among the stones put me asleep;
   If I grow drowsy I can pierce my foot.
Old Man. No, do not pierce it, for the foot is tender,
   It feels pain much. But find your sail again

And leave the well to me, for it belongs
   To all that's old and withered.
Young Man.   No, I stay.
               [*The Guardian of the Well gives the cry of the hawk.*
   There is that bird again.
Old Man.   There is no bird.
Young Man. It sounded like the sudden cry of a hawk,
   But there's no wing in sight. As I came hither
   A great grey hawk swept down out of the sky,
   And though I have good hawks, the best in the world
   I had fancied, I have not seen its like. It flew
   As though it would have torn me with its beak,
   Or blinded me, smiting with that great wing.
   I had to draw my sword to drive it off,
   And after that it flew from rock to rock.
   I pelted it with stones, a good half-hour,
   And just before I had turned the big rock there
   And seen this place, it seemed to vanish away.
   Could I but find a means to bring it down
   I'd hood it.
Old Man.   The Woman of the Sidhe herself,
   The mountain witch, the unappeasable shadow.
   She is always flitting upon this mountain-side,
   To allure or to destroy. When she has shown
   Herself to the fierce women of the hills
   Under that shape they offer sacrifice
   And arm for battle. There falls a curse
   On all who have gazed in her unmoistened eyes;
   So get you gone while you have that proud step
   And confident voice, for not a man alive
   Has so much luck that he can play with it.
   Those that have long to live should fear her most,
   The old are cursed already. That curse may be
   Never to win a woman's love and keep it;
   Or always to mix hatred in the love;
   Or it may be that she will kill your children,
   That you will find them, their throats torn and bloody,
   Or you will be so maddened that you kill them
   With your own hand.
Young Man.   Have you been set down there
   To threaten all who come, and scare them off?
   You seem as dried up as the leaves and sticks,

As though you had no part in life.

> [*The Guardian of the Well gives hawk cry again.*
>
> That cry!

There is that cry again. That woman made it,
But why does she cry out as the hawk cries?

Old Man. It was her mouth, and yet not she, that cried.
It was that shadow cried behind her mouth;
And now I know why she has been so stupid
All the day through, and had such heavy eyes.
Look at her shivering now, the terrible life
Is slipping through her veins. She is possessed.
Who knows whom she will murder or betray
Before she awakes in ignorance of it all,
And gathers up the leaves? But they'll be wet;
The water will have come and gone again;
That shivering is the sign. O, get you gone,
At any moment now I shall hear it bubble.
If you are good you will leave it. I am old,
And if I do not drink it now, will never;
I have been watching all my life and maybe
Only a little cupful will bubble up.

Young Man. I'll take it in my hands. We shall both drink,
And even if there are but a few drops,
Share them.

Old Man.   But swear that I may drink the first;
The young are greedy, and if you drink the first
You'll drink it all. Ah, you have looked at her;
She has felt your gaze and turned her eyes on us;
I cannot bear her eyes, they are not of this world,
Nor moist, nor faltering; they are no girl's eyes.

> [*He covers his head. The Guardian of the Well throws off her
> cloak and rises. Her dress under the cloak suggests a hawk.*

Young Man. Why do you fix those eyes of a hawk upon me?
I am not afraid of you, bird, woman, or witch.

> [*He goes to the side of the well, which the Guardian of the Well
> has left.*

Do what you will, I shall not leave this place
Till I have grown immortal like yourself.

> [*He has sat down; the Guardian of the Well has begun to dance,
> moving like a hawk. The Old Man sleeps. The dance goes on
> for some time.*

First Musician [*singing or half-singing*].

O God, protect me
From a horrible deathless body
Sliding through the veins of a sudden.

[*The dance goes on for some time. The Young Man rises slowly.*

First Musician [*speaking*]. The madness has laid hold upon him now,
For he grows pale and staggers to his feet.   [*The dance goes on.*

Young Man. Run where you will,
Grey bird, you shall be perched upon my wrist.
Some were called queens and yet have been perched there.

[*The dance goes on.*

First Musician [*speaking*]. I have heard water plash; it comes, it
comes;
Look where it glitters. He has heard the plash;
Look, he has turned his head.

[*The Guardian of the Well has gone out. The Young Man drops
his spear as if in a dream and goes out.*

Musicians [*singing*].

He has lost what may not be found
Till men heap his burial-mound
And all the history ends.
He might have lived at his ease,
An old dog's head on his knees,
Among his children and friends.

[*The Old Man creeps up to the well.*

Old Man. The accursed shadows have deluded me,
The stones are dark and yet the well is empty;
The water flowed and emptied while I slept.
You have deluded me my whole life through,
Accursed dancers, you have stolen my life.
That there should be such evil in a shadow!

Young man [*entering*]. She has fled from me and hidden in the rocks.

Old Man. She has but led you from the fountain. Look!
Though stones and leaves are dark where it has flowed,
There's not a drop to drink.

[*The Musicians cry* 'Aoife!' 'Aoife!' *and strike gong.*

Young Man.   What are those cries?
What is that sound that runs along the hill?
Who are they that beat a sword upon a shield?

Old Man. She has roused up the fierce women of the hills,
Aoife, and all her troop, to take your life,
And never till you are lying in the earth
Can you know rest.

Young Man.   The clash of arms again!
Old Man. O, do not go! The mountain is accursed;
   Stay with me, I have nothing more to lose,
   I do not now deceive you.
Young Man.   I will face them.
      [*He goes out, no longer as if in a dream, but shouldering his spear
         and calling:*
He comes! Cuchulain, son of Sualtim, comes!
      [*The Musicians stand up; one goes to centre with folded cloth.
         The others unfold it. While they do so they sing. During the
         singing, and while hidden by the cloth, the Old Man goes out.
         When the play is performed with Mr. Dulac's music, the Musi-
         cians do not rise or unfold the cloth till after they have sung the
         words* 'a bitter life'.

         [*Songs for the unfolding and folding of the cloth*]

              Come to me, human faces,
              Familiar memories;
              I have found hateful eyes
              Among the desolate places,
              Unfaltering, unmoistened eyes.

              Folly alone I cherish,
              I choose it for my share;
              Being but a mouthful of air,
              I am content to perish;
              I am but a mouthful of sweet air.

              O lamentable shadows,
              Obscurity of strife!
              I choose a pleasant life
              Among indolent meadows;
              Wisdom must live a bitter life.
                       [*They then fold up the cloth, singing.*
              'The man that I praise',
              Cries out the empty well,
              'Lives all his days
              Where a hand on the bell
              Can call the milch cows
              To the comfortable door of his house.
              Who but an idiot would praise
              Dry stones in a well?'

'The man that I praise',
Cries out the leafless tree,
'Has married and stays
By an old hearth, and he
On naught has set store
But children and dogs on the floor.
Who but an idiot would praise
A withered tree?'   [*They go out.*

THE END

THE GREEN HELMET

An Heroic Farce

1910

THE GREEN HELMET

An Heroic Farce

PERSONS IN THE PLAY

Laegaire (*pronounced* Leary)
Conall
Cuchulain (*pronounced* Cuhoolin)
Red Man, *a Spirit*
Emer

Laegaire's Wife
Conall's Wife
Laeg, *Cuchulain's chariot-driver*
Stable Boys and Scullions
Black Men, etc.

A house made of logs. There are two windows at the back and a door which cuts off one of the corners of the room. Through the door one can see low rocks which make the ground outside higher than it is within, and beyond the rocks a misty moon-lit sea. Through the windows one can see nothing but the sea. There is a great chair at the opposite side to the door, and in front of it a table with cups and a flagon of ale. Here and there are stools.

At the Abbey Theatre the house is orange-red and the chairs and tables and flagons black, with a slight purple tinge which is not clearly distinguishable from the black. The rocks are black with a few green touches. The sea is green and luminous, and all the characters except the Red Man and the Black Men are dressed in various shades of green, one or two with touches of purple which look nearly black. The Black Men all wear dark purple and have eared caps, and at the end their eyes should look green from the reflected light of the sea. The Red Man is altogether in red. He is very tall, and his height increased by horns on the Green Helmet. The effect is intentionally violent and startling.

Laegaire. What is that? I had thought that I saw, though but in the
    wink of an eye,
  A cat-headed man out of Connacht go pacing and spitting by;
  But that could not be.
Conall. You have dreamed it—there's nothing out there.
  I killed them all before daybreak—I hoked them out of their lair;
  I cut off a hundred heads with a single stroke of my sword,
  And then I danced on their graves and carried away their hoard.
Laegaire. Does anything stir on the sea?
Conall.   Not even a fish or a gull:

I can see for a mile or two, now that the moon's at the full.

> [*A distant shout.*

Laegaire. Ah—there—there is some one who calls us.

Conall.   But from the landward side,
And we have nothing to fear that has not come up from the tide;
The rocks and the bushes cover whoever made that noise,
But the land will do us no harm.

Laegaire.   It was like Cuchulain's voice.

Conall. But that's an impossible thing.

Laegaire.   An impossible thing indeed.

Conall. For he will never come home, he has all that he could need
In that high windy Scotland—good luck in all that he does.
Here neighbour wars on neighbour, and why there is no man knows,
And if a man is lucky all wish his luck away,
And take his good name from him between a day and a day.

Laegaire. I would he'd come for all that, and make his young wife
    know
That though she may be his wife, she has no right to go
Before your wife and my wife, as she would have done last night
Had they not caught at her dress, and pulled her as was right;
And she makes light of us though our wives do all that they can.
She spreads her tail like a peacock and praises none but her man.

Conall. A man in a long green cloak that covers him up to the chin
Comes down through the rocks and hazels.

Laegaire.   Cry out that he cannot come in.

Conall. He must look for his dinner elsewhere, for no one alive shall
    stop
Where a shame must alight on us two before the dawn is up.

Laegaire. No man on the ridge of the world must ever know that but
    us two.

Conall [*outside door*]. Go away, go away, go away.

Young Man [*outside door*]. I will go when the night is through
And I have eaten and slept and drunk to my heart's delight.

Conall. A law has been made that none shall sleep in this house to-night.

Young Man. Who made that law?

Conall.   We made it, and who has so good a right?
Who else has to keep the house from the Shape-Changers till day?

Young Man. Then I will unmake the law, so get you out of the way.

> [*He pushes past Conall and goes into house.*

Conall. I thought no living man could have pushed me from the door,
Nor could any living man do it but for the dip in the floor;
And had I been rightly ready there's no man living could do it,
Dip or no dip.

Laegaire.   Go out—if you have your wits, go out,
A stone's throw further on you will find a big house where
Our wives will give you supper, and you'll sleep sounder there,
For it's a luckier house.
Young Man.   I'll eat and sleep where I will.
Laegaire. Go out or I will make you.
Young Man [*forcing up Laegaire's arm, passing him and putting his
     shield on the wall over the chair*]. Not till I have drunk my fill,
But may some dog defend me, for a cat of wonder's up.
Laegaire and Conall are here, the flagon full to the top,
And the cups—
Laegaire.   It is Cuchulain.
Cuchulain.   The cups are dry as a bone.
                              [*He sits on chair and drinks.*
Conall. Go into Scotland again, or where you will, but begone
From this unlucky country that was made when the Devil spat.
Cuchulain. If I lived here a hundred years, could a worse thing come
     than that
     Laegaire and Conall should know me and bid me begone to my
     face?
Conall. We bid you begone from a house that has fallen on shame and
     disgrace.
Cuchulain. I am losing patience, Conall—I find you stuffed with pride,
The flagon full to the brim, the front door standing wide;
You'd put me off with words, but the whole thing's plain enough,
You are waiting for some message to bring you to war or love
In that old secret country beyond the wool-white waves,
Or it may be down beneath them in foam-bewildered caves
Where nine forsaken sea-queens fling shuttles to and fro;
But beyond them, or beneath them, whether you will or no,
I am going too.
Laegaire.   Better tell it all out to the end;
He was born to luck in the cradle, his good luck may amend
The bad luck we were born to.
Conall.   I'll lay the whole thing bare.
You saw the luck that he had when he pushed in past me there.
Does anything stir on the sea?
Laegaire.   Not even a fish or a gull.
Conall. You were gone but a little while. We were there and the ale-
     cup full.
We were half drunk and merry, and midnight on the stroke,
When a wide, high man came in with a red foxy cloak,
With half-shut foxy eyes and a great laughing mouth,

And he said, when we bid him drink, that he had so great a drouth
  He could drink the sea.
Cuchulain.   I thought he had come for one of you
  Out of some Connacht rath, and would lap up milk and mew;
  But if he so loved water I have the tale awry.
Conall. You would not be so merry if he were standing by,
  For when we had sung or danced as he were our next of kin
  He promised to show us a game, the best that ever had been;
  And when we had asked what game, he answered, 'Why, whip off
      my head!
  Then one of you two stoop down, and I'll whip off his', he said.
  'A head for a head', he said, 'that is the game that I play'.
Cuchulain. How could he whip off a head when his own had been
      whipped away?
Conall. We told him it over and over, and that ale had fuddled his wit,
  But he stood and laughed at us there, as though his sides would split,
  Till I could stand it no longer, and whipped off his head at a blow,
  Being mad that he did not answer, and more at his laughing so,
  And there on the ground where it fell it went on laughing at me.
Laegaire. Till he took it up in his hands—
Conall.   And splashed himself into the sea.
Cuchulain. I have imagined as good when I've been as deep in the cup.
Laegaire. You never did.
Cuchulain.   And believed it.
Conall.   Cuchulain, when will you stop
  Boasting of your great deeds and weighing yourself with us two,
  And crying out to the world, whatever we say or do,
  That you've said or done a better?—Nor is it a drunkard's tale,
  Though we said to ourselves at first that it all came out of the ale,
  And thinking that if we told it we should be a laughing-stock
  Swore we should keep it secret.
Laegaire.   But twelve months upon the clock—
Conall. A twelvemonth from the first time—
Laegaire.   And the jug full up to the brim:
  For we had been put from our drinking by the very thought of him—
Conall. We stood as we're standing now—
Laegaire.   The horns were as empty—
Conall.   When
  He ran up out of the sea with his head on his shoulders again.
Cuchulain. Why, this is a tale worth telling.
Conall.   And he called for his debt and his right,
  And said that the land was disgraced because of us two from that
      night

If we did not pay him his debt.

Laegaire.   What is there to be said
When a man with a right to get it has come to ask for your head?

Conall. If you had been sitting there you had been silent like us.

Laegaire. He said that in twelve months more he would come again
   to this house
And ask his debt again. Twelve months are up to-day.

Conall. He would have followed after if we had run away.

Laegaire. Will he tell every mother's son that we have broken our word?

Cuchulain. Whether he does or does not, we'll drive him out with
   the sword,
And take his life in the bargain if he but dare to scoff.

Conall. How can you fight with a head that laughs when you've
   whipped it off?

Laegaire. Or a man that can pick it up and carry it out in his hand?

Conall. He is coming now, there's a splash and a rumble along the
   strand
As when he came last.

Cuchulain.   Come, and put all your backs to the door.
   [*A tall red-headed, red-cloaked man stands upon the threshold
   against the misty green of the sea; the ground, higher without
   than within the house, makes him seem taller even than he is.
   He leans upon a great two-handed sword.*

Laegaire. It is too late to shut it, for there he stands once more
And laughs like the sea.

Cuchulain. Old herring—You whip off heads! Why, then,
   Whip off your own, for it seems you can clap it on again.
   Or else go down in the sea, go down in the sea, I say,
   Find that old juggler Manannan and whip his head away;
   Or the Red Man of the Boyne, for they are of your own sort,
   Or if the waves have vexed you and you would find a sport
   Of a more Irish fashion, go fight without a rest
   A caterwauling phantom among the winds of the West.
   But what are you waiting for? Into the water, I say!
   If there's no sword can harm you, I've an older trick to play,
   An old five-fingered trick to tumble you out of the place;
   I am Sualtim's son, Cuchulain—What, do you laugh in my face?

Red Man. So you too think me in earnest in wagering poll for poll!
   A drinking joke and a gibe and a juggler's feat, that is all,
   To make the time go quickly—for I am the drinker's friend,
   The kindest of all Shape-Changers from here to the world's end,
   The best of all tipsy companions. And now I bring you a gift:

I will lay it there on the ground for the best of you all to lift
                    [*He lays his Helmet on the ground.*
And wear upon his own head, and choose for yourselves the best.
O, Laegaire and Conall are brave, but they were afraid of my jest.
Well, maybe I jest too grimly when the ale is in the cup.
There, I'm forgiven now—
                    [*Then in a more solemn voice as he goes out.*
                    Let the bravest take it up.
          [*Conall takes up Helmet and gazes at it with delight.*
Laegaire [*singing, with a swaggering stride*].
                    Laegaire is best;
                    Between water and hill,
                    He fought in the West
                    With cat-heads, until
                    At the break of day
                    All fell by his sword,
                    And he carried away
                    Their hidden hoard.
                              [*He seizes the Helmet.*
Conall. Laegaire, that Helmet is mine, for what did you find in the bag
   But the straw and the broken delf and the bits of dirty rag
   You'd taken for good money?
Cuchulain.   No, no, but give it me.
                              [*He takes Helmet.*
Conall. The Helmet's mine or Laegaire's—you're the youngest of us
   three.
Cuchulain [*filling Helmet with ale*]. I did not take it to keep it—the
   Red Man gave it for one,
   But I shall give it to all—to all of us three or to none;
   That is as you look upon it—we will pass it to and fro,
   And time and time about, drink out of it and so
   Stroke into peace this cat that has come to take our lives.
   Now it is purring again, and now I drink to your wives,
   And I drink to Emer, my wife.
                    [*A great noise without and shouting.*
                    Why, what in God's name is that noise?
Conall. What else but the charioteers and the kitchen and stable boys
   Shouting against each other, and the worst of all is your own,
   That chariot-driver, Laeg, and they'll keep it up till the dawn,
   And there's not a man in the house that will close his eyes to-night,
   Or be able to keep them from it, or know what set them to fight.
                              [*A noise of horns without.*

There, do you hear them now? Such hatred has each for each
They have taken the hunting-horns to drown one another's speech
For fear the truth may prevail. —Here's your good health and long
    life
And, though she be quarrelsome, good health to Emer, your wife.
    [*The Charioteers, Stable Boys, and Scullions come running in.*
    They carry great horns and other instruments, ladles, and the
    like.

Laeg. I am Laeg, Cuchulain's driver, and my master's cock of the yard.
Another Charioteer. Conall would scatter his feathers.
                                     [*Confused murmurs.*
Laegaire [*to Cuchulain*]. No use, they won't hear a word.
Conall. They'll keep it up till the dawn.
Another Charioteer.   It is Laegaire that is the best,
    For he fought with cats in Connacht while Conall took his rest
    And drained his ale-pot.
Another.   Laegaire—what does a man of his sort
    Care for the like of us? He did it for his own sport.
Another. It was all mere luck at the best.
Another.   But Conall, I say—
Another.   Let me speak.
Laeg. You'd be dumb if the cock of the yard would but open his beak.
Another. Before your cock was born, my master was in the fight.
Laeg. Go home and praise your grand-dad. They took to the horns for
    spite,
    For I said that no cock of your sort had been born since the fight
    began.
Another. Conall has got it, the best man has got it, and I am his man.
Cuchulain. Who was it started this quarrel?
A Stable Boy.   It was Laeg.
Another.   It was Laeg done it all.
Laeg. A high, wide, foxy man came where we sat in the hall,
    Getting our supper ready, with a great voice like the wind,
    And cried that there was a helmet, or something of the kind,
    That was for the foremost man upon the ridge of the earth.
    So I cried your name through the hall,
        [*The others cry out and blow horns, partly drowning the rest of*
        his speech.
                            but they denied its worth,
    Preferring Laegaire or Conall, and they cried to drown my voice;
    But I have so strong a throat that I drowned all their noise
    Till they took to the hunting-horns and blew them into my face,

And as neither side would give in—we would settle it in this place.
Let the Helmet be taken from Conall.
A Stable Boy.   No, Conall is the best man here.
Another. Give it to Laegaire that made the murderous cats pay dear.
Cuchulain. It has been given to none: that our rivalry might cease,
We have turned that murderous cat into a cup of peace.
I drank the first; and then Conall; give it to Laegaire now
                                 [*Conall gives Helmet to Laegaire.*
That it may purr in his hand and all of our servants know
That, since the ale went in, its claws went out of sight.
A Servant. That's well—I will stop my shouting.
Another.   Cuchulain is in the right;
I am tired of this big horn that has made me hoarse as a rook.
Laegaire. Cuchulain, you drank the first.
Another.   By drinking the first he took
The whole of the honours himself.
Laegaire.   Cuchulain, you drank the first.
Another. If Laegaire drink from it now, he claims to be last and worst.
Another. Cuchulain and Conall have drunk.
Another.   He is lost if he taste a drop.
Laegaire [*laying Helmet on table*]. Did you claim to be better than us
     by drinking first from the cup?
Cuchulain [*his words are partly drowned by the murmurs of the crowd
     though he speaks very loud*]. That juggler from the sea, that old
     red herring it is
Who has set us all by the ears—he brought the Helmet for this,
And because we would not quarrel he ran elsewhere to shout
That Conall and Laegaire wronged me, till all had fallen out.
               [*The murmur grows less so that his words are heard.*
Who knows where he is now or whom he is spurring to fight?
So get you gone, and whatever may cry aloud in the night,
Or show itself in the air, be silent until morn.
A Servant. Cuchulain is in the right—I am tired of this big horn.
Cuchulain. Go!
     [*The Servants turn towards the door but stop on hearing the
     voices of women outside.*
Laegaire's Wife [*without*]. Mine is the better to look at.
Conall's Wife [*without*].   But mine is better born.
Emer [*without*]. My man is the pithier man.
Cuchulain.   Old hurricane, well done!
You've set our wives to the game that they may egg us on;
We are to kill each other that you may sport with us.

Ah, now they've begun to wrestle as to who'll be first in the house.

[*The women come to the door struggling.*

Emer. No, I have the right of the place, for I married the better man.

Conall's Wife [*pulling Emer back*]. My nails in your neck and shoulder.

Laegaire's Wife. And go before me if you can.

My husband fought in the West.

Conall's Wife [*kneeling in the door so as to keep the others out who pull at her*]. But what did he fight with there

But sidelong and spitting and helpless shadows of the dim air?

And what did he carry away but straw and broken delf?

Laegaire's Wife. Your own man made up that tale trembling alone by himself,

Drowning his terror.

Emer [*forcing herself in front*]. I am Emer, it is I go first through the door.

No one shall walk before me, or praise any man before

My man has been praised.

Cuchulain [*putting his spear across the door so as to close it*]. Come, put an end to their quarreling:

One is as fair as the other, each one the wife of a king.

Break down the painted walls, break them down, down to the floor!

Our wives shall come in together, each one at her own door.

[*Laegaire and Conall begin to break down the walls. Their wives go each to the hole her husband is making. Emer stands at the door and sings. Some of those who carry musical instruments may play an accompaniment.*

Emer.

> Nothing that he has done;
> His mind that is fire,
> His body that is sun,
> Have set my head higher
> Than all the world's wives.
> Himself on the wind
> Is the gift that he gives,
> Therefore women-kind,
> When their eyes have met mine,
> Grow cold and grow hot,
> Troubled as with wine
> By a secret thought,
> Preyed upon, fed upon
> By jealousy and desire,
> For I am moon to that sun,
> I am steel to that fire.

[*Holes have been broken in the walls. Cuchulain takes his spear from the door, and the three women come in at the same moment.*

Emer. Cuchulain, put off this sloth and awake:
I will sing till I've stiffened your lip against every knave that would take
A share of your honour.

Laegaire's Wife. You lie, for your man would take from my man.

Conall's Wife [*to Laegaire's Wife*]. You say that, you double-face, and your own husband began.

Cuchulain [*taking up Helmet from table*]. Townland may rail at townland till all have gone to wrack,
The very straws may wrangle till they've thrown down the stack;
The very door-posts bicker till they've pulled in the door,
The very ale-jars jostle till the ale is on the floor,
But this shall help no further. [*He throws Helmet into the sea.*

Laegaire's Wife. It was not for your head,
And so you would let none wear it, but fling it away instead.

Conall's Wife. But you shall answer for it, for you've robbed my man by this.

Conall. You have robbed us both, Cuchulain.

Laegaire. The greatest wrong there is
On the wide ridge of the world has been done to us two this day.

Emer [*drawing her dagger*]. Who is for Cuchulain?

Cuchulain. Silence!

Emer. Who is for Cuchulain, I say?
[*She sings the same words as before, flourishing her dagger about. While she is singing, Conall's Wife and Laegaire's Wife draw their daggers and run at her, but Cuchulain forces them back. Laegaire and Conall draw their swords to strike Cuchulain.*

Laegaire's Wife [*crying out so as to be heard through Emer's singing*]. Deafen her singing with horns!

Conall's Wife. Cry aloud! blow horns! make a noise!

Laegaire's Wife. Blow horns, clap hands, or shout, so that you smother her voice!
[*The Stable Boys and Scullions blow their horns or fight among themselves. There is a deafening noise and a confused fight. Suddenly three black hands come through the windows and put out the torches. It is now pitch-dark, but for a faint light outside the house which merely shows that there are moving forms, but not who or what they are, and in the darkness one can hear low terrified voices.*

A Voice. Coal-black, and headed like cats, they came up over the
strand.
Another Voice. And I saw one stretch to a torch and cover it with
his hand.
Another Voice. Another sooty fellow has plucked the moon from the
air.

   [*A light gradually comes into the house from the sea, on which
   the moon begins to show once more. There is no light within the
   house, and the great beams of the walls are dark and full of
   shadows, and the persons of the play dark too against the light.
   The Red Man is seen standing in the midst of the house. The
   black cat-headed men crouch and stand about the door. One
   carries the Helmet, one the great sword.*

Red Man. I demand the debt that's owing. Let some man kneel down
there
   That I may cut his head off, or all shall go to wrack.
Cuchulain. He played and paid with his head, and it's right that we
pay him back,
   And give him more than he gave, for he comes in here as a guest:
   So I will give him my head.   [*Emer begins to keen.*
                    Little wife, little wife, be at rest.
   Alive I have been far off in all lands under the sun,
   And been no faithful man; but when my story is done
   My fame shall spring up and laugh, and set you high above all.
Emer [*putting her arms about him*]. It is you, not your fame that I
love.
Cuchulain [*tries to put her from him*]. You are young, you are wise,
you can call
   Some kinder and comelier man that will sit at home in the house.
Emer. Live and be faithless still.
Cuchulain [*throwing her from him*]. Would you stay the great
barnacle-goose
   When its eyes are turned to the sea and its beak to the salt of the air?
Emer [*lifting her dagger to stab herself*]. I, too, on the grey wing's
path!
Cuchulain [*seizing dagger*]. Do you dare, do you dare, do you dare?
   Bear children and sweep the house.
                    [*Forcing his way through the servants who gather round.*
                              Wail, but keep from the road.
                    [*He kneels before Red Man. There is a pause.*
   Quick to your work, old Radish, you will fade when the cocks have
crowed.

[*A black cat-headed man holds out the Helmet. The Red Man
   takes it.*

Red Man. I have not come for your hurt, I'm the Rector of this land,
And with my spitting cat-heads, my frenzied moon-bred band,
Age after age I sift it, and choose for its championship
The man who hits my fancy.
                        [*He places the Helmet on Cuchulain's head.*
                        And I choose the laughing lip
That shall not turn from laughing, whatever rise or fall;
The heart that grows no bitterer although betrayed by all;
The hand that loves to scatter; the life like a gambler's throw;
And these things I make prosper, till a day come that I know,
When heart and mind shall darken that the weak may end the
   strong,
And the long-remembering harpers have matter for their song.

THE END

ON BAILE'S STRAND

1904

ON BAILE'S STRAND

PERSONS IN THE PLAY

A Fool
A Blind Man
Cuchulain, *King of Muirthemne*
Conchubar, *High King of Uladh*
A Young Man, *son of Cuchulain*
Kings and Singing Women

A great hall at Dundealgan, not 'Cuchulain's great ancient house' but an assembly-house nearer to the sea. A big door at the back, and through the door the misty light as of sea-mist. There are many chairs and one long bench. One of these chairs, which is towards the front of the stage, is bigger than the others. Somewhere at the back there is a table with flagons of ale upon it and drinking-horns. There is a small door at one side of the hall. A Fool and Blind Man, both ragged, and their features made grotesque and extravagant by masks, come in through the door at the back. The Blind Man leans upon a staff.

Fool. What a clever man you are though you are blind! There's nobody with two eyes in his head that is as clever as you are. Who but you could have thought that the henwife sleeps every day a little at noon? I would never be able to steal anything if you didn't tell me where to look for it. And what a good cook you are! You take the fowl out of my hands after I have stolen it and plucked it, and you put it into the big pot at the fire there, and I can go out and run races with the witches at the edge of the waves and get an appetite, and when I've got it, there's the hen waiting inside for me, done to the turn.

Blind Man [*who is feeling about with his stick*]. Done to the turn.

Fool [*putting his arm round Blind Man's neck*]. Come now, I'll have a leg and you'll have a leg, and we'll draw lots for the wish-bone. I'll be praising you, I'll be praising you while we're eating it, for your good plans and for your good cooking. There's nobody in the world like you, Blind Man. Come, come. Wait a minute. I shouldn't have closed the door. There are some that look for me, and I wouldn't like them not to find me. Don't tell it to anybody, Blind Man. There are some that follow me. Boann herself out of the river and Fand out of the deep sea. Witches they are, and they come by in the wind, and

they cry, 'Give a kiss, Fool, give a kiss', that's what they cry. That's
wide enough. All the witches can come in now. I wouldn't have them
beat at the door and say, 'Where is the Fool? Why has he put a lock
on the door?' Maybe they'll hear the bubbling of the pot and come
in and sit on the ground. But we won't give them any of the fowl.
Let them go back to the sea, let them go back to the sea.

Blind Man [*feeling legs of big chair with his hands*]. Ah! [*Then, in a
louder voice as he feels the back of it.*] Ah—ah—

Fool. Why do you say 'Ah-ah'?

Blind Man. I know the big chair. It is to-day the High King Conchubar is coming. They have brought out his chair. He is going to be
Cuchulain's master in earnest from this day out. It is that he's
coming for.

Fool. He must be a great man to be Cuchulain's master.

Blind Man. So he is. He is a great man. He is over all the rest of the
kings of Ireland.

Fool. Cuchulain's master! I thought Cuchulain could do anything he
liked.

Blind Man. So he did, so he did. But he ran too wild, and Conchubar
is coming to-day to put an oath upon him that will stop his rambling
and make him as biddable as a house-dog and keep him always at his
hand. He will sit in this chair and put the oath upon him.

Fool. How will he do that?

Blind Man. You have no wits to understand such things. [*The Blind
Man has got into the chair.*] He will sit up in this chair and he'll
say: 'Take the oath, Cuchulain. I bid you take the oath. Do as I tell
you. What are your wits compared with mine, and what are your
riches compared with mine? And what sons have you to pay your
debts and to put a stone over you when you die? Take the oath, I
tell you. Take a strong oath.'

Fool [*crumpling himself up and whining*]. I will not. I'll take no oath.
I want my dinner.

Blind Man. Hush, hush! It is not done yet.

Fool. You said it was done to a turn.

Blind Man. Did I, now? Well, it might be done, and not done. The
wings might be white, but the legs might be red. The flesh might
stick hard to the bones and not come away in the teeth. But, believe
me, Fool, it will be well done before you put your teeth in it.

Fool. My teeth are growing long with the hunger.

Blind Man. I'll tell you a story—the kings have story-tellers while they
are waiting for their dinner—I will tell you a story with a fight in it,
a story with a champion in it, and a ship and a queen's son that has
his mind set on killing somebody that you and I know.

Fool. Who is that? Who is he coming to kill?

Blind Man. Wait, now, till you hear. When you were stealing the fowl, I was lying in a hole in the sand, and I heard three men coming with a shuffling sort of noise. They were wounded and groaning.

Fool. Go on. Tell me about the fight.

Blind Man. There had been a fight, a great fight, a tremendous great fight. A young man had landed on the shore, the guardians of the shore had asked his name, and he had refused to tell it, and he had killed one, and others had run away.

Fool. That's enough. Come on now to the fowl. I wish it was bigger. I wish it was as big as a goose.

Blind Man. Hush! I haven't told you all. I know who that young man is. I heard the men who were running away say he had red hair, that he had come from Aoife's country, that he was coming to kill Cuchulain.

Fool. Nobody can do that.

> [*To a tune*]
> Cuchulain has killed kings,
> Kings and sons of kings,
> Dragons out of the water,
> And witches out of the air,

Banachas and Bonachas and people of the woods.

Blind Man. Hush! hush!

Fool [*still singing*].

> Witches that steal the milk,
> Fomor that steal the children,
> Hags that have heads like hares,
> Hares that have claws like witches,
> All riding a-cock-horse
> [*Spoken*]

Out of the very bottom of the bitter black North.

Blind Man. Hush, I say!

Fool. Does Cuchulain know that he is coming to kill him?

Blind Man. How would he know that with his head in the clouds? He doesn't care for common fighting. Why would he put himself out, and nobody in it but that young man? Now if it were a white fawn that might turn into a queen before morning—

Fool. Come to the fowl. I wish it was as big as a pig; a fowl with goose grease and pig's crackling.

Blind Man. No hurry, no hurry. I know whose son it is. I wouldn't tell anybody else, but I will tell you,—a secret is better to you than your dinner. You like being told secrets.

Fool. Tell me the secret.

Blind Man. That young man is Aoife's son. I am sure it is Aoife's son, it flows in upon me that it is Aoife's son. You have often heard me talking of Aoife, the great woman-fighter Cuchulain got the mastery over in the North?

Fool. I know, I know. She is one of those cross queens that live in hungry Scotland.

Blind Man. I am sure it is her son. I was in Aoife's country for a long time.

Fool. That was before you were blinded for putting a curse upon the wind.

Blind Man. There was a boy in her house that had her own red colour on him, and everybody said he was to be brought up to kill Cuchulain, that she hated Cuchulain. She used to put a helmet on a pillar-stone and call it Cuchulain and set him casting at it. There is a step outside—Cuchulain's step.

> [*Cuchulain passes by in the mist outside the big door.*

Fool. Where is Cuchulain going?

Blind Man. He is going to meet Conchubar that has bidden him to take the oath.

Fool. Ah, an oath, Blind Man. How can I remember so many things at once? Who is going to take an oath?

Blind Man. Cuchulain is going to take an oath to Conchubar who is High King.

Fool. What a mix-up you make of everything, Blind Man! You were telling me one story, and now you are telling me another story. . . . How can I get the hang of it at the end if you mix everything at the beginning? Wait till I settle it out. There now, there's Cuchulain [*he points to one foot*], and there is the young man [*he points to the other foot*] that is coming to kill him, and Cuchulain doesn't know. But where's Conchubar? [*Takes bag from side.*] That's Conchubar with all his riches—Cuchulain, young man, Conchubar.—And where's Aoife? [*Throws up cap.*] There is Aoife, high up on the mountains in high hungry Scotland. Maybe it is not true after all. Maybe it was your own making up. It's many a time you cheated me before with your lies. Come to the cooking-pot, my stomach is pinched and rusty. Would you have it to be creaking like a gate?

Blind Man. I tell you it's true. And more than that is true. If you listen to what I say, you'll forget your stomach.

Fool. I won't.

Blind Man. Listen. I know who the young man's father is, but I won't say. I would be afraid to say. Ah, Fool, you would forget everything if you could know who the young man's father is.

Fool. Who is it? Tell me now quick, or I'll shake you. Come, out with
   it, or I'll shake you.   [*A murmur of voices in the distance.*
Blind Man. Wait, wait. There's something coming. . . It is Cuchu-
   lain is coming. He's coming back with the High King. Go and ask
   Cuchulain. He'll tell you. It's little you'll care about the cooking-pot
   when you have asked Cuchulain that . . .
                              [*Blind Man goes out by side door.*
Fool. I'll ask him. Cuchulain will know. He was in Aoife's country.
   [*Goes up stage.*] I'll ask him. [*Turns and goes down stage.*] But, no,
   I won't ask him, I would be afraid. [*Going up again.*] Yes, I will
   ask him. What harm in asking? The Blind Man said I was to ask
   him. [*Going down.*] No, no. I'll not ask him. He might kill me. I
   have but killed hens and geese and pigs. He has killed kings. [*Goes
   up again almost to big door.*] Who says I'm afraid? I'm not afraid.
   I'm no coward. I'll ask him. No, no, Cuchulain, I'm not going to
   ask you.

                    He has killed kings,
                    Kings and the sons of kings,
                    Dragons out of the water,
                    And witches out of the air,
   Banachas and Bonachas and people of the woods.
      [*Fool goes out by side door, the last words being heard outside.
      Cuchulain and Conchubar enter through the big door at the
      back. While they are still outside, Cuchulain's voice is heard
      raised in anger. He is a dark man, something over forty years of
      age. Conchubar is much older and carries a long staff, elabor-
      ately carved or with an elaborate gold handle.*

Cuchulain. Because I have killed men without your bidding
   And have rewarded others at my own pleasure,
   Because of half a score of trifling things,
   You'd lay this oath upon me, and now—and now
   You add another pebble to the heap,
   And I must be your man, well-nigh your bondsman,
   Because a youngster out of Aoife's country
   Has found the shore ill-guarded.
Conchubar.   He came to land
   While you were somewhere out of sight and hearing,
   Hunting or dancing with your wild companions.
Cuchulain. He can be driven out. I'll not be bound.
   I'll dance or hunt, or quarrel or make love,
   Wherever and whenever I've a mind to.
   If time had not put water in your blood,
   You never would have thought it.

Conchubar.   I would leave
  A strong and settled country to my children.
Cuchulain. And I must be obedient in all things;
  Give up my will to yours; go where you please;
  Come when you call; sit at the council-board
  Among the unshapely bodies of old men;
  I whose mere name has kept this country safe,
  I that in early days have driven out
  Maeve of Cruachan and the northern pirates,
  The hundred kings of Sorcha, and the kings
  Out of the Garden in the East of the World.
  Must I, that held you on the throne when all
  Had pulled you from it, swear obedience
  As if I were some cattle-raising king?
  Are my shins speckled with the heat of the fire,
  Or have my hands no skill but to make figures
  Upon the ashes with a stick? Am I
  So slack and idle that I need a whip
  Before I serve you?
Conchubar.   No, no whip, Cuchulain,
  But every day my children come and say:
  'This man is growing harder to endure.
  How can we be at safety with this man
  That nobody can buy or bid or bind?
  We shall be at his mercy when you are gone;
  He burns the earth as if he were a fire,
  And time can never touch him.'
Cuchulain.   And so the tale
  Grows finer yet; and I am to obey
  Whatever child you set upon the throne,
  As if it were yourself!
Conchubar.   Most certainly.
  I am High King, my son shall be High King;
  And you for all the wildness of your blood,
  And though your father came out of the sun,
  Are but a little king and weigh but light
  In anything that touches government,
  If put into the balance with my children.
Cuchulain. It's well that we should speak our minds out plainly,
  For when we die we shall be spoken of
  In many countries. We in our young days
  Have seen the heavens like a burning cloud
  Brooding upon the world, and being more

Than men can be now that cloud's lifted up,
We should be the more truthful. Conchubar,
I do not like your children—they have no pith,
No marrow in their bones, and will lie soft
Where you and I lie hard.

Conchubar.   You rail at them
Because you have no children of your own.

Cuchulain. I think myself most lucky that I leave
No pallid ghost or mockery of a man
To drift and mutter in the corridors
Where I have laughed and sung.

Conchubar.   That is not true,
For all your boasting of the truth between us;
For there is no man having house and lands,
That have been in the one family, called
By that one family's name for centuries,
But is made miserable if he know
They are to pass into a stranger's keeping,
As yours will pass.

Cuchulain.   The most of men feel that,
But you and I leave names upon the harp.

Conchubar. You play with arguments as lawyers do,
And put no heart in them. I know your thoughts,
For we have slept under the one cloak and drunk
From the one wine-cup. I know you to the bone,
I have heard you cry, aye, in your very sleep,
'I have no son', and with such bitterness
That I have gone upon my knees and prayed
That it might be amended.

Cuchulain.   For you thought
That I should be as biddable as others
Had I their reason for it; but that's not true;
For I would need a weightier argument
Than one that marred me in the copying,
As I have that clean hawk out of the air
That, as men say, begot this body of mine
Upon a mortal woman.

Conchubar.   Now as ever
You mock at every reasonable hope,
And would have nothing, or impossible things.
What eye has ever looked upon the child
Would satisfy a mind like that?

Cuchulain.   I would leave

My house and name to none that would not face
Even myself in battle.
Conchubar.   Being swift of foot,
And making light of every common chance,
You should have overtaken on the hills
Some daughter of the air, or on the shore
A daughter of the Country-under-Wave.
Cuchulain. I am not blasphemous.
Conchubar.   Yet you despise
Our queens, and would not call a child your own,
If one of them had borne him.
Cuchulain.   I have not said it.
Conchubar. Ah! I remember I have heard you boast,
When the ale was in your blood, that there was one
In Scotland, where you had learnt the trade of war,
That had a stone-pale cheek and red-brown hair;
And that although you have loved other women,
You'd sooner that fierce woman of the camp
Bore you a son than any queen among them.
Cuchulain. You call her a 'fierce woman of the camp',
For, having lived among the spinning-wheels,
You'd have no woman near that would not say,
'Ah! how wise!' 'What will you have for supper?'
'What shall I wear that I may please you, sir?'
And keep that humming through the day and night
For ever. A fierce woman of the camp!
But I am getting angry about nothing.
You have never seen her. Ah! Conchubar, had you seen her
With that high, laughing, turbulent head of hers
Thrown backward, and the bowstring at her ear,
Or sitting at the fire with those grave eyes
Full of good counsel as it were with wine,
Or when love ran through all the lineaments
Of her wild body—although she had no child,
None other had all beauty, queen or lover,
Or was so fitted to give birth to kings.
Conchubar. There's nothing I can say that drifts you farther
From the one weighty matter. That very woman—
For I know well that you are praising Aoife—
Now hates you and will leave no subtlety
Unknotted that might run into a noose
About your throat, no army in idleness
That might bring ruin on this land you serve.

Cuchulain. No wonder in that, no wonder at all in that.
  I never have known love but as a kiss
  In the mid-battle, and a difficult truce
  Of oil and water, candles and dark night,
  Hillside and hollow, the hot-footed sun
  And the cold, sliding, slippery-footed moon—
  A brief forgiveness between opposites
  That have been hatreds for three times the age
  Of this long-'stablished ground.
Conchubar.   Listen to me.
  Aoife makes war on us, and every day
  Our enemies grow greater and beat the walls
  More bitterly, and you within the walls
  Are every day more turbulent; and yet,
  When I would speak about these things, your fancy
  Runs as it were a swallow on the wind.
      [*Outside the door in the blue light of the sea-mist are many old
      and young Kings; amongst them are three Women, two of whom
      carry a bowl of fire. The third, in what follows, puts from time
      to time fragrant herbs into the fire so that it flickers up into
      brighter flame.*
  Look at the door and what men gather there—
  Old counsellors that steer the land with me,
  And younger kings, the dancers and harp-players
  That follow in your tumults, and all these
  Are held there by the one anxiety.
  Will you be bound into obedience
  And so make this land safe for them and theirs?
  You are but half a king and I but half;
  I need your might of hand and burning heart,
  And you my wisdom.
Cuchulain [*going near to door*]. Nestlings of a high nest,
  Hawks that have followed me into the air
  And looked upon the sun, we'll out of this
  And sail upon the wind once more. This king
  Would have me take an oath to do his will,
  And having listened to his tune from morning,
  I will no more of it. Run to the stable
  And set the horses to the chariot-pole,
  And send a messenger to the harp-players.
  We'll find a level place among the woods,
  And dance awhile.

A Young King. Cuchulain, take the oath.
There is none here that would not have you take it.
Cuchulain. You'd have me take it? Are you of one mind?
The Kings. All, all, all, all!
A Young King. Do what the High King bids you.
Conchubar. There is not one but dreads this turbulence
Now that they're settled men.
Cuchulain. Are you so changed,
Or have I grown more dangerous of late?
But that's not it. I understand it all.
It's you that have changed. You've wives and children now,
And for that reason cannot follow one
That lives like a bird's flight from tree to tree.—
It's time the years put water in my blood
And drowned the wildness of it, for all's changed,
But that unchanged.—I'll take what oath you will:
The moon, the sun, the water, light, or air,
I do not care how binding.
Conchubar. On this fire
That has been lighted from your hearth and mine;
The older men shall be my witnesses,
The younger, yours. The holders of the fire
Shall purify the thresholds of the house
With waving fire, and shut the outer door,
According to the custom; and sing rhyme
That has come down from the old law-makers
To blow the witches out. Considering
That the wild will of man could be oath-bound,
But that a woman's could not, they bid us sing
Against the will of woman at its wildest
In the Shape-Changers that run upon the wind.
                    [*Conchubar has gone on to his throne.*
The Women. [*They sing in a very low voice after the first few words
            so that the others will all but drown their words.*
            May this fire have driven out
            The Shape-Changers that can put
            Ruin on a great king's house
            Until all be ruinous.
            Names whereby a man has known
            The threshold and the hearthstone,
            Gather on the wind and drive
            The women none can kiss and thrive,

For they are but whirling wind,
Out of memory and mind.
They would make a prince decay
With light images of clay
Planted in the running wave;
Or, for many shapes they have,
They would change them into hounds
Until he had died of his wounds,
Though the change were but a whim;
Or they'd hurl a spell at him,
That he follow with desire
Bodies that can never tire
Or grow kind, for they anoint
All their bodies, joint by joint,
With a miracle-working juice
That is made out of the grease
Of the ungoverned unicorn.
But the man is thrice forlorn,
Emptied, ruined, wracked, and lost,
That they follow, for at most
They will give him kiss for kiss
While they murmur, 'After this
Hatred may be sweet to the taste'.
Those wild hands that have embraced
All his body can but shove
At the burning wheel of love
Till the side of hate comes up.
Therefore in this ancient cup
May the sword-blades drink their fill
Of the home-brew there, until
They will have for masters none
But the threshold and hearthstone.

Cuchulain [*speaking, while they are singing*]. I'll take and keep this
    oath, and from this day
I shall be what you please, my chicks, my nestlings.
Yet I had thought you were of those that praised
Whatever life could make the pulse run quickly,
Even though it were brief, and that you held
That a free gift was better than a forced.—
But that's all over.—I will keep it, too;
I never gave a gift and took it again.
If the wild horse should break the chariot-pole,
It would be punished. Should that be in the oath?

[*Two of the Women, still singing, crouch in front of him holding
the bowl over their heads. He spreads his hands over the flame.*
I swear to be obedient in all things
To Conchubar, and to uphold his children.
Conchubar. We are one being, as these flames are one:
I give my wisdom, and I take your strength.
Now thrust the swords into the flame, and pray
That they may serve the threshold and the hearthstone
With faithful service.
[*The Kings kneel in a semicircle before the two Women and
Cuchulain, who thrusts his sword into the flame. They all put
the points of their swords into the flame. The third Woman is
at the back near the big door.*
Cuchulain.   O pure, glittering ones
That should be more than wife or friend or mistress,
Give us the enduring will, the unquenchable hope,
The friendliness of the sword!—
[*The song grows louder, and the last words ring out clearly. There
is a loud knocking at the door, and a cry of* 'Open! open!'
Conchubar. Some king that has been loitering on the way.
Open the door, for I would have all know
That the oath's finished and Cuchulain bound,
And that the swords are drinking up the flame.
[*The door is opened by the third Woman, and a Young Man with
a drawn sword enters.*
Young Man. I am of Aoife's country.
[*The Kings rush towards him. Cuchulain throws himself between.*
Cuchulain.   Put up your swords.
He is but one. Aoife is far away.
Young Man. I have come alone into the midst of you
To weigh this sword against Cuchulain's sword.
Conchubar. And are you noble? for if of common seed,
You cannot weigh your sword against his sword
But in mixed battle.
Young Man.   I am under bonds
To tell my name to no man; but it's noble.
Conchubar. But I would know your name and not your bonds.
You cannot speak in the Assembly House,
If you are not noble.
First Old King.   Answer the High King!
Young Man. I will give no other proof than the hawk gives
That it's no sparrow! [*He is silent for a moment, then speaks to all.*
                    Yet look upon me, Kings.

I, too, am of that ancient seed, and carry
The signs about this body and in these bones.
Cuchulain. To have shown the hawk's grey feather is enough,
And you speak highly, too. Give me that helmet.
I'd thought they had grown weary sending champions.
That sword and belt will do. This fighting's welcome.
The High King there has promised me his wisdom;
But the hawk's sleepy till its well-beloved
Cries out amid the acorns, or it has seen
Its enemy like a speck upon the sun.
What's wisdom to the hawk, when that clear eye
Is burning nearer up in the high air?
　　[*Looks hard at Young Man; then comes down steps and grasps
　　　　Young Man by shoulder.*
Hither into the light.
[*To Conchubar.*]　　　The very tint
Of her that I was speaking of but now.
Not a pin's difference.
[*To Young Man.*]　　　You are from the North,
Where there are many that have that tint of hair—
Red-brown, the light red-brown. Come nearer, boy,
For I would have another look at you.
There's more likeness—a pale, a stone-pale cheek.
What brought you, boy? Have you no fear of death?
Young Man. Whether I live or die is in the gods' hands.
Cuchulain. That is all words, all words; a young man's talk.
I am their plough, their harrow, their very strength;
For he that's in the sun begot this body
Upon a mortal woman, and I have heard tell
It seemed as if he had outrun the moon
That he must follow always through waste heaven,
He loved so happily. He'll be but slow
To break a tree that was so sweetly planted.
Let's see that arm. I'll see it if I choose.
That arm had a good father and a good mother,
But it is not like this.
Young Man.　　　　You are mocking me;
You think I am not worthy to be fought.
But I'll not wrangle but with this talkative knife.
Cuchulain. Put up your sword; I am not mocking you.
I'd have you for my friend, but if it's not
Because you have a hot heart and a cold eye,
I cannot tell the reason.

[*To Conchubar.*]   He has got her fierceness,
And nobody is as fierce as those pale women.
But I will keep him with me, Conchubar,
That he may set my memory upon her
When the day's fading.—You will stop with us,
And we will hunt the deer and the wild bulls;
And, when we have grown weary, light our fires
Between the wood and water, or on some mountain
Where the Shape-Changers of the morning come.
The High King there would make a mock of me
Because I did not take a wife among them.
Why do you hang your head? It's a good life:
The head grows prouder in the light of the dawn,
And friendship thickens in the murmuring dark
Where the spare hazels meet the wool-white foam.
But I can see there's no more need for words
And that you'll be my friend from this day out.

Conchubar. He has come hither not in his own name
     But in Queen Aoife's, and has challenged us
     In challenging the foremost man of us all.

Cuchulain. Well, well, what matter?

Conchubar.   You think it does not matter,
     And that a fancy lighter than the air,
     A whim of the moment, has more matter in it.
     For, having none that shall reign after you,
     You cannot think as I do, who would leave
     A throne too high for insult.

Cuchulain.   Let your children
     Re-mortar their inheritance, as we have,
     And put more muscle on.—I'll give you gifts,
     But I'd have something too—that arm-ring, boy.
     We'll have this quarrel out when you are older.

Young Man. There is no man I'd sooner have my friend
     Than you, whose name has gone about the world
     As if it had been the wind; but Aoife'd say
     I had turned coward.

Cuchulain.   I will give you gifts
     That Aoife'll know, and all her people know,
     To have come from me.   [*Showing cloak.*
                    My father gave me this.
     He came to try me, rising up at dawn
     Out of the cold dark of the rich sea.
     He challenged me to battle, but before

My sword had touched his sword, told me his name,
Gave me this cloak, and vanished. It was woven
By women of the Country-under-Wave
Out of the fleeces of the sea. O! tell her
I was afraid, or tell her what you will.
No; tell her that I heard a raven croak
On the north side of the house, and was afraid.
Conchubar. Some witch of the air has troubled Cuchulain's mind.
Cuchulain. No witchcraft. His head is like a woman's head
    I had a fancy for.
Conchubar.   A witch of the air
    Can make a leaf confound us with memories.
    They run upon the wind and hurl the spells
    That make us nothing, out of the invisible wind.
    They have gone to school to learn the trick of it.
Cuchulain. No, no—there's nothing out of common here;
    The winds are innocent.—That arm-ring, boy.
A King. If I've your leave I'll take this challenge up.
Another King. No, give it me, High King, for this wild Aoife
    Has carried off my slaves.
Another King.   No, give it me,
    For she has harried me in house and herd.
Another King. I claim this fight.
Other Kings [*together*].   And I! And I! And I!
Cuchulain. Back! back! Put up your swords! Put up your swords!
    There's none alive that shall accept a challenge
    I have refused. Laegaire, put up your sword!
Young Man. No, let them come. If they've a mind for it,
    I'll try it out with any two together.
Cuchulain. That's spoken as I'd have spoken it at your age.
    But you are in my house. Whatever man
    Would fight with you shall fight it out with me.
    They're dumb, they're dumb. How many of you would meet
                            [*Draws sword.*

    This mutterer, this old whistler, this sand-piper,
    This edge that's greyer than the tide, this mouse
    That's gnawing at the timbers of the world,
    This, this—Boy, I would meet them all in arms
    If I'd a son like you. He would avenge me
    When I have withstood for the last time the men
    Whose fathers, brothers, sons, and friends I have killed
    Upholding Conchubar, when the four provinces
    Have gathered with the ravens over them.

    But I'd need no avenger. You and I
    Would scatter them like water from a dish.
Young Man. We'll stand by one another from this out.
    Here is the ring.
Cuchulain.   No, turn and turn about.
    But my turn's first because I am the older.   [*Spreading out cloak.*
    Nine queens out of the Country-under-Wave
    Have woven it with the fleeces of the sea
    And they were long embroidering at it.—Boy,
    If I had fought my father, he'd have killed me,
    As certainly as if I had a son
    And fought with him, I should be deadly to him;
    For the old fiery fountains are far off
    And every day there is less heat o' the blood.
Conchubar [*in a loud voice*]. No more of this. I will not have this
      friendship.
    Cuchulain is my man, and I forbid it.
    He shall not go unfought, for I myself—
Cuchulain. I will not have it.
Conchubar.   You lay commands on me?
Cuchulain [*seizing Conchubar*]. You shall not stir, High King. I'll hold
    you there.
Conchubar. Witchcraft has maddened you.
The Kings [*shouting*].   Yes, witchcraft! witchcraft!
First Old King. Some witch has worked upon your mind, Cuchulain.
    The head of that young man seemed like a woman's
    You'd had a fancy for. Then of a sudden
    You laid your hands on the High King himself!
Cuchulain. And laid my hands on the High King himself?
Conchubar. Some witch is floating in the air above us.
Cuchulain. Yes, witchcraft! witchcraft! Witches of the air!
    [*To Young Man.*] Why did you? Who was it set you to this work?
    Out, out! I say, for now it's sword on sword!
Young Man. But . . . but I did not.
Cuchulain.   Out, I say, out, out!
    [*Young Man goes out followed by Cuchulain. The Kings follow
    them out with confused cries, and words one can hardly hear
    because of the noise. Some cry,* 'Quicker, quicker!' 'Why are you
    so long at the door?' 'We'll be too late!' 'Have they begun to
    fight?' 'Can you see if they are fighting?' *and so on. Their voices
    drown each other. The three Women are left alone.*
First Woman. I have seen, I have seen!
Second Woman.   What do you cry aloud?

First Woman. The Ever-living have shown me what's to come.
Third Woman. How? Where?
First Woman.   In the ashes of the bowl.
Second Woman. While you were holding it between your hands?
Third Woman. Speak quickly!
First Woman.   I have seen Cuchulain's roof-tree
   Leap into fire, and the walls split and blacken.
Second Woman. Cuchulain has gone out to die.
Third Woman.   O! O!
Second Woman. Who could have thought that one so great as he
   Should meet his end at this unnoted sword!
First Woman. Life drifts between a fool and a blind man
   To the end, and nobody can know his end.
Second Woman. Come, look upon the quenching of this greatness.
      [*The other two go to the door, but they stop for a moment upon
      the threshold and wail.*
First Woman. No crying out, for there'll be need of cries
   And rending of the hair when it's all finished.
      [*The Women go out. There is the sound of clashing swords from
      time to time during what follows.*
               Enter the Fool, dragging the Blind Man
Fool. You have eaten it, you have eaten it! You have left me nothing
   but the bones.   [*He throws Blind Man down by big chair.*
Blind Man. O, that I should have to endure such a plague! O, I ache
   all over! O, I am pulled to pieces! This is the way you pay me all
   the good I have done you.
Fool. You have eaten it! You have told me lies. I might have known
   you had eaten it when I saw your slow, sleepy walk. Lie there till the
   kings come. O, I will tell Conchubar and Cuchulain and all the kings
   about you!
Blind Man. What would have happened to you but for me, and you
   without your wits? If I did not take care of you, what would you do
   for food and warmth?
Fool. You take care of me? You stay safe, and send me into every kind
   of danger. You sent me down the cliff for gulls' eggs while you
   warmed your blind eyes in the sun; and then you ate all that were
   good for food. You left me the eggs that were neither egg nor bird.
   [*Blind Man tries to rise; Fool makes him lie down again.*] Keep
   quiet now, till I shut the door. There is some noise outside—a high
   vexing noise, so that I can't be listening to myself. [*Shuts the big
   door.*] Why can't they be quiet? Why can't they be quiet? [*Blind
   Man tries to get away.*] Oh! you would get away, would you? [*Follows Blind Man and brings him back.*] Lie there! lie there! No, you

won't get away! Lie there till the kings come. I'll tell them all about you. I will tell it all. How you sit warming yourself, when you have made me light a fire of sticks, while I sit blowing it with my mouth. Do you not always make me take the windy side of the bush when it blows, and the rainy side when it rains?

Blind Man. O, good Fool! listen to me. Think of the care I have taken of you. I have brought you to many a warm hearth, where there was a good welcome for you, but you would not stay there; you were always wandering about.

Fool. The last time you brought me in, it was not I who wandered away, but you that got put out because you took the crubeen out of the pot when nobody was looking. Keep quiet, now!

Cuchulain [*rushing in*]. Witchcraft! There is no witchcraft on the earth, or among the witches of the air, that these hands cannot break.

Fool. Listen to me, Cuchulain. I left him turning the fowl at the fire. He ate it all, though I had stolen it. He left me nothing but the feathers.

Cuchulain. Fill me a horn of ale!

Blind Man. I gave him what he likes best. You do not know how vain this Fool is. He likes nothing so well as a feather.

Fool. He left me nothing but the bones and feathers. Nothing but the feathers, though I had stolen it.

Cuchulain. Give me that horn. Quarrels here, too! [*Drinks.*] What is there between you two that is worth a quarrel? Out with it!

Blind Man. Where would he be but for me? I must be always think-ing—thinking to get food for the two of us, and when we've got it, if the moon is at the full or the tide on the turn, he'll leave the rabbit in the snare till it is full of maggots, or let the trout slip back through his hands into the stream.

[*The Fool has begun singing while the Blind Man is speaking.*
Fool [*singing*].

> When you were an acorn on the tree-top,
>   Then was I an eagle-cock;
> Now that you are a withered old block,
>   Still am I an eagle-cock.

Blind Man. Listen to him, now. That's the sort of talk I have to put up with day out, day in.

[*The Fool is putting the feathers into his hair. Cuchulain takes a handful of feathers out of a heap the Fool has on the bench beside him, and out of the Fool's hair, and begins to wipe the blood from his sword with them.*

Fool. He has taken my feathers to wipe his sword. It is blood that he is wiping from his sword.

Cuchulain [*goes up to door at back and throws away feathers*]. They are standing about his body. They will not awaken him, for all his witchcraft.

Blind Man. It is that young champion that he has killed. He that came out of Aoife's country.

Cuchulain. He thought to have saved himself with witchcraft.

Fool. That Blind Man there said he would kill you. He came from Aoife's country to kill you. That Blind Man said they had taught him every kind of weapon that he might do it. But I always knew that you would kill him.

Cuchulain [*to the Blind Man*]. You knew him, then?

Blind Man. I saw him, when I had my eyes, in Aoife's country.

Cuchulain. You were in Aoife's country?

Blind Man. I knew him and his mother there.

Cuchulain. He was about to speak of her when he died.

Blind Man. He was a queen's son.

Cuchulain. What queen? what queen? [*Seizes Blind Man, who is now sitting upon the bench.*] Was it Scathach? There were many queens. All the rulers there were queens.

Blind Man. No, not Scathach.

Cuchulain. It was Uathach, then? Speak! speak!

Blind Man. I cannot speak; you are clutching me too tightly. [*Cuchulain lets him go.*] I cannot remember who it was. I am not certain. It was some queen.

Fool. He said a while ago that the young man was Aoife's son.

Cuchulain. She? No, no! She had no son when I was there.

Fool. That Blind Man there said that she owned him for her son.

Cuchulain. I had rather he had been some other woman's son. What father had he? A soldier out of Alba? She was an amorous woman— a proud, pale, amorous woman.

Blind Man. None knew whose son he was.

Cuchulain. None knew! Did you know, old listener at doors?

Blind Man. No, no; I knew nothing.

Fool. He said a while ago that he heard Aoife boast that she'd never but the one lover, and he the only man that had overcome her in battle. [*Pause.*

Blind Man. Somebody is trembling, Fool! The bench is shaking. Why are you trembling? Is Cuchulain going to hurt us? It was not I who told you, Cuchulain.

Fool. It is Cuchulain who is trembling. It is Cuchulain who is shaking the bench.

Blind Man. It is his own son he has slain.

Cuchulain. 'Twas they that did it, the pale windy people.

Where? where? where? My sword against the thunder!
But no, for they have always been my friends;
And though they love to blow a smoking coal
Till it's all flame, the wars they blow aflame
Are full of glory, and heart-uplifting pride,
And not like this. The wars they love awaken
Old fingers and the sleepy strings of harps.
Who did it then? Are you afraid? Speak out!
For I have put you under my protection,
And will reward you well. Dubthach the Chafer?
He'd an old grudge. No, for he is with Maeve.
Laegaire did it! Why do you not speak?
What is this house? [*Pause.*] Now I remember all.

> [*Comes before Conchubar's chair, and strikes out with his sword,
> as if Conchubar was sitting upon it.*

'Twas you who did it—you who sat up there
With your old rod of kingship, like a magpie
Nursing a stolen spoon. No, not a magpie,
A maggot that is eating up the earth!
Yes, but a magpie, for he's flown away.
Where did he fly to?
Blind Man.   He is outside the door.
Cuchulain. Outside the door?
Blind Man.   Between the door and the sea.
Cuchulain. Conchubar, Conchubar! the sword into your heart!

> [*He rushes out. Pause. Fool creeps up to the big door and looks
> after him.*

Fool. He is going up to King Conchubar. They are all about the young
man. No, no, he is standing still. There is a great wave going to
break, and he is looking at it. Ah! now he is running down to the sea,
but he is holding up his sword as if he were going into a fight.
[*Pause.*] Well struck! well struck!
Blind Man. What is he doing now?
Fool. O! he is fighting the waves!
Blind Man. He sees King Conchubar's crown on every one of them.
Fool. There, he has struck at a big one! He has struck the crown off it;
he has made the foam fly. There again, another big one!
Blind Man. Where are the kings? What are the kings doing?
Fool. They are shouting and running down to the shore, and the people
are running out of the houses. They are all running.
Blind Man. You say they are running out of the houses? There will be
nobody left in the houses. Listen, Fool!
Fool. There, he is down! He is up again. He is going out in the deep

water. There is a big wave. It has gone over him. I cannot see him now. He has killed kings and giants, but the waves have mastered him, the waves have mastered him!

Blind Man. Come here, Fool!

Fool. The waves have mastered him.

Blind Man. Come here!

Fool. The waves have mastered him.

Blind Man. Come here, I say.

Fool [*coming towards him, but looking backwards towards the door*]. What is it?

Blind Man. There will be nobody in the houses. Come this way; come quickly! The ovens will be full. We will put our hands into the ovens.

[*They go out.*

THE END

THE ONLY JEALOUSY OF EMER
1919

THE ONLY JEALOUSY OF EMER

PERSONS IN THE PLAY

Three Musicians (*their faces made up to resemble masks*)
The Ghost of Cuchulain (*wearing a mask*)
The Figure of Cuchulain (*wearing a mask*)
Emer ⎱ (*masked, or their faces made up to resemble masks*)
Eithne Inguba ⎰
Woman of the Sidhe (*wearing a mask*)

Enter Musicians, who are dressed and made up as in 'At the Hawk's Well'. They have the same musical instruments, which can either be already upon the stage or be brought in by the First Musician before he stands in the centre with the cloth between his hands, or by a player when the cloth has been unfolded. The stage as before can be against the wall of any room, and the same black cloth can be used as in 'At the Hawk's Well'.
 [*Song for the folding and unfolding of the cloth*]
First Musician.

> A woman's beauty is like a white
> Frail bird, like a white sea-bird alone
> At daybreak after stormy night
> Between two furrows upon the ploughed land:
> A sudden storm, and it was thrown
> Between dark furrows upon the ploughed land.
> How many centuries spent
> The sedentary soul
> In toils of measurement
> Beyond eagle or mole,
> Beyond hearing or seeing,
> Or Archimedes' guess,
> To raise into being
> That loveliness?

> A strange, unserviceable thing,
> A fragile, exquisite, pale shell,
> That the vast troubled waters bring

To the loud sands before day has broken.
The storm arose and suddenly fell
Amid the dark before day had broken.
What death? what discipline?
What bonds no man could unbind,
Being imagined within
The labyrinth of the mind,
What pursuing or fleeing,
What wounds, what bloody press,
Dragged into being
This loveliness?

[*When the cloth is folded again the Musicians take their place against the wall. The folding of the cloth shows on one side of the stage the curtained bed or litter on which lies a man in his grave-clothes. He wears an heroic mask. Another man with exactly similar clothes and mask crouches near the front. Emer is sitting beside the bed.*

First Musician [*speaking*]. I call before the eyes a roof
With cross-beams darkened by smoke;
A fisher's net hangs from a beam,
A long oar lies against the wall.
I call up a poor fisher's house;
A man lies dead or swooning,
That amorous man,
That amorous, violent man, renowned Cuchulain,
Queen Emer at his side.
At her own bidding all the rest have gone;
But now one comes on hesitating feet,
Young Eithne Inguba, Cuchulain's mistress.
She stands a moment in the open door.
Beyond the open door the bitter sea,
The shining, bitter sea, is crying out,
[*singing*] White shell, white wing!
I will not choose for my friend
A frail, unserviceable thing
That drifts and dreams, and but knows
That waters are without end
And that wind blows.

Emer [*speaking*]. Come hither, come sit down beside the bed;
You need not be afraid, for I myself
Sent for you, Eithne Inguba.

Eithne Inguba.   No, Madam,
I have too deeply wronged you to sit there.

Emer. Of all the people in the world we two,
  And we alone, may watch together here,
  Because we have loved him best.
Eithne Inguba.   And is he dead?
Emer. Although they have dressed him out in his grave-clothes
  And stretched his limbs, Cuchulain is not dead;
  The very heavens when that day's at hand,
  So that his death may not lack ceremony,
  Will throw out fires, and the earth grow red with blood.
  There shall not be a scullion but foreknows it
  Like the world's end.
Eithne Inguba.   How did he come to this?
Emer. Towards noon in the assembly of the kings
  He met with one who seemed a while most dear.
  The kings stood round; some quarrel was blown up;
  He drove him out and killed him on the shore
  At Baile's tree, and he who was so killed
  Was his own son begot on some wild woman
  When he was young, or so I have heard it said;
  And thereupon, knowing what man he had killed,
  And being mad with sorrow, he ran out;
  And after, to his middle in the foam,
  With shield before him and with sword in hand,
  He fought the deathless sea. The kings looked on
  And not a king dared stretch an arm, or even
  Dared call his name, but all stood wondering
  In that dumb stupor like cattle in a gale,
  Until at last, as though he had fixed his eyes
  On a new enemy, he waded out
  Until the water had swept over him;
  But the waves washed his senseless image up
  And laid it at this door.
Eithne Inguba.   How pale he looks!
Emer. He is not dead.
Eithne Inguba.   You have not kissed his lips
  Nor laid his head upon your breast.
Emer.   It may be
  An image has been put into his place.
  A sea-borne log bewitched into his likeness,
  Or some stark horseman grown too old to ride
  Among the troops of Manannan, Son of the Sea,
  Now that his joints are stiff.
Eithne Inguba.   Cry out his name.

All that are taken from our sight, they say,
Loiter amid the scenery of their lives
For certain hours or days, and should he hear
He might, being angry, drive the changeling out.
Emer. It is hard to make them hear amid their darkness,
   And it is long since I could call him home;
   I am but his wife, but if you cry aloud
   With the sweet voice that is so dear to him
   He cannot help but listen.
Eithne Inguba.   He loves me best,
   Being his newest love, but in the end
   Will love the woman best who loved him first
   And loved him through the years when love seemed lost.
Emer. I have that hope, the hope that some day somewhere
   We'll sit together at the hearth again.
Eithne Inguba. Women like me, the violent hour passed over,
   Are flung into some corner like old nut-shells.
   Cuchulain, listen.
Emer.   No, not yet, for first
I'll cover up his face to hide the sea;
And throw new logs upon the hearth and stir
The half-burnt logs until they break in flame.
Old Manannan's unbridled horses come
Out of the sea, and on their backs his horsemen;
But all the enchantments of the dreaming foam
Dread the hearth-fire.
     [*She pulls the curtains of the bed so as to hide the sick man's face,*
     that the actor may change his mask unseen. She goes to one side
     of the platform and moves her hand as though putting logs on
     a fire and stirring it into a blaze. While she makes these move-
     ments the Musicians play, marking the movements with drum
     and flute perhaps.
          Having finished she stands beside the imaginary fire at a dis-
     tance from Cuchulain and Eithne Inguba.
                    Call on Cuchulain now.
Eithne Inguba. Can you not hear my voice?
Emer.   Bend over him;
   Call out dear secrets till you have touched his heart,
   If he lies there; and if he is not there,
   Till you have made him jealous.
Eithne Inguba.   Cuchulain, listen.
Emer. Those words sound timidly; to be afraid
   Because his wife is but three paces off,

When there is so great need, were but to prove
The man that chose you made but a poor choice:
We're but two women struggling with the sea.

Eithne Inguba. O my beloved, pardon me, that I
Have been ashamed. I thrust my shame away.
I have never sent a message or called out,
Scarce had a longing for your company
But you have known and come; and if indeed
You are lying there, stretch out your arms and speak;
Open your mouth and speak, for to this hour
My company has made you talkative.
What ails your tongue, or what has closed your ears?
Our passion had not chilled when we were parted
On the pale shore under the breaking dawn.
He cannot speak: or else his ears are closed
And no sound reaches him.

Emer.   Then kiss that image;
The pressure of your mouth upon his mouth
May reach him where he is.

Eithne Inguba [*starting back*]. It is no man.
I felt some evil thing that dried my heart
When my lips touched it.

Emer.   No, his body stirs;
The pressure of your mouth has called him home;
He has thrown the changeling out.

Eithne Inguba [*going further off*].   Look at that arm;
That arm is withered to the very socket.

Emer [*going up to the bed*]. What do you come for; and from where?

Figure of Cuchulain. I have come
From Manannan's court upon a bridleless horse.

Emer. What one among the Sidhe has dared to lie
Upon Cuchulain's bed and take his image?

Figure of Cuchulain. I am named Bricriu—not the man—that Bricriu,
Maker of discord among gods and men,
Called Bricriu of the Sidhe.

Emer.   Come for what purpose?

Figure of Cuchulain [*sitting up, parting curtain and showing its distorted face, as Inguba goes out*]. I show my face, and everything he loves
Must fly away.

Emer.   You people of the wind
Are full of lying speech and mockery:
I have not fled your face.

Figure of Cuchulain. You are not loved.

Emer. And therefore have no dread to meet your eyes
   And to demand him of you.

Figure of Cuchulain. For that I have come.
   You have but to pay the price and he is free.

Emer. Do the Sidhe bargain?

Figure of Cuchulain. When they would free a captive
   They take in ransom a less valued thing.
   The fisher, when some knowledgeable man
   Restores to him his wife, or son, or daughter,
   Knows he must lose a boat or net, or it may be
   The cow that gives his children milk; and some
   Have offered their own lives. I do not ask
   Your life, or any valuable thing;
   You spoke but now of the mere chance that some day
   You'd be the apple of his eye again
   When old and ailing, but renounce that chance
   And he shall live again.

Emer. I do not question
   But you have brought ill-luck on all he loves;
   And now, because I am thrown beyond your power
   Unless your words are lies, you come to bargain.

Figure of Cuchulain. You loved your mastery, when but newly married,
   And I love mine for all my withered arm;
   You have but to put yourself into that power
   And he shall live again.

Emer. No, never, never.

Figure of Cuchulain. You dare not be accursed, yet he has dared.

Emer. I have but two joyous thoughts, two things I prize.
   A hope, a memory, and now you claim that hope.

Figure of Cuchulain. He'll never sit beside you at the hearth
   Or make old bones, but die of wounds and toil
   On some far shore or mountain, a strange woman
   Beside his mattress.

Emer. You ask for my one hope
   That you may bring your curse on all about him.

Figure of Cuchulain. You've watched his loves and you have not been
      jealous,
   Knowing that he would tire, but do those tire
   That love the Sidhe? Come closer to the bed
   That I may touch your eyes and give them sight.

   [*He touches her eyes with his left hand, the right being withered.*

Emer [*seeing the crouching Ghost of Cuchulain*]. My husband is there.
Figure of Cuchulain.   I have dissolved the dark
  That hid him from your eyes, but not that other
  That's hidden you from his.
Emer.   O husband, husband!
Figure of Cuchulain. He cannot hear—being shut off, a phantom
  That can neither touch, nor hear, nor see;
  The longing and the cries have drawn him hither.
  He heard no sound, heard no articulate sound;
  They could but banish rest, and make him dream,
  And in that dream, as do all dreaming shades
  Before they are accustomed to their freedom,
  He has taken his familiar form; and yet
  He crouches there not knowing where he is
  Or at whose side he is crouched.
    [*A Woman of the Sidhe has entered and stands a little inside the
      door.*
Emer.   Who is this woman?
Figure of Cuchulain. She has hurried from the Country-under-Wave
  And dreamed herself into that shape that he
  May glitter in her basket; for the Sidhe
  Are dexterous fishers and they fish for men
  With dreams upon the hook.
Emer.   And so that woman
  Has hid herself in this disguise and made
  Herself into a lie.
Figure of Cuchulain. A dream is body;
  The dead move ever towards a dreamless youth
  And when they dream no more return no more;
  And those more holy shades that never lived
  But visit you in dreams.
Emer.   I know her sort.
  They find our men asleep, weary with war,
  Lap them in cloudy hair or kiss their lips;
  Our men awake in ignorance of it all,
  But when we take them in our arms at night
  We cannot break their solitude. [*She draws a knife from her girdle.*
Figure of Cuchulain.   No knife
  Can wound that body of air. Be silent; listen;
  I have not given you eyes and ears for nothing.
    [*The Woman of the Sidhe moves round the crouching Ghost of
      Cuchulain at front of stage in a dance that grows gradually
      quicker, as he slowly awakes. At moments she may drop her hair*

*upon his head, but she does not kiss him. She is accompanied by
string and flute and drum. Her mask and clothes must suggest
gold or bronze or brass or silver, so that she seems more an idol
than a human being. This suggestion may be repeated in her
movements. Her hair, too, must keep the metallic suggestion.*

Ghost of Cuchulain. Who is it stands before me there
    Shedding such light from limb and hair
    As when the moon, complete at last
    With every labouring crescent past,
    And lonely with extreme delight,
    Flings out upon the fifteenth night?

Woman of the Sidhe. Because I long I am not complete.
    What pulled your hands about your feet,
    Pulled down your head upon your knees,
    And hid your face?

Ghost of Cuchulain.   Old memories:
    A woman in her happy youth
    Before her man had broken troth,
    Dead men and women. Memories
    Have pulled my head upon my knees.

Woman of the Sidhe. Could you that have loved many a woman
    That did not reach beyond the human,
    Lacking a day to be complete,
    Love one that, though her heart can beat,
    Lacks it but by an hour or so?

Ghost of Cuchulain. I know you now, for long ago
    I met you on a cloudy hill
    Beside old thorn-trees and a well.
    A woman danced and a hawk flew,
    I held out arms and hands; but you,
    That now seem friendly, fled away,
    Half woman and half bird of prey.

Woman of the Sidhe. Hold out your arms and hands again;
    You were not so dumbfounded when
    I was that bird of prey, and yet
    I am all woman now.

Ghost of Cuchulain.   I am not
    The young and passionate man I was,
    And though that brilliant light surpass
    All crescent forms, my memories
    Weigh down my hands, abash my eyes.

Woman of the Sidhe. Then kiss my mouth. Though memory
    Be beauty's bitterest enemy

I have no dread, for at my kiss
Memory on the moment vanishes;
Nothing but beauty can remain.
Ghost of Cuchulain. And shall I never know again
  Intricacies of blind remorse?
Woman of the Sidhe. Time shall seem to stay his course;
  When your mouth and my mouth meet
  All my round shall be complete
  Imagining all its circles run;
  And there shall be oblivion
  Even to quench Cuchulain's drouth,
  Even to still that heart.
Ghost of Cuchulain.   Your mouth!
               [*They are about to kiss, he turns away.*

O Emer, Emer!
Woman of the Sidhe. So then it is she
  Made you impure with memory.
Ghost of Cuchulain. O Emer, Emer, there we stand;
  Side by side and hand in hand
  Tread the threshold of the house
  As when our parents married us.
Woman of the Sidhe. Being among the dead you love her
  That valued every slut above her
  While you still lived.
Ghost of Cuchulain.   O my lost Emer!
Woman of the Sidhe. And there is not a loose-tongued schemer
  But could draw you, if not dead,
  From her table and her bed.
  But what could make you fit to wive
  With flesh and blood, being born to live
  Where no one speaks of broken troth,
  For all have washed out of their eyes
  Wind-blown dirt of their memories
  To improve their sight?
Ghost of Cuchulain.   Your mouth, your mouth!
         [*She goes out followed by Ghost of Cuchulain.*
Figure of Cuchulain. Cry out that you renounce his love; make haste
  And cry that you renounce his love for ever.
Emer. No, never will I give that cry.
Figure of Cuchulain.   Fool, fool!
  I am Fand's enemy come to thwart her will,
  And you stand gaping there. There is still time.

Hear how the horses trample on the shore,
Hear how they trample! She has mounted up.
Cuchulain's not beside her in the chariot.
There is still a moment left; cry out, cry out!
Renounce him, and her power is at an end.
Cuchulain's foot is on the chariot-step.
Cry——
Emer.   I renounce Cuchulain's love for ever.

    [*The Figure of Cuchulain sinks back upon the bed, half-drawing
       the curtain. Eithne Inguba comes in and kneels by bed.*

Eithne Inguba. Come to me, my beloved, it is I.
  I, Eithne Inguba. Look! He is there.
He has come back and moved upon the bed.
And it is I that won him from the sea,
That brought him back to life.
Emer.   Cuchulain wakes.

     [*The figure turns round. It once more wears the heroic mask.*

Cuchulain. Your arms, your arms! O Eithne Inguba,
  I have been in some strange place and am afraid.

    [*The First Musician comes to the front of stage, the others from
      each side, and unfold the cloth singing.*

    [*Song for the unfolding and folding of the cloth*]

The Musicians.

        Why does your heart beat thus?
        Plain to be understood,
        I have met in a man's house
        A statue of solitude,
        Moving there and walking;
        Its strange heart beating fast
        For all our talking.
        O still that heart at last.

        O bitter reward
        Of many a tragic tomb!
        And we though astonished are dumb
        Or give but a sigh and a word,
        A passing word.

        Although the door be shut
        And all seem well enough,
        Although wide world hold not
        A man but will give you his love

The moment he has looked at you,
He that has loved the best
May turn from a statue
His too human breast.

O bitter reward
Of many a tragic tomb!
And we though astonished are dumb
Or give but a sigh and a word,
A passing word.

What makes your heart so beat?
What man is at your side?
When beauty is complete
Your own thought will have died
And danger not be diminished;
Dimmed at three-quarter light,
When moon's round is finished
The stars are out of sight.

O bitter reward
Of many a tragic tomb!
And we though astonished are dumb
Or give but a sigh and a word,
A passing word.
    [*When the cloth is folded again the stage is bare.*

THE END

THE HOUR-GLASS

1914

THE HOUR-GLASS

PERSONS IN THE PLAY

A Wise Man	Teigue, *a Fool*
Bridget, *his wife*	Angel
	Children and Pupils

The stage is brought out into the orchestra so as to leave a wide space in front of the stage curtain. Pupils come in and stand before the stage curtain, which is still closed. One Pupil carries a book.

First Pupil. He said we might choose the subject for the lesson.

Second Pupil. There is none of us wise enough to do that.

Third Pupil. It would need a great deal of wisdom to know what it is we want to know.

Fourth Pupil. I will question him.

Fifth Pupil. You?

Fourth Pupil. Last night I dreamt that some one came and told me to question him. I was to say to him, 'You were wrong to say there is no God and no soul—maybe, if there is not much of either, there is yet some tatters, some tag on the wind—so to speak—some rag upon a bush, some bob-tail of a god'. I will argue with him—nonsense though it be—according to my dream, and you will see how well I can argue, and what thoughts I have.

First Pupil. I'd as soon listen to dried peas in a bladder as listen to your thoughts.

Teigue the Fool comes in

Fool. Give me a penny.

Second Pupil. Let us choose a subject by chance. Here is his big book. Let us turn over the pages slowly. Let one of us put down his finger without looking. The passage his finger lights on will be the subject for the lesson.

Fool. Give me a penny.

Third Pupil [*taking up book*]. How heavy it is!

Fourth Pupil. Spread it on Teigue's back, and then we can all stand round and see the choice.

Second Pupil. Make him spread out his arms.

Fourth Pupil. Down on your knees. Hunch up your back. Spread your arms out now, and look like a golden eagle in a church. Keep still, keep still.

Fool. Give me a penny.

Third Pupil. Is that the right cry for an eagle-cock?

Second Pupil. I'll turn the pages—you close your eyes and put your finger down.

Third Pupil. That's it, and then he cannot blame us for the choice.

First Pupil. There, I have chosen. Fool, keep still—and if what's wise is strange and sounds like nonsense, we've made a good choice.

Fifth Pupil. The Master has come.

Fool. Will anybody give a penny to a fool?

> [*One of the Pupils draws back the stage curtains showing the Master sitting at his desk. There is an hour-glass upon his desk or in a bracket on the wall. One Pupil puts the books before him.*

First Pupil. We have chosen the passage for the lesson, Master. 'There are two living countries, one visible and one invisible, and when it is summer there, it is winter here, and when it is November with us, it is lambing-time there.'

Wise Man. That passage, that passage! What mischief has there been since yesterday?

First Pupil. None, Master.

Wise Man. Oh yes, there has; some craziness has fallen from the wind, or risen from the graves of old men, and made you choose that subject.—Diem noctemque contendo, sed quos elegi, quos amavi, in tirocinium vel hi labuntur.

Fourth Pupil. I knew that it was folly, but they would have it.

Third Pupil. Had we not better say we picked it by chance?

Second Pupil. No; he would say we were children still.

First Pupil. I have found a sentence under that one that says—as though to show it had a hidden meaning—a beggar wrote it upon the walls of Babylon.

Wise Man. Then find some beggar and ask him what it means, for I will have nothing to do with it.

Fourth Pupil. Come, Teigue, what is the old book's meaning when it says that there are sheep that drop their lambs in November?

Fool. To be sure—everybody knows, everybody in the world knows, when it is spring with us, the trees are withering there, when it is summer with us, the snow is falling there, and have I not myself heard the lambs that are there all bleating on a cold November day—to be sure, does not everybody with an intellect know that?

And maybe when it's night with us, it is day with them, for many a
time I have seen the roads lighted before me.

Wise Man. The beggar who wrote that on Babylon wall meant that
there is a spiritual kingdom that cannot be seen or known till the
faculties, whereby we master the kingdom of this world, wither away
like green things in winter. A monkish thought, the most mischievous
thought that ever passed out of a man's mouth.—Virgas ut partus
educant colligunt aves, mens hominis nugas.

First Pupil. If he meant all that, I will take an oath that he was
spindle-shanked, and cross-eyed, and had a lousy itching shoulder,
and that his heart was crosser than his eyes, and that he wrote it
out of malice.

Second Pupil. Let's come away and find a better subject.

Fourth Pupil. And maybe now you'll let me choose.

First Pupil. Come.

Wise Man. Were it but true, 'twould alter everything
  Until the stream of the world had changed its course,
  And that and all our thoughts had run
  Into some cloudy thunderous spring
  They dream to be its source—
  Aye, to some frenzy of the mind;
  And all that we have done would be undone,
  Our speculation but as the wind.   [*A pause.*
  I have dreamed it twice.

First Pupil. Something has troubled him.   [*Pupils go out.*

Wise Man. Twice have I dreamed it in a morning dream,
  Now nothing serves my pupils but to come
  With a like thought. Reason is growing dim;
  A moment more and Frenzy will beat his drum
  And laugh aloud and scream;
  And I must dance in the dream.
  No, no, but it is like a hawk, a hawk of the air,
  It has swooped down—and this swoop makes the third—
  And what can I, but tremble like a bird?

Fool. Give me a penny.

Wise Man. That I should dream it twice, and after that, that they
should pick it out!

Fool. Won't you give me a penny?

Wise Man. What do you want? What can it matter to you whether
the words I am reading are wisdom or sheer folly?

Fool. Such a great, wise teacher will not refuse a penny to a fool.

Wise Man. Seeing that everybody is a fool when he is asleep and
dreaming, why do you call me wise?

Fool. O, I know,—I know, I know what I have seen.

Wise Man. Well, to see rightly is the whole of wisdom, whatever dream be with us.

Fool. When I went by Kilcluan, where the bells used to be ringing at the break of every day, I could hear nothing but the people snoring in their houses. When I went by Tubber-vanach, where the young men used to be climbing the hill to the blessed well, they were sitting at the cross-roads playing cards. When I went by Carrick-orus, where the friars used to be fasting and serving the poor, I saw them drinking wine and obeying their wives. And when I asked what misfortune had brought all these changes, they said it was no misfortune, but that it was the wisdom they had learned from your teaching.

Wise Man. And you too have called me wise—you would be paid for that good opinion doubtless.—Run to the kitchen; my wife will give you food and drink.

Fool. That's foolish advice for a wise man to give.

Wise Man. Why, Fool?

Fool. What is eaten is gone—I want pennies for my bag. I must buy bacon in the shops, and nuts in the market, and strong drink for the time the sun is weak, and snares to catch the rabbits and the hares, and a big pot to cook them in.

Wise Man. I have more to think about than giving pennies to your like, so run away.

Fool. Give me a penny and I will bring you luck. The fishermen let me sleep among their nets in the loft because I bring them luck; and in the summer-time, the wild creatures let me sleep near their nests and their holes. It is lucky even to look at me, but it is much more lucky to give me a penny. If I was not lucky I would starve.

Wise Man. What are the shears for?

Fool. I won't tell you. If I told you, you would drive them away.

Wise Man. Drive them away! Whom would I drive away?

Fool. I won't tell you.

Wise Man. Not if I give you a penny?

Fool. No.

Wise Man. Not if I give you two pennies?

Fool. You will be very lucky if you give me two pennies, but I won't tell you.

Wise Man. Three pennies?

Fool. Four, and I will tell you.

Wise Man. Very well—four, but from this out I will not call you Teigue the Fool.

Fool. Let me come close to you, where nobody will hear me; but first you must promise not to drive them away. [*Wise Man nods.*] Every day men go out dressed in black and spread great black nets over the hills, great black nets.

Wise Man. A strange place that to fish in.

Fool. They spread them out on the hills that they may catch the feet of the angels; but every morning, just before the dawn, I go out and cut the nets with the shears and the angels fly away.

Wise Man [*speaking with excitement*]. Ah, now I know that you are Teigue the Fool. You say that I am wise, and yet I say there are no angels.

Fool. I have seen plenty of angels.

Wise Man. No, no, you have not.

Fool. They are plenty if you but look about you. They are like the blades of grass.

Wise Man. They are plenty as the blades of grass—I heard that phrase when I was but a child and was told folly.

Fool. When one gets quiet. When one is so quiet that there is not a thought in one's head maybe, there is something that wakes up inside one, something happy and quiet, and then all in a minute one can smell summer flowers, and tall people go by, happy and laughing, but they will not let us look at their faces. O no, it is not right that we should look at their faces.

Wise Man. You have fallen asleep upon a hill; yet even those that used to dream of angels dream now of other things.

Fool. I saw one but a moment ago—that is because I am lucky. It was coming behind me, but it was not laughing.

Wise Man. There's nothing but what men can see when they are awake. Nothing, nothing.

Fool. I knew you would drive them away.

Wise Man. Pardon me, Fool.

I had forgotten whom I spoke to.

Well, there are your four pennies—Fool you are called,

And all day long they cry, 'Come hither, Fool'.

                                   [*The Fool goes close to him.*

Or else it's, 'Fool, be gone'.   [*The Fool goes further off.*

Or, 'Fool, stand there'.   [*The Fool straightens himself up.*

Or, 'Fool, go sit in the corner'.   [*The Fool sits in the corner.*

                      And all the while

What were they all but fools before I came?

What are they now but mirrors that seem men

Because of my image? Fool, hold up your head. [*The Fool does so.*

What foolish stories they have told of the ghosts

That fumbled with the clothes upon the bed,
Or creaked and shuffled in the corridor,
Or else, if they were pious bred,
Of angels from the skies,
That coming through the door,
Or, it may be, standing there,
Would solidly out-stare
The steadiest eyes with their unnatural eyes,
Aye, on a man's own floor.

> [*An Angel has come in. It may be played by a man if a man can be found with the right voice, and in that case 'she' should be changed to 'he' throughout, and may wear a little golden domino and a halo made of metal. Or the whole face may be a beautiful mask, in which case the sentence in lines 21 and 22 on page 200 should not be spoken.*]

Yet it is strange, the strangest thing I have known,
That I should still be haunted by the notion
That there's a crisis of the spirit wherein
We get new sight, and that they know some trick
To turn our thoughts for their own needs to frenzy.
Why do you put your finger to your lip,
And creep away?   [*The Fool goes out.*

[*Wise Man sees Angel.*] What are you? Who are you?
I think I saw some like you in my dreams,
When but a child. That thing about your head,—
That brightness in your hair—that flowery branch;
But I have done with dreams, I have done with dreams.

Angel. I am the crafty one that you have called.

Wise Man. How that I called?

Angel.   I am the messenger.

Wise Man. What message could you bring to one like me?

Angel [*turning the hour-glass*]. That you will die when the last grain of sand
  Has fallen through this glass.

Wise Man.   I have a wife,
  Children and pupils that I cannot leave:
  Why must I die, my time is far away?

Angel. You have to die because no soul has passed
  The heavenly threshold since you have opened school,
  But grass grows there, and rust upon the hinge;
  And they are lonely that must keep the watch.

Wise Man. And whither shall I go when I am dead?

Angel. You have denied there is a Purgatory,
   Therefore that gate is closed; you have denied
   There is a Heaven, and so that gate is closed.
Wise Man. Where then? For I have said there is no Hell.
Angel. Hell is the place of those who have denied;
   They find there what they planted and what dug,
   A Lake of Spaces, and a Wood of Nothing,
   And wander there and drift, and never cease
   Wailing for substance.
Wise Man.   Pardon me, blessed Angel,
   I have denied and taught the like to others.
   But how could I believe before my sight
   Had come to me?
   Angel.   It is too late for pardon.
Wise Man. Had I but met your gaze as now I meet it—
   But how can you that live but where we go
   In the uncertainty of dizzy dreams
   Know why we doubt? Parting, sickness, and death,
   The rotting of the grass, tempest, and drouth,
   These are the messengers that came to me.
   Why are you silent? You carry in your hands
   God's pardon, and you will not give it me.
   Why are you silent? Were I not afraid,
   I'd kiss your hands—no, no, the hem of your dress.
Angel. Only when all the world has testified,
   May soul confound it, crying out in joy,
   And laughing on its lonely precipice.
   What's dearth and death and sickness to the soul
   That knows no virtue but itself? Nor could it,
   So trembling with delight and mother-naked,
   Live unabashed if the arguing world stood by.
Wise Man. It is as hard for you to understand
   Why we have doubted as it is for us
   To banish doubt.—What folly have I said?
   There can be nothing that you do not know.
   Give me a year—a month—a week—a day,
   I would undo what I have done—an hour—
   Give me until the sand has run in the glass.
Angel. Though you may not undo what you have done,
   I have this power—if you but find one soul,
   Before the sands have fallen, that still believes,
   One fish to lie and spawn among the stones

Till the great Fisher's net is full again,
You may, the purgatorial fire being passed,
Spring to your peace.
Pupils sing in the distance.

> Who stole your wits away
> And where are they gone?

Wise man.   My pupils come.
Before you have begun to climb the sky
I shall have found that soul. They say they doubt,
But what their mothers dinned into their ears
Cannot have been so lightly rooted up;
Besides, I can disprove what I once proved—
And yet give me some thought, some argument,
More mighty than my own.

Angel.   Farewell—farewell,
For I am weary of the weight of time.

> [*Angel goes out. Wise Man makes a step to follow and pauses.
> Some of his Pupils come in at the other side of the stage.*

First Pupil. Master, Master, you must choose the subject.

> [*Enter other Pupils with Fool, about whom they dance; all the
> Pupils may have little cushions on which presently they seat
> themselves.*

Second Pupil. Here is a subject—Where have the Fool's wits gone?

> [*singing.*

> Who dragged your wits away
> Where no one knows?
> Or have they run off
> On their own pair of shoes?

Fool. Give me a penny.
First Pupil. The Master will find your wits.
Second Pupil. And when they are found, you must not beg for pennies.
Third Pupil. They are hidden somewhere in the badger's hole,
   But you must carry an old candle-end
   If you would find them.
Fourth Pupil. They are up above the clouds.
Fool. Give me a penny, give me a penny.
First Pupil [*singing*].

> I'll find your wits again.
> Come, for I saw them roll
> To where old badger mumbles
> In the black hole.

Second Pupil [*singing*].

> No, but an angel stole them
> The night that you were born,
> And now they are but a rag
> On the moon's horn.

Wise Man. Be silent.

First Pupil. Can you not see that he is troubled?

> [*All the Pupils are seated.*

Wise Man. Nullum esse deum dixi, nullam dei matrem: mentitus vero: nam recte intelligenti sunt et deus et dei mater.

First Pupil. Argumentis igitur proba; nam argumenta poscit qui rationis est particeps.

Wise Man. Pro certo habeo e vobis unum quidem in fide perstitisse, unum altius quam me vidisse.

Second Pupil. You answer for us.

Third Pupil [*in a whisper to First Pupil*]. Be careful what you say;
> If he persuades you to an argument,
> He will but turn us all to mockery.

First Pupil. We had no minds until you made them for us.

Wise Man. Quae destruxi necesse est omnia reaedificem.

First Pupil. Haec rationibus nondum natis opinabamur: nunc vero adolevimus: exuimus incunabula.

Wise Man. You are afraid to tell me what you think
> Because I am hot and angry when I am crossed.
> I do not blame you for it; but have no fear,
> For if there's one that sat on smiling there
> As though my arguments were sweet as milk,
> Yet found them bitter, I will thank him for it,
> If he but speak his mind.

First Pupil.   There is no one, Master.
> There is not one but found them sweet as milk.

Wise Man. The things that have been told us in our childhood
> Are not so fragile.

Second Pupil.   We are not children now.

First Pupil. Non iam pueri sumus; corpus tantummodo ex matre fictum est.

Second Pupil. Docuisti; et nobis persuadetur.

Wise Man. Mendaciis vos imbui, mentisque simulacris.

Second Pupil. Nulli non persuasisti.

Other Pupils [*speaking together*]. Nulli, nulli, nulli.

Wise Man. I have deceived you—where shall I go for words?—
> I have no thoughts—my mind has been swept bare.
> The messengers that stand in the fiery cloud
> Fling themselves out, if we but dare to question,

And after that the Babylonian moon
Blots all away.

First Pupil [*to other Pupils*]. I take his words to mean
That visionaries and martyrs, when they are raised
Above translunary things, and there enlightened,
As the contention is, may lose the light,
And flounder in their speech when the eyes open.

Second Pupil. How well he imitates their trick of speech.

Third Pupil. Their air of mystery.

Fourth Pupil.   Their empty gaze
As though they'd looked upon some wingéd thing,
And would not condescend to mankind after.

First Pupil. Master, we all have learnt that truth is learnt
When the intellect's deliberate and cold,
As it were a polished mirror that reflects
An unchanged world; not when the steel dissolves
Bubbling and hissing, till there's naught but fume.

Wise Man. When it is melted, when it all fumes up,
They walk as when beside those three in the furnace
The form of the fourth.

First Pupil.   Master, there's none among us
That has not heard your mockery of these,
Or thoughts like these, and we have not forgot.

Wise Man. Something incredible has happened—some one has come
Suddenly like a grey hawk out of the air,
And all that I declared untrue is true.

First Pupil [*to other Pupils*]. You'd think, the way he says it, that
    he felt it.
There's not a mummer to compare with him.
He's something like a man.

Second Pupil. Argumentum, domine, profer.

Wise Man. What proof have I to give, but that an angel
An instant ago was standing on that spot?   [*The Pupils rise.*

Third Pupil. You dreamed it.

Wise Man.   I was awake as I am now.

First Pupil [*to the others*]. I may be dreaming now for all I know.
He wants to show we have no certain proof
Of anything in the world.

Second Pupil.   There is this proof
That shows we are awake—we have all one world
While every dreamer has a world of his own,
And sees what no one else can.

Third Pupil.   Teigue sees angels.

So when the Master says he has seen an angel,
He may have seen one.
First Pupil. Both may still be dreamers,
Unless it's proved the angels were alike.
Second Pupil. What sort are the angels, Teigue?
Third Pupil. That will prove nothing,
Unless we are sure prolonged obedience
Has made one angel like another angel
As they were eggs.
First Pupil. The Master's silent now:
For he has found that to dispute with us—
Seeing that he has taught us what we know—
Is but to reason with himself. Let us away,
And find if there is one believer left.
Wise Man. Yes, Yes. Find me but one that still can say:
Credo in patrem et filium et spiritum sanctum.
Third Pupil. He'll mock and maul him.
Fourth Pupil. From the first I knew
He wanted somebody to argue with. [*They go.*
Wise Man. I have no reason left. All dark, all dark!
[*Pupils return laughing. They push forward Fourth Pupil.*
First Pupil. Here, Master, is the very man you want.
He said, when we were studying the book,
That maybe after all the monks were right,
And you mistaken, and if we but gave him time,
He'd prove that it was so.
Fourth Pupil. I never said it.
Wise Man. Dear friend, dear friend, do you believe in God?
Fourth Pupil. Master, they have invented this to mock me.
Wise Man. You are afraid of me.
Fourth Pupil. They know well, Master,
That all I said was but to make them argue.
They've pushed me in to make a mock of me,
Because they know I could take either side
And beat them at it.
Wise Man. If you can say the creed
With but a grain, a mustard-grain of faith,
You are my soul's one friend. [*Pupils laugh.*
Mistress or wife
Can give us but our good or evil luck
Amid the howling world, but you shall give
Eternity, and those sweet-throated things

THE HOUR-GLASS

That drift above the moon.

              [Pupils look at one another and are silent.

Second Pupil.   How strange he is!

Wise Man. The angel that stood there upon that spot
  Said that my soul was lost unless I found
  One that had faith.

Fourth Pupil.   Cease mocking at me, Master,
  For I am certain that there is no God
  Nor immortality, and they that said it
  Made a fantastic tale from a starved dream
  To plague our hearts. Will that content you, Master?

Wise Man. The giddy glass is emptier every moment,
  And you stand there, debating, laughing and wrangling.
  Out of my sight! Out of my sight, I say.   *[He drives them out.*
  I'll call my wife, for what can women do,
  That carry us in the darkness of their bodies,
  But mock the reason that lets nothing grow
  Unless it grow in light? Bridget, Bridget!
  A woman never gives up all her faith,
  Say what we will. Bridget, come quickly, Bridget.
    [Bridget comes in wearing her apron. Her sleeves are turned up
    from her arms, which are covered with flour.
  Wife, what do you believe in? Tell me the truth,
  And not—as is the habit with you all—
  Something you think will please me. Do you pray?
  Sometimes when you're alone in the house, do you pray?

Bridget. Prayers—no, you taught me to leave them off long ago. At first
  I was sorry, but I am glad now, for I am sleepy in the evenings.

Wise Man. Do you believe in God?

Bridget. O, a good wife only believes in what her husband tells her.

Wise Man. But sometimes, when the children are asleep
  And I am in the school, do you not think
  About the martyrs and the saints and the angels,
  And all the things that you believed in once?

Bridget. I think about nothing. Sometimes I wonder if the linen is
  bleaching white, or I go out to see if the crows are picking up the
  chickens' food.

Wise Man. My God,—my God! I will go out myself.
  My pupils said they would find a man
  Whose faith I never shook—they may have found him.
  Therefore I will go out—but if I go,
  The glass will let the sands run out unseen.

I cannot go—I cannot leave the glass.
Go call my pupils—I can explain all now.
Only when all our hold on life is troubled,
Only in spiritual terror can the Truth
Come through the broken mind—as the pease burst
Out of a broken pease-cod.   [*He clutches Bridget as she is going.*
                                    Say to them
That Nature would lack all in her most need,
Could not the soul find truth as in a flash,
Upon the battle-field, or in the midst
Of overwhelming waves, and say to them—
But no, they would but answer as I bid.

Bridget. You want somebody to get up an argument with.

Wise Man. Look out and see if there is any one
    There in the street—I cannot leave the glass,
    For somebody might shake it, and the sand
    If it were shaken might run down on the instant.

Bridget. I don't understand a word you are saying.
    There's a crowd of people talking to your pupils.

Wise Man. Go out and find if they have found a man
    Who did not understand me when I taught,
    Or did not listen.

Bridget. It is a hard thing to be married to a man of learning that must
    always be having arguments.   [*She goes out.*

Wise Man. Strange that I should be blind to the great secret,
    And that so simple a man might write it out
    Upon a blade of grass with the juice of a berry,
    And laugh and cry, because it was so simple.
                Enter Bridget followed by the Fool

Fool. Give me something; give me a penny to buy bacon in the shops
    and nuts in the market, and strong drink for the time when the
    sun is weak.

Bridget. I have no pennies. [*To Wise Man.*] Your pupils cannot find
    anybody to argue with you. There's nobody in the whole country
    with religion enough for a lover's oath. Can't you be quiet now, and
    not always wanting to have arguments? It must be terrible to have
    a mind like that.

Wise Man. Then I am lost indeed.

Bridget. Leave me alone now, I have to make the bread for you and
    the children.   [*She goes into kitchen. The Fool follows her.*

Wise Man. Children, children!

Bridget. Your father wants you, run to him.   [*Children run in.*

Wise Man. Come to me, Children. Do not be afraid.

I want to know if you believe in Heaven,
God or the soul—no, do not tell me yet;
You need not be afraid I shall be angry;
Say what you please—so that it is your thought—
I wanted you to know before you spoke
That I shall not be angry.

First Child. We have not forgotten, father.

Second Child.   O no, father.

Both Children [*as if repeating a lesson*]. There is nothing we cannot
    see, nothing we cannot touch.

First Child. Foolish people used to say that there was, but you have
    taught us better.

Wise Man. Go to your mother, go—yet do not go.
    What can she say? If I am dumb you are lost;
    And yet, because the sands are running out,
    I have but a moment to show it all in. Children,
    The sap would die out of the blades of grass
    Had they a doubt. They understand it all,
    Being the fingers of God's certainty,
    Yet can but make their sign into the air;
    But could they find their tongues they'd show it all;
    But what am I to say that am but one,
    When they are millions and they will not speak?—

                               [*Children have run out.*

    But they are gone; what made them run away?

            The Fool comes in with a dandelion

    Look at me, tell me if my face is changed,
    Is there a notch of the Fiend's nail upon it
    Already? Is it terrible to sight
    Because the moment's near?   [*Going to glass.*

                    I dare not look,
    I dare not know the moment when they come.
    No, no, I dare not. [*Covers glass.*] Will there be a footfall,
    Or will there be a sort of rending sound,
    Or else a cracking, as though an iron claw
    Had gripped the threshold-stone?

                [*The Fool has begun to blow the dandelion.*
                    What are you doing?

Fool. Wait a minute—four—five—six—

Wise Man. What are you doing that for?

Fool. I am blowing the dandelion to find out what hour it is.

Wise Man. You have heard everything and that is why
    You'd find what hour it is—you'd find that out

That you may look upon a fleet of devils
Dragging my soul away. You shall not stop,
I will have no one here when they come in,
I will have no one sitting there—no one!
And yet—and yet—there is something strange about you.
I half remember something. What is it?
Do you believe in God and in the soul?

Fool. So you ask me now. I thought when you were asking your pupils, 'Will he ask Teigue the Fool? Yes, he will, he will; no, he will not— yes, he will'. But Teigue will say nothing. Teigue will say nothing.

Wise Man. Tell me quickly.

Fool. I said, 'Teigue knows everything, not even the green-eyed cats and the hares that milk the cows have Teigue's wisdom'; but Teigue will not speak, he says nothing.

Wise Man. Speak, speak, for underneath the cover there
The sand is running from the upper glass,
And when the last grain's through, I shall be lost.

Fool. I will not speak. I will not tell you what is in my mind. I will not tell you what is in my bag. You might steal away my thoughts. I met a bodach on the road yesterday, and he said, 'Teigue, tell me how many pennies are in your bag; I will wager three pennies that there are not twenty pennies in your bag; let me put in my hand and count them'. But I gripped the bag the tighter and when I go to sleep at night I hide the bag where nobody knows.

Wise Man. There's but one pinch of sand, and I am lost
If you are not he I seek.

Fool. O, what a lot the Fool knows, but he says nothing.

Wise Man. Yes, I remember now. You spoke of angels.
You said but now that you have seen an angel.
You are the one I seek, and I am saved.

Fool. O no. How could poor Teigue see angels? O, Teigue tells one tale here, another there, and everybody give him pennies. If Teigue had not his tales he would starve.   [*He breaks away and goes out.*

Wise Man. The last hope is gone,
And now that it's too late I see it all:
We perish into God and sink away
Into reality—the rest's a dream.

The Fool comes back

Fool. There was one there—there by the threshold, waiting there; and he said, 'Go in, Teigue, and tell him everything that he asks you. He will give you a penny if you tell him.'

Wise Man. I know enough, that know God's will prevails.

Fool. Waiting till the moment had come—That is what the one out there was saying, but I might tell you what you asked. That is what he was saying.

Wise Man. Be silent. May God's will prevail on the instant,
Although His will be my eternal pain.
I have no question:
It is enough, I know what fixed the station
Of star and cloud.
And knowing all, I cry
That whatso God has willed
On the instant be fulfilled,
Though that be my damnation.
The stream of the world has changed its course,
And with the stream my thoughts have run
Into some cloudy thunderous spring
That is its mountain source—
Aye, to some frenzy of the mind,
For all that we have done's undone,
Our speculation but as the wind.   [*He dies.*

Fool. Wise Man—Wise Man, wake up and I will tell you everything for a penny. It is I, poor Teigue the Fool. Why don't you wake up, and say, 'There is a penny for you, Teigue'? No, no, you will say nothing. You and I, we are the two fools, we know everything, but we will not speak.

Angel enters holding a casket

O, look what has come from his mouth! O, look what has come from his mouth—the white butterfly! He is dead, and I have taken his soul in my hands; but I know why you open the lid of that golden box. I must give it to you. There then [*he puts butterfly in casket*], he has gone through his pains, and you will open the lid in the Garden of Paradise. [*He closes curtain and remains outside it.*] He is gone, he is gone, he is gone, but come in, everybody in the world, and look at me.

I hear the wind a-blow,
I hear the grass a-grow,
And all that I know, I know.

But I will not speak, I will run away.   [*He goes out.*

THE END

THE UNICORN FROM THE STARS
1908

THE UNICORN FROM THE STARS

PERSONS IN THE PLAY

Father John
Thomas Hearne, *a coachbuilder*
Andrew Hearne, *his brother*
Martin Hearne, *his nephew*

Johnny Bocach
Paudeen
Biddy Lally
Nanny

} *beggars*

Period: early nineteenth century

ACT I

Interior of a coachbuilder's workshop. Parts of a gilded coach, among them an ornament representing a lion and unicorn. Thomas working at a wheel. Father John coming from door of inner room.

Father John. I have prayed over Martin. I have prayed a long time, but there is no move in him yet.

Thomas. You are giving yourself too much trouble, Father. It's as good for you to leave him alone till the doctor's bottle will come. If there is any cure at all for what is on him, it is likely the doctor will have it.

Father John. I think it is not doctor's medicine will help him in this case.

Thomas. It will, it will. The doctor has his business learned well. If Andrew had gone to him the time I bade him and had not turned again to bring yourself to the house, it is likely Martin would be walking at this time. I am loth to trouble you, Father, when the business is not of your own sort. Any doctor at all should be able and well able to cure the falling sickness.

Father John. It is not any common sickness that is on him now.

Thomas. I thought at the first it was gone to sleep he was. But when shaking him and roaring at him failed to rouse him, I knew well it was the falling sickness. Believe me, the doctor will reach it with his drugs.

Father John. Nothing but prayer can reach a soul that is so far beyond the world as his soul is at this moment.

Thomas. You are not saying that the life is gone out of him!

214

Father John. No, no, his life is in no danger. But where he himself, the spirit, the soul, is gone, I cannot say. It has gone beyond our imaginings. He is fallen into a trance.

Thomas. He used to be queer as a child, going asleep in the fields, and coming back with talk of white horses he saw, and bright people like angels or whatever they were. But I mended that. I taught him to recognise stones beyond angels with a few strokes of a rod. I would never give in to visions or to trances.

Father John. We who hold the Faith have no right to speak against trance or vision. Saint Elizabeth had them, Saint Benedict, Saint Anthony, Saint Columcille. Saint Catherine of Siena often lay a long time as if dead.

Thomas. That might be so in the olden time, but those things are gone out of the world now. Those that do their work fair and honest have no occasion to let the mind go rambling. What would send my nephew, Martin Hearne, into a trance, supposing trances to be in it, and he rubbing the gold on the lion and unicorn that he had taken in hand to make a good job of for the top of the coach?

Father John [*taking up ornament*]. It is likely it was that sent him off. The flashing of light upon it would be enough to throw one that had a disposition to it into a trance. There was a very saintly man, though he was not of our Church, he wrote a great book called *Mysterium Magnum*, was seven days in a trance. Truth, or whatever truth he found, fell upon him like a bursting shower, and he a poor tradesman at his work. It was a ray of sunlight on a pewter vessel that was the beginning of all. [*Goes to the door and looks in.*] There is no stir in him yet. It is either the best thing or the worst thing can happen to any one, that is happening to him now.

Thomas. And what in the living world can happen to a man that is asleep on his bed?

Father John. There are some would answer you that it is to those who are awake that nothing happens, and it is they that know nothing. He is gone where all have gone for supreme truth.

Thomas [*sitting down again and taking up tools*]. Well, maybe so. But work must go on and coachbuilding must go on, and they will not go on the time there is too much attention given to dreams. A dream is a sort of a shadow, no profit in it to any one at all. A coach, now, is a real thing and a thing that will last for generations and be made use of to the last, and maybe turn to be a hen-roost at its latter end.

Father John. I think Andrew told me it was a dream of Martin's that led to the making of that coach.

Thomas. Well, I believe he saw gold in some dream, and it led him to want to make some gold thing, and coaches being the handiest, nothing would do him till he put the most of his fortune into the making of this golden coach. It turned out better than I thought, for some of the lawyers came looking at it at Assize time, and through them it was heard of at Dublin Castle . . . and who now has it ordered but the Lord Lieutenant! [*Father John nods.*] Ready it must be and sent off it must be by the end of the month. It is likely King George will be visiting Dublin, and it is he himself will be sitting in it yet.

Father John. Martin has been working hard at it, I know.

Thomas. You never saw a man work the way he did, day and night, near ever since the time six months ago he first came home from France.

Father John. I never thought he would be so good at a trade. I thought his mind was only set on books.

Thomas. He should be thankful to myself for that. Any person I will take in hand, I make a clean job of them the same as I would make of any other thing in my yard—coach, half-coach, hackney-coach, ass-car, common-car, post-chaise, calash, chariot on two wheels, on four wheels. Each one has the shape Thomas Hearne put on it, and it in his hands; and what I can do with wood and iron, why would I not be able to do it with flesh and blood, and it in a way my own?

Father John. Indeed, I know you did your best for Martin.

Thomas. Every best. Checked him, taught him the trade, sent him to the monastery in France for to learn the language and to see the wide world; but who should know that if you did not know it, Father John, and I doing it according to your own advice?

Father John. I thought his nature needed spiritual guidance and teaching, the best that could be found.

Thomas. I thought myself it was best for him to be away for a while. There are too many wild lads about this place. He to have stopped here, he might have taken some fancies, and got into some trouble, going against the Government maybe the same as Johnny Gibbons that is at this time an outlaw, having a price upon his head.

Father John. That is so. That imagination of his might have taken fire here at home. It was better putting him with the Brothers, to turn it to imaginings of Heaven.

Thomas. Well, I will soon have a good hardy tradesman made of him now that will live quiet and rear a family, and be maybe appointed coachbuilder to the Royal Family at the last.

Father John [*at window*]. I see your brother Andrew coming back from the doctor; he is stopping to talk with a troop of beggars that are sitting by the side of the road.

Thomas. There, now, is another that I have shaped. Andrew used to be a bit wild in his talk and in his ways, wanting to go rambling, not content to settle in the place where he was reared. But I kept a guard over him; I watched the time poverty gave him a nip, and then I settled him into the business. He never was so good a worker as Martin, he is too fond of wasting his time talking vanities. But he is middling handy, and he is always steady and civil to customers. I have no complaint worth while to be making this last twenty years against Andrew.

Andrew comes in

Andrew. Beggars there outside going the road to the Kinvara Fair. They were saying there is news that Johnny Gibbons is coming back from France on the quiet; the King's soldiers are watching the ports for him.

Thomas. Let you keep now, Andrew, to the business you have in hand. Will the doctor be coming himself or did he send a bottle that will cure Martin?

Andrew. The doctor can't come, for he's down with the lumbago in the back. He questioned me as to what ailed Martin, and he got a book to go looking for a cure, and he began telling me things out of it, but I said I could not be carrying things of that sort in my head. He gave me the book then, and he has marks put in it for the places where the cures are. . . . Wait now. . . . [*Reads*] 'Compound medicines are usually taken inwardly, or outwardly applied; inwardly taken, they should be either liquid or solid; outwardly, they should be fomentations or sponges wet in some decoctions.'

Thomas. He had a right to have written it out himself upon a paper. Where is the use of all that?

Andrew. I think I moved the mark maybe. . . . Here, now, is the part he was reading to me himself. . . . 'The remedies for diseases belonging to the skins next the brain, headache, vertigo, cramp, convulsions, palsy, incubus, apoplexy, falling sickness.'

Thomas. It is what I bid you to tell him, that it was the falling sickness.

Andrew [*dropping book*]. O, my dear, look at all the marks gone out of it! Wait, now, I partly remember what he said . . . a blister he spoke of . . . or to be smelling hartshorn . . . or the sneezing powder . . . or if all fails, to try letting the blood.

Father John. All this has nothing to do with the real case. It is all waste of time.

Andrew. That is what I was thinking myself, Father. Sure it was I was the first to call out to you when I saw you coming down from the hillside, and to bring you in to see what could you do. I would have more trust in your means than in any doctor's learning. And in case you might fail to cure him, I have a cure myself I heard from my grandmother—God rest her soul!—and she told me she never knew it to fail. A person to have the falling sickness, to cut the top of his nails and a small share of the hair of his head, and to put it down on the floor, and to take a harry-pin and drive it down with that into the floor and to leave it there. 'That is the cure will never fail', she said, 'to rise up any person at all having the falling sickness.'

Father John [*hand on ear*]. I will go back to the hillside. I will go back to the hillside; but no, no, I must do what I can. I will go again, I will wrestle, I will strive my best to call him back with prayer.   [*Goes in and shuts door.*

Andrew. It is queer Father John is sometimes, and very queer. There are times when you would say that he believes in nothing at all.

Thomas. If you wanted a priest, why did you not get our own parish priest that is a sensible man, and a man that you would know what his thoughts are? You know well the Bishop should have something against Father John to have left him through the years in that poor mountainy place, minding the few unfortunate people that were left out of the last famine. A man of his learning to be going in rags the way he is, there must be some good cause for that.

Andrew. I had all that in mind and I bringing him. But I thought he would have done more for Martin than what he is doing. To read a Mass over him I thought he would, and to be convulsed in the reading it, and some strange thing to have gone out with a great noise through the doorway.

Thomas. It would give no good name to the place such a thing to be happening in it. It is well enough for labouring-men and for half-acre men. It would be no credit at all such a thing to be heard of in this house, that is for coachbuilding the capital of the county.

Andrew. If it is from the Devil this sickness comes, it would be best to put it out whatever way it would be put out. But there might no bad thing be on the lad at all. It is likely he was with wild companions abroad, and that knocking about might have shaken his health. I was that way myself one time.

Thomas. Father John said that it was some sort of a vision or trance, but I would give no heed to what he would say. It is his trade to see more than other people would see, the same as I myself might be seeing a split in a leather car-hood that no other person would find out at all.

Andrew. If it is the falling sickness is on him, I have no objection to that—a plain straight sickness that was cast as a punishment on the unbelieving Jews. It is a thing that might attack one of a family, and one of another family, and not to come upon their kindred at all.

A person to have it, all you have to do is not to go between him and the wind, or fire, or water. But I am in dread trance is a thing might run through the house the same as the cholera morbus.

Thomas. In my belief there is no such thing as a trance. Letting on people do be to make the world wonder the time they think well to rise up. To keep them to their work is best, and not to pay much attention to them at all.

Andrew. I would not like trances to be coming on myself. I leave it in my will if I die without cause, a holly-stake to be run through my heart the way I will lie easy after burial, and not turn my face downwards in my coffin. I tell you I leave it on you in my will.

Thomas. Leave thinking of your own comforts, Andrew, and give your mind to the business. Did the smith put the irons yet on the shafts of this coach?

Andrew. I will go see did he.

Thomas. Do so, and see did he make a good job of it. Let the shafts be sound and solid if they are to be studded with gold.

Andrew. They are, and the steps along with them—glass sides for the people to be looking in at the grandeur of the satin within—the lion and the unicorn crowning all. It was a great thought Martin had the time he thought of making this coach!

Thomas. It is best for me to go see the smith myself and leave it to no other one. You can be attending to that ass-car out in the yard wants a new tyre on the wheel—out in the rear of the yard it is. [*They go to door.*] To pay attention to every small thing, and to fill up every minute of time shaping whatever you have to do, that is the way to build up a business.   [*They go out.*

Father John [*bringing in Martin*]. They are gone out now—the air is fresher here in the workshop—you can sit here for a while. You are now fully awake, you have been in some sort of a trance or a sleep.

Martin. Who was it that pulled at me? Who brought me back?

Father John. It is I, Father John, did it. I prayed a long time over you and brought you back.

Martin. You, Father John, to be so unkind! O leave me, leave me alone!

Father John. You are in your dream still.

Martin. It was no dream, it was real. Do you not smell the broken fruit—the grapes? The room is full of the smell.

Father John. Tell me what you have seen, where you have been.

Martin. There were horses—white horses rushing by, with white shining riders—there was a horse without a rider, and some one caught me up and put me upon him and we rode away, with the wind, like the wind—

Father John. That is a common imagining. I know many poor persons have seen that.

Martin. We went on, on, on. We came to a sweet-smelling garden with a gate to it, and there were wheatfields in full ear around, and there were vineyards like I saw in France, and the grapes in bunches. I thought it to be one of the townlands of Heaven. Then I saw the horses we were on had changed to unicorns, and they began trampling the grapes and breaking them. I tried to stop them, but I could not.

Father John. That is strange, that is strange. What is it that brings to mind? I heard it in some place, *monoceros de astris,* the unicorn from the stars.

Martin. They tore down the wheat and trampled it on stones, and then they tore down what were left of the grapes and crushed and bruised and trampled them. I smelt the wine, it was flowing on every side— then everything grew vague. I cannot remember clearly, everything was silent; the trampling now stopped, we were all waiting for some command. O! was it given? I was trying to hear it; there was some one dragging, dragging me away from that. I am sure there was a command given, and there was a great burst of laughter. What was it? What was the command? Everything seemed to tremble round me.

Father John. Did you awake then?

Martin. I do not think I did, it all changed—it was terrible, wonderful! I saw the unicorns trampling, trampling, but not in the wine-troughs. O, I forget! Why did you waken me?

Father John. I did not touch you. Who knows what hands pulled you away? I prayed, that was all I did. I prayed very hard that you might awake. If I had not, you might have died. I wonder what it all meant? The unicorns—what did the French monk tell me?— strength they meant, virginal strength, a rushing, lasting, tireless strength.

Martin. They were strong. O, they made a great noise with their trampling.

Father John. And the grapes, what did they mean? It puts me in mind of the psalm, *Et calix meus inebrians quam praeclarus est.* It was a strange vision, a very strange vision, a very strange vision.

Martin. How can I get back to that place?

Father John. You must not go back, you must not think of doing that. That life of vision, of contemplation, is a terrible life, for it has far more temptation in it than the common life. Perhaps it would have been best for you to stay under rules in the monastery.

Martin. I could not see anything so clearly there. It is back here in my own place the visions come, in the place where shining people used to laugh around me, and I a little lad in a bib.

Father John. You cannot know but it was from the Prince of this world the vision came. How can one ever know unless one follows the discipline of the Church? Some spiritual director, some wise learned man, that is what you want. I do not know enough. What am I but a poor banished priest, with my learning forgotten, my books never handled and spotted with the damp!

Martin. I will go out into the fields where you cannot come to me to awake me. I will see that townland again; I will hear that command. I cannot wait. I must know what happened. I must bring that command to mind again.

Father John [*putting himself between Martin and the door*]. You must have patience as the Saints had it. You are taking your own way. If there is a command from God for you, you must wait His good time to receive it.

Martin. Must I live here forty years, fifty years . . . to grow as old as my uncles, seeing nothing but common things, doing work . . . some foolish work?

Father John. Here they are coming; it is time for me to go. I must think and I must pray. My mind is troubled about you. [*To Thomas as he and Andrew come in.*] Here he is; be very kind to him, for he has still the weakness of a little child. [*Goes out.*

Thomas. Are you well of the fit, lad?

Martin. It was no fit. I was away—for a while—no, you will not believe me if I tell you.

Andrew. I would believe it, Martin. I used to have very long sleeps myself and very queer dreams.

Thomas. You had, till I cured you, taking you in hand and binding you to the hours of the clock. The cure that will cure yourself, Martin, and will waken you, is to put the whole of your mind on to your golden coach; to take it in hand and to finish it out of face.

Martin. Not just now. I want to think—to try and remember what I saw, something that I heard, that I was told to do.

Thomas. No, but put it out of your mind. There is no man doing business that can keep two things in his head. A Sunday or a holy-day, now, you might go see a good hurling or a thing of the kind, but to be spreading out your mind on anything outside of the work-shop on common days, all coachbuilding would come to an end.

Martin. I don't think it is building I want to do. I don't think that is what was in the command.

Thomas. It is too late to be saying that, the time you have put the most of your fortune in the business. Set yourself now to finish your job, and when it is ended maybe I won't begrudge you going with the coach as far as Dublin.

Andrew. That is it, that will satisfy him. I had a great desire myself, and I young, to go traveling the roads as far as Dublin. The roads are the great things, they never come to an end. They are the same as the serpent having his tail swallowed in his own mouth.

Martin. It was not wandering I was called to. What was it? What was it?

Thomas. What you are called to, and what every one having no great estate is called to, is to work. Sure the world itself could not go on without work.

Martin. I wonder if that is the great thing, to make the world go on? No, I don't think that is the great thing—what does the Munster poet call it?—'this crowded slippery coach-loving world'. I don't think I was told to work for that.

Andrew. I often thought that myself. It is a pity the stock of the Hearnes to be asked to do any work at all.

Thomas. Rouse yourself, Martin, and don't be talking the way a fool talks. You started making that golden coach, and you were set upon it, and you had me tormented about it. You have yourself wore out working at it, and planning it, and thinking of it, and at the end of the race, when you have the winning-post in sight, and horses hired for to bring it to Dublin Castle, you go falling into sleeps and blathering about dreams, and we run to a great danger of letting the profit and the sale go by. Sit down on the bench now, and lay your hands to the work.

Martin [*sitting down*]. I will try. I wonder why I ever wanted to make it; it was no good dream set me doing that. [*He takes up wheel.*] What is there in a wooden wheel to take pleasure in it? Gilding it outside makes it no different.

Thomas. That is right, now. You had some good plan for making the axle run smooth.

Martin [*letting wheel fall and putting his hands to his head*]. It is no use. [*Angrily.*] Why did you send the priest to awake me? My soul is my own and my mind is my own. I will send them to where I like. You have no authority over my thoughts.

Thomas. That is no way to be speaking to me. I am head of this business. Nephew or no nephew, I will have no one come cold or unwilling to the work.

Martin. I had better go; I am of no use to you. I am going—I must be alone—I will forget if I am not alone. Give me what is left of my money and I will go out of this.

Thomas [*opening a press and taking out a bag and throwing it to him*]. There is what is left of your money! The rest of it you have spent on the coach. If you want to go, go, and I will not have to be annoyed with you from this out.

Andrew. Come now with me, Thomas. The boy is foolish, but it will soon pass over. He has not my sense to be giving attention to what you will say. Come along now, leave him for a while; leave him to me, I say, it is I will get inside his mind.

[*He leads Thomas out. Martin bangs door angrily after them and sits down, taking up lion and unicorn.*

Martin. I think it was some shining thing I saw. What was it?

Andrew [*opening door and putting in his head*]. Listen to me, Martin.

Martin. Go away, no more talking; leave me alone.

Andrew. O, but wait. I understand you. Thomas doesn't understand your thoughts, but I understand them. Wasn't I telling you I was just like you once?

Martin. Like me? Did you ever see the other things, the things beyond?

Andrew. I did. It is not the four walls of the house keep me content. Thomas doesn't know. O no, he doesn't know.

Martin. No, he has no vision.

Andrew. He has not, not any sort of a heart for a frolic.

Martin. He has never heard the laughter and the music beyond.

Andrew. He has not, nor the music of my own little flute. I have it hidden in the thatch outside.

Martin. Does the body slip from you as it does from me? They have not shut your window into eternity?

Andrew. Thomas never shut a window I could not get through. I knew you were one of my own sort. When I am sluggish in the morning, Thomas says, 'Poor Andrew is getting old'. That is all he knows. The way to keep young is to do the things youngsters do. Twenty years I have been slipping away, and he never found me out yet!

Martin. That is what they call ecstasy, but there is no word that can tell out very plain what it means. That freeing of the mind from its thoughts; when we put those wonders into words, those words seem as little like them as blackberries are like the moon and sun.

Andrew. I found that myself the time they knew me to be wild, and used to be asking me to say what pleasure did I find in cards, and women, and drink.

Martin. You might help me to remember that vision I had this morn-ing, to understand it. The memory of it has slipped from me. Wait, it is coming back, little by little. I know that I saw the unicorns trampling, and then a figure, a many-changing figure, holding some bright thing. I knew something was going to happen or to be said, something that would make my whole life strong and beautiful like the rushing of the unicorns, and then, and then—

Johnny Bocach's voice [*at window*]. A poor person I am, without food, without a way, without portion, without costs, without a person or a stranger, without means, without hope, without health, without warmth—

Andrew [*looking towards window*]. It is that troop of beggars. Bringing their tricks and their thieveries they are to the Kinvara Fair.

Martin [*impatiently*]. There is no quiet—come to the other room. I am trying to remember.

[*They go to door of inner room, but Andrew stops him.*

Andrew. They are a bad-looking fleet. I have a mind to drive them away, giving them a charity.

Martin. Drive them away or come away from their voices.

Another voice. I put under the power of my prayer
        All that will give me help.
        Rafael keep him Wednesday,
        Sachiel feed him Thursday,
        Hamiel provide him Friday,
        Cassiel increase him Saturday.
Sure giving to us is giving to the Lord and laying up a store in the treasury of Heaven.

Andrew. Whisht? He is entering by the window! [*Johnny climbs up.*

Johnny. That I may never sin, but the place is empty.

Paudeen [*outside*]. Go in and see what can you make a grab at.

Johnny [*getting in*]. That every blessing I gave may be turned to a curse on them that left the place so bare! [*He turns things over.*] I might chance something in this chest if it was open.

[*Andrew begins creeping towards him.*

Nanny [*outside*]. Hurry on, now, you limping crabfish, you! We can't be stopping here while you'll boil stirabout!

Johnny [*seizing bag of money and holding it up high in both hands.*] Look at this, now, look!   [*Andrew comes behind, seizes his arm.*

Johnny [*letting bag fall with a crash*]. Destruction on us all!

Martin [*running forward, seizes him. Heads at the window disappear*]. That is it! O, I remember. That is what happened. That is the command. Who was it sent you here with that command?

Johnny. It was misery sent me in, and starvation and the hard ways of the world.

Nanny [*outside*]. It was that, my poor child, and my one son only. Show mercy to him now and he after leaving gaol this morning.

Martin [*to Andrew*]. I was trying to remember it—when he spoke that word it all came back to me. I saw a bright many-changing figure; it was holding up a shining vessel [*holds up arms*]; then the vessel fell and was broken with a great crash; then I saw the unicorns trampling it. They were breaking the world to pieces—when I saw the cracks coming I shouted for joy! And I heard the command, 'Destroy, destroy, destruction is the life-giver! destroy!'

Andrew. What will we do with him? He was thinking to rob you of your gold.

Martin. How could I forget it or mistake it? It has all come upon me now; the reasons of it all, like a flood, like a flooded river.

Johnny [*weeping*]. It was the hunger brought me in and the drouth.

Martin. Were you given any other message? Did you see the unicorns?

Johnny. I saw nothing and heard nothing; near dead I am with the fright I got and with the hardship of the gaol.

Martin. To destroy, to overthrow all that comes between us and God, between us and that shining country. To break the wall, Andrew, to break the thing—whatever it is that comes between; but where to begin—?

Andrew. What is it you are talking about?

Martin. It may be that this man is the beginning. He has been sent— the poor, they have nothing, and so they can see Heaven as we cannot. He and his comrades will understand me. But how to give all men high hearts that they may all understand?

Johnny. It's the juice of the grey barley will do that.

Andrew. To rise everybody's heart, is it? Is it that was your meaning all the time? If you will take the blame of it all, I'll do what you want. Give me the bag of money then. [*He takes it up.*] O, I've a heart like your own. I'll lift the world, too. The people will be running from all parts. O, it will be a great day in this district.

Johnny. Will I go with you?

Martin. No, you must stay here; we have things to do and to plan.

Johnny. Destroyed we all are with the hunger and the drouth.

Martin. Go, then, get food and drink, whatever is wanted to give you strength and courage. Gather your people together here, bring them all in. We have a great thing to do, I have to begin—I want to tell it to the whole world. Bring them in, bring them in, I will make the house ready.

[*He stands looking up as if in ecstasy; Andrew and Johnny Bocach go out.*]

ACT II

The same workshop. Martin seen arranging mugs and bread, etc., on a table. Father John comes in, knocking at open door as he comes; his mind intensely absorbed.

Martin. Come in, come in, I have got the house ready. Here is bread and meat—everybody is welcome. [*Hearing no answer, turns round.*

Father John. Martin, I have come back. There is something I want to say to you.

Martin. You are welcome, there are others coming. They are not of your sort, but all are welcome.

Father John. I have remembered suddenly something that I read when I was in the seminary.

Martin. You seem very tired.

Father John [*sitting down*]. I had almost got back to my own place when I thought of it. I have run part of the way. It is very important; it is about the trance that you have been in. When one is inspired from above, either in trance or in contemplation, one remembers afterwards all that one has seen and read. I think there must be something about it in Saint Thomas. I know that I have read a long passage about it years ago. But, Martin, there is another kind of inspiration, or rather an obsession or possession. A diabolical power comes into one's body, or overshadows it. Those whose bodies are taken hold of in this way, jugglers, and witches, and the like, can often tell what is happening in distant places, or what is going to happen, but when they come out of that state they remember nothing. I think you said—

Martin. That I could not remember.

Father John. You remembered something, but not all. Nature is a great sleep; there are dangerous and evil spirits in her dreams, but God is above Nature. She is a darkness, but He makes everything clear; He is light.

Martin. All is clear now. I remember all, or all that matters to me. A poor man brought me a word, and I know what I have to do.

Father John. Ah, I understand, words were put into his mouth. I have read of such things. God sometimes uses some common man as His messenger.

Martin. You may have passed the man who brought it on the road. He left me but now.

Father John. Very likely, very likely, that is the way it happened. Some plain, unnoticed man has sometimes been sent with a command.

Martin. I saw the unicorns trampling in my dream. They were breaking the world. I am to destroy; destruction was the word the messenger spoke.

Father John. To destroy?

Martin. To bring again the old disturbed exalted life, the old splendour.

Father John. You are not the first that dream has come to. [*Gets up, and walks up and down.*] It has been wandering here and there, calling now to this man, now to that other. It is a terrible dream.

Martin. Father John, you have had the same thought.

Father John. Men were holy then, there were saints everywhere. There was reverence; but now it is all work, business, how to live a long time. Ah, if one could change it all in a minute, even by war and violence! There is a cell where Saint Ciaran used to pray; if one could bring that time again!

Martin. Do not deceive me. You have had the command.

Father John. Why are you questioning me? You are asking me things that I have told to no one but my confessor.

Martin. We must gather the crowds together, you and I.

Father John. I have dreamed your dream, it was long ago. I had your vision.

Martin. And what happened?

Father John [*harshly*]. It was stopped; that was an end. I was sent to the lonely parish where I am, where there was no one I could lead astray. They have left me there. We must have patience; the world was destroyed by water, it has yet to be consumed by fire.

Martin. Why should we be patient? To live seventy years, and others to come after us and live seventy years, it may be; and so from age to age, and all the while the old splendour dying more and more.

[*A noise of shouting. Andrew, who has been standing at the door, comes in.*

Andrew. Martin says truth, and he says it well. Planing the side of a cart or a shaft, is that life? It is not. Sitting at a desk writing letters to the man that wants a coach, or to the man that won't pay for the one he has got, is that life, I ask you? Thomas arguing at you and putting you down—'Andrew, dear Andrew, did you put the tyre on that wheel yet?' Is that life? No, it is not. I ask you all, what do you remember when you are dead? It's the sweet cup in the corner of the widow's drinking-house that you remember. Ha, ha, listen to that shouting! That is what the lads in the village will remember to the last day they live.

Martin. Why are they shouting? What have you told them?

Andrew. Never you mind; you left that to me. You bade me to lift their hearts and I did lift them. There is not one among them but will have his head like a blazing tar-barrel before morning. What did your friend the beggar say? The juice of the grey barley, he said.

Father John. You accursed villain! You have made them drunk!

Andrew. Not at all, but lifting them to the stars. That is what Martin bade me to do, and there is no one can say I did not do it.

[*A shout at door, and Beggars push in a barrel. They cry,* 'Hi! for the noble master!' *and point at Andrew.*

Johnny. It's not him, it's that one!   [*Points at Martin.*

Father John. Are you bringing this devil's work in at the very door? Go out of this, I say! get out! Take these others with you!

Martin. No, no; I asked them in, they must not be turned out. They are my guests.

Father John. Drive them out of your uncle's house!

Martin. Come, Father, it is better for you to go. Go back to your own place. I have taken the command. It is better perhaps for you that you did not take it.   [*Father John and Martin go out.*

Biddy. It is well for that old lad he didn't come between ourselves and our luck. Himself to be after his meal, and ourselves staggering with the hunger! It would be right to have flayed him and to have made bags of his skin.

Nanny. What a hurry you are in to get your enough! Look at the grease on your frock yet, with the dint of the dabs you put in your pocket! Doing cures and foretellings, is it? You starved pot-picker, you!

Biddy. That you may be put up to-morrow to take the place of that decent son of yours that had the yard of the gaol wore with walking it till this morning!

Nanny. If he had, he had a mother to come to, and he would know her when he did see her; and that is what no son of your own could do and he to meet you at the foot of the gallows.

Johnny. If I did know you, I knew too much of you since the first beginning of my life! What reward did I ever get travelling with you? What store did you give me of cattle or of goods? What provision did I get from you by day or by night but your own bad character to be joined on to my own, and I following at your heels, and your bags tied round about me!

Nanny. Disgrace and torment on you! Whatever you got from me, it was more than any reward or any bit I ever got from the father you had, or any honourable thing at all, but only the hurt and the harm of the world and its shame!

Johnny. What would he give you, and you going with him without leave! Crooked and foolish you were always, and you begging by the side of the ditch.

Nanny. Begging or sharing, the curse of my heart upon you! It's better off I was before ever I met with you to my cost! What was on me at all that I did not cut a scourge in the wood to put manners and decency on you the time you were not hardened as you are!

Johnny. Leave talking to me of your rods and your scourges! All you taught me was robbery, and it is on yourself and not on myself the scourges will be laid at the day of the recognition of tricks.

Paudeen. 'Faith, the pair of you together is better than Hector fighting before Troy!

Nanny. Ah, let you be quiet. It is not fighting we are craving, but the easing of the hunger that is on us and of the passion of sleep. Lend me a graineen of tobacco now till I'll kindle my pipe—a blast of it will take the weight of the road off my heart.

> [*Andrew gives her some. Nanny grabs it.*

Biddy. No, but it's to myself you should give it. I that never smoked a pipe this forty year without saying the tobacco prayer. Let that one say did ever she do that much.

Nanny. That the pain of your front tooth may be in your back tooth, you to be grabbing my share!   [*They snap at tobacco.*

Andrew. Pup, pup, pup! Don't be snapping and quarrelling now, and you so well treated in this house. It is strollers like yourselves should be for frolic and for fun. Have you ne'er a good song to sing, a song that will rise all our hearts?

Paudeen. Johnny Bocach is a good singer, it is what he used to be doing in the fairs, if the oakum of the gaol did not give him a hoarseness within the throat.

Andrew. Give it out so, a good song, a song will put courage and spirit into any man at all.

Johnny [*singing*].

> 'O come all ye airy bachelors,
>   A warning take by me,
> A sergeant caught me fowling,
>   And he fired his gun so free.
>
> His comrades came to his relief,
>   And I was soon trepanned,
> And bound up like a woodcock
>   That had fallen into their hands.
>
> The judge said transportation,
>   The ship was on the strand;
> They have yoked me to the traces
>   For to plough Van Diemen's Land!'

Andrew. That's no good of a song but a melancholy sort of a song. I'd as lief be listening to a saw going through timber. Wait, now, till you will hear myself giving out a tune on the flute.   [*Goes out for it.*

Johnny. It is what I am thinking, there must be a great dearth and a great scarcity of good comrades in this place, a man like that youngster, having means in his hand, to be bringing ourselves and our rags into the house.

Paudeen. You think yourself very wise, Johnny Bocach. Can you tell me, now, who that man is?

Johnny. Some decent lad, I suppose, with a good way of living and a mind to send up his name upon the roads.

Paudeen. You that have been gaoled this eight months know little of this countryside. It isn't a limping stroller like yourself the Boys would let come among them. But I know. I went to the drill a few nights and I skinning kids for the mountainy men. In a quarry beyond the drill is—they have their plans made—it's the Square House of the Brownes is to be made an attack on and plundered. Do you know, now, who is the leader they are waiting for?

Johnny. How would I know that?

Paudeen [*singing*].

'O, Johnny Gibbons, my five hundred healths to you!
It's long you are away from us over the sea!'

Johnny [*standing up excitedly*]. Sure, that man could not be Johnny Gibbons that is outlawed!

Paudeen. I asked news of him from the old lad, and I bringing in the drink along with him. 'Don't be asking questions', says he; 'take the treat he gives you', says he. 'If a lad that has a high heart has a mind to rouse the neighbours', says he, 'and to stretch out his hand to all that pass the road, it is in France he learned it', says he, 'the place he is but lately come from, and where the wine does be standing open in tubs. Take your treat when you get it', says he, 'and make no delay or all might be discovered and put an end to.'

Johnny. He came over the sea from France! It is Johnny Gibbons, surely, but it seems to me they were calling him by some other name.

Paudeen. A man on his keeping might go by a hundred names. Would he be telling it out to us that he never saw before, and we with that clutch of chattering women along with us? Here he is coming now. Wait till you see is he the lad I think him to be.

Martin [*coming in*]. I will make my banner, I will paint the unicorn on it. Give me that bit of canvas, there is paint over here. We will get no help from the settled men—we will call to the lawbreakers, the tinkers, the sievemakers, the sheepstealers.

[*He begins to make banner.*

Biddy. That sounds to be a queer name of an army. Ribbons I can understand, Whiteboys, Rightboys, Threshers, and Peep o' Days, but Unicorns I never heard of before.

Johnny. It is not a queer name but a very good name. [*Takes up lion and unicorn.*] It is often you saw that before you in the dock. There is the unicorn with the one horn, and what is it he is going against? The lion of course. When he has the lion destroyed, the crown must fall and be shivered. Can't you see it is the League of the Unicorns is the league that will fight and destroy the power of England and King George?

Paudeen. It is with that banner we will march and the lads in the quarry with us, it is they will have the welcome before him! It won't be long till we'll be attacking the Square House! Arms there are in it, riches that would smother the world, rooms full of guineas, we will put wax on our shoes walking them; the horses themselves shod with no less than silver!

Martin [*holding up banner*]. There it is ready! We are very few now, but the army of the Unicorns will be a great army! [*To Johnny.*] Why have you brought me the message? Can you remember any more? Has anything more come to you? You have been drinking, the clouds upon your mind have been destroyed. . . . Can you see anything or hear anything that is beyond the world?

Johnny. I can not. I don't know what do you want me to tell you at all.

Martin. I want to begin the destruction, but I don't know where to begin. . . . You do not hear any other voice?

Johnny. I do not. I have nothing at all to do with Freemasons or witch-craft.

Paudeen. It is Biddy Lally has to do with witchcraft. It is often she threw the cups and gave out prophecies the same as Columcille.

Martin. You are one of the knowledgeable women. You can tell where it is to begin, and what will happen in the end.

Biddy. I will foretell nothing at all. I rose out of it this good while, with the stiffness and the swelling it brought upon my joints.

Martin. If you have foreknowledge you have no right to keep silent. If you do not help me I may go to work in the wrong way. I know I have to destroy, but when I ask myself what I am to begin with, I am full of uncertainty.

Paudeen. Here now are the cups handy and the leavings in them.

Biddy [*taking cups and pouring one from another*]. Throw a bit of white money into the four corners of the house.

Martin. There! [*Throwing it.*]

Biddy. There can be nothing told without silver. It is not myself will

have the profit of it. Along with that I will be forced to throw out
gold.

Martin. There is a guinea for you. Tell me what comes before your
eyes.

Biddy. What is it you are wanting to have news of?

Martin. Of what I have to go out against at the beginning . . . There
is so much . . . the whole world, it may be.

Biddy [*throwing from one cup to another and looking*]. You have
no care for yourself. You have been across the sea, you are not long
back. You are coming within the best day of your life.

Martin. What is it? What is it I have to do?

Biddy. I see a great smoke, I see burning . . . There is a great smoke
overhead.

Martin. That means we have to burn away a great deal that men have
piled up upon the earth. We must bring men once more to the wildness of the clean green earth.

Biddy. Herbs for my healing, the big herb and the little herb, it is true
enough they get their great strength out of the earth.

Johnny. Who was it the green sod of Ireland belonged to in the olden
times? Wasn't it to the ancient race it belonged? And who has possession of it now but the race that came robbing over the sea? The
meaning of that is to destroy the big houses and the towns, and the
fields to be given back to the ancient race.

Martin. That is it. You don't put it as I do, but what matter? Battle
is all.

Paudeen. Columcille said, the four corners to be burned, and then the
middle of the field to be burned. I tell you it was Columcille's
prophecy said that.

Biddy. Iron handcuffs I see and a rope and a gallows, and it maybe
is not for yourself I see it, but for some I have acquaintance with a
good way back.

Martin. That means the Law. We must destroy the Law. That was the
first sin, the first mouthful of the apple.

Johnny. So it was, so it was. The Law is the worst loss. The ancient
Law was for the benefit of all. It is the Law of the English is the
only sin.

Martin. When there were no laws men warred on one another and
man to man, not with machines made in towns as they do now, and
they grew hard and strong in body. They were altogether alive like
Him that made them in His image, like people in that unfallen
country. But presently they thought it better to be safe, as if safety
mattered or anything but the exaltation of the heart, and to have

eyes that danger had made grave and piercing. We must overthrow the laws and banish them.

Johnny. It is what I say, to put out the laws is to put out the whole nation of the English. Laws for themselves they make for their own profit, and left us nothing at all, no more than a dog or a sow.

Biddy. An old priest I see, and I would not say is he the one was here or another. Vexed and troubled he is, kneeling fretting and ever-fretting in some lonesome ruined place.

Martin. I thought it would come to that. Yes, the Church too—that is to be destroyed. Once men fought with their desires and their fears, with all that they call their sins, unhelped, and their souls became hard and strong. When we have brought back the clean earth and destroyed the Law and the Church, all life will become like a flame of fire, like a burning eye . . . O, how to find words for it all . . . all that is not life will pass away.

Johnny. It is Luther's Church he means, and the hump-backed discourse of Seaghan Calvin's Bible. So we will break it, and make an end of it.

Martin. We will go out against the world and break it and unmake it. [*Rising.*] We are the army of the Unicorn from the Stars! We will trample it to pieces.—We will consume the world, we will burn it away—Father John said the world has yet to be consumed by fire. Bring me fire.

Andrew [*to Beggars*]. Here is Thomas. Hide—let you hide.

[*All except Martin hurry into next room.
Thomas comes in*

Thomas. Come with me, Martin. There is terrible work going on in the town! There is mischief gone abroad. Very strange things are happening!

Martin. What are you talking of? What has happened?

Thomas. Come along, I say, it must be put a stop to. We must call to every decent man. It is as if the Devil himself had gone through the town on a blast and set every drinking-house open!

Martin. I wonder how that has happened. Can it have anything to do with Andrew's plan?

Thomas. Are you giving no heed to what I'm saying? There is not a man, I tell you, in the parish and beyond the parish but has left the work he was doing whether in the field or in the mill.

Martin. Then all work has come to an end? Perhaps that was a good thought of Andrew's.

Thomas. There is not a man has come to sensible years that is not drunk or drinking! My own labourers and my own serving-men are sitting on counters and on barrels! I give you my word, the smell of the spirits and the porter, and the shouting and the cheering within, made the hair to rise up on my scalp.

Martin. And yet there is not one of them that does not feel that he could bridle the four winds.

Thomas [*sitting down in despair*]. You are drunk too. I never thought you had a fancy for it.

Martin. It is hard for you to understand. You have worked all your life. You have said to yourself every morning, 'What is to be done to-day?' and when you were tired out you have thought of the next day's work. If you gave yourself an hour's idleness, it was but that you might work the better. Yet it is only when one has put work away that one begins to live.

Thomas. It is those French wines that did it.

Martin. I have been beyond the earth. In Paradise, in that happy townland, I have seen the shining people. They were all doing one thing or another, but not one of them was at work. All that they did was but the overflowing of their idleness, and their days were a dance bred of the secret frenzy of their hearts, or a battle where the sword made a sound that was like laughter.

Thomas. You went away sober from out of my hands; they had a right to have minded you better.

Martin. No man can be alive, and what is Paradise but fulness of life, if whatever he sets his hand to in the daylight cannot carry him from exaltation to exaltation, and if he does not rise into the frenzy of contemplation in the night silence. Events that are not begotten in joy are misbegotten and darken the world, and nothing is begotten in joy if the joy of a thousand years has not been crushed into a moment.

Thomas. And I offered to let you go to Dublin in the coach!

Martin [*giving banner to Paudeen*]. Give me the lamp. The lamp has not yet been lighted, and the world is to be consumed!

[*Goes into inner room.*

Thomas [*seeing Andrew*]. Is it here you are, Andrew? What are these beggars doing? Was this door thrown open too? Why did you not keep order? I will go for the constables to help us!

Andrew. You will not find them to help you. They were scattering themselves through the drinking-houses of the town, and why wouldn't they?

Thomas. Are you drunk too? You are worse than Martin. You are a disgrace!

Andrew. Disgrace yourself! Coming here to be making an attack on

me and badgering me and disparaging me! And what about yourself
that turned me to be a hypocrite?

Thomas. What are you saying?

Andrew. You did, I tell you! Weren't you always at me to be regular
and to be working and to be going through the day and the night
without company and to be thinking of nothing but the trade? What
did I want with a trade? I got a sight of the faery gold one time in
the mountains. I would have found it again and brought riches from
it but for you keeping me so close to the work.

Thomas. O, of all the ungrateful creatures! You know well that I
cherished you, leading you to live a decent, respectable life.

Andrew. You never had respect for the ancient ways. It is after the
mother you take it, that was too soft and too lumpish, having too
much of the English in her blood. Martin is a Hearne like myself.
It is he has the generous heart! It is not Martin would make a
hypocrite of me and force me to do night-walking secretly, watching to be back by the setting of the seven stars!

> [*He begins to play his flute.*

Thomas. I will turn you out of this, yourself and this filthy troop! I
will have them lodged in gaol.

Johnny. Filthy troop, is it? Mind yourself! The change is coming. The
pikes will be up and the traders will go down.

All seize Thomas and sing

'O, the lion shall lose his strength,
    And the bracket-thistle pine,
And the harp shall sound sweet, sweet at length,
    Between the eight and nine!'

Thomas. Let me out of this, you villains!

Nanny. We'll make a sieve of holes of you, you old bag of treachery!

Biddy. How well you threatened us with gaol, you skim of a weasel's
milk!

Johnny. You heap of sicknesses! You blinking hangman! That you may
never die till you'll get a blue hag for a wife.

> [*Martin comes back with lighted lamp.*

Martin. Let him go. [*They let Thomas go, and fall back.*] Spread out
the banner. The moment has come to begin the war.

Johnny. Up with the Unicorn and destroy the Lion! Success to Johnny
Gibbons and all good men!

Martin. Heap all those things together there. Heap those pieces of the
coach one upon another. Put that straw under them. It is with this
flame I will begin the work of destruction. All nature destroys and
laughs.

Thomas. Destroy your own golden coach!

Martin [*kneeling before Thomas*]. I am sorry to go a way that you
do not like and to do a thing that will vex you. I have been a great
trouble to you since I was a child in the house, and I am a great
trouble to you yet. It is not my fault. I have been chosen for what
I have to do. [*Stands up.*] I have to free myself first and those that
are near me. The love of God is a very terrible thing! [*Thomas tries
to stop him, but is prevented by Beggars. Martin takes a wisp of
straw and lights it.*] We will destroy all that can perish! It is only
the soul that can suffer no injury. The soul of man is of the im-
perishable substance of the stars!

[*He throws wisp into heap—it blazes up.*

ACT III

*Before dawn. A wild rocky place. Nanny and Biddy Lally squatting
by a fire. Rich stuffs, etc., strewn about. Paudeen watching by Martin,
who is lying as if dead, a sack over him.*

Nanny [*to Paudeen*]. Well, you are great heroes and great warriors
and great lads altogether, to have put down the Brownes the way
you did, yourselves and the Whiteboys of the quarry. To have ran-
sacked the house and have plundered it! Look at the silks and the
satins and the grandeurs I brought away! Look at that now! [*Holds
up a velvet cloak.*] It's a good little jacket for myself will come out
of it. It's the singers will be stopping their songs and the jobbers turning from their cattle in the fairs to be taking a view of the laces of it
and the buttons! It's my far-off cousins will be drawing from far
and near!

Biddy. There was not so much gold in it all as what they were saying
there was. Or maybe that fleet of Whiteboys had the place ran·
sacked before we ourselves came in. Bad cess to them that put it in
my mind to go gather up the full of my bag of horseshoes out of the
forge. Silver they were saying they were, pure white silver; and what
are they in the end but only hardened iron! A bad end to them!
[*Flings away horseshoes.*] The time I will go robbing big houses
again it will not be in the light of the full moon I will go doing it,
that does be causing every common thing to shine out as if for a
deceit and a mockery. It's not shining at all they are at this time,
but duck-yellow and dark.

Nanny. To leave the big house blazing after us, it was that crowned
all! Two houses to be burned to ashes in the one night. It is likely

the servant-girls were rising from the feathers and the cocks crowing from the rafters for seven miles around, taking the flames to be the whitening of the dawn.

Biddy. It is the lad is stretched beyond you have to be thankful to for that. There was never seen a leader was his equal for spirit and for daring. Making a great scatter of the guards the way he did. Running up roofs and ladders, the fire in his hand, till you'd think he would be apt to strike his head against the stars.

Nanny. I partly guessed death was near him, and the queer shining look he had in his two eyes, and he throwing sparks east and west through the beams. I wonder now was it some inward wound he got, or did some hardy lad of the Brownes give him a tip on the skull unknownst in the fight? It was I myself found him, and the troop of the Whiteboys gone, and he lying by the side of a wall as weak as if he had knocked a mountain. I failed to waken him trying him with the sharpness of my nails, and his head fell back when I moved it, and I knew him to be spent and gone.

Biddy. It's a pity you not to have left him where he was lying and said no word at all to Paudeen or to that son you have, that kept us back from following on, bringing him here to this shelter on sacks and upon poles.

Nanny. What way could I help letting a screech out of myself, and the life but just gone out of him in the darkness, and not a living Christian by his side but myself and the great God?

Biddy. It's on ourselves the vengeance of the red soldiers will fall, they to find us sitting here the same as hares in a tuft. It would be best for us follow after the rest of the army of the Whiteboys.

Nanny. Whisht! I tell you. The lads are cracked about him. To get but the wind of the word of leaving him, it's little but they'd knock the head off the two of us. Whisht!

Enter Johnny Bocach with candles

Johnny [*standing over Martin*]. Wouldn't you say now there was some malice or some venom in the air, that is striking down one after another the whole of the heroes of the Gael?

Paudeen. It makes a person be thinking of the four last ends, death and judgment, Heaven and Hell. Indeed and indeed my heart lies with him. It is well I knew what man he was under his byname and his disguise.

[Sings]

'O, Johnny Gibbons, it's you were the prop to us.
You to have left us, we are foals astray!'

Johnny. It is lost we are now and broken to the end of our days. There is no satisfaction at all but to be destroying the English, and where now will we get so good a leader again? Lay him out fair and straight upon a stone, till I will let loose the secret of my heart keening him!

>   [*Sets out candles on a rock, propping them up with stones.*

Nanny. Is it mould candles you have brought to set around him, Johnny Bocach? It is great riches you should have in your pocket to be going to those lengths and not to be content with dips.

Johnny. It is lengths I will not be going to the time the life will be gone out of your own body. It is not your corpse I will be wishful to hold in honour the way I hold this corpse in honour.

Nanny. That's the way always, there will be grief and quietness in the house if it is a young person has died, but funning and springing and tricking one another if it is an old person's corpse is in it. There is no compassion at all for the old.

Paudeen. It is he would have got leave for the Gael to be as high as the Gall. Believe me, he was in the prophecies. Let you not be comparing yourself with the like of him.

Nanny. Why wouldn't I be comparing myself? Look at all that was against me in the world. Would you be matching me against a man of his sort, that had the people shouting him and that had nothing to do but to die and to go to Heaven?

Johnny. The day you go to Heaven that you may never come back alive out of it! But it is not yourself will ever hear the saints hammering at their musics! It is you will be moving through the ages, chains upon you, and you in the form of a dog or a monster. I tell you that one will go through Purgatory as quick as lightning through a thorn-bush.

Nanny. That's the way, that's the way.

[*Croons*]

> Three that are watching my time to run,
> The worm, the Devil, and my son,
> To see a loop around their neck,
> It's that would make my heart to lep!

Johnny. Five white candles. I wouldn't begrudge them to him indeed. If he had held out and held up, it is my belief he would have freed Ireland!

Paudeen. Wait till the full light of the day and you'll see the burying he'll have. It is not in this place we will be waking him. I'll make a call to the two hundred Ribbons he was to lead on to the attack on the barracks at Aughanish. They will bring him marching to his grave upon the hill. He had surely some gift from the other world, I wouldn't say but he had power from the other side.

Andrew [*coming in very shaky*]. Well, it was a great night he gave to the village, and it is long till it will be forgotten. I tell you the whole of the neighbours are up against him. There is no one at all this morning to set the mills going. There was no bread baked in the night-time, the horses are not fed in the stalls, the cows are not milked in the sheds. I met no man able to make a curse this night but he put it on my head and on the head of the boy that is lying there before us. . . . Is there no sign of life in him at all?

Johnny. What way would there be a sign of life and the life gone out of him this three hours or more?

Andrew. He was lying in his sleep for a while yesterday, and he wakened again after another while.

Nanny. He will not waken, I tell you. I held his hand in my own and it getting cold as if you were pouring on it the coldest cold water, and no running in his blood. He is gone, sure enough, and the life is gone out of him.

Andrew. Maybe so, maybe so. It seems to me yesterday his cheeks were bloomy all the while, and now he is as pale as wood ashes. Sure, we all must come to it at the last. Well, my white-headed darling, it is you were the bush among us all, and you to be cut down in your prime. Gentle and simple, every one liked you. It is no narrow heart you had, it is you were for spending and not for getting. It is you made a good wake for yourself, scattering your estate in one night only in beer and in wine for the whole province; and that you may be sitting in the middle of Paradise and in the chair of the Graces!

Johnny. Amen to that. It's pity I didn't think the time I sent for yourself to send the little lad of a messenger looking for a priest to overtake him. It might be in the end the Almighty is the best man for us all!

Andrew. Sure, I sent him on myself to bid the priest to come. Living or dead I would wish to do all that is rightful for the last and the best of my own race and generation.

Biddy [*jumping up*]. Is it the priest you are bringing in among us? Where is the sense in that? Aren't we robbed enough up to this with the expense of the candles and the like?

Johnny. If it is that poor starved priest he called to that came talking in secret signs to the man that is gone, it is likely he will ask nothing for what he has to do. There is many a priest is a Whiteboy in his heart.

Nanny. I tell you, if you brought him tied in a bag he would not say an Our Father for you, without you having a half-crown at the top of your fingers.

Biddy. There is no priest is any good at all but a spoiled priest. A one that would take a drop of drink, it is he would have courage to face the hosts of trouble. Rout them out he would, the same as a shoal of fish from out the weeds. It's best not to vex a priest, or to run against them at all.

Nanny. It's yourself humbled yourself well to one the time you were sick in the gaol and had like to die, and he bade you to give over the throwing of the cups.

Biddy. Ah, plaster of Paris I gave him. I took to it again and I free upon the roads.

Nanny. Much good you are doing with it to yourself or any other one. Aren't you after telling that corpse no later than yesterday that he was coming within the best day of his life?

Johnny. Whisht, let ye. Here is the priest coming.

Father John comes in

Father John. It is surely not true that he is dead?

Johnny. The spirit went from him about the middle hour of the night. We brought him here to this sheltered place. We were loth to leave him without friends.

Father John. Where is he?

Johnny [*taking up sacks*]. Lying there stiff and stark. He has a very quiet look as if there was no sin at all or no great trouble upon his mind.

Father John [*kneels and touches him*]. He is not dead.

Biddy [*pointing to Nanny*]. He is dead. If it was letting on he was, he would not have let that one rob him and search him the way she did.

Father John. It has the appearance of death, but it is not death. He is in a trance.

Paudeen. Is it Heaven and Hell he is walking at this time to be bringing back newses of the sinners in pain?

Biddy. I was thinking myself it might be away he was, riding on white horses with the riders of the forths.

Johnny. He will have great wonders to tell out, the time he will rise up from the ground. It is a pity he not to waken at this time and to lead us on to overcome the troop of the English. Sure, those that are in a trance get strength that they can walk on water.

Andrew. It was Father John wakened him yesterday the time he was lying in the same way. Wasn't I telling you it was for that I called to him?

Biddy. Waken him now till they'll see did I tell any lie in my fore-telling. I knew well by the signs, he was coming within the best day of his life.

Paudeen. And not dead at all! We'll be marching to attack Dublin itself within a week. The horn will blow for him, and all good men will gather to him. Hurry on, Father, and waken him.

Father John. I will not waken him. I will not bring him back from where he is.

Johnny. And how long will it be before he will waken of himself?

Father John. Maybe to-day, maybe to-morrow, it is hard to be certain.

Biddy. If it is *away* he is, he might be away seven years. To be lying like a stump of a tree and using no food and the world not able to knock a word out of him, I know the signs of it well.

Johnny. We cannot be waiting and watching through seven years. If the business he has started is to be done we have to go on here and now. The time there is any delay, that is the time the Government will get information. Waken him now, Father, and you'll get the blessing of the generations.

Father John. I will not bring him back. God will bring him back in His own good time. For all I know he may be seeing the hidden things of God.

Johnny. He might slip away in his dream. It is best to raise him up now.

Andrew. Waken him, Father John, I thought he was surely dead this time, and what way could I go face Thomas through all that is left of my lifetime, after me standing up to face him the way I did? And if I do take a little drop of an odd night, sure, I'd be very lonesome if I did not take it. All the world knows it's not for love of what I drink, but for love of the people that do be with me! Waken him, Father, or maybe I would waken him myself. [*Shakes him.*

Father John. Lift your hand from touching him. Leave him to himself and to the power of God.

Johnny. If you will not bring him back why wouldn't we ourselves do it? Go on now, it is best for you to do it yourself.

Father John. I woke him yesterday. He was angry with me, he could not get to the heart of the command.

Johnny. If he did not, he got a command from myself that satisfied him, and a message.

Father John. He did—he took it from you—and how do I know what devil's message it may have been that brought him into that devil's work, destruction and drunkenness and burnings? That was not a message from Heaven! It was I awoke him, it was I kept him from hearing what was maybe a divine message, a voice of truth, and he heard you speak and he believed the message was brought by you.

You have made use of your deceit and his mistaking—you have left him without house or means to support him, you are striving to destroy and to drag him to entire ruin. I will not help you, I would rather see him die in his trance and go into God's hands than awake him and see him go into Hell's mouth with vagabonds and outcasts like you!

Johnny [*turning to Biddy*]. You should have knowledge, Biddy Lally, of the means to bring back a man that is away.

Biddy. The power of the earth will do it through its herbs, and the power of the air will do it kindling fire into flame.

Johnny. Rise up and make no delay. Stretch out and gather a handful of an herb that will bring him back from whatever place he is in.

Biddy. Where is the use of herbs, and his teeth clenched the way he could not use them?

Johnny. Take fire so, in the Devil's name, and put it to the soles of his feet.   [*Takes a lighted sod from fire.*

Father John. Let him alone, I say!   [*Dashes away the sod.*

Johnny. I will not leave him alone! I will not give in to leave him swooning there and the country waiting for him to awake!

Father John. I tell you I awoke him! I sent him into thieves' company! I will not have him wakened again and evil things, it may be, waiting to take hold of him! Back from him, back, I say! Will you dare to lay a hand on me? You cannot do it! You cannot touch him against my will!

Biddy. Mind yourself, do not be bringing us under the curse of the Church.   [*Johnny steps back. Martin moves.*

Father John. It is God has him in His care. It is He is awaking him. [*Martin has risen to his elbow.*] Do not touch him, do not speak to him, he may be hearing great secrets.

Martin. That music, I must go nearer—sweet marvellous music— louder than the trampling of the unicorns; far louder, though the mountain is shaking with their feet—high joyous music.

Father John. Hush, he is listening to the music of Heaven!

Martin. Take me to you, musicians, wherever you are! I will go nearer to you; I hear you better now, more and more joyful; that is strange, it is strange.

Father John. He is getting some secret.

Martin. It is the music of Paradise, that is certain, somebody said that. It is certainly the music of Paradise. Ah, now I hear, now I understand. It is made of the continual clashing of swords!

Johnny. That is the best music. We will clash them sure enough. We will clash our swords and our pikes on the bayonets of the red soldiers. It is well you rose up from the dead to lead us! Come on, now, come on!

Martin. Who are you? Ah, I remember—where are you asking me to come to?

Paudeen. To come on, to be sure, to the attack on the barracks at Aughanish. To carry on the work you took in hand last night.

Martin. What work did I take in hand last night? O yes, I remember—some big house—we burned it down—but I had not understood the vision when I did that. I had not heard the command right. That was not the work I was sent to do.

Paudeen. Rise up now and bid us what to do. Your great name itself will clear the road before you. It is you yourself will have freed all Ireland before the stooks will be in stacks!

Martin. Listen, I will explain—I have misled you. It is only now I have the whole vision plain. As I lay there I saw through everything, I know all. It was but a frenzy, that going out to burn and to destroy. What have I to do with the foreign army? What I have to pierce is the wild heart of time. My business is not reformation but revelation.

Johnny. If you are going to turn back now from leading us, you are no better than any other traitor that ever gave up the work he took in hand. Let you come and face now the two hundred men you brought out daring the power of the Law last night, and give them your reason for failing them.

Martin. I was mistaken when I set out to destroy Church and Law. The battle we have to fight is fought out in our own mind. There is a fiery moment, perhaps once in a lifetime, and in that moment we see the only thing that matters. It is in that moment the great battles are lost and won, for in that moment we are a part of the host of Heaven.

Paudeen. Have you betrayed us to the naked hangman with your promise and with your drink? If you brought us out here to fail us and to ridicule us, it is the last day you will live!

Johnny. The curse of my heart on you! It would be right to send you to your own place on the flagstone of the traitors in Hell. When once I have made an end of you I will be as well satisfied to be going to my death for it as if I was going home!

Martin. Father John, Father John, can you not hear? Can you not see? Are you blind? Are you deaf?

Father John. What is it? What is it?

Martin. There on the mountain, a thousand white unicorns trampling; a thousand riders with their swords drawn—the swords clashing! O, the sound of the swords, the sound of the clashing of the swords!

[He goes slowly off stage. Johnny takes up a stone to throw at him.

Father John [seizing his arm]. Stop—do you not see he is beyond the world?

Biddy. Keep your hand off him, Johnny Bocach. If he is gone wild and cracked, that's natural. Those that have been wakened from a trance on a sudden are apt to go bad and light in the head.

Paudeen. If it is madness is on him, it is not he himself should pay the penalty.

Biddy. To prey on the mind it does, and rises into the head. There are some would go over any height and would have great power in their madness. It is maybe to some secret cleft he is going, to get knowledge of the great cure for all things, or of the Plough that was hidden in the old times, the Golden Plough.

Paudeen. It seemed as if he was talking through honey. He had the look of one that had seen great wonders. It is maybe among the old heroes of Ireland he went, raising armies for our help.

Father John. God take him in His care and keep him from lying spirits and from all delusions!

Johnny. We have got candles here, Father. We had them to put around his body. Maybe they would keep away the evil things of the air.

Paudeen. Light them so, and he will say out a Mass for him the same as in a lime-washed church. *[They light the candles.*

Thomas comes in

Thomas. Where is he? I am come to warn him. The destruction he did in the night-time has been heard of. The soldiers are out after him, and the constables—there are two of the constables not far off—there are others on every side—they heard he was here in the mountain—where is he?

Father John. He has gone up the path.

Thomas. Hurray after him! Tell him to hide himself—this attack he had a hand in is a hanging crime. Tell him to hide himself, to come to me when all is quiet—bad as his doings are, he is my own brother's son; I will get him on to a ship that will be going to France.

Father John. That will be best; send him back to the Brothers and to the wise Bishops. They can unravel this tangle, I cannot. I cannot be sure of the truth.

Thomas. Here are the constables; he will see them and get away. Say no word. The Lord be praised that he is out of sight.

Constables come in

Constable. The man we are looking for, where is he? He was seen coming here along with you. You have to give him up into the power of the Law.

Johnny. We will not give him up. Go back out of this or you will be sorry.

Paudeen. We are not in dread of you or the like of you.

Biddy. Throw them down over the rocks!

Nanny. Give them to the picking of the crows!

All. Down with the Law!

Father John. Hush! He is coming back. [*To Constables.*] Stop, stop—leave him to himself. He is not trying to escape, he is coming towards you.

Paudeen. There is a sort of a brightness about him. I misjudged him calling him a traitor. It is not to this world he belongs at all. He is over on the other side.

Martin [*standing beside the rock where the lighted candles are*]. *Et calix meus inebrians quam praeclarus est!*

Father John. I must know what he has to say. It is not from himself he is speaking.

Martin. Father John, Heaven is not what we have believed it to be. It is not quiet, it is not singing and making music, and all strife at an end. I have seen it, I have been there. The lover still loves, but with a greater passion, and the rider still rides, but the horse goes like the wind and leaps the ridges, and the battle goes on always, always. That is the joy of Heaven, continual battle. I thought the battle was here, and that the joy was to be found here on earth, that all one had to do was to bring again the old wild earth of the stories—but no, it is not here; we shall not come to that joy, that battle, till we have put out the senses, everything that can be seen and handled, as I put out this candle. [*He puts out candle.*] We must put out the whole world as I put out this candle [*puts out another candle*]. We must put out the light of the stars and the light of the sun and the light of the moon [*puts out the rest of the candles*], till we have brought everything to nothing once again. I saw in a broken vision, but now all is clear to me. Where there is nothing, where there is nothing—there is God!

Constable. Now we will take him!

Johnny. We will never give him up to the Law!

Paudeen. Make your escape! We will not let you be followed.

[*They struggle with Constables; the women help them; all disappear struggling. There is a shot. Martin stumbles and falls. Beggars come back with a shout.*

Johnny. We have done for them; they will not meddle with you again.

Paudeen. O, he is down!

Father John. He is shot through the breast, O, who has dared meddle with a soul that was in the tumults on the threshold of sanctity?

Johnny. It was that gun went off and I striking it from the constable's hand.

Martin [*looking at his hand, on which there is blood*]. Ah, that is blood! I fell among the rocks. It is a hard climb. It is a long climb to the vineyards of Eden. Help me up. I must go on. The Mountain of Abiegnos is very high—but the vineyards—the vineyards!

[*He falls back dead. The men uncover their heads.*

Paudeen [*to Biddy*]. It was you misled him with your foretelling that he was coming within the best day of his life.

Johnny. Madness on him or no madness, I will not leave that body to the Law to be buried with a dog's burial or brought away and maybe hanging upon a tree. Lift him on the sacks, bring him away to the quarry; it is there on the hillside the boys will give him a great burying, coming on horses and bearing white rods in their hands.

[*Nanny lays the velvet cloak over him. They lift him and carry the body away singing:*

'Our hope and our darling, our heart dies with you,
You to have failed us, we are foals astray!'

Father John. He is gone and we can never know where that vision came from. I cannot know—the wise Bishops would have known.

Thomas [*taking up banner*]. To be shaping a lad through his lifetime, and he to go his own way at the last, and a queer way. It is very queer the world itself is, whatever shape was put upon it at the first.

Andrew. To be too headstrong and too open, that is the beginning of trouble. To keep to yourself the thing that you know, and to do in quiet the thing you want to do. There would be no disturbance at all in the world, all people to bear that in mind!

THE END

THE PLAYER QUEEN

1922

THE PLAYER QUEEN

PERSONS IN THE PLAY

Decima
Septimus
Nona
The Queen
The Prime Minister
The Bishop

The Stage Manager
The Tapster
An Old Beggar
Old Men, Old Women, Citizens,
    Countrymen, Players, etc.

SCENE I: *An open space at the meeting of three streets*

SCENE II: *The Throne-Room*

SCENE I

An open space at the meeting of three streets. One can see for some way down one of these streets, and at some little distance it turns, showing a bare piece of wall lighted by a hanging lamp. Against this lighted wall are silhouetted the heads and shoulders of two Old Men. They are leaning from the upper windows, one on either side of the street. They wear grotesque masks. A little to one side of the stage is a great stone for mounting a horse from. The houses have knockers.

First Old Man. Can you see the Queen's castle? You have better sight than I.

Second Old Man. I can just see it rising over the tops of the houses yonder on its great rocky hill.

First Old Man. Is the dawn breaking? Is it touching the tower?

Second Old Man. It is beginning to break upon the tower, but these narrow streets will be dark for a long while. [*A pause.*] Do you hear anything? You have better hearing than I.

First Old Man. No, all is quiet.

Second Old Man. At least fifty passed by an hour since, a crowd of fifty men walking rapidly.

First Old Man. Last night was very quiet, not a sound, not a breath.

Second Old Man. And not a thing to be seen till the Tapster's old dog came down the street upon this very hour from Cooper Malachi's ash-pit.

First Old Man. Hush, I hear feet, many feet. Perhaps they are coming this way. [*Pause.*] No, they are going the other way, they are gone now.

Second Old Man. The young are at some mischief,—the young and the middle-aged.

First Old Man. Why can't they stay in their beds, and they can sleep too—seven hours, eight hours? I mind the time when I could sleep ten hours. They will know the value of sleep when they are near upon ninety years.

Second Old Man. They will never live so long. They have not the health and strength that we had. They wear themselves out. They are always in a passion about something or other.

First Old Man. Hush! I hear a step now, and it is coming this way. We had best pull in our heads. The world has grown very wicked and there is no knowing what they might do to us or say to us.

Second Old Man. Yes, better shut the windows and pretend to be asleep.

[*They pull in their heads. One hears a knocker being struck in the distance, then a pause, and a knocker is struck close at hand. Another pause, and Septimus, a handsome man of thirty-five, staggers on to the stage. He is very drunk.*

Septimus. An uncharitable place, an unchristian place. [*He begins banging at a knocker.*] Open there, open there. I want to come in and sleep. [*A third Old Man puts his head from an upper window.*

Third Old Man. Who are you? What do you want?

Septimus. I am Septimus. I have a bad wife. I want to come in and sleep.

Third Old Man. You are drunk.

Septimus. Drunk! So would you be if you had as bad a wife.

Third Old Man. Go away. [*He shuts the window.*

Septimus. Is there not one Christian in this town? [*He begins hammering the knocker of First Old Man, but there is no answer.*] No one there? All dead or drunk maybe—bad wives! There must be one Christian man.

[*He hammers a knocker at the other side of the stage. An Old Woman puts her head out of the window above.*

Old Woman [*in a shrill voice*]. Who's there? What do you want? Has something happened?

Septimus. Yes, that's it. Something has happened. My wife has hid herself, has run away, or has drowned herself.

Old Woman. What do I care about your wife? You are drunk.

Septimus. Not care about my wife! But I tell you that my wife has to play by order of the Prime Minister before all the people in the great hall of the Castle precisely at noon, and she cannot be found.

Old Woman. Go away, go away! I tell you, go away.

[She shuts the window.

Septimus. Treat Septimus, who has played before Kubla Khan, like this! Septimus, dramatist and poet! [*The Old Woman opens the window again and empties a jug of water over him.*] Water! drenched to the skin—must sleep in the street. [*Lies down.*] Bad wife—others have had bad wives, but others were not left to lie down in the open street under the stars, drenched with cold water, a whole jug of cold water, shivering in the pale light of the dawn, to be run over, to be trampled upon, to be eaten by dogs, and all because their wives have hidden themselves.

Enter two Men a little older than Septimus.
They stand still and gaze into the sky

First Man. Ah, my friend, the little fair-haired one is a minx.

Second Man. Never trust fair hair—I will have nothing but brown hair.

First Man. They have kept us too long—brown or fair.

Second Man. What are you staring at?

First Man. At the first streak of the dawn on the Castle tower.

Second Man. I would not have my wife find out for the world.

Septimus [*sitting up*]. Carry me, support me, drag me, roll me, pull me, or sidle me along, but bring me where I may sleep in comfort. Bring me to a stable—my Saviour was content with a stable.

First Man. Who are you? I don't know your face.

Septimus. I am Septimus, a player, a playwright, and the most famous poet in the world.

Second Man. That name, sir, is unknown to me.

Septimus. Unknown?

Second Man. But my name will not be unknown to you. I am called Peter of the Purple Pelican, after the best known of my poems, and my friend is called Happy Tom. He also is a poet.

Septimus. Bad, popular poets.

Second Man. You would be a popular poet if you could.

Septimus. Bad, popular poets.

First Man. Lie where you are if you can't be civil.

Septimus. What do I care for any one now except Venus and Adonis and the other planets of heaven?

Second Man. You can enjoy their company for yourself.

[The two Men go out.

Septimus. Robbed, so to speak; naked, so to speak—bleeding, so to speak—and they pass by on the other side of the street.

[*A crowd of Citizens and Countrymen enter. At first only a few, and then more and more till the stage is filled by an excited crowd.*

First Citizen. There is a man lying here.

Second Citizen. Roll him over.

First Citizen. He is one of those players who are housed at the Castle. They arrived yesterday.

Second Citizen. Drunk, I suppose. He'll be killed or maimed by the first milk-cart.

Third Citizen. Better roll him into the corner. If we are in for a bloody day's business, there is no need for him to be killed—an unnecessary death might bring a curse upon us.

First Citizen. Give me a hand here.   [*They begin rolling Septimus.*

Septimus [*muttering*]. Not allowed to sleep! Rolled off the street! Shoved into a stony place! Unchristian town!

[*He is left lying at the foot of the wall to one side of the stage.*

Third Citizen. Are we all friends here, are we all agreed?

First Citizen. These men are from the country. They came in last night. They know little of the business. They won't be against the people, but they want to know more.

First Countryman. Yes, that is it. We are with the people, but we want to know more.

Second Countryman. We want to know all, but we are with the people.

[*Other voices take up the words,* 'We want to know all, but we are with the people', *etc. There is a murmur of voices together.*

Third Citizen. Have you ever seen the Queen, countryman?

First Countryman. No.

Third Citizen. Our Queen is a witch, a bad evil-living witch, and we will have her no longer for Queen.

Third Countryman. I would be slow to believe her father's daughter a witch.

Third Citizen. Have you ever seen the Queen, countryman?

Third Countryman. No.

Third Citizen. Nor has any one else. Not a man here has set eyes on her. For seven years she has been shut up in that great black house on the great rocky hill. From the day her father died she has been there with the doors shut on her, but we know now why she has hidden herself. She has no good companions in the dark night.

Third Countryman. In my district they say that she is a holy woman and prays for us all.

Third Citizen. That story has been spread about by the Prime Minister. He has spies everywhere spreading stories. He is a crafty man.

First Countryman. It is true, they always deceive us country people.

We are not educated like the people of the town.

A Big Countryman. The Bible says, Suffer not a witch to live. Last Candlemas twelvemonth I strangled a witch with my own hands.

Third Citizen. When she is dead we will make the Prime Minister King.

Second Citizen. No, no, he is not a king's son.

Second Countryman. I'd send a bellman through the world. There are many kings in Arabia, they say.

Third Countryman. The people must be talking. If you and I were to hide ourselves, or to be someway hard to understand, maybe they would put some bad name on us. I am not against the people, but I want testimony.

Third Citizen. Come, Tapster, stand up there on the stone and tell what you know.   [*The Tapster climbs up on the mounting-stone.*

Tapster. I live in the quarter where her Castle is. The garden of my house and the gardens of all the houses in my row run right up to the rocky hill that has her Castle on the top. There is a lad in my quarter that has a goat in his garden.

First Citizen. That's Strolling Michael—I know him.

Tapster. That goat is always going astray. Strolling Michael got out of his bed early one morning to go snaring birds, and nowhere could he see that goat. So he began climbing up the rock, and up and up he went, till he was close under the wall, and there he found the goat and it shaking and sweating as though something had scared it. Presently he heard a thing neigh like a horse, and after that a something like a white horse ran by, but it was no horse, but a unicorn. He had his pistol, for he had thought to bring down a rabbit, and seeing it rushing at him as he imagined, he fired at the unicorn. It vanished all in a moment, but there was blood on a great stone.

Third Citizen. Seeing what company she keeps in the small hours, what wonder that she never sets foot out of doors!

Third Countryman. I wouldn't believe all that night rambler says—boys are liars. All that we have against her for certain is that she won't put her foot out of doors. I knew a man once that when he was five-and-twenty refused to get out of his bed. He wasn't ill—no, not he, but he said life was a vale of tears, and for forty and four years till they carried him out to the churchyard he never left that bed. All tried him—parson tried him, priest tried him, doctor tried him, and all he'd say was, 'Life is a vale of tears'. It's too snug he was in his bed, and believe me, that ever since she has had no father to rout her out of a morning she has been in her bed, and small blame to her maybe.

The Big Countryman. But that's the very sort that are witches. They know where to find their own friends in the lonely hours of the night.

There was a witch in my own district that I strangled last Candlemas twelvemonth. She had an imp in the shape of a red cat, that sucked three drops of blood from her poll every night a little before the cock crew. It's with their blood they feed them; until they have been fed with the blood they are images and shadows; but when they have it drunk they can be for a while stronger than you or me.

Third Countryman. The man I knew was no witch, he was no way active. 'Life is a vale of tears,' he said. Parson tried him, doctor tried him, priest tried him—but that was all he'd say.

First Citizen. We'd have no man go beyond evidence and reason, but hear the Tapster out, and when you have you'll say that we cannot leave her alive this day—no, not for one day longer.

Tapster. It's not a story that I like to be telling, but you are all married men. Another night that boy climbed up after his goat, and it was an hour earlier by his clock and no light in the sky, and when he came to the Castle wall he clambered along the wall among the rocks and bushes till he saw a light from a little window over his head. It was an old wall full of holes, where mortar had fallen out, and he climbed up, putting his toes into the holes, till he could look in through the window; and when he looked in, what did he see but the Queen!

First Countryman. And did he say what she was like?

Tapster. He saw more than that. He saw her coupling with a great white unicorn.   [*Murmurs among the crowd.*

Second Countryman. I will not have the son of the unicorn to reign over us, although you will tell me he would be no more than half a unicorn.

First Countryman. I'll not go against the people, but I'd let her live if the Prime Minister promised to rout her out of bed in the morning and to set a guard to drive off the unicorn.

The Big Countryman. I have strangled an old witch with these two hands, and to-day, I will strangle a young witch.

Septimus [*who has slowly got up and climbed up on to the mounting-stone which the Tapster has left*]. Did I hear somebody say that the Unicorn is not chaste? It is a most noble beast, a most religious beast. It has a milk-white skin and milk-white horn, and milk-white hooves, but a mild blue eye, and it dances in the sun. I will have no one speak against it, not while I am still upon the earth. It is written in 'The Great Beastery of Paris' that it is chaste, that it is the most chaste of all the beasts in the world.

The Big Countryman. Pull him out of that, he's drunk.

Septimus. Yes, I am drunk, I am very drunk, but that is no reason why I should permit any one to speak against the Unicorn.

Second Citizen. Let's hear him out. We can do nothing till the sun's up.

Septimus. Nobody shall speak against the Unicorn. No, my friends and poets, nobody. I will hunt it if you will, though it is a dangerous and cross-grained beast. Much virtue has made it cross-grained. I will go with you to the high tablelands of Africa where it lives, and we will there shoot it through the head, but I will not speak against its character, and if any man declares it is not chaste I will fight him, for I affirm that its chastity is equal to its beauty.

The Big Countryman. He is most monstrously drunk.

Septimus. No longer drunk, but inspired.

Second Citizen. Go on, go on, we'll never hear the like again.

The Big Countryman. Come away. I've enough of this—we have work to do.

Septimus. Go away, did you say, and my breast-feathers thrust out and my white wings buoyed up with divinity? Ah! but I can see it now— you are bent upon going to some lonely place where uninterrupted you can speak against the character of the Unicorn, but you shall not, I tell you that you shall not. [*He comes down off the stone and squares up at the crowd which tries to pass him.*] In the midst of this uncharitable town I will protect that noble, milk-white, flighty beast.

The Big Countryman. Let me pass.

Septimus. No, I will not let you pass.

First Countryman. Leave him alone.

Second Countryman. No violence—it might bring ill-luck upon us.

> [*They try to hold back the Big Countryman.*

Septimus. I will oppose your passing to the death. For I will not have it said that there is a smirch, or a blot, upon the most milky whiteness of an heroic brute that bathes by the sound of tabors at the rising of the sun and the rising of the moon, and the rising of the Great Bear, and above all, it shall not be said, whispered, or in any wise published abroad by you that stand there, so to speak, between two washings; for you were doubtless washed when you were born, and, it may be, shall be washed again after you are dead.

> [*The Big Countryman knocks him down.*

First Citizen. You have killed him.

The Big Countryman. Maybe I have, maybe I have not—let him lie there. A witch I strangled last Candlemas twelvemonth, a witch I will strange to-day. What do I care for the likes of him?

Third Citizen. Come round to the east quarter of the town. The basket-makers and the sieve-makers will be out by this.

Fourth Citizen. It is a short march from there to the Castle gate.

> [*They go up one of the side streets, but return quickly in confusion and fear.*

First Citizen. Are you sure that you saw him?

Second Citizen. Who could mistake that horrible old man?

Third Citizen. I was standing by him when the ghost spoke out of him seven years ago.

First Countryman. I never saw him before. He has never been in my district. I don't rightly know what sort he is, but I have heard of him, many a time I have heard of him.

First Citizen. His eyes become glassy, and that is the trance growing upon him, and when he is in the trance his soul slips away and a ghost takes its place and speaks out of him—a strange ghost.

Third Citizen. I was standing by him the last time. 'Get me straw,' said that old man, 'my back itches.' Then all of a sudden he lay down, with his eyes wide open and glassy, and he brayed like a donkey. At that moment the King died and the King's daughter was Queen.

First Countryman. They say it is the donkey that carried Christ into Jerusalem, and that is why it knows its rightful sovereign. He goes begging about the country and there is no man dare refuse him what he asks.

The Big Countryman. Then it is certain nobody will take my hand off her throat. I will make my grip tighter. He will be lying down on the straw and he will bray, and when he brays she will be dead.

First Countryman. Look! There he is coming over the top of the hill, and the mad look upon him.

Second Countryman. I wouldn't face him for the world this night. Come round to the market-place, we'll be less afraid in a big place.

The Big Countryman. I'm not afraid, but I'll go with you till I get my hand on her throat.

> [*They all go out but Septimus. Presently Septimus sits up; his head is bleeding. He rubs with his fingers his broken head and looks at the blood on his fingers.*

Septimus. Unchristian town! First I am, so to speak, thrown out into the street, and then I am all but murdered; and I drunk, and therefore in need of protection. All creatures are in need of protection at some time or other. Even my wife was once a frail child in need of milk, of smiles, of love, as if in the midst of a flood, in danger of drowning, so to speak.

> [*An Old Beggar with long matted hair and beard and in ragged clothes comes in.*

The Old Beggar. I want straw.

Septimus. Happy Tom and Peter of the Purple Pelican have done it all. They are bad, popular poets, and being jealous of my fame, they have stirred up the people. [*He catches sight of the Old Beggar.*]

There is a certain medicine which is made by distilling camphor, Peruvian bark, spurge and mandrake, and mixing all with twelve ounces of dissolved pearls and four ounces of the oil of gold; and this medicine is infallible to stop the flow of blood. Have you any of it, old man?

The Old Beggar. I want straw.

Septimus. I can see that you have not got it, but no matter, we shall be friends.

The Old Beggar. I want straw to lie down on.

Septimus. It is no doubt better that I should bleed to death. For that way, my friend, I shall disgrace Happy Tom and Peter of the Purple Pelican, but it is necessary that I shall die somewhere where my last words can be taken down. I am therefore in need of your support.

[*Having got up he now staggers over to the Old Beggar and leans upon him.*

The Old Beggar. Don't you know who I am—aren't you afraid? When something comes inside me, my back itches. Then I must lie down and roll, and then I bray and the crown changes.

Septimus. Ah! you are inspired. Then we are indeed brothers. Come, I will rest upon your shoulder and we will mount the hill side by side. I will sleep in the Castle of the Queen.

The Old Beggar. You will give me straw to lie upon?

Septimus. Asphodels! Yet, indeed, the asphodel is a flower much over-rated by the classic authors. Still if a man has a preference, I say, for the asphodel——

[*They go out and one hears the voice of Septimus murmuring in the distance about asphodels.*

[*The First Old Man opens his window and taps with his crutch at the opposite window. The Second Old Man opens his window.*

First Old Man. It is all right now. They are all gone. We can have our talk out.

Second Old Man. The whole Castle is lit by the dawn now, and it will begin to grow brighter in the street.

First Old Man. It's time for the Tapster's old dog to come down the street.

Second Old Man. Yesterday he had a bone in his mouth.

SCENE II

The Throne-Room in the Castle. Between pillars are gilded openwork doors, except at one side, where there is a large window. The morning light is slanting through the window, making dark shadows among the

*pillars. As the scene goes on, the light, at first feeble, becomes strong
and suffused, and the shadows disappear. Through the openwork doors
one can see down long passages, and one of these passages plainly leads
into the open air. One can see daylight at the end of it. There is a
throne in the centre of the room and a flight of steps that leads to it.*

*The Prime Minister, an elderly man with an impatient manner and
voice, is talking to a group of Players, among whom is Nona, a fair,
comely, comfortable-looking young woman of perhaps thirty-five; she
seems to take the lead.*

Prime Minister. I will not be trifled with. I chose the play myself; I
 chose 'The Tragical History of Noah's Deluge' because when Noah
 beats his wife to make her go into the Ark everybody understands,
 everybody is pleased, everybody recognises the mulish obstinacy of
 their own wives, sweethearts, sisters. And now, when it is of the
 greatest importance to the State that everybody should be pleased,
 the play cannot be given. The leading lady is lost, you say, and there
 is some unintelligible reason why nobody can take her place; but I
 know what you are all driving at—you object to the play I have
 chosen. You want some dull, poetical thing, full of long speeches.
 I will have that play and no other. The rehearsal must begin at once
 and the performance take place at noon punctually.

Nona. We have searched all night, sir, and we cannot find her anywhere. She was heard to say that she would drown rather than play
 a woman older than thirty. Seeing that Noah's wife is a very old
 woman, we are afraid that she has drowned herself indeed.

 [*Decima, a very pretty woman, puts her head out from under the
 throne where she has been lying hidden.*

Prime Minister. Nonsense! It is all a conspiracy. Your manager should
 be here. He is responsible. You can tell him when he does come that
 if the play is not performed, I will clap him into gaol for a year and
 pitch the rest of you over the border.

Nona. O, sir, he couldn't help it. She does whatever she likes.

Prime Minister. Does whatever she likes—I know her sort; would pull
 the world to pieces to spite her husband or her lover. I know her—a
 bladder full of dried peas for a brain, a brazen, bragging baggage.
 Of course he couldn't help it, but what do I care? [*Decima pulls in
 her head.*] To gaol he goes—somebody has got to go to gaol. Go and
 cry her name everywhere. Away with you! Let me hear you cry it
 out. Call the baggage. Louder. Louder. [*The Players go out crying,
 'Where are you, Decima?'*] O, Adam! why did you fall asleep in the
 garden? You might have known that, while you were lying there
 helpless, the Old Man in the Sky would play some prank upon
 you.

[*The Queen, who is young, with an ascetic timid face, enters in a badly fitting state dress.*

Ah!

Queen. I will show myself to the angry people as you have bidden me. I am almost certain that I am ready for martyrdom. I have prayed all night. Yes, I am almost certain.

Prime Minister. Ah!

Queen. I have now attained to the age of my patroness, Holy Saint Octema, when she was martyred at Antioch. You will remember that her unicorn was so pleased at the spectacle of her austerity that he caracoled in his excitement. Thereupon she dropped out of the saddle and was trampled to death under the feet of the mob. Indeed, but for the unicorn, the mob would have killed her long before.

Prime Minister. No, you will not be martyred. I have a plan to settle that. I will stop their anger with a word. Who made that dress?

Queen. It was my mother's dress. She wore it at her coronation. I would not have a new one made. I do not deserve new clothes. I am always committing sin.

Prime Minister. Is there sin in an egg that has never been hatched, that has never been warmed, in a chalk egg?

Queen. I wish I could resemble Holy Saint Octema in everything.

Prime Minister. What a dress! It is too late now. Nothing can be done. It may appear right to those on the edge of the crowd. The others must be conquered by charm, dignity, royal manner. As for the dress, I must think of some excuse, some explanation. Remember that they have never seen your face, and you will put them in a bad humour if you hang your head in that dumbfounded way.

Queen. I wish I could return to my prayers.

Prime Minister. Walk! Permit me to see your Majesty walk. No, no, no. Be more majestic. Ah! If you had known the queens I have known—they had a way with them. Morals of a dragoon, but a way, a way! Put on a kind of eagle look, a vulture look.

Queen. There are cobble-stones—if I might go barefoot it would be a blessed penance. It was especially the bleeding feet of Saint Octema that gave pleasure to the unicorn.

Prime Minister. Sleep of Adam! Barefoot—barefoot, did you say? [*A pause.*] There is not time to take off your shoes and stockings. If you were to look out of the window there, you would see the crowd becoming wickeder every minute. Come! [*He gives his arm to the Queen.*]

Queen. You have a plan to stop their anger so that I shall not be martyred?

Prime Minister. My plan will be disclosed before the face of the people and there alone.   [*They go out.*

[*Nona comes in with a bottle of wine and a boiled lobster and lays them on the middle of the floor. She puts her finger on her lip and stands in the doorway towards the back of the stage.*

Decima [*comes cautiously out of her hiding-place singing*].

'He went away', my mother sang,
'When I was brought to bed.'
And all the while her needle pulled
The gold and silver thread.

She pulled the thread and bit the thread
And made a golden gown,
She wept because she had dreamt that I
Was born to wear a crown.

[*She is just reaching her hand for the lobster when Nona comes forward holding out towards her the dress and mask of Noah's wife which she has been carrying over her left arm.*

Nona. Thank God you are found! [*Getting between her and the lobster.*] No, not until you have put on this dress and mask. I have caught you now, and you are not going to hide again.

Decima. Very well, when I have had my breakfast.

Nona. Not a mouthful till you are dressed ready for the rehearsal.

Decima. Do you know what song I was singing just now?

Nona. It is that song you're always singing. Septimus made it up.

Decima. It is the song of the mad singing daughter of a harlot. The only song she had. Her father was a drunken sailor waiting for the full tide, and yet she thought her mother had foretold that she would marry a prince and become a great queen. [*Singing.*]

'When she was got', my mother sang,
'I heard a seamew cry,
I saw a flake of yellow foam
That dropped upon my thigh.'

How therefore could she help but braid
The gold upon my hair,
And dream that I should carry
The golden top of care?

The moment ago as I lay here I thought I could play a queen's part, a great queen's part; the only part in the world I can play is a great queen's part.

Nona. You play a queen's part? You that were born in a ditch between two towns and wrapped in a sheet that was stolen from a hedge.

Decima. The Queen cannot play at all, but I could play so well. I could bow with my whole body down to my ankles and could be stern when hard looks were in season. O, I would know how to put all summer in a look and after that all winter in a voice.

Nona. Low comedy is what you are fit for.

Decima. I understood all this in a wink of the eye, and then just when I am saying to myself that I was born to sit up there with soldiers and courtiers, you come shaking in front of me that mask and that dress. I am not to eat my breakfast unless I play an old peaky-chinned, drop-nosed harridan that a foul husband beats with a stick because she won't clamber among the other brutes into his cattle-boat. [*She makes a dart at the lobster.*]

Nona. No, no, not a drop, not a mouthful till you have put these on. Remember that if there is no play Septimus must go to prison.

Decima. Would they give him dry bread to eat?

Nona. They would.

Decima. And water to drink and nothing in the water?

Nona. They would.

Decima. And a straw bed?

Nona. They would, and only a little straw maybe.

Decima. And iron chains that clanked.

Nona. They would.

Decima. And keep him there for a whole week?

Nona. A month maybe.

Decima. And he would say to the turnkey, 'I am here because of my beautiful cruel wife, my beautiful flighty wife'?

Nona. He might not, he'd be sober.

Decima. But he'd think it, and every time he was hungry, every time he was thirsty, every time he felt the hardness of the stone floor, every time he heard the chains clank, he would think it, and every time he thought it I would become more beautiful in his eyes.

Nona. No, he would hate you.

Decima. Little do you know what the love of man is. If that Holy Image of the church where you put all those candles at Easter was pleasant and affable, why did you come home with the skin worn off your two knees?

Nona [*in tears*]. I understand—you cruel, bad woman!—you won't play the part at all, and all that Septimus may go to prison, and he a great genius that can't take care of himself.

[*Seeing Nona distracted with tears Decima makes a dart and almost gets the lobster.*

Nona. No, no! Not a mouthful, not a drop. I will break the bottle if
you go near it. There is not another woman in the world would treat
a man like that, and you were sworn to him in church—yes, you
were, there is no good denying it. [*Decima makes another dart, but
Nona, who is still in tears, puts the lobster in her pocket.*] Leave the
food alone; not one mouthful will you get. I have never sworn to
a man in church, but if I did swear, I would not treat him like a
tinker's donkey—before God I would not—I was properly brought
up; my mother always told me it was no light thing to take a man
in church.

Decima. You are in love with my husband.

Nona. Because I don't want to see him gaoled you say I am in love
with him. Only a woman with no heart would think one can't be
sorry for a man without being in love with him—a woman who
has never been sorry for anybody! But I won't have him gaoled;
if you won't play the part I'll play it myself.

Decima. When I married him, I made him swear never to play with
anybody but me, and well you know it.

Nona. Only this once, and in a part nobody can do anything with.

Decima. That is the way it begins, and all the time you would be saying things the audience couldn't hear.

Nona. Septimus will break his oath, and I have learnt the part. Every
line of it.

Decima. Septimus would not break his oath for anybody in the world.

Nona. There is one person in the world for whom he will break his
oath.

Decima. What have you in your head now?

Nona. He will break it for me.

Decima. You are crazy.

Nona. Maybe I have my secrets.

Decima. What are you keeping back? Have you been sitting in corners
with Septimus? giving him sympathy because of the bad wife he
has, and all the while he has sat there to have the pleasure of talking
about me?

Nona. You think that you have his every thought because you are a
devil.

Decima. Because I am a devil I have his every thought. You know how
his own song runs. The man speaks first—[*singing*]

> Put off that mask of burning gold
> With emerald eyes,

and then the woman answers—

> O no, my dear, you make so bold
> To find if hearts be wild and wise
> And yet not cold.

Nona. His every thought—that is a lie. He forgets all about you the moment you're out of his sight.

Decima. Then look what I carry under my bodice. This is a poem praising me, all my beauties one after the other—eyes, hair, complexion, shape, disposition, mind—everything. And there are a great many verses to it. And here is a little one he gave me yesterday morning. I had turned him out of bed and he had to lie alone by himself.

Nona. Alone by himself!

Decima. And as he lay there alone, unable to sleep, he made it up, wishing that he were blind so as not to be troubled by looking at my beauty. Hear how it goes! [*sings again*]

> O would that I were an old beggar
> Without a friend on this earth
> But a thieving rascally cur,
> A beggar blind from his birth;
> Or anything else but a man
> Lying alone on a bed
> Remembering a woman's beauty,
> Alone with a crazy head.

Nona. Alone in his bed indeed. I know that long poem, that one with all the verses; I know it to my hurt, though I haven't read a word of it. Four lines in every verse, four beats in every line, and fourteen verses—my curse upon it!

Decima [*taking out a manuscript from her bodice*]. Yes, fourteen verses. There are numbers to them.

Nona. You have another there—ten verses all in fours and threes.

Decima [*looking at another manuscript*]. Yes, the verses are in fours and threes. But how do you know all this? I carry them here. They are a secret between him and me, and nobody can see them till they have lain a long while upon my heart.

Nona. They have lain upon your heart, but they were made upon my shoulder. Ay, and down along my spine in the small hours of the morning; so many beats a line, and for every beat a tap of the fingers.

Decima. My God!

Nona. That one with the fourteen verses kept me from my sleep two

hours, and when the lines were finished he lay upon his back another
hour waving one arm in the air, making up the music. I liked him
well enough to seem to be asleep through it all, and many another
poem too—but when he made up that short one you sang he was so
pleased that he muttered the words all about his lying alone in his
bed thinking of you, and that made me mad. So I said to him, 'Am
I not beautiful? Turn round and look.' O, I cut it short, for even I
can please a man when there is but one candle. [*She takes a pair
of scissors that are hanging round her neck and begins snipping at
the dress for Noah's wife.*] And now you know why I can play the
part in spite of you and not be driven out. Work upon Septimus if
you have a mind for it. Little need I care. I will clip this a trifle
and re-stitch it again—I have a needle and thread ready.

[*The Stage Manager comes in ringing a bell. He is followed by
various players all dressed up in the likeness of various beasts.*
Stage Manager. Put on that mask—get into your clothes. Why are you
standing there as if in a trance?
Nona. Decima and I have talked the matter over and we have settled
that I am to play the part.
Stage Manager. Do as you please. Thank God it's a part that anybody can play. All you have got to do is to copy an old woman's
squeaky voice. We are all here now but Septimus, and we cannot
wait for him. I will read the part of Noah. He will be here before
we are finished, I daresay. We will suppose that the audience is
upon this side, and that the Ark is over there with a gangway for
the beasts to climb. All you beasts are to crowd up on the prompt
side. Lay down Noah's hat and cloak there till Septimus comes. As
the first scene is between Noah and the beasts, you can go on with
your sewing.
Decima. No, I must first be heard. My husband has been spending his
nights with Nona, and that is why she sits clipping and stitching
with that vainglorious air.
Nona. She made him miserable, she knows every trick of breaking a
man's heart—he came to me with his troubles—I seemed to be a
comfort to him, and now—why should I deny it?—he is my lover.
Decima. I will take the vainglory out of her. I have been a plague to
him. O, I have been a badger and a weasel and a hedgehog and
pole-cat, and all because I was dead sick of him. And, thank God!,
she has got him and I am free. I threw away a part and I threw
away a man—she has picked both up.
Stage Manager. It seems to me that it all concerns you two. It's your
business and not ours. I don't see why we should delay the rehearsal.

Decima. I will have no rehearsal yet. I'm too happy now that I am free. I must find somebody who will dance with me for a while. Come, we must have music. [*She picks up a lute which has been laid down amongst some properties.*] You can't all be claws and hoofs.

Stage Manager. We've only an hour and the whole play to go through.

Nona. O, she has taken my scissors, she is only pretending not to care. Look at her! She is mad! Take them away from her! Hold her hand! She is going to kill me or to kill herself. [*To Stage Manager.*] Why don't you interfere? My God! She is going to kill me.

Decima. Here, Peter.

[*She begins cutting through the breast-feathers of the Swan.*

Nona. She is doing it all to stop the rehearsal, out of vengeance; and you stand there and do nothing.

Stage Manager. If you have taken her husband, why didn't you keep the news till the play was over? She is going to make them all mad now, I can see that much in her eyes.

Decima. Now that I have thrown Septimus into her lap, I will choose a new man. Shall it be you, Turkeycock? or you, Bullhead?

Stage Manager. There is nothing to be done. It is all your fault. If Septimus can't manage his wife, it's certain that I can't.

[*He sits down helplessly.*

Decima. Dance, Bullhead, dance—no—no—stop. I will not have you for my man, slow on the feet and heavy of build, and that means jealousy, and there is a sort of melancholy in your voice. What a folly that I should find love nothing, and yet through sympathy with that voice should stretch and yawn as if I loved! Dance, Turkeycock, dance—no, stop. I cannot have you, for my man must be lively on his feet and have a quick eye. I will not have that round eye fixed upon me now that I have sent my mind asleep. Yet what do I care who it is, so that I choose and get done with it? Dance, all dance, and I will choose the best dancer among you. Quick, quick, begin to dance. [*All dance round Decima.*

Decima [*singing*].

> Shall I fancy beast or fowl?
> Queen Pasiphae chose a bull,
> While a passion for a swan
> Made Queen Leda stretch and yawn,
> Wherefore spin ye, whirl ye, dance ye,
> Till Queen Decima's found her fancy.

> *Chorus*
> Wherefore spin ye, whirl ye, dance ye,
> Till Queen Decima's found her fancy.

Decima.

> Spring and straddle, stride and strut,
> Shall I chose a bird or brute?
> Name the feather or the fur
> For my single comforter?

> *Chorus*
> Wherefore spin ye, whirl ye, dance ye,
> Till Queen Decima's found her fancy.

Decima.

> None has found, that found out love,
> Single bird or brute enough;
> Any bird or brute may rest
> An empty head upon my breast.

> *Chorus*
> Wherefore spin ye, whirl ye, dance ye,
> Till Queen Decima's found her fancy.

Stage Manager. Stop, stop, here is Septimus.

Septimus [*the blood still upon his face, and but little soberer*]. Gather about me, for I announce the end of the Christian Era, the coming of a New Dispensation, that of the New Adam, that of the Unicorn; but alas, he is chaste, he hesitates, he hesitates.

Stage Manager. This is not a time for making up speeches for your new play.

Septimus. His unborn children are but images; we merely play with images.

Stage Manager. Let us get on with the rehearsal.

Septimus. No; let us prepare to die. The mob is climbing up the hill with pitchforks to stick into our vitals and burning wisps to set the roof on fire.

First Player [*who has gone to the window*]. My God, it's true. There is a great crowd at the bottom of the hill.

Second Player. But why should they attack us?

Septimus. Because we are the servants of the Unicorn.

Third Player [*at window*]. My God, they have dung-forks and scythes set on poles and they are coming this way.

> [*Many Players gather round the window.*

Septimus [*who has found the bottle and is drinking*]. Some will die like Cato, some like Cicero, some like Demosthenes, triumphing over death in sonorous eloquence, or, like Petronius Arbiter, will tell witty, scandalous tales; but I will speak, no, I will sing, as if the mob did not exist. I will rail upon the Unicorn for his chastity. I will bid him trample mankind to death and beget a new race. I will even put my railing into rhyme, and all shall run sweetly, sweetly, for, even if they blow up the floor with gunpowder, they are merely the mob.

Upon the round blue eye I rail,
Damnation on the milk-white horn.

A telling sound, a sound to linger in the ear—hale, tale, bale, gale— my God, I am even too sober to find a rhyme! [*He drinks and then picks up a lute*]—a tune that my murderers may remember my last words and croon them to their grandchildren.

[*For the next few speeches he is busy making his tune.*

First Player. The players of this town are jealous. Have we not been chosen before them all, because we are the most famous players in the world? It is they who have stirred up the mob.

Second Player. It is of me they are jealous. They know what happened at Xanadu. At the end of that old play 'The Fall of Troy' Kubla Khan sent for me and said that he would give his kingdom for such a voice, and for such a presence. I stood before him dressed as Agamemnon just as when in a great scene at the end I had re-proached Helen for all the misery she had wrought.

First Player. My God, listen to him! Is it not always the comedian who draws the crowd? Am I dreaming, or was it not I who was called six times before the curtain? Answer me that——

Second Player. What if you were called six dozen times? The players of this town are not jealous because of the crowd's applause. They have that themselves. The unendurable thought, the thought that wrenches their hearts, the thought that puts murder into their minds is that I alone, alone of all the world's players, have looked as an equal into the eyes of Kubla Khan.

Stage Manager. Stop quarrelling with one another and listen to what is happening out there. There is a man making a speech, and the crowd is getting angrier and angrier, and which of you they are jealous of I don't know, but they are all coming this way and maybe they will burn the place down as if it were Troy, and if you will do what I say you will get out of this.

First Player. Must we go dressed like this?

Second Player. There is not time to change, and besides, should the hill be surrounded, we can gather in some cleft of the rocks where we can be seen only from a distance. They will suppose we are a drove of cattle or a flock of birds.

[*All go out except Septimus, Decima, and Nona. Nona is making a bundle of Noah's hat and cloak and other properties. Decima is watching Septimus.*

Septimus [*while the Players are going out*]. Leave me to die alone? I do not blame you. There is courage in red wine, in white wine, in beer, even in thin beer sold by a blear-eyed potboy in a bankrupt tavern, but there is none in the human heart. When my master the Unicorn bathes by the light of the Great Bear, and to the sound of tabors, even the sweet river-water makes him drunk; but it is cold, it is cold, alas! it is cold.

Nona. I'll pile these upon your back. I shall carry the rest myself and so we shall save all.

[*She begins tying a great bundle of properties on Septimus' back.*

Septimus. You are right. I accept the reproach. It is necessary that we who are the last artists—all the rest have gone over to the mob—shall save the images and implements of our art. We must carry into safety the cloak of Noah, the high-crowned hat of Noah, and the mask of the sister of Noah. She was drowned because she thought her brother was telling lies; certainly we must save her rosy cheeks and rosy mouth, that drowned, wicked mouth.

Nona. Thank God you can still stand upright on your legs.

Septimus. Tie all upon my back and I will tell you the great secret that came to me at the second mouthful of the bottle. Man is nothing till he is united to an image. Now the Unicorn is both an image and beast; that is why he alone can be the new Adam. When we have put all in safety we will go to the high tablelands of Africa and find where the Unicorn is stabled and sing a marriage song. I will stand before the terrible blue eye.

Nona. There, now, I have tied them on.

[*She begins making another bundle for herself, but forgets the mask of the sister of Noah. It lies near the throne.*

Septimus. You will make Ionian music—music with its eyes upon that voluptuous Asia—the Dorian scale would but confirm him in his chastity. One Dorian note might undo us, and above all we must be careful not to speak of Delphi. The oracle is chaste.

Nona. Come, let us go.

Septimus. If we cannot fill him with desire he will deserve death. Even unicorns can be killed. What they dread most in the world is a blow from a knife that has been dipped in the blood of a serpent that died gazing upon an emerald.

[*Nona and Septimus are about to go out, Nona leading Septimus.*

Decima. Stand back, do not dare to move a step.

Septimus. Beautiful as the Unicorn, but fierce.

Decima. I have locked the gates that we may have a talk.

> [*Nona lets the hat of Noah fall in her alarm.*

Septimus. That is well, very well. You would talk with me because to-day I am extraordinarily wise.

Decima. I will not unlock the gate till I have a promise that you will drive her from the company.

Nona. Do not listen to her; take the key from her.

Septimus. If I were not her husband I would take the key, but because I am her husband she is terrible. The Unicorn will be terrible when it loves.

Nona. You are afraid.

Septimus. Could not you yourself take it? She does not love you, therefore she will not be terrible.

Nona. If you are a man at all you will take it.

Septimus. I am more than a man, I am extraordinarily wise. I will take the key.

Decima. If you come a step nearer I will shove the key through the grating of the door.

Nona [*pulling him back*]. Don't go near her; if she shoves it through the door we shall not be able to escape. The crowd will find us and murder us.

Decima. I will unlock this gate when you have taken an oath to drive her from the company, an oath never to speak with her or look at her again, a terrible oath.

Septimus. You are jealous; it is very wrong to be jealous. An ordinary man would be lost—even I am not yet wise enough. [*Drinks again.*] Now all is plain.

Decima. You have been unfaithful to me.

Septimus. I am only unfaithful when I am sober. Never trust a sober man. All the world over they are unfaithful. Never trust a man who has not bathed by the light of the Great Bear. I warn you against all sober men from the bottom of my heart. I am extraordinarily wise.

Nona. Promise, if it is only an oath she wants. Take whatever oath she bids you. If you delay we shall all be murdered.

Septimus. I can see your meaning. You would explain to me that an oath can be broken, more especially an oath under compulsion, but no, I say to you, no, I say to you, certainly not. Am I a rascally sober man, such a man as I have warned you against? Shall I be forsworn before the very eyes of Delphi, so to speak, before the very eyes of that cold, rocky oracle? What I promise I perform, therefore, my little darlings, I will not promise anything at all.

Decima. Then we shall wait here. They will come in through this door, they will carry dung-forks with burning wisps. They will put the burning wisps into the roof and we shall be burnt.

Septimus. I shall die railing upon that beast. The Christian era has come to an end, but because of the machinations of Delphi he will not become the new Adam.

Decima. I shall be avenged. She starved me, but I shall have killed her.

Nona [*who has crept behind Decima and snatched the key*]. I have it, I have it!

> [*Decima tries to take the key again, but Septimus holds her.*

Septimus. Because I am an unsworn man I am strong: a violent virginal creature, that is how it is put in 'The Great Beastery of Paris'.

Decima. Go, then, I shall stay here and die.

Nona. Let us go. A half hour since she offered herself to every man in the company.

Decima. If you would be faithful to me, Septimus, I would not let a man of them touch me.

Septimus. Flighty, but beautiful.

Nona. She is a bad woman.   [*Nona runs out.*

Septimus. A beautiful, bad, flighty woman I will follow, but follow slowly. I will take with me this noble hat. [*He picks up Noah's hat with difficulty.*] No, it may lie there, what have I to do with that drowned, wicked mouth—beautiful, drowned, flighty mouth? I will have nothing to do with it, but I will save the noble, high-crowned hat of Noah. I will carry it thus with dignity. I will go slowly that they may see I am not afraid.   [*Singing.*

> Upon the round blue eye I rail,
> Damnation on the milk-white horn.

But not one word of Delphi. I am extraordinarily wise.   [*He goes.*

Decima. Betrayed, betrayed, and for a nobody. For a woman that a man can shake and twist like so much tallow. A woman that till now never looked higher than a prompter or a property man. [*The Old Beggar comes in.*] Have you come to kill me, old man?

Old Beggar. I am looking for straw. I must soon lie down and roll, and where will I get straw to roll on? I went round to the kitchen, and 'Go away', they said. They made the sign of the cross as if it were a devil that puts me rolling.

Decima. When will the mob come to kill me?

Old Beggar. Kill you? It is not you they are going to kill. It's the itching in my back that drags them hither, for when I bray like a donkey, the crown changes.

Decima. The crown? So it is the Queen they are going to kill.

Old Beggar. But, my dear, she can't die till I roll and bray, and I will whisper to you what it is that rolls. It is the donkey that carried Christ into Jerusalem, and that is why he is so proud; and that is why he knows the hour when there is to be a new King or a new Queen.

Decima. Are you weary of the world, old man?

Old Beggar. Yes, yes, because when I roll and bray I am asleep. I know nothing about it, and that is a great pity. I remember nothing but the itching in my back. But I must stop talking and find some straw.

Decima [*picking up the scissors*]. Old man, I am going to drive this into my heart.

Old Beggar. No, no; don't do that. You don't know what you will be put to when you are dead, into whose gullet you will be put to sing or to bray. You have a look of a foretelling sort. Who knows but you might be put to foretell the death of kings; and bear in mind I will have no rivals, I could not endure a rival.

Decima. I have been betrayed by a man, I have been made a mockery of. Do those who are dead, old man, make love and do they find good lovers?

Old Beggar. I will whisper you another secret. People talk, but I have never known of anything to come from there but an old jackass. Maybe there is nothing else. Who knows but he has the whole place to himself? But there, my back is beginning to itch, and I have not yet found any straw.

　　[*He goes out. Decima leans the scissors upon the arm of the throne and is about to press herself upon them when the Queen enters.*

Queen [*stopping her*]. No, no—that would be a great sin.

Decima. Your Majesty!

Queen. I thought I would like to die a martyr, but that would be different, that would be to die for God's glory. The Holy Saint Octema was a martyr.

Decima. I am very unhappy.

Queen. I, too, am very unhappy. When I saw the great angry crowd and knew that they wished to kill me, though I had wanted to be a martyr, I was afraid and ran away.

Decima. I would not have run away, O no; but it is hard to drive a knife into one's own flesh.

Queen. In a moment they will have come and they will beat in the door, and how shall I escape them?

Decima. If they could mistake me for you, you would escape.

Queen. I could not let another die instead of me. That would be very wrong.

Decima. O, your Majesty, I shall die whatever you do, and if only I could wear that gold brocade and those gold slippers for one moment, it would not be so hard to die.

Queen. They say that those who die to save a rightful sovereign show great virtue.

Decima. Quick! the dress.

Queen. If you killed yourself your soul would be lost, and now you will be sure of Heaven.

Decima. Quick, I hear them coming.

[*Decima puts on the Queen's robe of state and her slippers. Underneath her robe of state the Queen wears some kind of nun-like dress.*

The following speech is spoken by the Queen while she is helping Decima to fasten the dress and the slippers.

Queen. Was it love? [*Decima nods.*] O, that is a great sin. I have never known love. Of all things, that is what I have had most fear of. Saint Octema shut herself up in a tower on a mountain because she was loved by a beautiful prince. I was afraid it would come in at the eye and seize upon me in a moment. I am not naturally good, and they say people will do anything for love, there is so much sweetness in it. Even Saint Octema was afraid of it. But you will escape all that and go up to God as a pure virgin. [*The change is now complete.*] Good-bye, I know how I can slip away. There is a convent that will take me in. It is not a tower, it is only a convent, but I have long wanted to go there to lose my name and disappear. Sit down upon the throne and turn your face away. If you do not turn your face away, you will be afraid. [*The Queen goes out.*

[*Decima is seated upon the throne. A great crowd gathers outside the gates. A Bishop enters.*

Bishop. Your loyal people, your Majesty, offer you their homage. I bow before you in their name. Your royal will has spoken by the mouth of the Prime Minister—has filled them with gratitude. All misunderstandings are at an end, all has been settled by your condescension in bestowing your royal hand upon the Prime Minister. [*To crowd.*] Her Majesty, who has hitherto shut herself away from all men's eyes that she might pray for this kingdom undisturbed, will henceforth show herself to her people. [*To Player Queen.*] So beautiful a Queen need never fear the disobedience of her people [*shouts from crowd of 'Never'*].

Prime Minister [*entering hurriedly*]. I will explain all, your Majesty—

there was nothing else to be done—this Bishop has been summoned
to unite us [*seeing the Queen*]; but, sleep of Adam!—this—who is
this?

Decima. Your emotion is too great for words. Do not try to speak.

Prime Minister. This—this . . . !

Decima [*standing up*]. I am Queen. I know what it is to be Queen.
If I were to say to you I had an enemy you would kill him—you
would tear him in pieces, would you not? [*Shouts:* 'We would kill
him', 'We would tear him in pieces', *etc.*] But I do not bid you kill
any one—I bid you obey my husband when I have raised him to the
throne. He is not of royal blood, but I choose to raise him to the
throne. That is my will. Show me that you will obey him so long as
I bid you to obey.　　　　　　　　　　　　　　　[*Great cheering.*

　　[*Septimus, who has been standing among the crowd, comes for-
　　ward and takes the Prime Minister by the sleeve. Various persons
　　kiss the hand of the supposed Queen.*

Septimus. My lord, that is not the Queen; that is my bad wife.

　　　　　　　　　　　　　　　　　　　[*Decima looks at them.*

Prime Minister. Did you see that? Did you see the devil in her eye?
They are mad after her pretty face, and she knows it. They would
not believe a word I say; there is nothing to be done till they cool.

Decima. Are all here my faithful servants?

Bishop. All, your Majesty.

Decima. All?

Prime Minister [*bowing low*]. All, your Majesty.

Decima [*singing*].

　　　　　She pulled the thread, and bit the thread
　　　　　And made a golden gown.

Hand me that plate. While I am eating I will have a good look at
my new man.

　　[*The plate and a bottle of wine are handed to her. The bray of a
　　donkey is heard and the Old Beggar is dragged in.*

Bishop. At last we have found this impostor out. He has been accepted
by the whole nation as if he were the Voice of God. As if the crown
could not be settled firmly on any head without his help. It's plain
that he has been in league with the conspirators, and believed that
your Majesty had been killed. He is keeping it up still. Look at his
glassy eye. But his madman airs won't help him now.

Prime Minister. Carry him to prison, we will hang him in the morning.
　　[*Shaking Septimus.*] Do you understand that there has been a
miracle, that God or the Fiend has spoken, and that the crown is

on her head for good, that fate has brayed on that man's lips?
[*Aloud.*] We will hang him in the morning.

Septimus. She is my wife.

Prime Minister. The crown has changed and there is no help for it.
Sleep of Adam, I must have that woman for wife. The Oracle has
settled that.

Septimus. She is my wife, she is my bad, flighty wife.

Prime Minister. Seize this man. He has been whispering slanders
against Her Majesty. Cast him beyond the borders of the kingdom,
and his players after him.

Decima. He must not return upon pain of death. He has wronged me,
and I will never look upon his face again.

Prime Minister. Away with him.

Decima. My good name is dearer than my life, but I will see the
players before they go.

Prime Minister. Sleep of Adam! What has she got into her head?
Fetch the players.

Decima [*picking up the mask of the sister of Noah*]. My loyal subjects
must forgive me if I hide my face—it is not yet used to the light of
day, it is a modest face. I will be much happier if His Holiness will
help me to tie the mask.

Prime Minister. The players come.

> *Enter Players, who all bow to the new Queen*

Decima. They had some play they were to perform, but I will make
them dance instead, and after that they must be richly rewarded.

Prime Minister. It shall be as you will.

Decima. You are banished and must not return upon pain of death,
and yet not one of you shall be poorer because banished. That I
promise. But you have lost one thing that I will not restore. A
woman player has left you. Do not mourn her. She was a bad, headstrong, cruel woman, and seeks destruction somewhere and with
some man she knows nothing of; such a woman they tell me that
this mask would well become, this foolish, smiling face! Come,
dance.

> [*They dance, and at certain moments she cries* 'Good-bye, good-
> bye' *or else* 'Farewell'. *And she throws them money.*]

THE END

THE DREAMING OF THE BONES
1919

THE DREAMING OF THE BONES

PERSONS IN THE PLAY

Three Musicians (*their faces made up to resemble masks*)
A Young Man
A Stranger (*wearing a mask*)
A Young Girl (*wearing a mask*)

Time—1916

The stage is any bare place in a room close to the wall. A screen, with a pattern of mountain and sky, can stand against the wall, or a curtain with a like pattern hang upon it, but the pattern must only symbolise or suggest. One Musician enters and then two others; the first stands singing, as in preceding plays, while the others take their places. Then all three sit down against the wall by their instruments, which are already there—a drum, a zither, and a flute. Or they unfold a cloth as in 'At the Hawk's Well', while the instruments are carried in.

[*Song for the folding and unfolding of the cloth*]

First Musician [*or all three Musicians, singing*].

> Why does my heart beat so?
> Did not a shadow pass?
> It passed but a moment ago.
> Who can have trod in the grass?
> What rogue is night-wandering?
> Have not old writers said
> That dizzy dreams can spring
> From the dry bones of the dead?
> And many a night it seems
> That all the valley fills
> With those fantastic dreams.
> They overflow the hills,
> So passionate is a shade,
> Like wine that fills to the top
> A grey-green cup of jade,
> Or maybe an agate cup.

[*The three Musicians are now seated by the drum, flute, and zither at the back of the stage. The First Musician speaks.*

The hour before dawn and the moon covered up;
The little village of Abbey is covered up;
The little narrow trodden way that runs
From the white road to the Abbey of Corcomroe
Is covered up; and all about the hills
Are like a circle of agate or of jade.
Somewhere among great rocks on the scarce grass
Birds cry, they cry their loneliness.
Even the sunlight can be lonely here,
Even hot noon is lonely. I hear a footfall—
A young man with a lantern comes this way.
He seems an Aran fisher, for he wears
The flannel bawneen and the cow-hide shoe.
He stumbles wearily, and stumbling prays.

[*A Young Man enters, praying in Irish.*

Once more the birds cry in their loneliness,
But now they wheel about our heads; and now
They have dropped on the grey stone to the northeast.

[*A Stranger and a Young Girl, in the costume of a past time, come in. They wear heroic masks.*

Young Man [*raising his lantern*]. Who is there? I cannot see what you
    are like.
    Come to the light.
Stranger.   But what have you to fear?
Young Man. And why have you come creeping through the dark?

[*The Girl blows out lantern.*

The wind has blown my lantern out. Where are you?
I saw a pair of heads against the sky
And lost them after; but you are in the right,
I should not be afraid in County Clare;
And should be, or should not be, have no choice,
I have to put myself into your hands,
Now that my candle's out.
Stranger.   You have fought in Dublin?
Young Man. I was in the Post Office, and if taken
    I shall be put against a wall and shot.
Stranger. You know some place of refuge, have some plan
    Or friend who will come to meet you?
Young Man   I am to lie
    At daybreak on the mountain and keep watch
    Until an Aran coracle puts in

> At Muckanish or at the rocky shore
> Under Finvara, but would break my neck
> If I went stumbling there alone in the dark.

Stranger. We know the pathways that the sheep tread out,
> And all the hiding-places of the hills,
> And that they had better hiding-places once.

Young Man. You'd say they had better before English robbers
> Cut down the trees or set them upon fire
> For fear their owners might find shelter there.
> What is that sound?

Stranger.   An old horse gone astray.
> He has been wandering on the road all night.

Young Man. I took him for a man and horse. Police
> Are out upon the roads. In the late Rising
> I think there was no man of us but hated
> To fire at soldiers who but did their duty
> And were not of our race, but when a man
> Is born in Ireland and of Irish stock,
> When he takes part against us——

Stranger.   I will put you safe,
> No living man shall set his eyes upon you;
> I will not answer for the dead.

Young Man.   The dead?

Stranger. For certain days the stones where you must lie
> Have in the hour before the break of day
> Been haunted.

Young Man.   But I was not born at midnight.

Stranger. Many a man that was born in the full daylight
> Can see them plain, will pass them on the high-road
> Or in the crowded market-place of the town,
> And never know that they have passed.

Young Man.   My Grandam
> Would have it they did penance everywhere;
> Some lived through their old lives again.

Stranger.   In a dream;
> And some for an old scruple must hang spitted
> Upon the swaying tops of lofty trees;
> Some are consumed in fire, some withered up
> By hail and sleet out of the wintry North,
> And some but live through their old lives again.

Young Man. Well, let them dream into what shape they please
> And fill waste mountains with the invisible tumult
> Of the fantastic conscience. I have no dread;

They cannot put me into gaol or shoot me;
And seeing that their blood has returned to fields
That have grown red from drinking blood like mine,
They would not if they could betray.
Stranger.   This pathway
Runs to the ruined Abbey of Corcomroe;
The Abbey passed, we are soon among the stone
And shall be at the ridge before the cocks
Of Aughanish or Bailevelehan
Or grey Aughtmana shake their wings and cry.

                    [*They go round the stage once.*
First Musician [*speaking*]. They've passed the shallow well and the
    flat stone
Fouled by the drinking cattle, the narrow lane
Where mourners for five centuries have carried
Noble or peasant to his burial;
An owl is crying out above their heads.

[*Singing*]
Why should the heart take fright?
What sets it beating so?
The bitter sweetness of the night
Has made it but a lonely thing.
Red bird of March, begin to crow!
Up with the neck and clap the wing,
Red cock, and crow!

[*They go round the stage once. The First Musician speaks.*
And now they have climbed through the long grassy field
And passed the ragged thorn-trees and the gap
In the ancient hedge; and the tomb-nested owl
At the foot's level beats with a vague wing.

[*Singing*]
My head is in a cloud;
I'd let the whole world go;
My rascal heart is proud
Remembering and remembering.
Red bird of March, begin to crow!
Up with the neck and clap the wing,
Red cock, and crow!

[*They go round the stage once. The First Musician speaks.*
They are among the stones above the ash,

Above the briar and thorn and the scarce grass;
Hidden amid the shadow far below them
The cat-headed bird is crying out.

[*Singing*]
The dreaming bones cry out
Because the night winds blow
And heaven's a cloudy blot.
Calamity can have its fling.
Red bird of March, begin to crow!
Up with the neck and clap the wing,
Red cock, and crow!

Stranger. We're almost at the summit and can rest.
The road is a faint shadow there; and there
The Abbey lies amid its broken tombs.
In the old days we should have heard a bell
Calling the monks before day broke to pray;
And when the day had broken on the ridge,
The crowing of its cocks.
Young Man.   Is there no house
Famous for sanctity or architectural beauty
In Clare or Kerry, or in all wide Connacht,
The enemy has not unroofed?
Stranger.   Close to the altar
Broken by wind and frost and worn by time
Donough O'Brien has a tomb, a name in Latin.
He wore fine clothes and knew the secrets of women,
But he rebelled against the King of Thomond
And died in his youth.
Young Man.   And why should he rebel?
The King of Thomond was his rightful master.
It was men like Donough who made Ireland weak—
My curse on all that troop, and when I die
I'll leave my body, if I have any choice,
Far from his ivy-tod and his owl. Have those
Who, if your tale is true, work out a penance
Upon the mountain-top where I am to hide,
Come from the Abbey graveyard?
Young Girl.   They have not that luck,
But are more lonely; those that are buried there
Warred in the heat of the blood; if they were rebels
Some momentary impulse made them rebels,
Or the commandment of some petty king

Who hated Thomond. Being but common sinners,
No callers-in of the alien from oversea,
They and their enemies of Thomond's party
Mix in a brief dream-battle above their bones:
Or make one drove; or drift in amity;
Or in the hurry of the heavenly round
Forget their earthly names. These are alone,
Being accursed.
Young Man.   But if what seems is true
And there are more upon the other side
Than on this side of death, many a ghost
Must meet them face to face and pass the word
Even upon this grey and desolate hill.
Young Girl. Until this hour no ghost or living man
Has spoken, though seven centuries have run
Since they, weary of life and of men's eyes,
Flung down their bones in some forgotten place,
Being accursed.
Young man.   I have heard that there are souls
Who, having sinned after a monstrous fashion,
Take on them, being dead, a monstrous image
To drive the living, should they meet its face,
Crazy, and be a terror to the dead.
Young Girl.   But these
Were comely even in their middle life
And carry, now that they are dead, the image
Of their first youth, for it was in that youth
Their sin began.
Young Man.   I have heard of angry ghosts
Who wander in a wilful solitude.
Young Girl. These have no thought but love; nor any joy
But that upon the instant when their penance
Draws to its height, and when two hearts are wrung
Nearest to breaking, if hearts of shadows break,
His eyes can mix with hers; nor any pang
That is so bitter as that double glance,
Being accursed.
Young Man.   But what is this strange penance—
That when their eyes have met can wring them most?
Young Girl. Though eyes can meet, their lips can never meet.
Young Man. And yet it seems they wander side by side.
But doubtless you would say that when lips meet
And have not living nerves, it is no meeting.

Young Girl. Although they have no blood, or living nerves,
   Who once lay warm and live the live-long night
   In one another's arms, and know their part
   In life, being now but of the people of dreams,
   Is a dream's part; although they are but shadows,
   Hovering between a thorn-tree and a stone,
   Who have heaped up night on wingéd night; although
   No shade however harried and consumed
   Would change his own calamity for theirs,
   Their manner of life were blessed could their lips
   A moment meet; but when he has bent his head
   Close to her head, or hand would slip in hand,
   The memory of their crime flows up between
   And drives them apart.
Young Man.   The memory of a crime—
   He took her from a husband's house, it may be,
   But does the penance for a passionate sin
   Last for so many centuries?
Young Girl.   No, no;
   The man she chose, the man she was chosen by,
   Cared little and cares little from whose house
   They fled towards dawn amid the flights of arrows,
   Or that it was husband's and a king's;
   And how, if that were all, could she lack friends,
   On crowded roads or on the unpeopled hill?
   Helen herself had opened wide the door
   Where night by night she dreams herself awake
   And gathers to her breast a dreaming man.
Young Man. What crime can stay so in the memory?
   What crime can keep apart the lips of lovers
   Wandering and alone?
Young Girl.   Her king and lover
   Was overthrown in battle by her husband,
   And for her sake and for his own, being blind
   And bitter and bitterly in love, he brought
   A foreign army from across the sea.
Young Man. You speak of Diarmuid and Dervorgilla
   Who brought the Norman in?
Young Girl.   Yes, yes, I spoke
   Of that most miserable, most accursed pair
   Who sold their country into slavery; and yet
   They were not wholly miserable and accursed

If somebody of their race at last would say,
'I have forgiven them'.
Young Man.   O, never, never
Shall Diarmuid and Dervorgilla be forgiven.
Young Girl. If some one of their race forgave at last
Lip would be pressed on lip.
Young Man.   O, never, never
Shall Diarmuid and Dervorgilla be forgiven.
You have told your story well, so well indeed
I could not help but fall into the mood
And for a while believe that it was true,
Or half believe; but better push on now.
The horizon to the east is growing bright.
                    [*They go round stage once. The Musicians play.*
So here we're on the summit. I can see
The Aran Islands, Connemara Hills,
The Galway in the breaking light; there too
The enemy has toppled roof and gable,
And torn the panelling from ancient rooms;
What generations of old men had known
Like their own hands, and children wondered at,
Has boiled a trooper's porridge. That town had lain,
But for the pair that you would have me pardon,
Amid its gables and its battlements
Like any old admired Italian town;
For though we have neither coal, nor iron ore,
To make us wealthy and corrupt the air,
Our country, if that crime were uncommitted,
Had been most beautiful. Why do you dance?
Why do you gaze, and with so passionate eyes,
One on the other; and then turn away,
Covering your eyes, and weave it in a dance?
Who are you? what are you? you are not natural.
Young Girl. Seven hundred years our lips have never met.
Young Man. Why do you look so strangely at one another,
So strangely and so sweetly?
Young Girl.   Seven hundred years.
Young Man. So strangely and so sweetly. All the ruin,
All, all their handiwork is blown away
As though the mountain air had blown it away
Because their eyes have met. They cannot hear,
Being folded up and hidden in their dance.

The dance is changing now. They have dropped their eyes,
They have covered up their eyes as though their hearts
Had suddenly been broken—never, never
Shall Diarmuid and Dervorgilla be forgiven.
They have drifted in the dance from rock to rock.
They have raised their hands as though to snatch the sleep
That lingers always in the abyss of the sky
Though they can never reach it. A cloud floats up
And covers all the mountain-head in a moment;
And now it lifts and they are swept away.

> [*The Stranger and the Young Girl go out.*

I had almost yielded and forgiven it all—
Terrible the temptation and the place!

> [*The Musicians begin unfolding and folding a black cloth. The First Musician comes forward to the front of the stage, at the centre. He holds the cloth before him. The other two come one on either side and unfold it. They afterwards fold it up in the same way. While it is unfolded, the Young Man leaves the stage.*
> [*Songs for the unfolding and folding of the cloth*]

The Musicians [*singing*].

I

At the grey round of the hill
Music of a lost kingdom
Runs, runs and is suddenly still.
The winds out of Clare-Galway
Carry it: suddenly it is still.

I have heard in the night air
A wandering airy music;
And moidered in that snare
A man is lost of a sudden,
In that sweet wandering snare.

What finger first began
Music of a lost kingdom?
They dream that laughed in the sun.
Dry bones that dream are bitter,
They dream and darken our sun.

Those crazy fingers play
A wandering airy music;
Our luck is withered away,

And wheat in the wheat-ear withered,
And the wind blows it away.

II

My heart ran wild when it heard
The curlew cry before dawn
And the eddying cat-headed bird;
But now the night is gone.
I have heard from far below
The strong March birds a-crow.
Stretch neck and clap the wing,
Red cocks, and crow!

THE END

CALVARY

1920

CALVARY

Three Musicians (*their faces made up to resemble masks*)
Christ (*wearing a mask*)
Lazarus (*wearing a mask*)
Judas (*wearing a mask*)
Three Roman Soldiers (*their faces masked or made up to resemble masks*)

At the beginning of the play the First Musician comes to the front of the bare place, round three sides of which the audience are seated, with a folded cloth hanging from his joined hands. Two other Musicians come, as in the preceding play, one from either side, and unfold the cloth so that it shuts out the stage, and then fold it again, singing and moving rhythmically. They do the same at the end of the play, which enables the players to leave the stage unseen.
[Song for the folding and unfolding of the cloth]
First Musician.

> Motionless under the moon-beam,
> Up to his feathers in the stream;
> Although fish leap, the white heron
> Shivers in a dumbfounded dream.

Second Musician.

> God has not died for the white heron.

Third Musician.

> Although half famished he'll not dare
> Dip or do anything but stare
> Upon the glittering image of a heron,
> That now is lost and now is there.

Second Musician.

> God has not died for the white heron.

First Musician.

> But that the full is shortly gone
> And after that is crescent moon,
> It's certain that the moon-crazed heron
> Would be but fishes' diet soon.

288

Second Musician.
>God has not died for the white heron.
>[*The three Musicians are now seated by the drum, flute, and zither at the back of stage.*

First Musician. The road to Calvary, and I beside it
Upon an ancient stone. Good Friday's come,
The day whereon Christ dreams His passion through.
He climbs up hither but as a dreamer climbs.
The cross that but exists because He dreams it
Shortens His breath and wears away His strength.
And now He stands amid a mocking crowd,
Heavily breathing.
>[*A player with the mask of Christ and carrying a cross has entered and now stands leaning upon the cross.*

>Those that are behind
Climb on the shoulders of the men in front
To shout their mockery: 'Work a miracle',
Cries one, 'and save yourself'; another cries,
'Call on your father now before your bones
Have been picked bare by the great desert birds';
Another cries, 'Call out with a loud voice
And tell him that his son is cast away
Amid the mockery of his enemies'.

>[*Singing*]
>O, but the mockers' cry
>Makes my heart afraid,
>As though a flute of bone
>Taken from a heron's thigh,
>A heron crazed by the moon,
>Were cleverly, softly played.

>[*Speaking*]
Who is this from whom the crowd has shrunk,
As though he had some look that terrified?
He has a deathly face, and yet he moves
Like a young foal that sees the hunt go by
And races in the field.
>[*A player with the mask of Lazarus has entered.*

Lazarus. He raised me up.
I am the man that died and was raised up;
I am called Lazarus.

Christ. Seeing that you died,
Lay in the tomb four days and were raised up,

You will not mock at me.

Lazarus.   For four whole days
  I had been dead and I was lying still
  In an old comfortable mountain cavern
  When you came climbing there with a great crowd
  And dragged me to the light.

Christ.   I called your name:
  'Lazarus, come out', I said, and you came out
  Bound up in cloths, your face bound in a cloth.

Lazarus. You took my death, give me your death instead.

Christ. I gave you life.

Lazarus.   But death is what I ask.
  Alive I never could escape your love,
  And when I sickened towards my death I thought,
  'I'll to the desert, or chuckle in a corner,
  Mere ghost, a solitary thing.' I died
  And saw no more until I saw you stand
  In the opening of the tomb; 'Come out!' you called;
  You dragged me to the light as boys drag out
  A rabbit when they have dug its hole away;
  And now with all the shouting at your heels
  You travel towards the death I am denied.
  And that is why I have hurried to this road
  And claimed your death.

Christ.   But I have conquered death,
  And all the dead shall be raised up again.

Lazarus. Then what I heard is true. I thought to die
  When my allotted years ran out again;
  And that, being done, you could not hinder it;
  But now you will blind with light the solitude
  That death has made; you will disturb that corner
  Where I had thought I might lie safe for ever.

Christ. I do my Father's will.

Lazarus.   And not your own;
  And I was free four days, four days being dead.
  Climb up to Calvary, but turn your eyes
  From Lazarus that cannot find a tomb
  Although he search all height and depth: make way,
  Make way for Lazarus that must go search
  Among the desert places where there is nothing
  But howling wind and solitary birds.   [*He goes out.*

First Musician. The crowd shrinks backward from the face that seems

Death-stricken and death-hungry still; and now
Martha, and those three Marys, and the rest
That live but in His love are gathered round Him.
He holds His right arm out, and on His arm
Their lips are pressed and their tears fall; and now
They cast them on the ground before His dirty
Blood-dabbled feet and clean them with their hair.

[*Sings*]
Take but His love away,
Their love becomes a feather
Of eagle, swan or gull,
Or a drowned heron's feather
Tossed hither and thither
Upon the bitter spray
And the moon at the full.

Christ. I felt their hair upon my feet a moment
And then they fled away—why have they fled?
Why has the street grown empty of a sudden
As though all fled in terror?
Judas [*who has just entered*].   I am Judas
That sold you for the thirty pieces of silver.
Christ. You were beside me every day, and saw
The dead raised up and blind men given their sight,
And all that I have said and taught you have known,
Yet doubt that I am God.
Judas.   I have not doubted;
I knew it from the first moment that I saw you;
I had no need of miracles to prove it.
Christ. And yet you have betrayed me.
Judas.   I have betrayed **you**
Because you seemed all-powerful.
Christ.   My Father
Even now, if I were but to whisper it,
Would break the world in His miraculous fury
To set me free.
Judas.   And is there not one man
In the wide world that is not in your power?
Christ. My Father put all men into my hands.
Judas. That was the very thought that drove me wild.
I could not bear to think you had but to whistle
And I must do; but after that I thought,

'Whatever man betrays Him will be free';
And life grew bearable again. And now
Is there a secret left I do not know,
Knowing that if a man betrays a God
He is the stronger of the two?

Christal.   But if
'Twere the commandment of that God Himself,
That God were still the stronger.

Judas.   When I planned it
There was no live thing near me but a heron
So full of itself that it seemed terrified.

Christ. But my betrayal was decreed that hour
When the foundations of the world were laid.

Judas. It was decreed that somebody betray you—
I'd thought of that—but not that I should do it,
I the man Judas, born on such a day,
In such a village, such and such his parents;
Nor that I'd go with my old coat upon me
To the High Priest, and chuckle to myself
As people chuckle when alone, and do it
For thirty pieces and no more, no less,
And neither with a nod nor a sent message,
But with a kiss upon your cheek. I did it,
I, Judas, and no other man, and now
You cannot even save me.

Christ.   Begone from me.
                  [*Three Roman Soldiers have entered.*
First Roman Soldier. He has been chosen to hold up the cross.
      [*During what follows, Judas holds up the cross while Christ stands
      with His arms stretched out upon it.*
Second Roman Soldier. We'll keep the rest away; they are too per-
      sistent;
They are always wanting something.

Third Roman Soldier.   Die in peace.
There's no one here but Judas and ourselves.

Christ. And who are you that ask your God for nothing?

Third Roman Soldier. We are the gamblers, and when you are dead
We'll settle who is to have that cloak of yours
By throwing dice.

Second Roman Soldier.   Our dice were carved
Out of an old sheep's thigh at Ephesus.

First Roman Soldier. Although but one of us can win the cloak

That will not make us quarrel; what does it matter?
One day one loses and the next day wins.
Second Roman Soldier. Whatever happens is the best, we say,
    So that it's unexpected.
Third Roman Soldier.   Had you sent
    A crier through the world you had not found
    More comfortable companions for a death-bed
    Than three old gamblers that have asked for nothing.
First Roman Soldier. They say you're good and that you made the
    world,
    But it's no matter.
Second Roman Soldier.   Come now; let us dance
    The dance of the dice-throwers, for it may be
    He cannot live much longer and has not seen it.
Third Roman Soldier. If he were but the God of dice he'd know it,
    But he is not that God.
First Roman Soldier.   One thing is plain,
    To know that he has nothing that we need
    Must be a comfort to him.
Second Roman Soldier.   In the dance
    We quarrel for a while, but settle it
    By throwing dice, and after that, being friends,
    Join hand to hand and wheel about the cross.   *[They dance.*
Christ. My Father, why hast Thou forsaken Me?
    [*Song for the folding and unfolding of the cloth*]
First Musician.
            Lonely the sea-bird lies at her rest,
            Blown like a dawn-blenched parcel of spray
            Upon the wind, or follows her prey
            Under a great wave's hollowing crest.
Second Musician.
            God has not appeared to the birds.
Third Musician.
            The ger-eagle has chosen his part
            In blue deep of the upper air
            Where one-eyed day can meet his stare;
            He is content with his savage heart.
Second Musician.
            God has not appeared to the birds.
First Musician.
            But where have last year's cygnets gone?
            The lake is empty; why do they fling

White wing out beside white wing?
What can a swan need but a swan?

Second Musician.

God has not appeared to the birds.

THE END

THE CAT AND THE MOON
1926

TO

JOHN MASEFIELD

THE CAT AND THE MOON

PERSONS IN THE PLAY

A Blind Beggar
A Lame Beggar
Three Musicians

SCENE.—*The scene is any bare place before a wall against which stands a patterned screen, or hangs a patterned curtain suggesting Saint Colman's Well. Three Musicians are sitting close to the wall, with zither, drum, and flute. Their faces are made up to resemble masks.*

First Musician [*singing*].

> The cat went here and there
> And the moon spun round like a top,
> And the nearest kin of the moon,
> The creeping cat, looked up.
> Black Minnaloushe stared at the moon,
> For, wander and wail as he would,
> The pure cold light in the sky
> Troubled his animal blood.

    [*Two beggars enter—a blind man with a lame man on his back. They wear grotesque masks. The Blind Beggar is counting the paces.*

Blind Beggar. One thousand and six, one thousand and seven, one thousand and nine. Look well now, for we should be in sight of the holy well of Saint Colman. The beggar at the cross-roads said it was one thousand paces from where he stood and a few paces over. Look well now, can you see the big ash-tree that's above it?

Lame Beggar [*getting down*]. No, not yet.

Blind Beggar. Then we must have taken a wrong turn; flighty you always were, and maybe before the day is over you will have me drowned in Kiltartan River or maybe in the sea itself.

Lame Beggar. I have brought you the right way, but you are a lazy man, Blind Man, and you make very short strides.

Blind Beggar. It's great daring you have, and how could I make a long stride and you on my back from the peep o' day?

Lame Beggar. And maybe the beggar of the cross-roads was only mak-ing it up when he said a thousand paces and a few paces more. You and I, being beggars, know the way of beggars, and maybe he never paced it at all, being a lazy man.

Blind Beggar. Get up. It's too much talk you have.

Lame Beggar [*getting up*]. But as I was saying, he being a lazy man—O, O, O, stop pinching the calf of my leg and I'll not say another word till I'm spoken to.

> [*They go round the stage once, moving to drum-taps, and as they move the following song is sung.*

First Musician [*singing*].

> Minnaloushe runs in the grass
> Lifting his delicate feet.
> Do you dance, Minnaloushe, do you dance?
> When two close kindred meet
> What better than call a dance?
> Maybe the moon may learn,
> Tired of that courtly fashion,
> A new dance turn.

Blind Beggar. Do you see the big ash-tree?

Lame Beggar. I do then, and the wall under it, and the flat stone, and the things upon the stone; and here is a good dry place to kneel in.

Blind Beggar. You may get down so. [*Lame Beggar gets down.*] I begin to have it in my mind that I am a great fool, and it was you who egged me on with your flighty talk.

Lame Beggar. How should you be a great fool to ask the saint to give you back your two eyes?

Blind Beggar. There is many gives money to a blind man and would give nothing but a curse to a whole man, and if it was not for one thing—but no matter anyway.

Lame Beggar. If I speak out all that's in my mind you won't take a blow at me at all?

Blind Beggar. I will not this time.

Lame Beggar. Then I'll tell you why you are not a great fool. When you go out to pick up a chicken, or maybe a stray goose on the road, or a cabbage from a neighbour's garden, I have to go riding on your back; and if I want a goose, or a chicken, or a cabbage, I must have your two legs under me.

Blind Beggar. That's true now, and if we were whole men and went different ways, there'd be as much again between us.

Lame Beggar. And your own goods keep going from you because you are blind.

Blind Beggar. Rogues and thieves ye all are, but there are some I may have my eyes on yet.

Lame Beggar. Because there's no one to see a man slipping in at the door, or throwing a leg over the wall of a yard, you are a bitter temptation to many a poor man, and I say it's not right, it's not right at all. There are poor men that because you are blind will be delayed in Purgatory.

Blind Beggar. Though you are a rogue, Lame Man, maybe you are in the right.

Lame Beggar. And maybe we'll see the blessed saint this day, for there's an odd one sees him, and maybe that will be a grander thing than having my two legs, though legs are a grand thing.

Blind Beggar. You're getting flighty again, Lame Man; what could be better for you than to have your two legs?

Lame Beggar. Do you think now will the saint put an ear on him at all, and we without an Ave or a Paternoster to put before the prayer or after the prayer?

Blind Beggar. Wise though you are and flighty though you are, and you throwing eyes to the right of you and eyes to the left of you, there's many a thing you don't know about the heart of man.

Lame Beggar. But it stands to reason that he'd be put out and he maybe with a great liking for the Latin.

Blind Beggar. I have it in mind that the saint will be better pleased at us not knowing a prayer at all, and that we had best say what we want in plain language. What pleasure can he have in all that holy company kneeling at his well on holidays and Sundays, and they as innocent maybe as himself?

Lame Beggar. That's a strange thing to say, and do you say it as I or another might say it, or as a blind man?

Blind Beggar. I say it as a blind man, I say it because since I went blind in the tenth year of my age, I have been hearing and remembering the knowledges of the world.

Lame Beggar. And you who are a blind man say that a saint, and he living in a pure well of water, would soonest be talking with a sinful man.

Blind Beggar. Do you mind what the beggar told you about the holy man in the big house at Laban?

Lame Beggar. Nothing stays in my head, Blind Man.

Blind Beggar. What does he do but go knocking about the roads with an old lecher from the county of Mayo, and he a woman-hater from the day of his birth! And what do they talk of by candle-light and by daylight? The old lecher does be telling over all the sins he committed, or maybe never committed at all, and the man of Laban does be trying to head him off and quiet him down that he may quit telling them.

Lame Beggar. Maybe it is converting him he is.

Blind Beggar. If you were a blind man you wouldn't say a foolish thing the like of that. He wouldn't have him different, no, not if he was to get all Ireland. If he was different, what would they find to talk about, will you answer me that now?

Lame Beggar. We have great wisdom between us, that's certain.

Blind Beggar. Now the Church says that it is a good thought, and a sweet thought, and a comfortable thought, that every man may have a saint to look after him, and I, being blind, give it out to all the world that the bigger the sinner the better pleased is the saint. I am sure and certain that Saint Colman would not have us two different from what we are.

Lame Beggar. I'll not give in to that, for, as I was saying, he has a great liking maybe for the Latin.

Blind Beggar. Is it contradicting me you are? Are you in reach of my arm? [*swinging stick*].

Lame Beggar. I'm not, Blind Man, you couldn't touch me at all; but as I was saying—

First Musician [*speaking*]. Will you be cured or will you be blessed?

Lame Beggar. Lord save us, that is the saint's voice and we not on our knees.   [*They kneel.*

Blind Beggar. Is he standing before us, Lame Man?

Lame Beggar. I cannot see him at all. It is in the ash-tree he is, or up in the air.

First Musician. Will you be cured or will you be blessed?

Lame Beggar. There he is again.

Blind Beggar. I'll be cured of my blindness.

First Musician. I am a saint and lonely. Will you become blessed and stay blind and we will be together always?

Blind Beggar. No, no, your Reverence, if I have to choose, I'll have the sight of my two eyes, for those that have their sight are always stealing my things and telling me lies, and some maybe that are near me. So don't take it bad of me, Holy Man, that I ask the sight of my two eyes.

Lame Beggar. No one robs him and no one tells him lies; it's all in his head, it is. He's had his tongue on me all day because he thinks I stole a sheep of his.

Blind Beggar. It was the feel of his sheepskin coat put it into my head, but my sheep was black, they say, and he tells me, Holy Man, that his sheepskin is of the most lovely white wool so that it is a joy to be looking at it.

First Musician. Lame Man, will you be cured or will you be blessed?

Lame Beggar. What would it be like to be blessed?

First Musician. You would be of the kin of the blessed saints and of the martyrs.

Lame Beggar. Is it true now that they have a book and that they write the names of the blessed in that book?

First Musician. Many a time I have seen the book, and your name would be in it.

Lame Beggar. It would be a grand thing to have two legs under me, but I have it in my mind that it would be a grander thing to have my name in that book.

First Musician. It would be a grander thing.

Lame Beggar. I will stay lame, Holy Man, and I will be blessed.

First Musician. In the name of the Father, the Son and the Holy Spirit I give this Blind Man sight and I make this Lame Man blessed.

Blind Beggar. I see it all now, the blue sky and the big ash-tree and the well and the flat stone,—all as I have heard the people say—and the things the praying people put on the stone, the beads and the candles and the leaves torn out of prayer-books, and the hairpins and the buttons. It is a great sight and a blessed sight, but I don't see yourself, Holy Man—is it up in the big tree you are?

Lame Beggar. Why, there he is in front of you and he laughing out of his wrinkled face.

Blind Beggar. Where, where?

Lame Beggar. Why, there, between you and the ash-tree.

Blind Beggar. There's nobody there—you're at your lies again.

Lame Beggar. I am blessed, and that is why I can see the holy saint.

Blind Beggar. But if I don't see the saint, there's something else I can see.

Lame Beggar. The blue sky and green leaves are a great sight, and a strange sight to one that has been long blind.

Blind Beggar. There is a stranger sight than that, and that is the skin of my own black sheep on your back.

Lame Beggar. Haven't I been telling you from the peep o' day that my sheepskin is that white it would dazzle you?

Blind Beggar. Are you so swept with the words that you've never thought that when I had my own two eyes, I'd see what colour was on it?

Lame Beggar [*very dejected*]. I never thought of that.

Blind Beggar. Are you that flighty?

Lame Beggar. I am that flighty. [*Cheering up.*] But am I not blessed, and it's a sin to speak against the blessed?

Blind Beggar. Well, I'll speak against the blessed, and I'll tell you something more that I'll do. All the while you were telling me how, if I had my two eyes, I could pick up a chicken here and a goose there, while my neighbours were in bed, do you know what I was thinking?

Lame Beggar. Some wicked blind man's thought.

Blind Beggar. It was, and it's not gone from me yet. I was saying to myself, I have a long arm and a strong arm and a very weighty arm, and when I get my own two eyes I shall know where to hit.

Lame Beggar. Don't lay a hand on me. Forty years we've been knocking about the roads together, and I wouldn't have you bring your soul into mortal peril.

Blind Beggar. I have been saying to myself, I shall know where to hit and how to hit and who to hit.

Lame Beggar. Do you not know that I am blessed? Would you be as bad as Caesar and as Herod and Nero and the other wicked emperors of antiquity?

Blind Beggar. Where'll I hit him, for the love of God, where'll I hit him?

[*Blind Beggar beats Lame Beggar. The beating takes the form of a dance and is accompanied on drum and flute. The Blind Beggar goes out.*

Lame Beggar. That is a soul lost, Holy Man.

First Musician. Maybe so.

Lame Beggar. I'd better be going, Holy Man, for he'll rouse the whole country against me.

First Musician. He'll do that.

Lame Beggar. And I have it in my mind not to even myself again with the martyrs, and the holy confessors, till I am more used to being blessed.

First Musician. Bend down your back.

Lame Beggar. What for, Holy Man?

First Musician. That I may get up on it.

Lame Beggar. But my lame legs would never bear the weight of you.

First Musician. I'm up now.

Lame Beggar. I don't feel you at all.

First Musician. I don't weigh more than a grasshopper.

Lame Beggar. You do not.

First Musician. Are you happy?

Lame Beggar. I would be if I was right sure I was blessed.

First Musician. Haven't you got me for a friend?

Lame Beggar. I have so.

First Musician. Then you're blessed.

Lame Beggar. Will you see that they put my name in the book?

First Musician. I will then.

Lame Beggar. Let us be going, Holy Man.

First Musician. But you must bless the road.

Lame Beggar. I haven't the right words.

First Musician. What do you want words for? Bow to what is before you, bow to what is behind you, bow to what is to the left of you, bow to what is to the right of you. [*The Lame Beggar begins to bow.*

First Musician. That's no good.

Lame Beggar. No good, Holy Man?

First Musician. No good at all. You must dance.

Lame Beggar. But how can I dance? Ain't I a lame man?

First Musician. Aren't you blessed?

Lame Beggar. Maybe so.

First Musician. Aren't you a miracle?

Lame Beggar. I am, Holy Man.

First Musician. Then dance, and that'll be a miracle.

[*The Lame Beggar begins to dance, at first clumsily, moving about with his stick, then he throws away the stick and dances more and more quickly. Whenever he strikes the ground strongly with his lame foot the cymbals clash. He goes out dancing, after which follows the First Musician's song.*

First Musician [*singing*].

>Minnaloushe creeps through the grass
>From moonlit place to place.
>The sacred moon overhead
>Has taken a new phase.
>Does Minnaloushe know that his pupils
>Will pass from change to change,
>And that from round to crescent,
>From crescent to round they range?
>Minnaloushe creeps through the grass
>Alone, important and wise,
>And lifts to the changing moon
>His changing eyes.

THE END

SOPHOCLES' KING OEDIPUS

A Version for the Modern Stage

1928

SOPHOCLES' KING OEDIPUS

A Version for the Modern Stage

PERSONS IN THE PLAY

Oedipus, *King of Thebes*
Jocasta, *wife of Oedipus*
Antigone, *daughter of Oedipus*
Ismene, *daughter of Oedipus*
Creon, *brother-in-law of Oedipus*

Tiresias, *a seer*
A Priest
Messengers
A Herdsman

Chorus

SCENE

The Palace of King Oedipus at Thebes

Oedipus. Children, descendants of old Cadmus, why do you come before me, why do you carry the branches of suppliants, while the city smokes with incense and murmurs with prayer and lamentation? I would not learn from any mouth but yours, old man, therefore I question you myself. Do you know of anything that I can do and have not done? How can I, being the man I am, being King Oedipus, do other than all I know? I were indeed hard of heart did I not pity such suppliants.

Priest. Oedipus, King of my country, we who stand before your door are of all ages, some too young to have walked so many miles, some —priests of Zeus such as I—too old. Among us stand the pick of the young men, and behind in the market-places the people throng, carrying suppliant branches. We all stand here because the city stumbles towards death, hardly able to raise up its head. A blight has fallen upon the fruitful blossoms of the land, a blight upon flock and field and upon the bed of marriage—plague ravages the city. Oedipus, King, not God but foremost of living men, seeing that when you first came to this town of Thebes you freed us from that harsh singer, the riddling Sphinx, we beseech you, all we suppliants, to find some help; whether you find it by your power as a man, or because, being near the Gods, a God has whispered you. Uplift our

State; think upon your fame; your coming brought us luck, be lucky to us still; remember that it is better to rule over men than over a waste place, since neither walled town nor ship is anything if it be empty and no man within it.

Oedipus. My unhappy children! I know well what need has brought you, what suffering you endure; yet, sufferers though you be, there is not a single one whose suffering is as mine—each mourns himself, but my soul mourns the city, myself, and you. It is not therefore as if you came to arouse a sleeping man. No! Be certain that I have wept many tears and searched hither and thither for some remedy. I have already done the only thing that came into my head for all my search. I have sent the son of Menoeceus, Creon, my own wife's brother, to the Pythian House of Phoebus, to hear if deed or word of mine may yet deliver this town. I am troubled, for he is a long time away—a longer time than should be—but when he comes I shall not be an honest man unless I do whatever the God commands.

Priest. You have spoken at the right time. They have just signalled to us that Creon has arrived.

Oedipus. O King Apollo, may he bring brighter fortune, for his face is shining!

Priest. He brings good news, for he is crowned with bay.

Oedipus. We shall know soon. Brother-in-law, Menoeceus' son, what news from the God?

Creon. Good news; for pain turns to pleasure when we have set the crooked straight.

Oedipus. But what is the oracle?—so far the news is neither good nor bad.

Creon. If you would hear it with all these about you, I am ready to speak. Or do we go within?

Oedipus. Speak before all. The sorrow I endure is less for my own life than these.

Creon. Then, with your leave, I speak. Our lord Phoebus bids us drive out a defiling thing that has been cherished in this land.

Oedipus. By what purification?

Creon. King Laius was our King before you came to pilot us.

Oedipus. I know—but not of my own knowledge, for I never saw him.

Creon. He was killed; and the God now bids us revenge it on his murderers, whoever they be.

Oedipus. Where shall we come upon their track after all these years? Did he meet his death in house or field, at home or in some foreign land?

Creon. In a foreign land: he was journeying to Delphi.

Oedipus. Did no fellow-traveller see the deed? Was there none there who could be questioned?

Creon. All perished but one man who fled in terror and could tell for certain but one thing of all he had seen.

Oedipus. One thing might be a clue to many things.

Creon. He said that they were fallen upon by a great troop of robbers.

Oedipus. What robbers would be so daring unless bribed from here?

Creon. Such things were indeed guessed at, but Laius once dead no avenger arose. We were amid our troubles.

Oedipus. But when royalty had fallen what troubles could have hindered search?

Creon. The riddling Sphinx put those dark things out of our thoughts —we thought of what had come to our own doors.

Oedipus. But I will start afresh and make the dark things plain. In doing right by Laius I protect myself, for whoever slew Laius might turn a hand against me. Come, my children, rise up from the altar steps; lift up these suppliant boughs and let all the children of Cadmus be called hither that I may search out everything and find for all happiness or misery as God wills.

Priest. May Phoebus, sender of the oracle, come with it and be our saviour and deliverer!

The Chorus enter

Chorus

What message comes to famous Thebes from the Golden House?
What message of disaster from that sweet-throated Zeus?
What monstrous thing our fathers saw do the seasons bring?
Or what that no man ever saw, what new monstrous thing?
Trembling in every limb I raise my loud importunate cry,
And in a sacred terror wait the Delian God's reply.

Apollo chase the God of Death that leads no shouting men,
Bears no rattling shield and yet consumes this form with pain.
Famine takes what the plague spares, and all the crops are lost;
No new life fills the empty place—ghost flits after ghost
To that God-trodden western shore, as flit benighted birds.
Sorrow speaks to sorrow, but no comfort finds in words.

Hurry him from the land of Thebes with a fair wind behind
Out on to that formless deep where not a man can find
Hold for an anchor-fluke, for all is world-enfolding sea;
Master of the thunder-cloud, set the lightning free,

And add the thunder-stone to that and fling them on his head,
For death is all the fashion now, till even Death be dead.

We call against the pallid face of this God-hated God
The springing heel of Artemis in the hunting sandal shod,
The tousle-headed Maenads, blown torch and drunken sound,
The stately Lysian king himself with golden fillet crowned,
And in his hands the golden bow and the stretched golden string,
And Bacchus' wine-ensanguined face that all the Maenads sing.

Oedipus. You are praying, and it may be that your prayer will be answered; that if you hear my words and do my bidding you may find help out of all your trouble. This is my proclamation, children of Cadmus. Whoever among you knows by what man Laius, son of Labdacus, was killed, must tell all he knows. If he fear for himself and being guilty denounce himself, he shall be in the less danger, suffering no worse thing than banishment. If on the other hand there be one that knows that a foreigner did the deed, let him speak, and I shall give him a reward and my thanks: but if any man keep silent from fear or to screen a friend, hear all what I will do to that man. No one in this land shall speak to him, nor offer sacrifice beside him; but he shall be driven from their homes as if he himself had done the deed. And in this I am the ally of the Pythian God and of the murdered man, and I pray that the murderer's life may, should he be so hidden and screened, drop from him and perish away, whoever he may be, whether he did the deed with others or by himself alone: and on you I lay it to make—so far as man may—these words good, for my sake, and for the God's sake, and for the sake of this land. And even if the God had not spurred us to it, it were a wrong to leave the guilt unpurged, when one so noble, and he your King, had perished; and all have sinned that could have searched it out and did not: and now since it is I who hold the power which he held once, and have his wife for wife—she who would have borne him heirs had he but lived—I take up this cause even as I would were it that of my own father. And if there be any who do not obey me in it, I pray that the Gods send them neither harvest of the earth nor fruit of the womb; but let them be wasted by this plague, or by one more dreadful still. But may all be blessed for ever who hear my words and do my will!

Chorus. We do not know the murderer, and it were indeed more fitting that Phoebus, who laid the task upon us, should name the man.

Oedipus. No man can make the Gods speak against their will.

Chorus. Then I will say what seems the next best thing.

Oedipus. If there is a third course, show it.

Chorus. I know that our lord Tiresias is the seer most like to our lord Phoebus, and through him we may unravel all.

Oedipus. So I was advised by Creon, and twice already have I sent to bring him.

Chorus. If we lack his help we have nothing but vague and ancient rumours.

Oedipus. What rumours are they? I would examine every story.

Chorus. Certain wayfarers were said to have killed the King.

Oedipus. I know, I know. But who was there that saw it?

Chorus. If there is such a man, and terror can move him, he will not keep silence when they have told him of your curses.

Oedipus. He that such a deed did not terrify will not be terrified because of a word.

Chorus. But there is one who shall convict him. For the blind prophet comes at last—in whom alone of all men the truth lives.

Enter Tiresias, led by a boy

Oedipus. Tiresias, master of all knowledge, whatever may be spoken, whatever is unspeakable, whatever omens of earth and sky reveal, the plague is among us, and from that plague, Great Prophet, protect us and save us. Phoebus in answer to our question says that it will not leave us till we have found the murderers of Laius, and driven them into exile or put them to death. Do you therefore neglect neither the voice of birds, nor any other sort of wisdom, but rescue yourself, rescue the State, rescue me, rescue all that are defiled by the deed. For we are in your hands, and what greater task falls to a man than to help other men with all he knows and has?

Tiresias. Aye, and what worse task than to be wise and suffer for it? I know this well; it slipped out of mind, or I would never have come.

Oedipus. What now?

Tiresias. Let me go home. You will bear your burden to the end more easily, and I bear mine—if you but give me leave for that.

Oedipus. Your words are strange and unkind to the State that bred you.

Tiresias. I see that you, on your part, keep your lips tight shut, and therefore I have shut mine that I may come to no misfortune.

Oedipus. For God's love do not turn away—if you have knowledge. We suppliants implore you on our knees.

Tiresias. You are fools—I will bring misfortune neither upon you nor upon myself.

Oedipus. What is this? You know all and will say nothing? You are minded to betray me and Thebes?

Tiresias. Why do you ask these things? You will not learn them from me.

Oedipus. What! Basest of the base! You would enrage the very stones. Will you never speak out? Cannot anything touch you?

Tiresias. The future will come of itself though I keep silent.

Oedipus. Then seeing that come it must, you had best speak out.

Tiresias. I will speak no further. Rage if you have a mind to; bring out all the fierceness that is in your heart.

Oedipus. That will I. I will not spare to speak my thoughts. Listen to what I have to say. It seems to me that you have helped to plot the deed; and, short of doing it with your own hands, have done the deed yourself. Had you eyesight I would declare that you alone had done it.

Tiresias. So that is what you say? I charge you to obey the decree that you yourself have made, and from this day out to speak neither to these nor to me. You are the defiler of this land.

Oedipus. So brazen in your impudence? How do you hope to escape punishment?

Tiresias. I have escaped; my strength is in my truth.

Oedipus. Who taught you this? You never got it by your art.

Tiresias. You, because you have spurred me to speech against my will.

Oedipus. What speech? Speak it again that I may learn it better.

Tiresias. You are but tempting me—you understood me well enough.

Oedipus. No; not so that I can say I know it; speak it again.

Tiresias. I say that you are yourself the murderer that you seek.

Oedipus. You shall rue it for having spoken twice such outrageous words.

Tiresias. Would you that I say more that you may be still angrier?

Oedipus. Say what you will. I will not let it move me.

Tiresias. I say that you are living with your next of kin in unimagined shame.

Oedipus. Do you think you can say such things and never smart for it?

Tiresias. Yes, if there be strength in truth.

Oedipus. There is; yes—for everyone but you. But not for you that are maimed in ear and in eye and in wit.

Tiresias. You are but a poor wretch flinging taunts that in a little while everyone shall fling at you.

Oedipus. Night, endless night has covered you up so that you can neither hurt me nor any man that looks upon the sun.

Tiresias. Your doom is not to fall by me. Apollo is enough: it is his business to work out your doom.

Oedipus. Was it Creon that planned this or you yourself?

Tiresias. Creon is not your enemy; you are your own enemy.

Oedipus. Power, ability, position, you bear all burdens, and yet what envy you create! Great must that envy be if envy of my power in this town—a power put into my hands unsought—has made trusty Creon, my old friend Creon, secretly long to take that power from me; if he has suborned this scheming juggler, this quack and trickster, this man with eyes for his gains and blindness in his art. Come, come, where did you prove yourself a seer? Why did you say nothing to set the townsmen free when the riddling Sphinx was here? Yet that riddle was not for the first-comer to read; it needed the skill of a seer. And none such had you! Neither found by help of birds, nor straight from any God. No, I came; I silenced her, I the ignorant Oedipus, it was I that found the answer in my mother-wit, untaught by any birds. And it is I that you would pluck out of my place, thinking to stand close to Creon's throne. But you and the plotter of all this shall mourn despite your zeal to purge the land. Were you not an old man, you had already learnt how bold you are and learnt it to your cost.

Chorus. Both this man's words and yours, Oedipus, have been said in anger. Such words cannot help us here, nor any but those that teach us to obey the oracle.

Tiresias. King though you are, the right to answer when attacked belongs to both alike. I am not subject to you, but to Loxias; and therefore I shall never be Creon's subject. And I tell you, since you have taunted me with blindness, that though you have your sight, you cannot see in what misery you stand, nor where you are living, nor with whom, unknowing what you do—for you do not know the stock you come of—you have been your own kin's enemy be they living or be they dead. And one day a mother's curse and father's curse alike shall drive you from this land in dreadful haste with darkness upon those eyes. Therefore, heap your scorn on Creon and on my message if you have a mind to; for no one of living men shall be crushed as you shall be crushed.

Oedipus. Begone this instant! Away, away! Get you from these doors!

Tiresias. I had never come but that you sent for me.

Oedipus. I did not know you were mad.

Tiresias. I may seem mad to you, but your parents thought me sane.

Oedipus. My parents! Stop! Who was my father?

Tiresias. This day shall you know your birth; and it will ruin you.

Oedipus. What dark words you always speak!

Tiresias. But are you not most skilful in the unravelling of dark words?

Oedipus. You mock me for that which made me great?

Tiresias. It was that fortune that undid you.

Oedipus. What do I care? For I delivered all this town.

Tiresias. Then I will go: boy, lead me out of this.

Oedipus. Yes, let him lead you. You take vexation with you.

Tiresias. I will go: but first I will do my errand. For frown though you may you cannot destroy me. The man for whom you look, the man you have been threatening in all the proclamations about the death of Laius, that man is here. He seems, so far as looks go, an alien; yet he shall be found a native Theban and shall nowise be glad of that fortune. A blind man, though now he has his sight; a beggar, though now he is most rich; he shall go forth feeling the ground before him with his stick; so you go in and think on that, and if you find I am in fault say that I have no skill in prophecy.

[*Tiresias is led out by the boy. Oedipus enters the palace.*

Chorus

The Delphian rock has spoken out, now must a wicked mind,
Planner of things I dare not speak and of this bloody wrack,
Pray for feet that are as fast as the four hoofs of the wind:
Cloudy Parnassus and the Fates thunder at his back.

That sacred crossing-place of lines upon Parnassus' head,
Lines that have run through North and South, and run through
    West and East,
That navel of the world bids all men search the mountain wood,
The solitary cavern, till they have found that infamous beast.

Creon enters from the house

Creon. Fellow-citizens, having heard that King Oedipus accuses me of dreadful things, I come in my indignation. Does he think that he has suffered wrong from me in these present troubles, or anything that could lead to wrong, whether in word or deed? How can I live under blame like that? What life would be worth having if by you here, and by my nearest friends, called a traitor through the town?

Chorus. He said it in anger, and not from his heart out.

Creon. He said it was I put up the seer to speak those falsehoods.

Chorus. Such things were said.

Creon. And had he his right mind saying it?

Chorus. I do not know—I do not know what my masters do.

Oedipus enters

Oedipus. What brought you here? Have you a face so brazen that you come to my house—you, the proved assassin of its master—the certain robber of my crown? Come, tell me in the face of the Gods what cowardice, or folly, did you discover in me that you plotted this? Did you think that I would not see what you were at till you had

crept upon me, or seeing it would not ward it off? What madness to
seek a throne, having neither friends nor followers!

Creon. Now, listen, hear my answer, and then you may with knowledge
judge between us.

Oedipus. You are plausible, but waste words now that I know you.

Creon. Hear what I have to say. I can explain it all.

Oedipus. One thing you will not explain away—that you are my enemy.

Creon. You are a fool to imagine that senseless stubbornness sits well
upon you.

Oedipus. And you to imagine that you can wrong a kinsman and escape
the penalty.

Creon. That is justly said, I grant you; but what is this wrong that
you complain of?

Oedipus. Did you advise, or not, that I should send for that notorious
prophet?

Creon. And I am of the same mind still.

Oedipus. How long is it, then, since Laius—

Creon. What, what about him?

Oedipus. Since Laius was killed by an unknown hand?

Creon. That was many years ago.

Oedipus. Was this prophet at his trade in those days?

Creon. Yes; skilled as now and in equal honour.

Oedipus. Did he ever speak of me?

Creon. Never certainly when I was within earshot.

Oedipus. And did you enquire into the murder?

Creon. We did enquire but learnt nothing.

Oedipus. And why did he not tell out his story then?

Creon. I do not know. When I know nothing I say nothing.

Oedipus. This much at least you know and can say out.

Creon. What is that? If I know it I will say it.

Oedipus. That if he had not consulted you he would never have said
that it was I who killed Laius.

Creon. You know best what he said; but now, question for question.

Oedipus. Question your fill—I cannot be proved guilty of that blood.

Creon. Answer me then. Are you not married to my sister?

Oedipus. That cannot be denied.

Creon. And do you not rule as she does? And with a like power?

Oedipus. I give her all she asks for.

Creon. And am not I the equal of you both?

Oedipus. Yes: and that is why you are so false a friend.

Creon. Not so; reason this out as I reason it, and first weigh this: who
would prefer to lie awake amid terrors rather than to sleep in peace,
granting that his power is equal in both cases? Neither I nor any

sober-minded man. You give me what I ask and let me do what I want, but were I King I would have to do things I did not want to do. Is not influence and no trouble with it better than any throne, am I such a fool as to hunger after unprofitable honours? Now all are glad to see me, every one wishes me well, all that want a favour from you ask speech of me—finding in that their hope. Why should I give up these things and take those? No wise mind is treacherous. I am no contriver of plots, and if another took to them he would not come to me for help. And in proof of this go to the Pythian Oracle, and ask if I have truly told what the Gods said: and after that, if you have found that I have plotted with the Soothsayer, take me and kill me; not by the sentence of one mouth only—but of two mouths, yours and my own. But do not condemn me in a corner, upon some fancy and without proof. What right have you to declare a good man bad or a bad good? It is as bad a thing to cast off a true friend as it is for a man to cast away his own life—but you will learn these things with certainty when the time comes; for time alone shows a just man; though a day can show a knave.

Chorus. King! He has spoken well, he gives himself time to think; a headlong talker does not know what he is saying.

Oedipus. The plotter is at his work, and I must counterplot headlong, or he will get his ends and I miss mine.

Creon. What will you do then? Drive me from the land?

Oedipus. Not so; I do not desire your banishment—but your death.

Creon. You are not sane.

Oedipus. I am sane at least in my own interest.

Creon. You should be in mine also.

Oedipus. No, for you are false.

Creon. But if you understand nothing?

Oedipus. Yet I must rule.

Creon. Not if you rule badly.

Oedipus. Hear him, O Thebes!

Creon. Thebes is for me also, not for you alone.

Chorus. Cease, princes: I see Jocasta coming out of the house; she comes just in time to quench the quarrel.

Jocasta enters

Jocasta. Unhappy men! Why have you made this crazy uproar? Are you not ashamed to quarrel about your own affairs when the whole country is in trouble? Go back into the palace, Oedipus, and you, Creon, to your own house. Stop making all this noise about some petty thing.

Creon. Your husband is about to kill me—or to drive me from the land of my fathers.

Oedipus. Yes: for I have convicted him of treachery against me.

Creon. Now may I perish accursed if I have done such a thing!

Jocasta. For God's love believe it, Oedipus. First, for the sake of his oath, and then for my sake, and for the sake of these people here.

Chorus [*all*]. King, do what she asks.

Oedipus. What would you have me do?

Chorus. Not to make a dishonourable charge, with no more evidence than rumour, against a friend who has bound himself with an oath.

Oedipus. Do you desire my exile or my death?

Chorus. No, by Helios, by the first of all the Gods, may I die abandoned by Heaven and earth if I have that thought! What breaks my heart is that our public griefs should be increased by your quarrels.

Oedipus. Then let him go, though I am doomed thereby to death or to be thrust dishonoured from the land; it is your lips, not his, that move me to compassion; wherever he goes my hatred follows him.

Creon. You are as sullen in yielding as you were vehement in anger, but such natures are their own heaviest burden.

Oedipus. Why will you not leave me in peace and begone?

Creon. I will go away; what is your hatred to me? In the eyes of all here I am a just man.   [*He goes.*

Chorus. Lady, why do you not take your man in to the house?

Jocasta. I will do so when I have learned what has happened.

Chorus. The half of it was blind suspicion bred of talk; the rest the wounds left by injustice.

Jocasta. It was on both sides?

Chorus. Yes.

Jocasta. What was it?

Chorus. Our land is vexed enough. Let the thing alone now that it is over.   [*Exit leader of Chorus.*

Jocasta. In the name of the Gods, King, what put you in this anger?

Oedipus. I will tell you; for I honour you more than these men do. The cause is Creon and his plots against me.

Jocasta. Speak on, if you can tell clearly how this quarrel arose.

Oedipus. He says that I am guilty of the blood of Laius.

Jocasta. On his own knowledge, or on hearsay?

Oedipus. He has made a rascal of a seer his mouthpiece.

Jocasta. Do not fear that there is truth in what he says. Listen to me, and learn to your comfort that nothing born of woman can know what is to come. I will give you proof of that. An oracle came to Laius once, I will not say from Phoebus, but from his ministers, that he was doomed to die by the hand of his own child sprung from him and me. When his child was but three days old, Laius bound its feet together and had it thrown by sure hands upon a trackless mountain; and when Laius was murdered at the place where three highways meet, it was, or so at least the rumour says, by foreign robbers. So Apollo did not bring it about that the child should kill its father, nor did Laius die in the dreadful way he feared by his child's hand. Yet that was how the message of the seers mapped out the future. Pay no attention to such things. What the God would show he will need no help to show it, but bring it to light himself.

Oedipus. What restlessness of soul, lady, has come upon me since I heard you speak, what a tumult of the mind!

Jocasta. What is this new anxiety? What has startled you?

Oedipus. You said that Laius was killed where three highways meet.

Jocasta. Yes: that was the story.

Oedipus. And where is the place?

Jocasta. In Phocis where the road divides branching off to Delphi and to Daulia.

Oedipus. And when did it happen? How many years ago?

Jocasta. News was published in this town just before you came into power.

Oedipus. O Zeus! What have you planned to do unto me?

Jocasta. He was tall; the silver had just come into his hair; and in shape not greatly unlike to you.

Oedipus. Unhappy that I am! It seems that I have laid a dreadful curse upon myself, and did not know it.

Jocasta. What do you say? I tremble when I look on you, my King.

Oedipus. And I have a misgiving that the seer can see indeed. But I will know it all more clearly, if you tell me one thing more.

Jocasta. Indeed, though I tremble I will answer whatever you ask.

Oedipus. Had he but a small troop with him; or did he travel like a great man with many followers?

Jocasta. There were but five in all—one of them a herald; and there was one carriage with Laius in it.

Oedipus. Alas! It is now clear indeed. Who was it brought the news, lady?

Jocasta. A servant—the one survivor.

Oedipus. Is he by chance in the house now?

Jocasta. No; for when he found you reigning instead of Laius he besought me, his hand clasped in mine, to send him to the fields among the cattle that he might be far from the sight of this town; and I sent him. He was a worthy man for a slave and might have asked a bigger thing.

Oedipus. I would have him return to us without delay.

Jocasta. Oedipus, it is easy. But why do you ask this?

Oedipus. I fear that I have said too much, and therefore I would question him.

Jocasta. He shall come, but I too have a right to know what lies so heavy upon your heart, my King.

Oedipus. Yes: and it shall not be kept from you now that my fear has grown so heavy. Nobody is more to me than you, nobody has the same right to learn my good or evil luck. My father was Polybus of Corinth, my mother the Dorian Merope, and I was held the foremost man in all that town until a thing happened—a thing to startle a man, though not to make him angry as it made me. We were sitting at the table, and a man who had drunk too much cried out that I was not my father's son—and I, though angry, restrained my anger for that day; but the next day went to my father and my mother and questioned them. They were indignant at the taunt and that comforted me—and yet the man's words rankled, for they had spread a rumour through the town. Without consulting my father or my mother I went to Delphi, but Phoebus told me nothing of the thing for which I came, but much of other things—things of sorrow and of terror: that I should live in incest with my mother, and beget a brood that men would shudder to look upon; that I should be my father's murderer. Hearing those words I fled out of Corinth, and from that day have but known where it lies when I have found its direction by the stars. I sought where I might escape those infamous things—the doom that was laid upon me. I came in my flight to that very spot where you tell me this king perished. Now, lady, I will tell you the truth. When I had come close up to those three roads, I came upon a herald, and a man like him you have described seated in a carriage. The man who held the reins and the old man himself would not give me room, but thought to force me from the path, and I struck the driver in my anger. The old man, seeing what I had done, waited till I was passing him and then struck me upon the head. I paid him back in full, for I knocked him out of the carriage with a blow of my stick. He rolled on his back, and after that I killed them all. If this stranger were indeed Laius, is there a more miserable man in the world than the man before you? Is there a man more hated of Heaven? No stranger, no citizen, may receive him into his house, not a soul may speak to him, and no mouth but my own mouth has laid this curse upon me. Am I not wretched? May I be swept from this world before I have endured this doom!

Chorus. These things, O King, fill us with terror; yet hope till you speak with him that saw the deed, and have learnt all.

Oedipus. Till I have learnt all, I may hope. I await the man that is coming from the pastures.

Jocasta. What is it that you hope to learn?

Oedipus. I will tell you. If his tale agrees with yours, then I am clear.

Jocasta. What tale of mine?

Oedipus. He told you that Laius met his death from robbers; if he keeps to that tale now and speaks of several slayers, I am not the slayer. But if he says one lonely wayfarer, then beyond a doubt the scale dips to me.

Jocasta. Be certain of this much at least, his first tale was of robbers. He cannot revoke that tale—the city heard it and not I alone. Yet, if he should somewhat change his story, King, at least he cannot make the murder of Laius square with prophecy; for Loxias plainly said of Laius that he would die by the hand of my child. That poor innocent did not kill him, for it died before him. Therefore from this out I would not, for all divination can do, so much as look to my right hand or to my left hand, or fear at all.

Oedipus. You have judged well; and yet for all that, send and bring this peasant to me.

Jocasta. I will send without delay. I will do all that you would have of me—but let us come in to the house.   [*They go in to the house.*

Chorus

For this one thing above all I would be praised as a man,
That in my words and my deeds I have kept those laws in mind
Olympian Zeus, and that high clear Empyrean,
Fashioned, and not some man or people of mankind,
Even those sacred laws nor age nor sleep can blind.

A man becomes a tyrant out of insolence,
He climbs and climbs, until all people call him great,
He seems upon the summit, and God flings him thence;
Yet an ambitious man may lift up a whole State,
And in his death be blessed, in his life fortunate.

And all men honour such; but should a man forget
The holy images, the Delphian Sibyl's trance,
And the world's navel-stone, and not be punished for it
And seem most fortunate, or even blessed perchance,
Why should we honour the Gods, or join the sacred dance?

Jocasta enters from the palace

Jocasta. It has come into my head, citizens of Thebes, to visit every altar of the Gods, a wreath in my hand and a dish of incense. For all manner of alarms trouble the soul of Oedipus, who instead of weighing new oracles by old, like a man of sense, is at the mercy of every mouth that speaks terror. Seeing that my words are nothing to him, I cry to you, Lysian Apollo, whose altar is the first I meet: I come, a suppliant, bearing symbols of prayer; O, make us clean, for now we are all afraid, seeing him afraid, even as they who see the helmsman afraid.

Enter Messenger

Messenger. May I learn from you, strangers, where is the home of King Oedipus? Or better still, tell me where he himself is, if you know.

Chorus. This is his house, and he himself, stranger, is within it, and this lady is the mother of his children.

Messenger. Then I call a blessing upon her, seeing what man she has married.

Jocasta. May God reward those words with a like blessing, stranger! But what have you come to seek or to tell?

Messenger. Good news for your house, lady, and for your husband.

Jocasta. What news? From whence have you come?

Messenger. From Corinth, and you will rejoice at the message I am about to give you; yet, maybe, it will grieve you.

Jocasta. What is it? How can it have this double power?

Messenger. The people of Corinth, they say, will take him for king.

Jocasta. How then? Is old Polybus no longer on the throne?

Messenger. No. He is in his tomb.

Jocasta. What do you say? Is Polybus dead, old man?

Messenger. May I drop dead if it is not the truth.

Jocasta. Away! Hurry to your master with this news. O oracle of the Gods, where are you now? This is the man whom Oedipus feared and shunned lest he should murder him, and now this man has died a natural death, and not by the hand of Oedipus.

Enter Oedipus

Oedipus. Jocasta, dearest wife, why have you called me from the house?

Jocasta. Listen to this man, and judge to what the oracles of the Gods have come.

Oedipus. And he—who may he be? And what news has he?

Jocasta. He has come from Corinth to tell you that your father, Polybus, is dead.

Oedipus. How, stranger? Let me have it from your own mouth.

Messenger. If I am to tell the story, the first thing is that he is dead and gone.

Oedipus. By some sickness or by treachery?

Messenger. A little thing can bring the aged to their rest.

Oedipus. Ah! He died, it seems, from sickness?

Messenger. Yes; and of old age.

Oedipus. Alas! Alas! Why, indeed, my wife, should one look to that Pythian seer, or to the birds that scream above our heads? For they would have it that I was doomed to kill my father. And now he is dead—hid already beneath the earth. And here am I—who had no part in it, unless indeed he died from longing for me. If that were so, I may have caused his death; but Polybus has carried the oracles with him into Hades—the oracles as men have understood them— and they are worth nothing.

Jocasta. Did I not tell you so, long since?

Oedipus. You did, but fear misled me.

Jocasta. Put this trouble from you.

Oedipus. Those bold words would sound better, were not my mother living. But as it is—I have some grounds for fear; yet you have said well.

Jocasta. Yet your father's death is a sign that all is well.

Oedipus. I know that: but I fear because of her who lives.

Messenger. Who is this woman who makes you afraid?

Oedipus. Merope, old man, the wife of Polybus.

Messenger. What is there in her to make you afraid?

Oedipus. A dreadful oracle sent from Heaven, stranger.

Messenger. Is it a secret, or can you speak it out?

Oedipus. Loxias said that I was doomed to marry my own mother, and to shed my father's blood. For that reason I fled from my house in Corinth; and I did right, though there is great comfort in familiar faces.

Messenger. Was it indeed for that reason that you went into exile?

Oedipus. I did not wish, old man, to shed my father's blood.

Messenger. King, have I not freed you from that fear?

Oedipus. You shall be fittingly rewarded.

Messenger. Indeed, to tell the truth, it was for that I came; to bring you home and be the better for it——

Oedipus. No! I will never go to my parents' home.

Messenger. Oh, my son, it is plain enough, you do not know what you do.

Oedipus. How, old man? For God's love, tell me.

Messenger. If for these reasons you shrink from going home.

Oedipus. I am afraid lest Phoebus has spoken true.

Messenger. You are afraid of being made guilty through Merope?

Oedipus. That is my constant fear.

Messenger. A vain fear.

Oedipus. How so, if I was born of that father and mother?

Messenger. Because they were nothing to you in blood.

Oedipus. What do you say? Was Polybus not my father?

Messenger. No more nor less than myself.

Oedipus. How can my father be no more to me than you who are nothing to me?

Messenger. He did not beget you any more than I.

Oedipus. No? Then why did he call me his son?

Messenger. He took you as a gift from these hands of mine.

Oedipus. How could he love so dearly what came from another's hands?

Messenger. He had been childless.

Oedipus. If I am not your son, where did you get me?

Messenger. In a wooded valley of Cithaeron.

Oedipus. What brought you wandering there?

Messenger. I was in charge of mountain sheep.

Oedipus. A shepherd—a wandering, hired man.

Messenger. A hired man who came just in time.

Oedipus. Just in time—had it come to that?

Messenger. Have not the cords left their marks upon your ankles?

Oedipus. Yes, that is an old trouble.

Messenger. I took your feet out of the spancel.

Oedipus. I have had those marks from the cradle.

Messenger. They have given you the name you bear.

Oedipus. Tell me, for God's sake, was that deed my mother's or my father's?

Messenger. I do not know—he who gave you to me knows more of that than I.

Oedipus. What? You had me from another? You did not chance on me yourself?

Messenger. No. Another shepherd gave you to me.

Oedipus. Who was he? Can you tell me who he was?

Messenger. I think that he was said to be of Laius' household.

Oedipus. The king who ruled this country long ago?

Messenger. The same—the man was herdsman in his service.

Oedipus. Is he alive, that I might speak with him?

Messenger. You people of this country should know that.

Oedipus. Is there any one here present who knows the herd he speaks of? Any one who has seen him in the town pastures? The hour has come when all must be made clear.

Chorus. I think he is the very herd you sent for but now; Jocasta can tell you better than I.

Jocasta. Why ask about that man? Why think about him? Why waste a thought on what this man has said? What he has said is of no account.

Oedipus. What, with a clue like that in my hands and fail to find out my birth?

Jocasta. For God's sake, if you set any value upon your life, give up this search—my misery is enough.

Oedipus. Though I be proved the son of a slave, yes, even of three generations of slaves, you cannot be made base-born.

Jocasta. Yet, hear me, I implore you. Give up this search.

Oedipus. I will not hear of anything but searching the whole thing out.

Jocasta. I am only thinking of your good—I have advised you for the best.

Oedipus. Your advice makes me impatient.

Jocasta. May you never come to know who you are, unhappy man!

Oedipus. Go, some one, bring the herdsman here—and let that woman glory in her noble blood.

Jocasta. Alas, alas, miserable man! Miserable! That is all that I can call you now or for ever. [*She goes out.*

Chorus. Why has the lady gone, Oedipus, in such a transport of despair? Out of this silence will burst a storm of sorrows.

Oedipus. Let come what will. However lowly my origin I will discover it. That woman, with all a woman's pride, grows red with shame at my base birth. I think myself the child of Good Luck, and that the years are my foster-brothers. Sometimes they have set me up, and sometimes thrown me down, but he that has Good Luck for mother can suffer no dishonour. That is my origin, nothing can change it, so why should I renounce this search into my birth?

Chorus

Oedipus' nurse, mountain of many a hidden glen,
Be honoured among men;
A famous man, deep-thoughted, and his body strong;
Be honoured in dance and song.
Who met in the hidden glen? Who let his fancy run
Upon nymph of Helicon?
Lord Pan or Lord Apollo or the mountain Lord
By the Bacchantes adored?

Oedipus. If I, who have never met the man, may venture to say so, I think that the herdsman we await approaches; his venerable age matches with this stranger's, and I recognize as servants of mine those who bring him. But you, if you have seen the man before, will know the man better than I.

Chorus. Yes, I know the man who is coming; he was indeed in Laius' service, and is still the most trusted of the herdsmen.

Oedipus. I ask you first, Corinthian stranger, is this the man you mean?

Messenger. He is the very man.

Oedipus. Look at me, old man! Answer my questions. Were you once in Laius' service?

Herdsman. I was: not a bought slave, but reared up in the house.

Oedipus. What was your work—your manner of life?

Herdsman. For the best part of my life I have tended flocks.

Oedipus. Where, mainly?

Herdsman. Cithaeron or its neighbourhood.

Oedipus. Do you remember meeting with this man there?

Herdsman. What man do you mean?

Oedipus. This man. Did you ever meet him?

Herdsman. I cannot recall him to mind.

Messenger. No wonder in that, master; but I will bring back his memory. He and I lived side by side upon Cithaeron. I had but one flock and he had two. Three full half-years we lived there, from spring to autumn, and every winter I drove my flock to my own fold, while he drove his to the fold of Laius. Is that right? Was it not so?

Herdsman. True enough; though it was long ago.

Messenger. Come, tell me now—do you remember giving me a boy to rear as my own foster-son?

Herdsman. What are you saying? Why do you ask me that?

Messenger. Look at that man, my friend, he is the child you gave me.

Herdsman. A plague upon you! Cannot you hold your tongue?

Oedipus. Do not blame him, old man; your own words are more blameable.

Herdsman. And how have I offended, master?

Oedipus. In not telling of that boy he asks of.

Herdsman. He speaks from ignorance, and does not know what he is saying.

Oedipus. If you will not speak with a good grace you shall be made to speak.

Herdsman. Do not hurt me for the love of God, I am an old man.

Oedipus. Some one there, tie his hands behind his back.

Herdsman. Alas! Wherefore! What more would you learn?

Oedipus. Did you give this man the child he speaks of?

Herdsman. I did: would I had died that day!

Oedipus. Well, you may come to that unless you speak the truth.

Herdsman. Much more am I lost if I speak it.

Oedipus. What! Would the fellow make more delay?

Herdsman. No, no. I said before that I gave it to him.

Oedipus. Where did you come by it? Your own child, or another?

Herdsman. It was not my own child—I had it from another.

Oedipus. From any of those here? From what house?

Herdsman. Do not ask any more, master; for the love of God do not ask.

Oedipus. You are lost if I have to question you again.

Herdsman. It was a child from the house of Laius.

Oedipus. A slave? Or one of his own race?

Herdsman. Alas! I am on the edge of dreadful words.

Oedipus. And I of hearing: yet hear I must.

Herdsman. It was said to have been his own child. But your lady within can tell you of these things best.

Oedipus. How? It was she who gave it to you?

Herdsman. Yes, King.

Oedipus. To what end?

Herdsman. That I should make away with it.

Oedipus. Her own child?

Herdsman. Yes: from fear of evil prophecies.

Oedipus. What prophecies?

Herdsman. That he should kill his father.

Oedipus. Why, then, did you give him up to this old man?

Herdsman. Through pity, master, believing that he would carry him to whatever land he had himself come from—but he saved him for dreadful misery; for if you are what this man says, you are the most miserable of all men.

Oedipus. O! O! All brought to pass! All truth! Now, O light, may I look my last upon you, having been found accursed in bloodshed, accursed in marriage, and in my coming into the world accursed!

[*He rushes into the palace.*

Chorus

What can the shadow-like generations of man attain

But build up a dazzling mockery of delight that under their touch dissolves again?

Oedipus seemed blessed, but there is no man blessed amongst men.

Oedipus overcame the woman-breasted Fate;

He seemed like a strong tower against Death and first among the fortunate;

He sat upon the ancient throne of Thebes, and all men called him great.

But, looking for a marriage-bed, he found the bed of his birth,

Tilled the field his father had tilled, cast seed into the same abounding earth;
Entered through the door that had sent him wailing forth.

Begetter and begot as one! How could that be hid?
What darkness cover up that marriage-bed? Time watches, he is
 eagle-eyed,
And all the works of man are known and every soul is tried.

Would you had never come to Thebes, nor to this house,
Nor riddled with the woman-breasted Fate, beaten off Death and
 succoured us,
That I had never raised this song, heartbroken Oedipus!

Second Messenger [*coming from the house*]. Friends and kinsmen of
 this house! What deeds must you look upon, what burden of sorrow
 bear, if true to race you still love the House of Labdacus. For not
 Ister nor Phasis could wash this house clean, so many misfortunes have
 been brought upon it, so many has it brought upon itself, and those
 misfortunes are always the worst that a man brings upon himself.
Chorus. Great already are the misfortunes of this house, and you bring
 us a new tale.
Second Messenger. A short tale in the telling: Jocasta, our Queen,
 is dead.
Chorus. Alas, miserable woman, how did she die?
Second Messenger. By her own hand. It cannot be as terrible to you
 as to one that saw it with his eyes, yet so far as words can serve, you
 shall see it. When she had come into the vestibule, she ran half
 crazed towards her marriage-bed, clutching at her hair with the
 fingers of both hands, and once within the chamber dashed the doors
 together behind her. Then called upon the name of Laius, long since
 dead, remembering that son who killed the father and upon the
 mother begot an accursed race. And wailed because of that marriage wherein she had borne a two-fold race—husband by husband,
 children by her child. Then Oedipus with a shriek burst in and
 running here and there asked for a sword, asked where he would
 find the wife that was no wife but a mother who had borne his
 children and himself. Nobody answered him, we all stood dumb; but
 supernatural power helped him, for, with a dreadful shriek, as
 though beckoned, he sprang at the double doors, drove them in,
 burst the bolts out of their sockets, and ran into the room. There
 we saw the woman hanging in a swinging halter, and with a terrible

cry he loosened the halter from her neck. When that unhappiest woman lay stretched upon the ground, we saw another dreadful sight. He dragged the golden brooches from her dress and lifting them struck them upon his eyeballs, crying out, 'You have looked enough upon those you ought never to have looked upon, failed long enough to know those that you should have known; henceforth you shall be dark'. He struck his eyes, not once, but many times, lifting his hands and speaking such or like words. The blood poured down and not with a few slow drops, but all at once over his beard in a dark shower as it were hail.

[*The Chorus wails and he steps further on to the stage.* Such evils have come forth from the deeds of those two and fallen not on one alone but upon husband and wife. They inherited much happiness, much good fortune; but to-day, ruin, shame, death, and loud crying, all evils that can be counted up, all, all are theirs.

Chorus. Is he any quieter?

Second Messenger. He cries for someone to unbar the gates and to show to all the men of Thebes his father's murderer, his mother's— the unholy word must not be spoken. It is his purpose to cast himself out of the land that he may not bring all this house under his curse. But he has not the strength to do it. He must be supported and led away. The curtain is parting; you are going to look upon a sight which even those who shudder must pity.

Enter Oedipus

Oedipus. Woe, woe is me! Miserable, miserable that I am! Where am I? Where am I going? Where am I cast away? Who hears my words?

Chorus. Cast away indeed, dreadful to the sight of the eye, dreadful to the ear.

Oedipus. Ah, friend, the only friend left to me, friend still faithful to the blind man! I know that you are there; blind though I am, I recognise your voice.

Chorus. Where did you get the courage to put out your eyes? What unearthly power drove you to that?

Oedipus. Apollo, friends, Apollo, but it was my own hand alone, wretched that I am, that quenched these eyes.

Chorus. You were better dead than blind.

Oedipus. No, it is better to be blind. What sight is there that could give me joy? How could I have looked into the face of my father when I came among the dead, aye, or on my miserable mother, since against them both I sinned such things that no halter can punish? And what to me this spectacle, town, statue, wall, and what to me this people, since I, thrice wretched, I, noblest of Theban men, have doomed myself to banishment, doomed myself when I commanded all to thrust out the unclean thing?

Chorus. It had indeed been better if that herdsman had never taken your feet out of the spancel or brought you back to life.

Oedipus. O three roads, O secret glen; O coppice and narrow way where three roads met; you that drank up the blood I spilt, the blood that was my own, my father's blood: remember what deeds I wrought for you to look upon, and then, when I had come hither, the new deeds that I wrought. O marriage-bed that gave me birth and after that gave children to your child, creating an incestuous kindred of fathers, brothers, sons, wives, and mothers. Yes, all the shame and the uncleanness that I have wrought among men.

Chorus. For all my pity I shudder and turn away.

Oedipus. Come near, condescend to lay your hands upon a wretched man; listen, do not fear. My plague can touch no man but me. Hide me somewhere out of this land for God's sake, or kill me, or throw me into the sea where you shall never look upon me more.

Enter Creon and attendants

Chorus. Here Creon comes at a fit moment; you can ask of him what you will, help or counsel, for he is now in your place. He is King.

Oedipus. What can I say to him? What can I claim, having been altogether unjust to him.

Creon. I have not come in mockery, Oedipus, nor to reproach you. Lead him in to the house as quickly as you can. Do not let him display his misery before strangers.

Oedipus. I must obey, but first, since you have come in so noble a spirit, you will hear me.

Creon. Say what you will.

Oedipus. I know that you will give her that lies within such a tomb as befits your own blood, but there is something more, Creon. My sons are men and can take care of themselves, but my daughters, my two unhappy daughters, that have ever eaten at my own table and shared my food, watch over my daughters, Creon. If it is lawful, let me touch them with my hands. Grant it, Prince, grant it, noble heart. I would believe, could I touch them, that I still saw them.

[*Ismene and Antigone are led in by attendants.*
But do I hear them sobbing? Has Creon pitied me and sent my children, my darlings? Has he done this?

Creon. Yes, I ordered it, for I know how greatly you have always loved them.

Oedipus. Then may you be blessed, and may Heaven be kinder to you than it has been to me! My children, where are you? Come hither—

hither—come to the hands of him whose mother was your mother; the hands that put out your father's eyes, eyes once as bright as your own; his who, understanding nothing, seeing nothing, became your father by her that bore him. I weep when I think of the bitter life that men will make you live, and the days that are to come. Into what company dare you go, to what festival, but that you shall return home from it not sharing in the joys, but bathed in tears? When you are old enough to be married, what man dare face the reproach that must cling to you and to your children? What misery is there lacking? Your father killed his father, he begat you at the spring of his own being, offspring of her that bore him. That is the taunt that would be cast upon you and on the man that you should marry. That man is not alive; my children, you must wither away in barrenness. Ah, son of Menoeceus, listen. Seeing that you are the only father now left to them, for we their parents are lost, both of us lost, do not let them wander in beggary—are they not your own kindred?—do not let them sink down into my misery. No, pity them, seeing them utterly wretched in helpless childhood if you do not protect them. Show me that you promise, generous man, by touching me with your hand. [*Creon touches him.*] My children, there is much advice that I would give you were you but old enough to understand, but all I can do now is bid you pray that you may live wherever you are let live, and that your life be happier than your father's.

Creon. Enough of tears. Pass into the house.

Oedipus. I will obey, though upon conditions.

Creon. Conditions?

Oedipus. Banish me from this country. I know that nothing can destroy me, for I wait some incredible fate; yet cast me upon Cithaeron, chosen by my father and my mother for my tomb.

Creon. Only the Gods can say yes or no to that.

Oedipus. No, for I am hateful to the Gods.

Creon. If that be so you will get your wish the quicker. They will banish that which they hate.

Oedipus. Are you certain of that?

Creon. I would not say it if I did not mean it.

Oedipus. Then it is time to lead me within.

Creon. Come, but let your children go.

Oedipus. No, do not take them from me.

Creon. Do not seek to be master; you won the mastery but could not keep it to the end.

[*He leads Oedipus into the palace, followed by Ismene, Antigone, and attendants.*

Chorus

Make way for Oedipus. All people said,
'That is a fortunate man';
And now what storms are beating on his head!
'That is a fortunate man';
Call no man fortunate that is not dead.
The dead are free from pain.

THE END

SOPHOCLES' OEDIPUS AT COLONUS

A Version for the Modern Stage

1934

SOPHOCLES' OEDIPUS AT COLONUS

A Version for the Modern Stage

PERSONS IN THE PLAY

Oedipus
Antigone }
Ismene } daughters of Oedipus
Polyneices, son of Oedipus
Theseus, King of Athens

Creon, King of Thebes, brother-in-law
    of Oedipus
A Stranger
A Messenger
Chorus
Servants and Soldiers

SCENE

The neighbourhood of Athens, near a shrine

Oedipus. To what town or country have we come, Antigone? Who to-day gives alms to the blind man, to wandering Oedipus? I ask little and get less and am content; where there is nobility of character suffering teaches patience, and we have been long enough together to learn that lesson. Bring me, daughter, to some place, to some sacred place perhaps, where we can rest and speak to a passer-by, and find out where we are and what we are to do. We must do whatever they bid us.

Antigone. I can see the distant towers of a city, and this place seem to be sacred; it is shaded with laurels, olives and vines, and nightingales are singing. So sit down upon this stone; you have travelled far for an old man.

Oedipus. Seat me upon it and keep a watch over the blind man.

Antigone. I have no need to learn that.

Oedipus. Where are we?

Antigone. I do not know this place, but the town I see is Athens.

Oedipus. Every passer-by has told us that.

Antigone. Shall I find somebody to tell us where we are?

Oedipus. Yes, child, if the place is inhabited.

Antigone. Inhabited it certainly is, but I need not search; somebody is coming.

330

Oedipus. Coming towards us?

Antigone. He is already beside us; ask whatever you want to know.

Enter Stranger, a man of Colonus

Oedipus. Stranger, this girl who has sight both for herself and for me tells me that you are there. There is something I would ask.

Stranger. Get up from that seat before you ask it. You are in a place where no man is permitted to set his foot.

Oedipus. What place? And to what God sacred?

Stranger. A place where none may set his foot, for it belongs to the Dreadful Goddesses, daughters of the earth and of darkness.

Oedipus. I will pray to them if you tell me their names.

Stranger. We natives call them the Furies, but there are pleasanter names.

Oedipus. I beseech them to be gracious to me and to welcome me, for never will I leave this place.

Stranger. What do you mean by those words?

Oedipus. My fate.

Stranger. I cannot remove you by force until I have reported to the authorities and got their warrant.

Oedipus. Seeing that I am an unlucky wanderer, do not for God's love refuse to answer my questions.

Stranger. Question and I will answer.

Oedipus. Into what manner of country have I come?

Stranger. The whole neighbourhood is sacred, sacred to Poseidon and to Prometheus the Firebringer; but the spot where you are seated protects Athens and is called the Brazen Threshold. And the first Lord of the Manor was named Colonus, and all his people bear his name as well as their own. Such is this neighbourhood. It is not famous in history, but it is dear to those that inhabit it.

Oedipus. So, then, there are inhabitants?

Stranger. Yes, all that bear the name of that settler.

Oedipus. Have they a king? Or do they decide everything for themselves?

Stranger. The King of Athens rules them.

Oedipus. What is his name?

Stranger. Theseus, son of Aegeus.

Oedipus. Could some one go to him with a message?

Stranger. With what object? To bring him here?

Oedipus. That he may win a great profit by doing a small service.

Stranger. What profit can he get from a blind man?

Oedipus. My words shall not be blind.

Stranger. Attend to what I say, friend. If I can judge by a man's looks and not by his clothes, you are no common man. I would not have you get into trouble. I will send no messenger to the town, but I will say what you have said to the neighbours; and so stay there where I found you until they decide whether you may stay there or not.   [*The Stranger goes out.*

Oedipus. Is that man gone?

Antigone. He is gone: say whatever comes into your head; no ear listens but mine.

Oedipus. Dreadful apparitions, Furies, Queens, your shrine is the first in this land at which I have bent my knees; therefore be gracious to me and gracious to the God Phoebus. When he proclaimed my doom, my countless sorrows, the God proclaimed that after many years I should come to a shrine of yours and find there rest, hospitality, and death, and bring good fortune to those that did me good, and ruin upon those that had driven me into wandering. Furthermore, he warned me that thunder and lightning and earthquake would announce my death. If I am not too base for your notice, Queens, I who have borne the worst burden in the world, and if it has been by your guidance, as I think, that I have found this sacred wood, fulfil the words of Phoebus and show me how to bring all to an end. Dear daughters of ancient darkness, and Athens, most honoured among cities, have mercy upon this ghost of Oedipus, upon this ghost, for the man Oedipus is dead, the man men knew.

Antigone. Hush. Some old men are coming, doubtless to ask what we are doing here.

Oedipus. I will be silent, but lead me into the wood and away from the road, till we have learnt what their intentions are.

　　[*She leads him into the wood. The Elders of Colonus, the Chorus, enter as if searching for some one. At first there are confused voices, then one man speaks for all. Where the words are in rhyme all may join in the singing.*

Chorus. Where is he gone? Where has he hidden himself? Look carefully, search every place, for this must be the most insolvent man alive. He must be a foreigner, a man from a distant country. No native would dare to enter this untrodden wood, profane a spot sacred to the apparitions whose very name we dare not speak. A shrine which we pass turning our eyes away, and pray to so silently that we dare not even move our lips.

Oedipus [*led from his hiding-place by Antigone*]. I am the man you are looking for. I can see with the mind's eye that have no other sight.

Chorus. O! O! Dreadful to look upon!

Oedipus. Do not consider me a lawless man.

Chorus. God protect us! Who is this old man?

Oedipus. Not so fortunate a man that you need envy him. This girl lets me walk with her strength and look through her eyes.

Chorus. Alas! Have you been blind from birth? Your life has indeed been accursed, and as it seems to me long, but do not add a new curse to the other. I can save you from that at any rate. Turn back from there before you have wandered into the silent depths of the wood where the sacred pool is. Come back. Come back. Do you not hear me, road-weary man? If you have anything to say to us, come first out of that forbidden spot, come to some place where it is lawful to speak, but keep silent until you have found it.

Oedipus. How shall we answer him, daughter?

Antigone. We must obey the customs of this place, listening to its people, and, as far as we can, doing what they ask.

Oedipus. Then give me your hand.

Antigone. I put it into yours.

Oedipus. No one dare touch me while I stand upon this spot. Promise me, therefore, that when I leave it and put myself into your hands I shall not suffer injury.

Chorus. We promise that, old man.

> [*Oedipus begins to move forward and then stops.*

Oedipus. Further?

Chorus. Yes, still further.

Oedipus. Further yet?

Chorus. Lead him further yet, lady.

Antigone. Follow me as I lead.

Chorus. We would have you learn what our people hate that you may hate it also, and what we reverence that you may reverence it also.

Oedipus. Lead on, child, to some spot where I may speak and hear, for I would hear what is customary, and so not set myself up against fate.

> [*Oedipus is brought to a ledge of rock at the edge of the road.*

Chorus. Stay your feet at that edge of rock.

Oedipus. Have I gone far enough?

Chorus. I tell you that is far enough.

Oedipus. Shall I sit down?

Chorus. Move him sideways and put him down on the edge of the rock.

Antigone. This is my work; father, step carefully.   [*Oedipus groans.*

Antigone. Another step; lean your old body upon my arm.

Oedipus. It is a dreadful thing to be blind.

> [*Antigone seats him upon the rock.*

Chorus. Tell me now, unhappy man, what your name is, in what country you were born, and from what country you come.

Oedipus. I am an exile, strangers, but forbear.

Chorus. From what would you have us forbear, old man?

Oedipus. From asking my name, from asking anything.

Chorus. Why do you say that?

Oedipus. My birth was horrible.

Chorus. You must answer.

Oedipus [*to Antigone*]. My child, what am I to say?

Chorus. Who was your father, stranger? And of what family?

Oedipus. O misery, misery, what will become of me, my child?

Antigone. Speak: necessity compels it.

Oedipus. I will speak, if speak I must.

Chorus. You make a great delay between you; come, speak out.

Oedipus. I am the son of Laius—[*cry from the Chorus*] and my family the Labdacidae.

Chorus. O God!

Oedipus. And my name Oedipus.

Chorus. That man!

Oedipus. But why should my words make you afraid?

> [*The Chorus half turn away, cover their eyes with their cloaks, and cry out.*

Oedipus. Miserable that I am! [*Clamour goes on.*] Daughter, what is going to happen?

Chorus. Away with you, away out of this land!

Oedipus. And your promise? Will you not keep your promise?

Chorus. The Gods do not punish any man for doing to another what that other has done to him. You knew I did not know your name; you let me promise in ignorance of that, and so I but pay deceit by deceit. Get you gone from this sacred spot, and gone from this neighbourhood before you have brought a curse upon it.

Antigone. Strangers, good honourable men, you will not listen to my father because of what he did against his will, but you should have compassion upon me; there is nothing to set me apart from you! I can still look at you with eyes that might be those of your own kin, and I beseech you that you may have compassion also upon this old man. We come to you in our misery as if you were a God—no, do not turn away—we scarce dare hope; and yet grant our prayer. I implore you by everything that you hold dear, by wife, by child, by your home, by the God you worship. My father was driven on by a God; how could he help himself?

Chorus. We pity your father and you his daughter, we pity both alike; you have shared misfortune together: but we dread the anger of the Gods and cannot add anything to what we have already said.

Oedipus. It is said that Athens of all the cities of the world has most will and power to succour and protect the exile, but that is fame and therefore but a breath of wind. You persuaded me to leave the rocky place where none dared touch me that you might drive me from your country. Was that succour and protection? What are you afraid of? What can I do against you? My life has been suffering, not doing. I need not tell you that story of my father and my mother; you know it already: it has put terror into you. But tell me this, how does it prove my nature evil? Even had I struck my father knowingly it would have been in self-defence, and I did it in ignorance; but the men that wronged me knew all that they did. Remember, strangers, that I left under a promise a place where the Gods protected me, and that if you do not keep your promise you do dishonour to those Gods, and the Gods know well how to separate those that do them honour from those that do not, and what man ever made them angry and prospered afterwards? Give the Gods their due, avoid what would blast the fair name of Athens. Do not despise me because my face is maimed and hideous. I came to you as a suppliant, I hold your pledge, fulfil that pledge. To you at any rate I should be sacred, for I can bring luck to all this neighbourhood if I have a mind to. When your master comes, whatever his name be, I shall explain my meaning; and as for the rest, see that you are not treacherous.

Chorus. You have spoken words that fill me with awe. I cannot understand, for they are full of hints and mysteries, but it is for my betters to find out their meaning.

Oedipus. Where is your master, strangers?

Chorus. At Athens, and the messenger who has brought us here has gone to fetch him. We sent him when you named yourself.

Oedipus. Do you think that he will come, that he will have respect enough for a blind man to come himself?

Chorus. Yes, certainly; for he will hear your name. Your name has gone through all countries, and whatever he is doing, resting or working, he will put it aside and come upon the instant.

Oedipus. May he act so that he may call down a blessing not upon me alone but upon his city! Only a fool is his own enemy.

Antigone. O God! Can I believe my own eyes? Can I be mistaken?

Oedipus. What is it, my child? What is it, Antigone?

Antigone. A girl in a Thessalian sunbonnet upon one of those young horses from Etna. But can it be she, or does my sight deceive me? Is it all my imagination? No, I cannot be certain, but it is, it is; she is waving her hand. She is flinging herself from her horse. She is here.

Enter Ismene

Oedipus. What are you saying, child?

Antigone. It is your daughter and my sister, Ismene. You will know in a moment, for she is going to speak.

Ismene. Father and sister, I had long search before I found you—you who are more dear to me than anybody in the world,—and now can hardly see because of my tears.

Oedipus. You have come, my child.

Ismene. Old man, you have had a dreadful life.

Oedipus. But you are here, my child.

Ismene. Yes, after much toil.

Oedipus. Touch me, my daughter.

Ismene. A hand for both of you.

Oedipus. Children—sisters.

Ismene. Yes, child and sister, a twice wretched life.

Oedipus. Her life and mine.

Ismene. Mine also.

Oedipus. Child, what has brought you?

Ismene. Care for you, father.

Oedipus. That you may see me?

Ismene. Yes, and because there is news that I cannot trust to any mouth but my own.

Oedipus. Your brothers might have brought it.

Ismene. They are—where they are. It is their dark hour.

Oedipus. Their dark hour? A true saying, for both in character and in life they are like those Egyptians who send out their wives to earn their daily bread but keep the house themselves. My daughters carry their father's burden while their brothers stay at home in comfort like women. One, since she came into a woman's strength, has been the guide of the old blind man. Often hungry and barefoot, often vexed by rain or summer's heat, often travel-weary amid waste places; and always that her father might have protection, indifferent to her own comfort. And you, my child, have been my messenger and my watcher, bringing, unknown to the men of Thebes, every oracle that touched upon my fate. And now what news, what message, what oracle have you brought? What words of terror? For you have not come empty-handed.

Ismene. I went through much before I found you, father, but let that pass, for I will not talk of myself but of the misfortunes that afflict your two sons. I have come to tell you of those misfortunes. At first they had only one thought, to save the city from the curse our family has brought upon it; that it might escape further pollution they made no claim upon the throne but let Creon have it. But now, driven mad by some God or stirred up by their own wickedness, they have both claimed the throne. The younger, and therefore the more excitable of the two, has seized it and driven the elder son Polyneices into banishment; but he, or so it has been rumoured, is in Argos, and has gathered soldiers there. He plans to bring Thebes under the rule of Argos. I have brought you an evil tale, father; when will the Gods have pity upon you?

Oedipus. You still hope that they will have pity?

Ismene. Yes, father, I have that hope. There have been new oracles.

Oedipus. What are they? What has been foretold that I can fix my hopes upon?

Ismene. A day will come when the men of Thebes will long for the living man that he may bequeath to them his bones.

Oedipus. So they know it at last, know that I am good still for something.

Ismene. You shall make them strong or weak as you please.

Oedipus. I have been made into nothing; am I to be made into a man once more?

Ismene. Yes, the Gods unmade you and the Gods remake you.

Oedipus. A poor gift to a man to abase his youth and exalt his age.

Ismene. However that may be, Creon is coming to talk of these things and may be here sooner than you think.

Oedipus. What brings him, daughter?

Ismene. To set you somewhere outside the Theban border, yet near enough to be within their power.

Oedipus. What good can I do beyond the border?

Ismene. If an enemy's country possess your bones, they will bring it victory.

Oedipus. So the oracle has spoken at last.

Ismene. Yes, you must not be your own master, so they will have you for a neighbour but not for a Theban.

Oedipus. But if I die in that place, will they bury me in Theban earth?

Ismene. No, father, they dread pollution.

Oedipus. Then never shall they be my masters.

Ismene. A day is coming when that shall be a great grief to Thebes.

Oedipus. What do you know of that?

Ismene. They will come in arms and you will blast them from the tomb.

Oedipus. Where had you these things, child?

Ismene. I had them from the messengers of Delphi.

Oedipus. Yes; Apollo has said these things?

Ismene. Men went from Thebes to Delphi and brought back the news.

Oedipus. Do my sons know it?

Ismene. Both. They know it well.

Oedipus. Then they are base indeed not to have used the oracle for my recall.

Ismene. And not to the border but into the city itself.

Oedipus. They are afraid of offending; they think more of the kingship and of their struggle for it than of their own father.

Ismene. Your words fill me with grief, but I cannot contradict you.

Oedipus. Then may no God turn them from this war, may spear meet spear till I blast them from the tomb! I shall permit neither the son that now holds the throne to keep his throne, nor the son that is banished to return. They neither raised up their hands nor their voices to defend me driven out to shame and wandering. Say if you will that when the city drove me out it did the very thing I asked of it. No, I say, no! Upon that first day, when my soul was all in tumult and the dearest wish of my heart was to die, though I were to be stoned to death, no man would grant me my desire; but later on, when a long time had passed, when the tumult in my soul had passed, when I began to feel that in my anger against myself I had asked for punishments beyond my deserts, the city drove me out. My sons, who might have hindered, did nothing, though one word could have changed everything, and I their father was driven out to wander through my whole life as a beggar and an outcast. I owe my daily bread and whatever I have found of care and shelter to my daughters, to these two girls. Their brothers have preferred the mob's favour; yes, they have trafficked with it and bartered away their father for throne and sceptre. Never, never shall Oedipus be ally of one or the other, never shall the throne of Thebes be lucky to one or the other. I meditate upon the new prophecies the girl has brought, and when I speak, Phoebus Apollo speaks. Nor shall I help the men of Thebes whether it be Creon that they send or any other that may be great amongst them. But, strangers, if you are willing to help, if these Dreadful Goddesses are willing, I shall deliver your country from all its enemies.

Chorus. Who could refuse compassion to Oedipus and his daughters?— and you have added another claim upon us, that you can deliver this country. Yet I have advice to give, and you shall be the better for it.

Oedipus. Advise me, sir, and whatever that advice be I shall take it.

Chorus. Make prayer and atonement to the Dark Goddesses, for you have trespassed upon their ground.

Oedipus. How shall I go about it, stranger?

Chorus. Draw water from the spring well over there.

Oedipus. And when I have drawn the water?

Chorus. There are three bowls made by a famous potter.

Oedipus. Yes; what must I do?

Chorus. Pour out three streams of water, facing to the spot where the sun rises.

Oedipus. A stream from each bowl?

Chorus. Yes; and be careful to empty the last bowl completely.

Oedipus. And when the earth has drunk it?

Chorus. Put three times nine sprays from an olive-tree upon that earth, and pray.

Oedipus. What are the words that I must say? That is what chiefly matters.

Chorus. Remind them to be good to suppliants, seeing that they are called the Good People, and then pray for whatever you most need, but do not move your lips, or if you move your lips do not permit them to make any sound, and having prayed come from the place without looking behind you. Do this, and I will help you all I can.

Oedipus. These are men of the neighbourhood, daughters; you have heard them.

Antigone. We have heard them; what would you have us do?

Oedipus. I cannot go, for I have neither sight nor strength, but let one of you two go, for I think that one can perform a rite of this kind. If it be done with goodwill, one can make an atonement for ten thousand men. Go quickly, but one must remain here, for I am helpless without a guide.

Ismene. I will go. I will perform the rite, but where shall I find the spot? Direct me.

Chorus. On the further side of the wood, lady, and there is a custodian of the shrine who has everything that you will want.

Ismene. Take care of our father, Antigone, until I return.   [*She goes.*

Chorus. It is a terrible thing, stranger, to stir that old grief of yours, but there are things I long to know.

Oedipus. Must I tell all again?

Chorus. I am thinking of that heavy sorrow, that sorrow for which there is no cure, of all that heavy burden which you have borne.

Oedipus. You should be too considerate to probe into my shame; am I not your guest?

Chorus. I only speak of it because that tale has gone everywhere. I would know the true facts.

Oedipus. O misery!

Chorus. Do not deny me.

Oedipus. Misery! Misery!

Chorus. I have answered all your questions.

Oedipus. Every misfortune that I have suffered came from what I did in ignorance. I swear to God that I did nothing of my own will.

Chorus. How did that come about?

Oedipus. Thebes gave me the wife that brought the curse upon me.
I knew nothing.

Chorus. Is it true then that you lay with your own mother?

Oedipus. O misery! For you have spoken words that are cruel as death,
and those two girls that I begot—

Chorus. What is it that you say?

Oedipus. Those two daughters, those two curses.

Chorus. O God!

Oedipus. The womb that bore me bore them also.

Chorus. They are at once your children and—

Oedipus. My children and my sisters!

Chorus. O horror!

Oedipus. Horror indeed, every horror has again swept back upon me;
my soul is drowned.

Chorus. You have suffered.

Oedipus. Suffered dreadful things.

Chorus. But you have sinned.

Oedipus. Sinned without knowledge.

Chorus. I do not understand.

Oedipus. I tell you that Thebes gave her to me. Would that I had
never served that city, never been rewarded by it, miserable that I
am.

Chorus. But that is not all the tale; there was somebody that you killed.

Oedipus. So you must still question?

Chorus. You killed your own father!

Oedipus. Another stab! Have I not suffered enough?

Chorus. You killed him!

Oedipus. Yes; but I can plead—

Chorus. What can you plead?

Oedipus. And plead justly.

Chorus. And what can you plead?

Oedipus. That those whom I slew would have taken my own life, and
that therefore I am innocent before the law. No evil intent brought
me into this misery.

Chorus. Our King Theseus comes, summoned by the messenger. Theseus, son of Aegeus, will hear and judge all that you have to say.

Enter Theseus

Theseus. Son of Laius, I have long known you by hearsay and of the
cruel putting out of your eyes, and now you stand visible before me,
a ragged man with a disfigured face. I am full of compassion,
Oedipus; I have come to find out why you have taken up your stand
in this place, you and this luckless girl, and what you would ask

of Athens and of myself? I will not refuse it, for I myself have been in exile, nor has any living man been in greater peril of his life than I. Never will I reject such a wanderer; what am I but a man, and I may suffer to-morrow what you suffer to-day.

Oedipus. Theseus, you have put great nobleness into a few words, and why should I speak many words? You have named me aright and named my father aright, and you know from what land I come; I will say what I must and so finish the tale.

Theseus. Say it, for I am all ears.

Oedipus. I offer you as a gift this battered body; though hideous to look upon, it brings a blessing greater than beauty.

Theseus. What blessing?

Oedipus. That you shall know later.

Theseus. But the blessing? When does it come?

Oedipus. When I am dead and you have given me a grave.

Theseus. That is the last gift of all, the last service hands can do. Is there nothing that you would have between this and then?

Oedipus. Nothing. Give me that and I have all the rest.

Theseus. This is a trifling thing you ask.

Oedipus. It is no trifling thing. Weigh well what you do; it will stir up rancour.

Theseus. What? Between your sons and me?

Oedipus. Yes, and before you bury me.

Theseus. How could that be?

Oedipus. They may come to carry me to Thebes.

Theseus. But if they come, why remain in exile?

Oedipus. When I would, they would not.

Theseus. It is folly to make ill-fortune worse by temper.

Oedipus. Blame me when you have heard my story, not before.

Theseus. Speak. I would not blame you from ignorance.

Oedipus. I have suffered an unheard-of wrong.

Theseus. You mean that ancient misery?

Oedipus. No. Who in all Hellas but knows that?

Theseus. What new grief is this that no man has seen the like of?

Oedipus. I have been driven from my country by my own children, banished by them as my father's murderer.

Theseus. Then why should they come to fetch you?

Oedipus. Compelled by an oracle from the God.

Theseus. Because of some misfortune it foretells?

Oedipus. That they shall be conquered if they do not, conquered by Athens.

Theseus. Why should Thebes and Athens fight? What can disturb the friendship between myself and Thebes?

Oedipus. Friendly son of Aegeus, the Gods neither grow old nor die, but all else is subject to change. Bodily strength and earth's fertility decay, man's trust in man dies out and enmity takes its place. Not even the best of friends can keep in the same mood toward one another, nor can city toward city, for be it soon or late men find the bitter better than the sweet, and then again, it may be, turn to the sweet. All is sweet to-day between Thebes and you, but the known goes and the unknown comes in its stead, and men take to the spear for any trifle. My body shall be asleep and buried, and yet, if Phoebus, son of God, spoke truth and God be God, it shall, though cold in death, drink hot Theban blood. But these are mysteries I may not speak. Ask no more. I end the tale where I began it—do that which you have promised and you shall not, unless the God has cheated me, make Oedipus welcome and get nothing in return.

Chorus. From the first moment, King, he has promised this or some like thing.

Theseus. Who would reject the friendship of such a man? His house and mine are ancient allies, he promises great gifts to our city, and he is the suppliant of the Gods. I cannot refuse what he asks. I admit his claim and establish him as citizen amongst us. Whatever choice you make, Oedipus, whether to remain here under the protection of these men or to live with me in my own house, your will shall be my will.

Oedipus. The blessing of God upon such men as this!

Theseus. What is your decision? Will you come into my house?

Oedipus. I would were it lawful—but this is the place.

Theseus. The place for what? I will not thwart you—

Oedipus. To vanquish those that drove me out, and to blast them from the ground.

Theseus. Your presence may bring us a great destiny.

Oedipus. It shall—if you keep faith.

Theseus. Have no fear of that—I shall not fail you.

Oedipus. I will not bind you with an oath as we bind unworthy men.

Theseus. You would have gained nothing if you had; my word is my oath.

Oedipus. What will you do? How will you keep faith?

Theseus. What do you fear?

Oedipus. Men will come.

Theseus. There are those here who will see to that.

Oedipus. Beware—for if you leave me—

Theseus. It is not for you to teach me my business.

Oedipus. My fear drives me on.

Theseus. I see nothing to be afraid of.

Oedipus. You do not know what they have threatened.

Theseus. Let these Thebans threaten as they will, there shall be foul
weather between the threat and the act. Be of good courage. If God
sent you hither, you need no protection of mine, but God or no God
my mere name will protect. [*Theseus goes out.*

Chorus

Come praise Colonus' horses, and come praise
The wine-dark of the wood's intricacies,
The nightingale that deafens daylight there,
If daylight ever visit where,
Unvisited by tempest or by sun,
Immortal ladies tread the ground
Dizzy with harmonious sound,
Semele's lad a gay companion.

And yonder in the gymnasts' garden thrives
The self-sown, self-begotten shape that gives
Athenian intellect its mastery,
Even the grey-leaved olive-tree
Miracle-bred out of the living stone;
Nor accident of peace nor war
Shall wither that old marvel, for
The great grey-eyed Athene stares thereon.

Who comes into this country, and has come
Where golden crocus and narcissus bloom,
Where the Great Mother, mourning for her daughter
And beauty-drunken by the water
Glittering among grey-leaved olive-trees,
Has plucked a flower and sung her loss;
Who finds abounding Cephisus
Has found the loveliest spectacle there is.

Because this country has a pious mind
And so remembers that when all mankind
But trod the road, or splashed about the shore,
Poseidon gave it bit and oar,
Every Colonus lad or lass discourses
Of that oar and of that bit;
Summer and winter, day and night,
Of horses and horses of the sea, white horses.

Antigone. O country that all men praise, the time has come to pay for
praise.

Oedipus. Why do you say that? What has happened, daughter?

Antigone. To pay with deeds—Creon approaches, with many at his heels.

Oedipus. Kind old men, prove that I am safe indeed.

Chorus. You shall have that proof. Put away all fear; though age has robbed me of my strength my country is as strong as ever.

Enter Creon with attendants

Creon. Sirs, worthy countrymen, my coming has alarmed you; I can see it by your eyes. Why do you shrink away? I have no hostile purpose. I come, an old man, to the strongest city in all Greece; I come, old as I am, to persuade that man there to return to Thebes. And I have been sent, not by any one man, but by the whole people, chosen for this embassy since being of his own blood I mourn for his misfortune as no other Theban can. Hear me, luckless Oedipus, come home. All the people call you hither, and I in chief, because I would be the basest of men if it did not grieve me more than it can any other to see you standing there, old man, a stranger and a wanderer, and to think that you have gone, one woman for attendant, hither and thither in beggary; and never did I think to see that woman sunk into such a state of misery, chained to your blindness and your penury, and she a ripe unmarried girl at every brute's mercy. That such a thing should be is a public scandal, a shame that affects me and all our family. End this shame, Oedipus, by returning to your native city and to the house of your fathers; say goodbye in all friendship to this land, worthy though it be, for your own land has the first claim since you were born and bred there.

Oedipus. Audacity, professing the highest motives that you may deceive! You would carry me away bound and shackled to that very place where captivity would be the most bitter. In old days, driven mad by all the evil that I had brought upon myself, I cried out that you should cast me out of the land, but you were deaf and would not grant me what I asked; and when the violence of grief had passed and the seclusion of the house grown dear to me, then it was that you cast me from the house and from the land. You did not remember that I was of your blood, but now you remember it. Now that I have been welcomed by Athens and her children you would drag me away, covering up your purpose with specious words. What good is kindness done against our will? If a man gave no help in need, no gift when you asked it, but offered help and gift when you had no need of either, would you take pleasure in that man? Or thank him? Yet that is what you offer me, and, therefore, though it looks good it is evil. I will tell you what that evil is and prove how false you are. You have come to fetch me, but not that

you may take me home, but to plant me somewhere on the borders
that you may keep me in your power and therefore escape defeat in
war, defeat from this land. But you shall not escape, that shall not
be your portion, but this—the vengeance of my ghost; and for my
two sons this heritage, a place in Thebes where they may die, a place
in my kingdom just large enough for that. What do you know of the
fortune of that kingdom? But I know it. My knowledge comes from
Phoebus and his father God most high, aye, from truth itself, while
you have come with fraudulent lips and between them a tongue like
a sword; yet plead however you may, you shall not gain your case.
What is the use of words? No words of mine can alter you. Get you
gone; she and I live where we have chosen, and no matter what a
plight we are in, our life, so long as we are contented with it, shall
not be altogether wretched.

Creon. Whom has this debate made the more wretched? You who injure yourself thereby, or me that you have injured?

Oedipus. I am well content with your part in it, for you have moved
neither me nor these that stand beside us.

Creon. Do you want everybody to know, miserable man, that age
has not brought you sense? Do you want to make yourself a by-
word?

Oedipus. Your tongue is too ready to be honest.

Creon. And you speak many words and nothing to the point.

Oedipus. And yours, it seems, are to the point and few.

Creon. Who could speak to the point that had you for a listener?

Oedipus. Begone, I tell you to be begone, in my own name, and in the
name of these others. And stop spying upon me in this place where
I am predestined to remain.

Creon. These others will bear me out in what I have said, and as to
the answer that you have sent to your own kith and kin, if ever I
take you—

Oedipus. Can you take me in spite of these?

Creon. No need to take you; I can make you smart enough without
that.

Oedipus. No matter how you bluster, what can you do?

Creon. One of your daughters has been seized and sent hence, and
now I shall seize the other and send her after.

Oedipus. O misery!

Creon. You shall be more miserable yet.

Oedipus. You have taken my child.

Creon. And I shall take this one in a moment.

Oedipus. What will you do to help me, friends? Will you forsake me,
or will you drive away this godless man?

Chorus. Get you gone, stranger; you have done a most wicked act and plan another.

Creon [*to his attendants*]. Take that girl by force if she will not come of her own will.

Antigone. What am I to do, miserable that I am? Where shall I find help from Gods or men?

Chorus [*to Creon*]. What are you doing, stranger?

Creon. I will not touch that man, but his daughter is mine.

Oedipus. Worthy old men—

Chorus. Stranger, what you do is unjust.

Creon. No. Just.

Chorus. How can it be just?

Creon. I take one of my own kin.   [*Lays his hand on Antigone.*

Oedipus. Hear me, Athens.

Chorus. Be careful, stranger, let her go. We shall soon find out whether you or we are the stronger.   [*They gather round him, threatening.*

Creon. Stand back.

Chorus. We shall not stand back unless you change your mind.

Creon. If you injure me it will be war between Thebes and Athens.

Oedipus. War. I said so.

Chorus. Take your hands from that girl.

Creon. You are not the master here.

Chorus. Leave hold, I tell you.

Creon [*to one of his guards who seizes Antigone*]. Take her and be-gone.

Chorus. To the rescue, men of Colonus, to the rescue! The might of Athens is insulted. Help! Help!

Antigone. They are dragging me away—friends—friends—

Oedipus [*blindly seeking for her*]. Where are you, my child?

Antigone. They are dragging me away.

Oedipus. Your hands, my child.

Antigone. I am helpless.

Creon [*to his guards*]. Away with you.

Oedipus. O misery!   [*Guards go out with Antigone.*

Creon. Never will those two crutches prop your steps again. It is your will to ruin friends and country, and I can do nothing to prevent you. I though a prince have been their messenger, and I have failed, but you have done yourself no good in giving way to anger, and you will know that in times to come. You have always given yourself up to anger, no friend could ever turn you from it, and that has been your curse.   [*He turns to follow his guard.*

Chorus. Stop! Stop!

Creon. Hands off!

Chorus. You shall not go until those two girls have been given back.

Creon. Then I shall take what is, it seems, dearer to Athens than those two girls.

Chorus. What are you planning now?

Creon. To take that man there captive.

Chorus. A brave threat!

Creon. It shall be made a deed upon the instant.

Chorus. Yes, unless the King of this country intervenes.

Oedipus. Will you dare to touch me?

Creon. Be silent.

Oedipus. No, no, but by permission of the powers of this place I speak yet one more curse. Wretch, I am blind, and you have taken by force the unhappy creature who gave me sight. Therefore I call upon the Sun-God that sees all things, to give you an old age like mine.

Creon. Hear him, men of Colonus.

Oedipus. They hear both you and me, and they know that my wrongs can strike, that my revenge shall not be in words.

Creon. Then I will do what I threatened; alone and slow with age though I am, I will take that man by force.

[*Approaches Oedipus to seize him.*

Oedipus. O misfortune!

Chorus. You are a foolhardy man to think that you can do it.

Creon. I think it.

Chorus. If you do it there is no such city as Athens.

Creon. Even a weak man is strong in a good cause.

Oedipus. Hear what he is saying.

Chorus. Let him say what he likes. He cannot do it, by God, he cannot.

Creon. What do you know of God?

Chorus. Insolence!

Creon. Insolence that you must put up with.

Enter Theseus

Theseus. What is this quarrel? What is the trouble? High words have reached me at the altar of the Sea-God, the patron saint of your own Colonus. Speak out—you have interrupted the sacrifice.

Oedipus. Friend, I know your voice. That man there has done me a foul wrong.

Theseus. What wrong? What man? Speak out.

Oedipus. The man that is before your eyes—Creon. He has taken my children from me, all that I had.

Theseus. What is that you say?

Oedipus. My tale is finished.

Theseus [*to his attendants*]. Let one of you run to the altars, bid every one to leave the sacrifice and hurry to the cross-roads, whether upon foot or upon horseback. Let the horsemen ride with a loose rein, for if they do not get there before the girls I shall be made a mockery. Away, away. [*Turning to Creon.*] As for this man, if I had not kept a tight hold upon myself he would already have had something to remember me by, but it is better to deal out to him the law that he dealt to Oedipus. [*To Creon.*] You shall not leave this country until you have brought back those girls and set them there in my sight, for what you have done is a disgrace to me and to my people as it is to you and to your people. You have come to a city that observes justice, that does all things according to the law, and you have set aside the laws of that city, taken captives at your own pleasure, taken what you wanted by violence, as though my city were uninhabited, or inhabited by slaves, and I a mere nothing. Thebes never taught you this—her men are honourable—nor would Thebes approve an act of robbery against me, not that you should commit an act of robbery against the Gods, and carry away their suppliants. Do you suppose that I, if I trod your soil, would take anything without licence from its ruler, even if my claim were of all claims the most just? I know how to deport myself among the people of another nation. But you who are old and should have learnt wisdom, you have brought disgrace upon an honourable city. I therefore repeat, unless those girls are brought to me you shall remain here, a captive in their stead, and do not think what I say mere words, for I say them with my whole heart and soul.

Chorus. Think where you stand, stranger; you come of a just race, but your actions have been weighed and they are unjust.

Creon. I have done what I have done, not because I thought this city lacked law, lacked men for its defence, as you have declared, but because I did not believe that its people were so much in love with my own kindred that they would keep them against my will. I thought they would not protect a parricide, a pollution, a man who had taken his own mother to wife. That is why I dared to act, nor had I done so even then, but that he called down curses upon my people and upon myself. I thought I could requite such wrong. Only the dead are free from anger, and anger does not grow less as a man grows old. I have a just cause, but I am in your power, so do what you think right, and yet remember that however old I may be I can requite one deed with another.

Oedipus. Do such taunts disgrace most the man at whom they are aimed or the man that makes them? All that I am taunted with, parricide, incest, misery, I have borne indeed, but by no choice of mine, but at the pleasure of the Gods. Set me apart from these acts, apart from all that they, enraged, it may be, against my ancestors, have made me do against my family and myself, and there is nobody can accuse me of anything. They settled before my birth all that I was to do. The oracle had announced that my father was to die by the hand of his son. How then can I be blamed? I met my father not knowing who he was, and killed him not knowing what I did, but misery is not guilt. Are you not ashamed to have spoken of my mother, and to make me speak of my marriage with her, seeing that she was your own sister? You drive me to shameless speech and speak I must, whether I will or no—Misery! Misery! She was my mother indeed, and a mother bore children to her son, but one thing is plain as day, that what we did we did unknowingly, but that you knowingly have reviled her and me. You throw all that has happened in my teeth, and yet no man can judge me guilty either of that marriage or of my father's death. Answer this one question—if an armed man were to start up before you now, would you out of your righteousness ask before you drew to defend yourself if he were, perchance, your father? I think that you would have at him without further words and not search here and there to find the rights of it, seeing that you love your life. Yet that was how it was with me; into that dilemma had the Gods led me. If my father could come back to life he would not contradict what I have said. Yet you in a frenzy of speech, not caring what you say or do not say, have accused me, and before these strangers. You began with flattery, praising Theseus and Athens for their justice, and then when you could not get your way showed how little you thought of that justice by stealing my daughters and by laying your hands on me, yes, upon the old man and the suppliant. And therefore I call upon those Goddesses whom this land worships to fight upon my side, and I call upon this land that you may learn what men serve it.

Chorus. King, he is a good man though under a curse, and worthy of our help.

Theseus. Enough of words; the doers of the wrong are in flight and we do nothing.

Creon. Well, what would you have me do? I am in your power.

Theseus. Bring me to the girls if near at hand, put me upon their track if your men have carried them away. They will never cross the border. Come, set out, for the robber has been robbed and the hunter taken in the net. I will see to it that no accomplice helps you. I am very certain that you would never have dared to commit this outrage without some treachery among my people. If you have any wits you will pay more attention to my words than you paid to the warnings these others spoke a while back.

Creon. You are in your own country, say what you will, but when I get
　home to mine I shall know how to act.

Theseus. Threaten if you have a fancy for it, but set out. Oedipus, stay
　here in peace, be satisfied with this pledge: I shall bring those chil-
　dren or die attempting it.

Oedipus. May Heaven reward you, Theseus, for you are a noble and
　faithful man.　　　　　　　　　[*Theseus, Creon, and attendants go out.*

Chorus

Would I were there when they turn and Theban robbers face,
Amid the brazen roar of shields, Colonus in chase;
Whether by the Pythian strand, or further away to the west
Where immortal spirits reveal the life of the blessed
To the living man that has sworn to let none living know;
Or it may be north and west amid Oea's desolate snow.
No matter how steep the climb Colonus follows the track,
No matter how loose the rein Theseus rides at their back;
And the captives turn in the saddle, turn their heads at his call.
Swords upon brazen shields and brazen helmets fall.
Creon is captured or slain, many are captured or slain.
Terrible the men of Colonus, terrible Theseus' men.
O glitter of bridle and bit; O lads in company
To the son of Rhea that rides upon the horses of the sea
Vowed, and to the Goddess Pallas Athene vowed!
O that I had seen it all mounted upon a cloud!
O that I had run thither, a bird upon the wind!
I have but imagined it all, seen it in the eye of the mind,
And cannot know what happened for all the words I say,
And therefore to God's daughter Pallas Athene pray
To bring the lads and the horses and the luckless ladies home,
And when that prayer is finished that a double blessing come
From the running ground of the deer, from the mountain land to this,
Pray to the brother and sister, Apollo and Artemis.

Chorus. I have not raised false hopes. The men return with your
　daughters in the midst of them.

Oedipus. Where? Where? What is that you say?

　　　　Enter Antigone, Ismene, Theseus, and attendants

Antigone. O father, father! that God would restore your sight that you
　might see how noble a man stands there!

Oedipus. My child, so you have come back to me.

Antigone. Yes, thanks to the strong arms of Theseus and his men.

Oedipus. Come to me, children; let me embrace you. I never thought
to have touched you with my hands again.

Antigone. We come, for we too long to embrace you.

Oedipus. Where are you?

Antigone. Here, approaching you together.

Oedipus. My darlings—props of my old age.

Antigone. We three are under the same curse.

Oedipus. I draw my darlings to me, and now should I die I shall not
be altogether wretched since you have come to me again. Come
closer on either side, children; cling to your father; rest, for you are
tired out after all that has happened. Tell me of it all; but no, you
are young girls and so afraid to speak before such a crowd as this.

Antigone. There is nothing we need say, for our deliverer is there, and
he can tell you all.

Oedipus. Do not wonder, sir, that I have so much to say to these
children lost and found when hope itself seemed lost. I have not
forgotten that by you and you alone were they rescued. May the Gods
give you all the good that I wish, give it to you and to this land, for
through you and through you alone, and here alone, here in this
one place out of the whole world, have I found truth and piety and
justice, and I have nothing to give you in return but words. Stretch
out your hand towards me that I may take it in mine and kiss you
upon the cheek. But what am I saying? I am miserable and sinful
and polluted. I would not have you touch me; no, no, I dare not
permit it even if you would. No one may touch me but those that
lie under the same curse. Take my greeting there where you stand,
and be as favourable in the future as in this hour.

Theseus. What more natural than to dwell upon your joy and speak of
it to these children; what more natural than to think of these before
you thought of me? My fame comes from what I do and not from
the words of any man. Your daughters are there; I have carried out
my promise, old man, and all those threats came to nothing; they
will tell you all in good time, for I will tell no tale and make no
boast. But as I returned here something happened that I must speak
of and get your advice about, for though no great matter in itself I
do not know what it may mean.

Oedipus. What is it, son of Aegeus? For I have heard nothing of it.

Theseus. When the noise of the quarrel with Creon reached me I was
sacrificing at the altar of Poseidon, and as I brought your daughters
hither I passed that altar and there I found a man who was, they
told me, a kinsman of yours, though not your countryman.

Oedipus. Of what country? What does he want?

Theseus. I know nothing but this one thing: he wants to speak with you, but as he promises to be brief it will not trouble you much.

Oedipus. What brings him? A man does not go to the altar of Poseidon about nothing.

Theseus. All that he has asked of the God is that he may speak with you and return home uninjured.

Oedipus. But who can this man be?

Theseus. He is of Argos. Have you a kinsman there?

Oedipus. Do not plead for that man, King.

Theseus. What ails you?

Oedipus. Do not ask me.

Theseus. Ask what?

Oedipus. I know that suppliant.

Theseus. But what has he done that I should not plead for him?

Oedipus. My son, the hateful son whose voice would vex me more than that of any living man.

Theseus. Are you afraid that he will persuade you to something against your will? It can do you no harm to hear what he has to say.

Oedipus. The voice of that son is hateful to his father; do not compel me to give way.

Theseus. Remember that he is a suppliant to the God and that you have a duty to the God.

Antigone. Father, let me speak, though I am too young to advise anyone. Do what the King asks, seeing that he asks it for his own sake and that of the God, and let my brother come. He cannot force you to anything against your will, nor will he be able to deceive you. It is far more likely that he will betray his own foolish plan. What harm, therefore, can come of hearing what he has to say? You are his father, and no matter what wrongs he may do against you, you must not wrong him in return. Let him come. Other men have been driven to anger by evil children and have been none the worse when friends have talked away their anger. Turn your eyes from the present moment; think of all the evils that have come upon you through your own father and mother; think what you did in your anger against your own father and against your own sight. What good ever came of intemperate anger? Give way because we all ask it of you. It is not right to receive a favour and give nothing in return, nor to keep a suppliant waiting.

Oedipus. What you have asked goes bitterly against the grain, my child, but let it be as you will. But promise me this, my friend, that if this man comes hither neither he nor any other shall be put over me as a master.

Theseus. No need to ask that, old man. I will not boast, but you may be certain that while God keeps me in the world no man shall be put over you as a master.   [*Theseus goes out.*

Chorus

Endure what life God gives and ask no longer span;
Cease to remember the delights of youth, travel-wearied aged man;
Delight becomes death-longing if all longing else be vain.

Even from that delight memory treasures so,
Death, despair, division of families, all entanglements of mankind grow,
As that old wandering beggar and these God-hated children know.

In the long echoing streets the laughing dancers throng,
The bride is carried to the bridegroom's chamber through torch-light and tumultuous song;
I celebrate the silent kiss that ends short life or long.

Never to have lived is best, ancient writers say;
Never to have drawn the breath of life, never to have looked into the eye of day;
The second best's a gay goodnight and quickly turn away.

Antigone. Father, I can see the suppliant coming, a man without attendants, the tears pouring from his eyes.
Oedipus. Who is he?
Antigone. The man who was in your thoughts from the first—Polyneices.

Polyneices enters

Polyneices. What shall I do or say? Must I mourn first for my own sorrow or first for my father, for that man there, that man lost among strangers, you two his only friends, his eyeballs blind, his clothing in squalid rags, his hair tossed by the wind, and his food— Heaven knows what scraps—in that old wallet? That is how I find him. I know now—now that it is too late—that I have proved myself, father, by neglect of you, the basest of living men. I proclaim it aloud, admit all that I am. And yet Mercy is the Queen of Heaven, and wherever God goes Mercy goes at His side, and that emboldens me to pray that she may stand at your side also. I have committed a great wrong, and yet all may be set right again. [*A pause.*] Why do you keep silent? Speak, father; do not turn away; will you not even answer? Will you drive me away with a contempt so great that you will not even explain why you are angry? Do what you can, sisters, to make our father speak to me: persuade him not to drive me away without even an answer. Remind him that I have come from the altar of the God.

Antigone. Say why you come, my unhappy brother, for words full of emotion, joy, anger, tenderness, whatever it is, can move a dumb man and make him speak.

Polyneices. I will tell everything—you have given me good advice; but first put myself under the God's protection. The King of this country brought me from the altar and promised that I should say whatever I had to say and suffer no wrong thereby, and I appeal to those here, to those who are strangers, and to my father and to my sisters, not to dishonour the King's word. And now, father, I will say what brings me here. I have been driven into exile, driven out of my own country, because being your eldest son I had claimed the throne. Eteocles, though younger than I, drove me into exile, though he neither worsted me in battle nor won the people from me by any sound argument. His cajolery and intrigue prevailed against me because of the curse that is upon your house; so at least do I think, and so I have been told by the oracle. And I am the more certain because when I reached Argos all went well. I married the daughter of Adrastus, lately King there, gathered about me seven companies of spearmen, and all the men most famous in war, and all sworn to die to drive out my enemies. But why have I come? I come to entreat you, father, in my own name and in that of my allies. Seven leaders, each with his troop of spearmen, gathering against Thebes. Amphiaraus, incomparable in war and divination alike; Tydeus the Aetolian; Eteoclus of Argos; Hippomedon, sent by Talaos his father; Capaneus, who boasts that he will burn Thebes to the ground; Parthenopaeus of Arcadia, son of Atalanta; and last of the seven, I, the son of Oedipus, but no, not his, but son of an accursed destiny. We seven who beleaguer Thebes and lead the men of Argos implore, pray, and beseech you. Remember your own children, remember your own exile, and turn away your anger. Do not let your anger follow when I march against the brother who has driven me out and stolen my inheritance. For victory, if truth be in the oracles, shall be with that party that you favour, and upon whatever side you claim to be your own. So by the Gods and by the founders of our race, I ask that you favour our party and our side. I too am a beggar and an exile—you and I eat the bread of strangers, and share a common doom, while he reigns as king, and strutting in our house mocks us both alike. With you to help, I shall conquer without toil or delay, and thereupon, my brother driven out, establish myself upon the throne and you in your own house once more. Favour our party, all shall be accomplished, but if you do not I shall not even return alive.

Chorus. Remember the man that brought him hither, Oedipus; say something, speak, speak to your son before you send him away.

Oedipus. If I did not remember that Theseus brought him and begged me to speak, I would not speak a word. But now he shall hear words that shall bring no comfort to his heart, and after that let him be gone. Villain, when you had the throne that your brother has taken, when you had the sceptre in your own hand, you drove me into exile, you made me a nationless man, aye, clapped these rags upon my back. And now that you are driven out in your turn you cannot look upon these rags without tears, but the time for tears is past. I bear my burden while I live, and while I live think you my murderer, for it was you that sent me wandering and begging for my bread. And but for these, these daughters, my nurses and preservers, these girls that have the strength of a man, I had been dead by now. But you and your brother are strangers and no sons of mine. Therefore the eye of God has seen you; punishment has begun, but it shall not ruin you utterly until your army marches upon Thebes. You shall not overthrow that city. No, but you shall fall and your brother fall, each drowned in the other's blood. I have called down that curse upon you, and now I call upon God that you may learn before your death what it is to mock a blind father. These are good, they are different, altogether different. But you, throne and supplication alike, are in the power of my curse, if indeed God's justice exists and his eternal law. Begone with my abhorrence, son that I have made no son, vilest of the vile, begone, orphan, begone, carry my curses away—all that I have called down upon your head. Never shall you vanquish your own country, your own kin, never shall you return to Argos among its hills, but find your death at the hand of kin and kill the man that gives that death, aye, kill the brother that drove you out of Thebes. And I call on the ancestral Night, I, the blind man, to gather you into itself, I call upon the spirits of this place and I call upon that power that has put such fearful hatred between brother and brother, I call upon the destroying God himself. Go, carry away these words in your ears; publish them abroad that the men of Thebes and your faithful allies may know that Oedipus pays as much honour to the one son as to the other.

Chorus. Get you gone: as I do not approve of your plottings I cannot wish you good luck.

Polyneices. I mourn for my lost hope and for my useless journey, and

I mourn for my comrades. What an end to all our plans; little did we think it when we marched from Argos. Misery, misery, such an end that I dare not speak of it to any, but must go in silence to this doom. Promise, you who are my sisters though his daughters, that if our father's curses be fulfilled, and if you be recalled to Thebes, you will give me fitting burial. Promise that my body suffer no dishonour; be praised among men for a double service—that done to a father, that done to a brother.

Antigone. One thing I entreat of you, Polyneices.

Polyneices. What is it, dear Antigone?

Antigone. Order your army back to Argos. Do not destroy yourself and Thebes.

Polyneices. No, it is impossible; I never could lead that army again once it were known that I had blenched.

Antigone. So you would lead it again—why rage against Thebes? If you destroy your native city at last, how will you be the better?

Polyneices. It is shameful to be an exile, an elder brother mocked at by a younger.

Antigone. Then it is you that make all certain, you that bring about the fulfilment of his prophecies, the killing of a brother by a brother.

Polyneices. Yes, that is what he wants, but I must not yield.

Antigone. Alas! Alas! But who dare follow you when he has heard the prophecy?

Polyneices. He will never hear it; no good leader brings bad news.

Antigone. So then, my brother, your decision is taken?

Polyneices. Yes, taken. Do not delay me further. Henceforth I run my race followed by demons and my father's curse; but I call down God's blessing upon you, my sister, if after my death you do my will, for while I live I am beyond your help. Take away your arms. Good-bye, sisters, for never will you look again upon my living body.

Antigone. Alas!

Polyneices. Do not mourn for me.

Antigone. Who would not mourn you, brother, hurrying away to a foreknown death?

Polyneices. How can I help it if I am fated to die?

Antigone. No, no; hear me, I beseech.

Polyneices. You waste breath.

Antigone. If wasted, then indeed am I wretched, for I must lose you.

Polyneices. Fortune will decide, but I pray to God that only good fortune attend you two, for there is not a man in the world but knows that you deserve it.　　　　　　　　　　　　　　　　　[*He goes out.*

Chorus

What is this portent? What does it shadow forth?
Have Heaven and Earth in dreadful marriage lain?
What shall the allotted season bring to birth?
This blind old ragged, rambling beggar-man
Calls curses upon cities, upon the great,
And scatters at his pleasure rich estate.

[*Thunder.*

Chorus. What an uproar! God protect us!

Oedipus. My children, my children, if there is any man who can be
sent, send to Theseus and summon him hither.

Antigone. Why should he be summoned, father?

Oedipus. God's winged thunder comes to lead me down to Hades;
send for him, send for him upon the instant.

[*A second peal of thunder.*

Chorus

Thunder has stirred the hair upon my head.
What horror comes to birth? What shall be found,
That travail finished, on the lowly bed?
Never in vain the dreadful thunder sounds,
Nor can the living lightning flash in vain;
Heaven has borne a child and shrieks from pain.

Oedipus. Daughters, your father comes to his predestined end; he can
no more turn away his face.

Antigone. How do you know it? What have you heard or seen?

Oedipus. Enough that I know it. Let a man go quickly and bring the
lord of this country.   [*Thunder.*

Chorus

Once more that dreadful sound! God pity us
When all is finished on the bed of earth,
Nor hold us all unclean for Oedipus.
Whatever fate maternal sky bring forth,
Pity Colonus, nor lay us under ban
Because of Oedipus the beggar-man.

Oedipus. Has Theseus come? Will he find me living, children? and
with all my wits?

Antigone. What would you say to him? What are you afraid of for-
getting?

Oedipus. He has heaped benefits upon me. The time has come to pay
for all.

Chorus

Come, King of Athens, father of the land—
Whether at Poseidon's altars and the still
Unfinished sacrifice, or close at hand—
A blind old beggar-man proclaims God's will,
Proclaims a blessing on the land and us;
Come, King of Athens, come, King Theseus.

Enter Theseus

Theseus. Why this sudden clamor? Why am I called hither, called as it seems by this stranger and by my own people alike? Have you been terrified by the thunder? No wonder indeed if you are terrified by such a storm.

Oedipus. Welcome! God has sent you, King; good fortune waits you here.

Theseus. What has happened, son of Laius?

Oedipus. I am about to die, and before I die I would accomplish for you and for this city what has been foretold.

Theseus. Why do you say you are about to die?

Oedipus. The Gods have sent the signs that they promised.

Theseus. What signs, old man?

Oedipus. Prolonged loud thunder and abundant lightning.

Theseus. You have foretold many things, and what you have foretold has come true. Therefore I believe your words and I ask what I must do.

Oedipus. Son of Aegeus, I shall expound a mystery and give your city that which time shall never take away. First I shall lead you to my place of death, and though blind I shall need no guiding hand. But that place you must never show to any living man, for it shall be, while it stays hidden, more protection than a multitude of Athenian shields or than the borrowed might of an ally; and there by that place mysteries shall be revealed, revealed to you alone, things that I dare not speak to my own daughters, much as I love them, things it is not lawful to put into words; and these you must guard in your heart and reveal to your successor, and then only upon your death-bed, that they may be revealed to his successor in turn and so through all time. So shall this city and countryside be kept unharmed from the dragon's teeth and from the men of Thebes, but keep it secret: while you keep all secret you shall be safe from your own citizens as from the enemy. Even the best-governed cities are turbulent, and though the Gods punish turbulence they are slow to act. But why should I warn you? the son of Aegeus knows how to guard himself. Now let us hurry to that place, for the heavens call and I dare not linger. Follow me, children, though but for a portion of the way. It is my turn to guide those that long have been their father's guide; come, come, but lay no hand upon me; all unhelped I shall discover my predestined plot of ground, my sacred tomb. Come this way, this way; Hermes guides and the Goddess of the Dead. O light bathing my body for the last time; O light, my light long ago, I tread the road to Hades; blessed be this land, blessed be its people, you, best of friends, be blessed, and when your fortune mounts, remember me in the tomb.

[*He goes out, followed by his daughters, Theseus, and attendants.*

Chorus

I call upon Persephone, queen of the dead,
And upon Hades, king of night, I call;
Chain all the Furies up that he may tread
The perilous pathway to the Stygian hall
And rest among his mighty peers at last,
For the entanglements of God are past.

Nor may the hundred-headed dog give tongue
Until the daughter of Earth and Tartarus
That even bloodless shades call Death has sung
The travel-broken shade of Oedipus
Through triumph of completed destiny
Into eternal sleep, if such there be.

Enter Messenger

Messenger. Fellow-countrymen, three words can sum up all I have to say—Oedipus is dead. But it all took time to happen and it will take time in the telling.

Chorus. So that unhappy man is dead.

Messenger. He is dead indeed.

Chorus. How? In a God-appointed, painless way?

Messenger. There indeed you touch upon the wonder of it. You saw with your own eyes how the man went out from here, none to show him where to set his feet, but he the guide of all. We followed to the sacrificial hollow in the rock where the footpaths cross and to the sacred threshold where brazen steps go down into the earth, and there, midway between the four sacred things, the basin of brass, the hollow pear-tree, the marble tomb, the stone from Thoricus, he sat upon the ground and began to loosen his miserable rags. Then he bade his children find spring water for washing and libation, and they climbed the neighbouring hill, found spring water there, and brought it to their father. They washed and dressed him as we wash and dress the dead, and no sooner had all been done according to his commands than there came from under our feet, as if from the place of shades, a sound of thunder. The two children trembled, threw themselves down upon their father's knees, beat upon their breasts, wept and cried aloud. And thereupon he cast his arms about them and said, 'From this day you are left without a father, and all that is mine comes to an end. Your attendance upon me has been a heavy burden, children; I know how heavy, and yet it seemed to you light. A word, a solitary word tells all, and that word is love. No living man could have loved as I have loved. But now I go, and never again shall you look upon me through all your days of life.' After he had spoken all three clung to one another, sobbing and crying out; but presently they ceased to sob and to cry out and there was silence, and then a voice spoke and summoned Oedipus, and the hair stood up upon our heads, for it was a God that spoke. It summoned Oedipus not once but many times. 'Oedipus, Oedipus,' it said, 'what keeps you there? We must set out upon our journey.' He, knowing what voice had spoken, called King Theseus to his side and said, 'O best of friends, put your right hand into the hands of my daughters; promise to be their guardian and never forsake them.' King Theseus, that most magnanimous man, promised and swore an oath, and yet fearing to wring the children's hearts anew spoke no word of grief. That oath being sworn, Oedipus groped for his daughters with blind hands and said, 'My children, be brave and go from this place, for there are things it is not lawful for you to see or hear. Go quickly, and let these others go, but let King Theseus stay and hear and see everything, for that is his right.' When he had spoken the children left and we followed with streaming eyes, but after a little time turned our heads. Oedipus had gone and the King stood there, a hand raised to shade his eyes as from some dreadful sight. Then, after a little, he bent down and kissed the earth, and after raised his arms to heaven praying, as it seemed, to heaven and earth in the same prayer. But by what death Oedipus died no man can say but Theseus. Neither did thunderbolt descend nor storm come up out of the sea, but some messenger carried him away or the foundations of the earth were riven to receive him, riven not by pain but by love. For I affirm, and care not if my words seem folly, that this man has gone without the pang of death and in a manner altogether wonderful.

Chorus. But where are the others? And where are the two girls?

Messenger. That sound of mourning tells where they are.

Enter Antigone, Ismene, and attendants

Ismene. Where shall we wander, where find our daily bread? I dread what is to come.

Chorus. Why should you, remembering the bitterness of your past, dread the future?

Ismene. Things that were most bitter can seem most sweet in memory. How should those days seem bitter when we could take him in our arms? Our beloved is gone down under the earth.

Chorus. He has found a blessed end.

Antigone. Sister, I will go back there.

Ismene. Why?

Antigone. I have a great longing.

Ismene. For what?

Antigone. To find a bed under the earth.

Ismene. What bed?

Antigone. Our father's bed.

Ismene. I thought you understood.

Antigone. Understood what?

Ismene. That he had no tomb, that nobody can tell where he lies, that he went alone to his death.

Antigone. Bring me to where we saw him last and kill me there.

Ismene. But if you died I should be friendless.

Chorus. Do not be afraid, my children.

Antigone. What refuge have we but our father's tomb?

Chorus. A refuge has been found.

Enter Theseus

Theseus. Your father is with the Powers under the earth; you have his promise and their protection. Do not vex them with lamentation. I bring you the protection of Athens.

Antigone. Promise me, son of Aegeus.

Theseus. What must I promise?

Antigone. To bring me to my father's tomb.

Theseus. The law forbids.

Antigone. But you are King of Athens.

Theseus. He had a charge upon me that never human foot approach that place.

Antigone. If that be my father's will I must obey.

Theseus. In all else it shall be as you will. I will omit nothing that can profit you or gratify the dead.

Chorus. Raise no funeral song. God's will has been accomplished.

THE END

THE RESURRECTION

1931

TO
JUNZO SATO

THE RESURRECTION

PERSONS IN THE PLAY

The Hebrew   The Syrian
The Greek   Christ
            Three Musicians

Before I had finished this play I saw that its subject-matter might make it unsuited for the public stage in England or in Ireland. I had begun it with an ordinary stage scene in the mind's eye, curtained walls, a window and door at back, a curtained door at left. I now changed the stage directions and wrote songs for the unfolding and folding of the curtain that it might be played in a studio or a drawing-room like my dance plays, or at the Peacock Theatre before a specially chosen audience. If it is played at the Peacock Theatre the Musicians may sing the opening and closing songs, as they pull apart or pull together the proscenium curtain; the whole stage may be hung with curtains with an opening at the left. While the play is in progress the Musicians will sit towards the right of the audience; if at the Peacock, on the step which separates the stage from the audience, or one on either side of the proscenium.

[*Song for the unfolding and folding of the curtain*]

I

I saw a staring virgin stand
Where holy Dionysus died,
And tear the heart out of his side,
And lay the heart upon her hand
And bear that beating heart away;
And then did all the Muses sing
Of Magnus Annus at the spring,
As though God's death were but a play.

II

Another Troy must rise and set,
Another lineage feed the crow,

364

Another Argo's painted prow
Drive to a flashier bauble yet.
The Roman Empire stood appalled:
It dropped the reins of peace and war
When that fierce virgin and her Star
Out of the fabulous darkness called.

[*The Hebrew is discovered alone upon the stage; he has a sword
or spear. The Musicians make faint drum-taps, or sound a
rattle; the Greek enters through the audience from the left.*

The Hebrew. Did you find out what the noise was?

The Greek. Yes, I asked a Rabbi.

The Hebrew. Were you not afraid?

The Greek. How could he know that I am called a Christian? I wore
the cap I brought from Alexandria. He said the followers of Dionysus
were parading the streets with rattles and drums; that such a thing
had never happened in this city before; that the Roman authorities
were afraid to interfere. The followers of Dionysus have been out
among the fields tearing a goat to pieces and drinking its blood, and
are now wandering through the streets like a pack of wolves. The
mob was so terrified of their frenzy that it left them alone, or, as
seemed more likely, so busy hunting Christians it had time for nothing else. I turned to go, but he called me back and asked where I
lived. When I said outside the gates, he asked if it was true that the
dead had broken out of the cemeteries.

The Hebrew. We can keep the mob off for some minutes, long enough
for the Eleven to escape over the roofs. I shall defend the narrow
stair between this and the street until I am killed, then you will take
my place. Why is not the Syrian here?

The Greek. I met him at the door and sent him on a message; he will
be back before long.

The Hebrew. The three of us will be few enough for the work in hand.

The Greek [*glancing towards the opening at the left*]. What are they
doing now?

The Hebrew. While you were down below, James brought a loaf out
of a bag, and Nathanael found a skin of wine. They put them on the
table. It was a long time since they had eaten anything. Then they
began to speak in low voices, and John spoke of the last time they
had eaten in that room.

The Greek. They were thirteen then.

The Hebrew. He said that Jesus divided bread and wine amongst them.
When John had spoken they sat still, nobody eating or drinking. If
you stand here you will see them. That is Peter close to the window.

He has been quite motionless for a long time, his head upon his breast.

The Greek. Is it true that when the soldier asked him if he were a follower of Jesus he denied it?

The Hebrew. Yes, it is true. James told me. Peter told the others what he had done. But when the moment came they were all afraid. I must not blame. I might have been no braver. What are we all but dogs who have lost their master?

The Greek. Yet you and I if the mob come will die rather than let it up that stair.

The Hebrew. Ah! That is different. I am going to draw that curtain; they must not hear what I am going to say.   [*He draws curtain.*

The Greek. I know what is in your mind.

The Hebrew. They are afraid because they do not know what to think. When Jesus was taken they could no longer believe him the Messiah. We can find consolation, but for the Eleven it was always complete light or complete darkness.

The Greek. Because they are so much older.

The Hebrew. No, no. You have only to look into their faces to see they were intended to be saints. They are unfitted for anything else. What makes you laugh?

The Greek. Something I can see through the window. There, where I am pointing. There, at the end of the street.

     [*They stand together looking out over the heads of the audience.*

The Hebrew. I cannot see anything.

The Greek. The hill.

The Hebrew. That is Calvary.

The Greek. And the three crosses on the top of it.   [*He laughs again.*

The Hebrew. Be quiet. You do not know what you are doing. You have gone out of your mind. You are laughing at Calvary.

The Greek. No, no. I am laughing because they thought they were nailing the hands of a living man upon the Cross, and all the time there was nothing there but a phantom.

The Hebrew. I saw him buried.

The Greek. We Greeks understand these things. No god has ever been buried; no god has ever suffered. Christ only seemed to be born, only seemed to eat, seemed to sleep, seemed to walk, seemed to die. I did not mean to tell you until I had proof.

The Hebrew. Proof?

The Greek. I shall have proof before nightfall.

The Hebrew. You talk wildly, but a masterless dog can bay the moon.

The Greek. No Jew can understand these things.

The Hebrew. It is you who do not understand. It is I and those men in there, perhaps, who begin to understand at last. He was nothing more than a man, the best man who ever lived. Nobody before him had so pitied human misery. He preached the coming of the Messiah because he thought the Messiah would take it all upon himself. Then some day when he was very tired, after a long journey perhaps, he thought that he himself was the Messiah. He thought it because of all destinies it seemed the most terrible.

The Greek. How could a man think himself the Messiah?

The Hebrew. It was always foretold that he would be born of a woman.

The Greek. To say that a god can be born of a woman, carried in her womb, fed upon her breast, washed as children are washed, is the most terrible blasphemy.

The Hebrew. If the Messiah were not born of a woman he could not take away the sins of man. Every sin starts a stream of suffering, but the Messiah takes it all away.

The Greek. Every man's sins are his property. Nobody else has a right to them.

The Hebrew. The Messiah is able to exhaust human suffering as though it were all gathered together in the spot of a burning-glass.

The Greek. That makes me shudder. The utmost possible suffering as an object of worship! You are morbid because your nation has no statues.

The Hebrew. What I have described is what I thought until three days ago.

The Greek. I say that there is nothing in the tomb.

The Hebrew. I saw him carried up the mountain and the tomb shut upon him.

The Greek. I have sent the Syrian to the tomb to prove that there is nothing there.

The Hebrew. You knew the danger we were all in and yet you weakened our guard?

The Greek. I have risked the apostles' lives and our own. What I have sent the Syrian to find out is more important.

The Hebrew. None of us are in our right mind to-day. I have got something in my own head that shocks me.

The Greek. Something you do not want to speak about?

The Hebrew. I am glad that he was not the Messiah; we might all have been deceived to our lives' end, or learnt the truth too late. One had to sacrifice everything that the divine suffering might, as it were, descend into one's mind and soul and make them pure. [*A sound of rattles and drums, at first in short bursts that come between sentences, but gradually growing continuous.*] One had to give up all worldly knowledge, all ambition, do nothing of one's own will.

Only the divine could have any reality. God had to take complete possession. It must be a terrible thing when one is old, and the tomb round the corner, to think of all the ambitions one has put aside; to think, perhaps, a great deal about women. I want to marry and have children.

The Greek [*who is standing facing the audience, and looking out over their heads*]. It is the worshippers of Dionysus. They are under the window now. There is a group of women who carry upon their shoulders a bier with an image of the dead god upon it. No, they are not women. They are men dressed as women. I have seen something like it in Alexandria. They are all silent, as if something were going to happen. My God! What a spectacle! In Alexandria a few men paint their lips vermilion. They imitate women that they may attain in worship a woman's self-abandonment. No great harm comes of it—but here! Come and look for yourself.

The Hebrew. I will not look at such madmen.

The Greek. Though the music has stopped some men are still dancing, and some of the dancers have gashed themselves with knives, imagining themselves, I suppose, at once the god and the Titans that murdered him. A little further off a man and woman are coupling in the middle of the street. She thinks the surrender to some man the dance threw into her arms may bring her god back to life. All are from the foreign quarter, to judge by face and costume, and are the most ignorant and excitable class of Asiatic Greeks, the dregs of the population. Such people suffer terribly and seek forgetfulness in monstrous ceremonies. Ah, that is what they were waiting for. The crowd has parted to make way for a singer. It is a girl. No, not a girl; a boy from the theatre. I know him. He acts girls' parts. He is dressed as a girl, but his finger-nails are gilded and his wig is made of gilded cords. He looks like a statue out of some temple. I remember something of the kind in Alexandria. Three days after the full moon, a full moon in March, they sing the death of the god and pray for his resurrection.

[*One of the Musicians sings the following song*]
             Astrea's holy child!
             A rattle in the wood
             Where a Titan strode!
             His rattle drew the child
             Into that solitude.
Barrum, barrum, barrum
             [*Drum-taps accompany and follow the words.*
             We wandering women,
             Wives for all that come,

Tried to draw him home;
And every wandering woman
Beat upon a drum.
Barrum, barrum, barrum   [*Drum-taps as before.*
But the murderous Titans
Where the woods grow dim
Stood and waited him.
The great hands of those Titans
Tore limb from limb.
Barrum, barrum, barrum   [*Drum-taps as before.*
On virgin Astrea
That can succour all
Wandering women call;
Call out to Astrea
That the moon stood at the full.
Barrum, barrum, barrum   [*Drum-taps as before.*

The Greek. I cannot think all that self-surrender and self-abasement is Greek, despite the Greek name of its god. When the goddess came to Achilles in the battle she did not interfere with his soul, she took him by his yellow hair. Lucretius thinks that the gods appear in the visions of the day and night but are indifferent to human fate; that, however, is the exaggeration of a Roman rhetorician. They can be discovered by contemplation, in their faces a high keen joy like the cry of a bat, and the man who lives heroically gives them the only earthly body that they covet. He, as it were, copies their gestures and their acts. What seems their indifference is but their eternal possession of themselves. Man, too, remains separate. He does not surrender his soul. He keeps his privacy.

[*Drum-taps to represent knocking at the door.*

The Hebrew. There is someone at the door, but I dare not open with that crowd in the street.

The Greek. You need not be afraid. The crowd has begun to move away. [*The Hebrew goes down into the audience towards the left.*] I deduce from our great philosophers that a god can overwhelm man with disaster, take health and wealth away, but man keeps his privacy. If that is the Syrian he may bring such confirmation that mankind will never forget his words.

The Hebrew [*from amongst the audience*]. It is the Syrian. There is something wrong. He is ill or drunk.

[*He helps the Syrian on to the stage.*

The Syrian. I am like a drunken man. I can hardly stand upon my feet. Something incredible has happened. I have run all the way.

The Hebrew. Well?

The Syrian. I must tell the Eleven at once. Are they still in there? Everybody must be told.

The Hebrew. What is it? Get your breath and speak.

The Syrian. I was on my way to the tomb. I met the Galilean women, Mary the mother of Jesus, Mary the mother of James, and the other women. The younger women were pale with excitement and began to speak all together. I did not know what they were saying; but Mary the mother of James said that they had been to the tomb at daybreak and found that it was empty.

The Greek. Ah!

The Hebrew. The tomb cannot be empty. I will not believe it.

The Syrian. At the door stood a man all shining, and cried out that Christ had arisen. [*Faint drum-taps and the faint sound of a rattle.*] As they came down the mountain a man stood suddenly at their side; that man was Christ himself. They stooped down and kissed his feet. Now stand out of my way that I may tell Peter and James and John.

The Hebrew [*standing before the curtained entrance of the inner room*]. I will not stand out of the way.

The Syrian. Did you hear what I said? Our master has arisen.

The Hebrew. I will not have the Eleven disturbed for the dreams of women.

The Greek. The women were not dreaming. They told you the truth, and yet this man is in the right. He is in charge here. We must all be convinced before we speak to the Eleven.

The Syrian. The Eleven will be able to judge better than we.

The Greek. Though we are so much younger we know more of the world than they do.

The Hebrew. If you told your story they would no more believe it than I do, but Peter's misery would be increased. I know him longer than you do and I know what would happen. Peter would remember that the women did not flinch; that not one amongst them denied her master; that the dream proved their love and faith. Then he would remember that he had lacked both, and imagine that John was looking at him. He would turn away and bury his head in his hands.

The Greek. I said that we must all be convinced, but there is another reason why you must not tell them anything. Somebody else is coming. I am certain that Jesus never had a human body; that he is a phantom and can pass through that wall; that he will so pass; that he will pass through this room; that he himself will speak to the apostles.

The Syrian. He is no phantom. We put a great stone over the mouth of the tomb, and the women say that it has been rolled back.

The Hebrew. The Romans heard yesterday that some of our people planned to steal the body, and to put abroad a story that Christ had arisen; and so escape the shame of our defeat. They probably stole it in the night.

The Syrian. The Romans put sentries at the tomb. The women found the sentries asleep. Christ had put them asleep that they might not see him move the stone.

The Greek. A hand without bones, without sinews, cannot move a stone.

The Syrian. What matter if it contradicts all human knowledge?—another Argo seeks another fleece, another Troy is sacked.

The Greek. Why are you laughing?

The Syrian. What is human knowledge?

The Greek. The knowledge that keeps the road from here to Persia free from robbers, that has built the beautiful humane cities, that has made the modern world, that stands between us and the barbarian.

The Syrian. But what if there is something it cannot explain, something more important than anything else?

The Greek. You talk as if you wanted the barbarian back.

The Syrian. What if there is always something that lies outside knowledge, outside order? What if at the moment when knowledge and order seem complete that something appears?

            [He has begun to laugh.

The Hebrew. Stop laughing.

The Syrian. What if the irrational return? What if the circle begin again?

The Hebrew. Stop! He laughed when he saw Calvary through the window, and now you laugh.

The Greek. He too has lost control of himself.

The Hebrew. Stop, I tell you.   *[Drums and rattles.*

The Syrian. But I am not laughing. It is the people out there who are laughing.

The Hebrew. No, they are shaking rattles and beating drums.

The Syrian. I thought they were laughing. How horrible!

The Greek [*looking out over heads of audience*]. The worshippers of Dionysus are coming this way again. They have hidden their image of the dead god, and have begun their lunatic cry, 'God has arisen! God has arisen!'

  [*The Musicians who have been saying* 'God has arisen!' *fall silent.* They will cry 'God has arisen!' through all the streets of the city. They can make their god live and die at their pleasure; but why are they silent? They are dancing silently. They are coming nearer and nearer, dancing all the while, using some kind of ancient step unlike anything I have seen in Alexandria. They are almost under the window now.

The Hebrew. They have come back to mock us, because their god arises every year, whereas our god is dead for ever.

The Greek. How they roll their painted eyes as the dance grows quicker and quicker! They are under the window. Why are they all suddenly motionless? Why are all those unseeing eyes turned upon this house? Is there anything strange about this house?

The Hebrew. Somebody has come into the room.

The Greek. Where?

The Hebrew. I do not know; but I thought I heard a step.

The Greek. I knew that he would come.

The Hebrew. There is no one here. I shut the door at the foot of the steps.

The Greek. The curtain over there is moving.

The Hebrew. No, it is quite still, and besides there is nothing behind it but a blank wall.

The Greek. Look, look!

The Hebrew. Yes, it has begun to move.

[*During what follows he backs in terror towards the left-hand corner of the stage.*

The Greek. There is someone coming through it.

[*The figure of Christ wearing a recognisable but stylistic mask enters through the curtain. The Syrian slowly draws back the curtain that shuts off the inner room where the apostles are. The three young men are towards the left of the stage, the figure of Christ is at the back towards the right.*

The Greek. It is the phantom of our master. Why are you afraid? He has been crucified and buried, but only in semblance, and is among us once more. [*The Hebrew kneels.*] There is nothing here but a phantom, it has no flesh and blood. Because I know the truth I am not afraid. Look, I will touch it. It may be hard under my hand like a statue—I have heard of such things—or my hand may pass through it—but there is no flesh and blood. [*He goes slowly up to the figure and passes his hand over its side.*] The heart of a phantom is beating! The heart of a phantom is beating!

[*He screams. The figure of Christ crosses the stage and passes into the inner room.*

The Syrian. He is standing in the midst of them. Some are afraid. He looks at Peter and James and John. He smiles. He has parted the clothes at his side. He shows them his side. There is a great wound there. Thomas has put his hand into the wound. He has put his hand where the heart is.

The Greek. O Athens, Alexandria, Rome, something has come to destroy you. The heart of a phantom is beating. Man has begun to die.

Your words are clear at last, O Heraclitus. God and man die each
other's life, live each other's death.

[*The Musicians rise, one or more singing the following words. If
the performance is in a private room or studio, they unfold and
fold a curtain as in my dance plays; if at the Peacock Theatre,
they draw the proscenium curtain across.*

I

In pity for man's darkening thought
He walked that room and issued thence
In Galilean turbulence;
The Babylonian starlight brought
A fabulous, formless darkness in;
Odour of blood when Christ was slain
Made all Platonic tolerance vain
And vain all Doric discipline.

II

Everything that man esteems
Endures a moment or a day:
Love's pleasure drives his love away,
The painter's brush consumes his dreams;
The herald's cry, the soldier's tread
Exhaust his glory and his might:
Whatever flames upon the night
Man's own resinous heart has fed.

THE END

THE WORDS UPON THE
WINDOW-PANE

1934

IN MEMORY OF
LADY GREGORY
IN WHOSE HOUSE IT WAS WRITTEN

THE WORDS UPON THE WINDOW-PANE

PERSONS IN THE PLAY

Dr. Trench	Cornelius Patterson
Miss Mackenna	Abraham Johnson
John Corbet	Mrs. Mallet
Mrs. Henderson	

A lodging-house room, an armchair, a little table in front of it, chairs on either side. A fireplace and window. A kettle on the hob and some tea-things on a dresser. A door to back and towards the right. Through the door one can see an entrance hall. The sound of a knocker. Miss Mackenna passes through and then she re-enters hall together with John Corbet, a man of twenty-two or twenty-three, and Dr. Trench, a man of between sixty and seventy.

Dr. Trench [*in hall*]. May I introduce John Corbet, one of the Corbets of Ballymoney, but at present a Cambridge student? This is Miss Mackenna, our energetic secretary.

        [They come into room, take off their coats.

Miss Mackenna. I thought it better to let you in myself. This country is still sufficiently medieval to make spiritualism an undesirable theme for gossip. Give me your coats and hats, I will put them in my own room. It is just across the hall. Better sit down; your watches must be fast. Mrs. Henderson is lying down, as she always does before a séance. We won't begin for ten minutes yet.

        [She goes out with hats and coats.

Dr. Trench. Miss Mackenna does all the real work of the Dublin Spiritualists' Association. She did all the correspondence with Mrs. Henderson, and persuaded the landlady to let her this big room and a small room upstairs. We are a poor society and could not guarantee anything in advance. Mrs. Henderson has come from London at her own risk. She was born in Dublin and wants to spread the movement here. She lives very economically and does not expect a great deal. We all give what we can. A poor woman with the soul of an apostle.

John Corbet. Have there been many séances?

Dr. Trench. Only three so far.

John Corbet. I hope she will not mind my scepticism. I have looked into Myers' *Human Personality* and a wild book by Conan Doyle, but am unconvinced.

Dr. Trench. We all have to find the truth for ourselves. Lord Dunraven, then Lord Adare, introduced my father to the famous David Home. My father often told me that he saw David Home floating in the air in broad daylight, but I did not believe a word of it. I had to investigate for myself, and I was very hard to convince. Mrs. Piper, an American trance medium, not unlike Mrs. Henderson, convinced me.

John Corbet. A state of somnambulism and voices coming through her lips that purport to be those of dead persons?

Dr. Trench. Exactly: quite the best kind of mediumship if you want to establish the identity of a spirit. But do not expect too much. There has been a hostile influence.

John Corbet. You mean an evil spirit?

Dr. Trench. The poet Blake said that he never knew a bad man that had not something very good about him. I say a hostile influence, an influence that disturbed the last séance very seriously. I cannot tell you what happened, for I have not been at any of Mrs. Henderson's séances. Trance mediumship has nothing new to show me—I told the young people when they made me their President that I would probably stay at home, that I could get more out of Emanuel Swedenborg than out of any séance. [*A knock.*] That is probably old Cornelius Patterson; he thinks they race horses and whippets in the other world, and is, so they tell me, so anxious to find out if he is right that he is always punctual. Miss Mackenna will keep him to herself for some minutes. He gives her tips for Harold's Cross.

[*Miss Mackenna crosses to hall door and admits Cornelius Patterson. She brings him to her room across the hall.*

John Corbet [*who has been wandering about*]. This is a wonderful room for a lodging-house.

Dr. Trench. It was a private house until about fifty years ago. It was not so near the town in those days, and there are large stables at the back. Quite a number of notable people lived here. Grattan was born upstairs; no, not Grattan, Curran perhaps—I forget—but I do know that this house in the early part of the eighteenth century belonged to friends of Jonathan Swift, or rather of Stella. Swift chaffed her in the *Journal to Stella* because of certain small sums of money she lost at cards probably in this very room. That was before Vanessa appeared upon the scene. It was a country-house in those days, surrounded by trees and gardens. Somebody cut some

lines from a poem of hers upon the window-pane—tradition says
Stella herself. [*A knock.*] Here they are, but you will hardly make
them out in this light.

> [*They stand in the window. Corbet stoops down to see better.
> Miss Mackenna and Abraham Johnson enter and stand near
> door.*

Abraham Johnson. Where is Mrs. Henderson?

Miss Mackenna. She is upstairs; she always rests before a séance.

Abraham Johnson. I must see her before the séance. I know exactly
what to do to get rid of this evil influence.

Miss Mackenna. If you go up to see her there will be no séance at all.
She says it is dangerous even to think, much less to speak, of an
evil influence.

Abraham Johnson. Then I shall speak to the President.

Miss Mackenna. Better talk the whole thing over first in my room.
Mrs. Henderson says that there must be perfect harmony.

Abraham Johnson. Something must be done. The last séance was completely spoiled.   [*A knock.*

Miss Mackenna. That may be Mrs. Mallet; she is a very experienced
spiritualist. Come to my room, old Patterson and some others are
there already.

> [*She brings him to the other room and later crosses to hall door to
> admit Mrs. Mallet.*

John Corbet. I know those lines well—they are part of a poem Stella
wrote for Swift's fifty-fourth birthday. Only three poems of hers
—and some lines she added to a poem of Swift's—have come down
to us, but they are enough to prove her a better poet than Swift.
Even those few words on the window make me think of a seven-
teenth-century poet, Donne or Crashaw.   [*He quotes.*

> 'You taught how I might youth prolong
> By knowing what is right and wrong,
> How from my heart to bring supplies
> Of lustre to my fading eyes.'

How strange that a celibate scholar, well on in life, should keep the
love of two such women! He met Vanessa in London at the height
of his political power. She followed him to Dublin. She loved him
for nine years, perhaps died of love, but Stella loved him all her life.

Dr. Trench. I have shown that writing to several persons, and you are
the first who has recognised the lines.

John Corbet. I am writing an essay on Swift and Stella for my doctorate at Cambridge. I hope to prove that in Swift's day men of

intellect reached the height of their power—the greatest position they ever attained in society and the State, that everything great in Ireland and in our character, in what remains of our architecture, comes from that day; that we have kept its seal longer than England.

Dr. Trench. A tragic life: Bolingbroke, Harley, Ormonde, all those great Ministers that were his friends, banished and broken.

John Corbet. I do not think you can explain him in that way—his tragedy had deeper foundations. His ideal order was the Roman Senate, his ideal men Brutus and Cato. Such an order and such men had seemed possible once more, but the movement passed and he foresaw the ruin to come. Democracy, Rousseau, the French Revolution; that is why he hated the common run of men,—'I hate lawyers, I hate doctors,' he said, 'though I love Dr. So-and-so and Judge So-and-so'—that is why he wrote *Gulliver,* that is why he wore out his brain, that is why he felt *saeva indignatio,* that is why he sleeps under the greatest epitaph in history. You remember how it goes? It is almost finer in English than in Latin: 'He has gone where fierce indignation can lacerate his heart no more.'

[*Abraham Johnson comes in, followed by Mrs. Mallet and Cornelius Patterson.*

Abraham Johnson. Something must be done, Dr. Trench, to drive away the influence that has destroyed our séances. I have come here week after week at considerable expense. I am from Belfast. I am by profession a minister of the Gospel, I do a great deal of work among the poor and ignorant. I produce considerable effect by singing and preaching, but I know that my effect should be much greater than it is. My hope is that I shall be able to communicate with the great Evangelist Moody. I want to ask him to stand invisible beside me when I speak or sing, and lay his hands upon my head and give me such a portion of his power that my work may be blessed as the work of Moody and Sankey was blessed.

Mrs. Mallet. What Mr. Johnson says about the hostile influence is quite true. The last two séances were completely spoilt. I am thinking of starting a tea-shop in Folkestone. I followed Mrs. Henderson to Dublin to get my husband's advice, but two spirits kept talking and would not let any other spirit say a word.

Dr. Trench. Did the spirits say the same thing and go through the same drama at both séances?

Mrs. Mallet. Yes—just as if they were characters in some kind of horrible play.

Dr. Trench. That is what I was afraid of.

Mrs. Mallet. My husband was drowned at sea ten years ago, but constantly speaks to me through Mrs. Henderson as if he were still alive. He advises me about everything I do, and I am utterly lost if I cannot question him.

Cornelius Patterson. I never did like the Heaven they talk about in churches: but when somebody told me that Mrs. Mallet's husband ate and drank and went about with his favourite dog, I said to myself, 'That is the place for Corney Patterson'. I came here to find out if it was true, and I declare to God I have not heard one word about it.

Abraham Johnson. I ask you, Dr. Trench, as President of the Dublin Spiritualists' Association, to permit me to read the ritual of exorcism appointed for such occasions. After the last séance I copied it out of an old book in the library of Belfast University. I have it here.

[*He takes paper out of his pocket.*

Dr. Trench. The spirits are people like ourselves, we treat them as our guests and protect them from discourtesy and violence, and every exorcism is a curse or a threatened curse. We do not admit that there are evil spirits. Some spirits are earth-bound—they think they are still living and go over and over some action of their past lives, just as we go over and over some painful thought, except that where they are thought is reality. For instance, when a spirit which has died a violent death comes to a medium for the first time, it re-lives all the pains of death.

Mrs. Mallet. When my husband came for the first time the medium gasped and struggled as if she was drowning. It was terrible to watch.

Dr. Trench. Sometimes a spirit re-lives not the pain of death but some passionate or tragic moment of life. Swedenborg describes this and gives the reason for it. There is an incident of the kind in the *Odyssey,* and many in Eastern literature; the murderer repeats his murder, the robber his robbery, the lover his serenade, the soldier hears the trumpet once again. If I were a Catholic I would say that such spirits were in Purgatory. In vain do we write *requiescat in pace* upon the tomb, for they must suffer, and we in our turn must suffer until God gives peace. Such spirits do not often come to séances unless those séances are held in houses where those spirits lived, or where the event took place. This spirit which speaks those incomprehensible words and does not answer when spoken to is of such a nature. The more patient we are, the more quickly will it pass out of its passion and its remorse.

Abraham Johnson. I am still convinced that the spirit which disturbed the last séance is evil. If I may not exorcise it I will certainly pray for protection.

Dr. Trench. Mrs. Henderson's control, Lulu, is able and experienced and can protect both medium and sitters, but it may help Lulu if you pray that the spirit find rest.

[*Abraham Johnson sits down and prays silently, moving his lips. Mrs. Henderson comes in with Miss Mackenna and others. Miss Mackenna shuts the door.*

Dr. Trench. Mrs. Henderson, may I introduce to you Mr. Corbet, a young man from Cambridge and a sceptic, who hopes that you will be able to convince him?

Mrs. Henderson. We were all sceptics once. He must not expect too much from a first séance. He must persevere.

[*She sits in the armchair, and the others begin to seat themselves. Miss Mackenna goes to John Corbet and they remain standing.*

Miss Mackenna. I am glad that you are a sceptic.

John Corbet. I thought you were a spiritualist.

Miss Mackenna. I have seen a good many séances, and sometimes think it is all coincidence and thought-transference. [*She says this in a low voice.*] Then at other times I think as Dr. Trench does, and then I feel like Job—you know the quotation—the hair of my head stands up. A spirit passes before my face.

Mrs. Mallet. Turn the key, Dr. Trench, we don't want anybody blundering in here. [*Dr. Trench locks door.*] Come and sit here, Miss Mackenna.

Miss Mackenna. No, I am going to sit beside Mr. Corbet.

[*Corbet and Miss Mackenna sit down.*

John Corbet. You feel like Job to-night?

Miss Mackenna. I feel that something is going to happen, that is why I am glad that you are a sceptic.

John Corbet. You feel safer?

Miss Mackenna. Yes, safer.

Mrs. Henderson. I am glad to meet all my dear friends again and to welcome Mr. Corbet amongst us. As he is a stranger I must explain that we do not call up spirits, we make the right conditions and they come. I do not know who is going to come; sometimes there are a great many and the guides choose between them. The guides try to send somebody for everybody but do not always succeed. If you want to speak to some dear friend who has passed over, do not be discouraged. If your friend cannot come this time, maybe he can next time. My control is a dear little girl called Lulu who died when she was five or six years old. She describes the spirits present and tells us what spirit wants to speak. Miss Mackenna, a verse of a hymn, please, the same we had last time, and will everyone join in the singing.

[*They sing the following lines from Hymn 564, Irish Church Hymnal.*

'Sun of my soul, Thou Saviour dear,
It is not night if Thou be near:
O may no earth-born cloud arise
To hide Thee from Thy servant's eyes.'
[*Mrs. Henderson is leaning back in her chair asleep.*

Miss Mackenna [*to John Corbet*]. She always snores like that when she is going off.

Mrs. Henderson [*in a child's voice*]. Lulu so glad to see all her friends.

Mrs. Mallet. And we are glad you have come, Lulu.

Mrs. Henderson [*in a child's voice*]. Lulu glad to see new friend.

Miss Mackenna [*to John Corbet*]. She is speaking to you.

John Corbet. Thank you, Lulu.

Mrs. Henderson [*in a child's voice*]. You mustn't laugh at the way I talk.

John Corbet. I am not laughing, Lulu.

Mrs. Henderson [*in a child's voice*]. Nobody must laugh. Lulu does her best but can't say big long words. Lulu sees a tall man here, lots of hair on face [*Mrs. Henderson passes her hands over her cheeks and chin*], not much on the top of his head [*Mrs. Henderson passes her hand over the top of her head*], red necktie, and such a funny sort of pin.

Mrs. Mallet. Yes. . . . Yes. . . .

Mrs. Henderson [*in a child's voice*]. Pin like a horseshoe.

Mrs. Mallet. It's my husband.

Mrs. Henderson [*in a child's voice*]. He has a message.

Mrs. Mallet. Yes.

Mrs. Henderson [*in a child's voice*]. Lulu cannot hear. He is too far off. He has come near. Lulu can hear now. He says . . . he says, 'Drive that man away!' He is pointing to somebody in the corner, that corner over there. He says it is the bad man who spoilt everything last time. If they won't drive him away, Lulu will scream.

Miss Mackenna. That horrible spirit again.

Abraham Johnson. Last time he monopolised the séance.

Mrs. Mallet. He would not let anybody speak but himself.

Mrs. Henderson [*in a child's voice*]. They have driven that bad man away. Lulu sees a young lady.

Mrs. Mallet. Is not my husband here?

Mrs. Henderson [*in a child's voice*]. Man with funny pin gone away. Young lady here—Lulu thinks she must be at a fancy dress party, such funny clothes, hair all in curls—all bent down on floor near that old man with glasses.

Dr. Trench. No, I do not recognize her.

Mrs. Henderson [*in a child's voice*]. That bad man, that bad old man in the corner, they have let him come back. Lulu is going to scream. O. . . . O. . . . [*In a man's voice*]. How dare you write to her? How dare you ask if we were married? How dare you question her?

Dr. Trench. A soul in its agony—it cannot see us or hear us.

Mrs. Henderson [*upright and rigid, only her lips moving, and still in a man's voice*]. You sit crouching there. Did you not hear what I said? How dared you question her? I found you an ignorant little girl without intellect, without moral ambition. How many times did I not stay away from great men's houses, how many times forsake the Lord Treasurer, how many times neglect the business of the State that we might read Plutarch together!

[*Abraham Johnson half rises. Dr. Trench motions him to remain seated.*

Dr. Trench. Silence!

Abraham Johnson. But, Dr. Trench . . .

Dr. Trench. Hush—we can do nothing.

Mrs. Henderson [*speaking as before*]. I taught you to think in every situation of life not as Hester Vanhomrigh would think in that situation, but as Cato or Brutus would, and now you behave like some common slut with her ear against the keyhole.

John Corbet [*to Miss Mackenna*]. It is Swift, Jonathan Swift, talking to the woman he called Vanessa. She was christened Hester Vanhomrigh.

Mrs. Henderson [*in Vanessa's voice*]. I questioned her, Jonathan, because I love. Why have you let me spend hours in your company if you did not want me to love you? [*In Swift's voice.*] When I rebuilt Rome in your mind it was as though I walked its streets. [*In Vanessa's voice.*] Was that all, Jonathan? Was I nothing but a painter's canvas? [*In Swift's voice.*] My God, do you think it was easy? I was a man of strong passions and I had sworn never to marry. [*In Vanessa's voice.*] If you and she are not married, why should we not marry like other men and women? I loved you from the first moment when you came to my mother's house and began to teach me. I thought it would be enough to look at you, to speak to you, to hear you speak. I followed you to Ireland five years ago and I can bear it no longer. It is not enough to look, to speak, to hear. Jonathan, Jonathan, I am a woman, the women Brutus and Cato loved were not different. [*In Swift's voice.*] I have something in my blood that no child must inherit. I have constant attacks of dizziness; I pretend they come from a surfeit of fruit when I was a child. I had them in London. . . . There was a great doctor there, Dr. Arbuthnot; I told him of those attacks of dizziness, I told him of worse things. It was he who explained. There is a line of Dryden's. . . . [*In Vanessa's voice.*] O, I know—'Great wits are sure to madness near allied'. If you had children, Jonathan, my blood would make them healthy. I will take your hand, I will lay it upon my heart— upon the Vanhomrigh blood that has been healthy for generations. [*Mrs. Henderson slowly raises her left hand.*] That is the first time you have touched my body, Jonathan. [*Mrs. Henderson stands up and remains rigid. In Swift's voice.*] What do I care if it be healthy? What do I care if it could make mine healthy? Am I to add another to the healthy rascaldom and knavery of the world? [*In Vanessa's voice.*] Look at me, Jonathan. Your arrogant intellect separates us. Give me both your hands. I will put them upon my breast. [*Mrs. Henderson raises her right hand to the level of her left and then raises both to her breast.*] O, it is white—white as the gambler's dice—white ivory dice. Think of the uncertainty. Perhaps a mad child—perhaps a rascal—perhaps a knave—perhaps not, Jonathan. The dice of the intellect are loaded, but I am the common ivory dice. [*Her hands are stretched out as though drawing somebody towards her.*] It is not my hands that draw you back. My hands are weak, they could not draw you back if you did not love as I love. You said that you have strong passions; that is true, Jonathan—no man in Ireland is so passionate. That is why you need me, that is why you need children, nobody has greater need. You are growing old. An old man without children is very solitary. Even his friends, men as old as he, turn away, they turn towards the young, their children or their children's children. They cannot endure an old man like themselves. [*Mrs. Henderson moves away from the chair, her movements gradually growing convulsive.*] You are not too old for the dice, Jonathan, but a few years if you turn away will make you an old miserable childless man. [*In Swift's voice.*] O God, hear the prayer of Jonathan Swift, that afflicted man, and grant that he may leave to posterity nothing but his intellect that came to him from Heaven. [*In Vanessa's voice.*] Can you face solitude with that mind, Jonathan? [*Mrs. Henderson goes to the door, finds that it is closed.*] Dice, white ivory dice. [*In Swift's voice.*] My God, I am left alone with my enemy. Who locked the door, who locked me in with my enemy? [*Mrs. Henderson beats upon the door, sinks to the floor and then speaks as Lulu.*] Bad old man! Do not let him come back. Bad old man does not know he is dead. Lulu cannot find fathers, mothers, sons that have passed over. Power almost gone. [*Mrs. Mallet leads Mrs. Henderson, who seems very exhausted, back to her chair. She is still asleep. She speaks again as Lulu.*] Another verse of hymn. Everybody sing. Hymn will bring good influence.

[*They sing*]
'If some poor wandering child of Thine
Have spurned to-day the voice divine,
Now, Lord, the gracious work begin;
Let him no more lie down in sin.'

[*During the hymn Mrs. Henderson has been murmuring 'Stella', but the singing has almost drowned her voice. The singers draw one another's attention to the fact that she is speaking. The singing stops.*]

Dr. Trench. I thought she was speaking.

Mrs. Mallet. I saw her lips move.

Dr. Trench. She would be more comfortable with a cushion, but we might wake her.

Mrs. Mallet. Nothing can wake her out of a trance like that until she wakes up herself.

[*She brings a cushion and she and Dr. Trench put Mrs. Henderson into a more comfortable position.*

Mrs. Henderson [*in Swift's voice*]. Stella.

Miss Mackenna [*to John Corbet*]. Did you hear that? She said 'Stella'.

John Corbet. Vanessa has gone, Stella has taken her place.

Miss Mackenna. Did you notice the change while we were singing? The new influence in the room?

John Corbet. I thought I did, but it must have been fancy.

Mrs. Mallet. Hush!

Mrs. Henderson [*in Swift's voice*]. Have I wronged you, beloved Stella? Are you unhappy? You have no children, you have no lover, you have no husband. A cross and ageing man for friend—nothing but that. But no, do not answer—you have answered already in that poem you wrote for my last birthday. With what scorn you speak of the common lot of women 'with no endowments but a face—'

'Before the thirtieth year of life
A maid forlorn or hated wife.'

It is the thought of the great Chrysostom who wrote in a famous passage that women loved according to the soul, loved as saints can love, keep their beauty longer, have greater happiness than women loved according to the flesh. That thought has comforted me, but it is a terrible thing to be responsible for another's happiness. There are moments when I doubt, when I think Chrysostom may have been wrong. But now I have your poem to drive doubt away. You have addressed me in these noble words:

> 'You taught how I might youth prolong
> By knowing what is right and wrong;
> How from my heart to bring supplies
> Of lustre to my fading eyes;
> How soon a beauteous mind repairs
> The loss of chang'd or falling hairs;
> How wit and virtue from within
> Can spread a smoothness o'er the skin.'

John Corbet. The words upon the window-pane!

Mrs. Henderson [*in Swift's voice*]. Then, because you understand that I am afraid of solitude, afraid of outliving my friends—and myself—you comfort me in that last verse—you overpraise my moral nature when you attribute to it a rich mantle, but O how touching those words which describe your love:

> 'Late dying may you cast a shred
> Of that rich mantle o'er my head;
> To bear with dignity my sorrow,
> One day alone, then die to-morrow.'

Yes, you will close my eyes, Stella. O, you will live long after me, dear Stella, for you are still a young woman, but you will close my eyes. [*Mrs. Henderson sinks back in chair and speaks as Lulu.*] Bad old man gone. Power all used up. Lulu can do no more. Good-bye, friends. [*Mrs. Henderson, speaking in her own voice.*] Go away, go away! [*She wakes.*] I saw him a moment ago, has he spoilt the séance again?

Mrs. Mallet. Yes, Mrs. Henderson, my husband came, but he was driven away.

Dr. Trench. Mrs. Henderson is very tired. We must leave her to rest. [*To Mrs. Henderson.*] You did your best and nobody can do more than that.   [*He takes out money.*

Mrs. Henderson. No. . . . No. . . . I cannot take any money, not after a séance like that.

Dr. Trench. Of course you must take it, Mrs. Henderson.

[*He puts money on table, and Mrs. Henderson gives a furtive glance to see how much it is. She does the same as each sitter lays down his or her money.*

Mrs. Mallet. A bad séance is just as exhausting as a good séance, and you must be paid.

Mrs. Henderson. No. . . . No. . . . Please don't. It is very wrong to take money for such a failure.   [*Mrs. Mallet lays down money*

Cornelius Patterson. A jockey is paid whether he wins or not.

[*He lays down money.*

Miss Mackenna. That spirit rather thrilled me.

[*She lays down money.*

Mrs. Henderson. If you insist, I must take it.

Abraham Johnson. I shall pray for you to-night. I shall ask God to bless and protect your séances.

[*He lays down money. All go out except John Corbet and Mrs. Henderson.*

John Corbet. I know you are tired, Mrs. Henderson, but I must speak to you. I have been deeply moved by what I have heard. This is my contribution to prove that I am satisfied, completely satisfied.

[*He puts a note on the table.*

Mrs. Henderson. A pound note—nobody ever gives me more than ten shillings, and yet the séance was a failure.

John Corbet [*sitting down near Mrs. Henderson*]. When I say I am satisfied I do not mean that I am convinced it was the work of spirits. I prefer to think that you created it all, that you are an accomplished actress and scholar. In my essay for my Cambridge doctorate I examine all the explanations of Swift's celibacy offered by his biographers and prove that the explanation you selected was the only plausible one. But there is something I must ask you. Swift was the chief representative of the intellect of his epoch, that arrogant intellect free at last from superstition. He foresaw its collapse. He foresaw Democracy, he must have dreaded the future. Did he refuse to beget children because of that dread? Was Swift mad? Or was it the intellect itself that was mad?

Mrs. Henderson. Who are you talking of, sir?

John Corbet. Swift, of course.

Mrs. Henderson. Swift? I do not know anybody called Swift.

John Corbet. Jonathan Swift, whose spirit seemed to be present to-night.

Mrs. Henderson. What? That dirty old man?

John Corbet. He was neither old nor dirty when Stella and Vanessa loved him.

Mrs. Henderson. I saw him very clearly just as I woke up. His clothes were dirty, his face covered with boils. Some disease had made one of his eyes swell up, it stood out from his face like a hen's egg.

John Corbet. He looked like that in his old age. Stella had been dead a long time. His brain had gone, his friends had deserted him. The man appointed to take care of him beat him to keep him quiet.

Mrs. Henderson. Now they are old, now they are young. They change all in a moment as their thought changes. It is sometimes a terrible thing to be out of the body, God help us all.

Dr. Trench [*at doorway*]. Come along, Corbet, Mrs. Henderson is tired out.

John Corbet. Good-bye, Mrs. Henderson.

[*He goes out with Dr. Trench. All the sitters except Miss Mackenna, who has returned to her room, pass along the passage on their way to the front door. Mrs. Henderson counts the money, finds her purse, which is in a vase on the mantelpiece, and puts the money in it.*

Mrs. Henderson. How tired I am! I'd be the better of a cup of tea. [*She finds the teapot and puts kettle on fire, and then as she crouches down by the hearth suddenly lifts up her hands and counts her fingers, speaking in Swift's voice.*] Five great Ministers that were my friends are gone, ten great Ministers that were my friends are gone. I have not fingers enough to count the great Ministers that were my friends and that are gone. [*She wakes with a start and speaks in her own voice.*] Where did I put that tea-caddy? Ah! there it is. And there should be a cup and saucer. [*She finds the saucer.*] But where's the cup? [*She moves aimlessly about the stage and then, letting the saucer fall and break, speaks in Swift's voice.*] Perish the day on which I was born!

THE END

A FULL MOON IN MARCH

1935

A FULL MOON IN MARCH

PERSONS IN THE PLAY

First Attendant   The Queen
Second Attendant   The Swineherd

The Swineherd wears a half-savage mask covering the upper part of his face. He is bearded. When the inner curtain rises for the second time the player who has hitherto taken the part of the Queen is replaced by a dancer.

When the stage curtain rises, two Attendants, an elderly woman and a young man, are discovered standing before an inner curtain.

First Attendant. What do we do?
  What part do we take?
  What did he say?
Second Attendant. Join when we like,
  Singing or speaking.
First Attendant. Before the curtain rises on the play?
Second Attendant. Before it rises.
First Attendant. What do we sing?
Second Attendant. 'Sing anything, sing any old thing,' said he.
First Attendant. Come then and sing about the dung of swine.
    [*They slowly part the inner curtain. The Second Attendant sings
    —the First Attendant may join in the singing at the end of the
    first or second verse. The First Attendant has a soprano, the
    Second a bass voice.*
Second Attendant. Every loutish lad in love
               Thinks his wisdom great enough,
               What cares love for this and that?
               To make all his parish stare,
               As though Pythagoras wandered there.
               Crown of gold or dung of swine.

               Should old Pythagoras fall in love
               Little may he boast thereof.

What cares love for this and that?
Days go by in foolishness.
O how great their sweetness is!
Crown of gold or dung of swine.

Open wide those gleaming eyes,
That can make the loutish wise.
What cares love for this and that?
Make a leader of the schools
Thank the Lord, all men are fools.
Crown of gold or dung of swine.

[*They sit at one side of stage near audience. If they are musicians, they have beside them drum, flute and zither. The Queen is discovered seated and veiled.*

The Queen [*stretching and yawning*]. What man is at the door?
Second Attendant. Nobody, Queen.
The Queen. Some man has come, some terrifying man,
    For I have yawned and stretched myself three times.
    Admit him, Captain of the Guard. . . .
Second Attendant [*speaking as Captain of the Guard*]. He comes.
                    Enter the Swineherd
The Swineherd. The beggars of my country say that he
    That sings you best shall take you for a wife.
The Queen. He that best sings his passion.
The Swineherd.   And they say
    The kingdom is added to the gift.
The Queen.   I swore it.
The Swineherd. But what if some blind aged cripple sing
    Better than wholesome men?
The Queen.   Some I reject.
    Some I have punished for their impudence.
    None I abhor can sing.
The Swineherd.   So that's the catch.
    Queen, look at me, look long at these foul rags,
    At hair more foul and ragged than my rags;
    Look on my scratched foul flesh. Have I not come
    Through dust and mire? There in the dust and mire
    Beasts scratched my flesh; my memory too is gone,
    Because great solitudes have driven me mad.
    But when I look into a stream, the face
    That trembles upon the surface makes me think
    My origin more foul than rag or flesh.

The Queen. But you have passed through perils for my sake;
  Come a great distance. I permit the song.

The Swineherd. Kingdom and lady, if I sing the best?
  But who decides?

The Queen.   I and my heart decide.
  We say that song is best that moves us most.
  No song has moved us yet.

The Swineherd.   You must be won
  At a full moon in March, those beggars say.
  That moon has come, but I am here alone.

The Queen. No other man has come.

The Swineherd.   The moon is full.

The Queen. Remember through what perils you have come;
  That I am crueller than solitude,
  Forest or beast. Some I have killed or maimed
  Because their singing put me in a rage,
  And some because they came at all. Men hold
  That woman's beauty is a kindly thing,
  But they that call me cruel speak the truth,
  Cruel as the winter of virginity.
  But for a reason that I cannot guess
  I would not harm you. Go before I change.
  Why do you stand, your chin upon your breast?

The Swineherd. My mind is running on our marriage night,
  Imagining all from the first touch and kiss.

The Queen. What gives you that strange confidence? What makes
  You think that you can move my heart and me?

The Swineherd. Because I look upon you without fear.

The Queen. A lover in railing or in flattery said
  God only looks upon me without fear.

The Swineherd. Desiring cruelty, he made you cruel.
  I shall embrace body and cruelty,
  Desiring both as though I had made both.

The Queen. One question more. You bring like all the rest
  Some novel simile, some wild hyperbole
  Praising my beauty?

The Swineherd.   My memory has returned.
  I tended swine, when I first heard your name.
  I rolled among the dung of swine and laughed.
  What do I know of beauty?

The Queen.   Sing the best
  And you are not a swineherd, but a king.

The Swineherd. What do I know of kingdoms?
                              [*Snapping his fingers*] That for kingdoms!
The Queen. If trembling of my limbs or sudden tears
  Proclaim your song beyond denial best,
  I leave these corridors, this ancient house,
  A famous throne, the reverence of servants—
  What do I gain?
The Swineherd.   A song—the night of love,
  An ignorant forest and the dung of swine.
                              [*Queen leaves throne and comes down stage.*
The Queen. All here have heard the man and all have judged.
  I led him, that I might not seem unjust,
  From point to point, established in all eyes
  That he came hither not to sing but to heap
  Complexities of insult upon my head.
The Swineherd. She shall bring forth her farrow in the dung.
  But first my song—what nonsense shall I sing?
The Queen. Send for the headsman, Captain of the Guard.
Second Attendant [*speaking as Captain of the Guard*]. I have already
    sent. He stands without.
The Queen. I owe my thanks to God that this foul wretch,
  Foul in his rags, his origin, his speech,
  In spite of all his daring has not dared
  Ask me to drop my veil. Insulted ears
  Have heard and shuddered, but my face is pure.
  Had it but known the insult of his eyes
  I had torn it with these nails.
The Swineherd [*going up stage*]. Why should I ask?
  What do those features matter? When I set out
  I picked a number on the roulette wheel.
  I trust the wheel, as every lover must.
The Queen. Pray, if your savagery has learnt to pray,
  For in a moment they will lead you out
  Then bring your severed head.
The Swineherd.   My severed head.   [*Laughs.*
  There is a story in my country of a woman
  That stood all bathed in blood—a drop of blood
  Entered her womb and there begat a child.
The Queen. A severed head! She took it in her hands;
  She stood all bathed in blood; the blood begat.
  O foul, foul, foul!
The Swineherd.   She sank in bridal sleep.

The Queen. Her body in that sleep conceived a child.
  Begone! I shall not see your face again.
    [*She turns towards him, her back to the audience, and slowly
    drops her veil.*
    The Attendants close the inner curtain.
Second Attendant. What do we sing?
First Attendant.   An ancient Irish Queen
  That stuck a head upon a stake.
Second Attendant.   Her lover's head;
  But that's a different queen, a different story.
First Attendant. He had famished in a wilderness,
                  Braved lions for my sake,
                  And all men lie that say that I
                  Bade that swordsman take
                  His head from off his body
                  And set it on a stake.

                  He swore to sing my beauty
                  Though death itself forbade.
                  They lie that say, in mockery
                  Of all that lovers said,
                  Or in mere woman's cruelty
                  I bade them fetch his head.
                              [*They begin to part the inner curtain.*
                  O what innkeeper's daughter
                  Shared the Byzantine crown?
                  Girls that have governed cities,
                  Or burned great cities down,
                  Have bedded with their fancy-man
                  Whether a king or clown;

                  Gave their bodies, emptied purses
                  For praise of clown or king,
                  Gave all the love that women know!
                  O they had their fling,
                  But never stood before a stake
                  And heard the dead lips sing.

  [*The Queen is discovered standing exactly as before, the dropped
  veil at her side, but she holds above her head the severed head
  of the Swineherd. Her hands are red. There are red blotches
  upon her dress, not realistically represented: red gloves, some
  pattern of red cloth.*

First Attendant. Her lips are moving.

Second Attendant.   She has begun to sing.

First Attendant. I cannot hear what she is singing.
  Ah, now I can hear.

[*singing as Queen*]
Child and darling, hear my song
Never cry I did you wrong;
Cry that wrong came not from me
But my virgin cruelty.
Great my love before you came,
Greater when I loved in shame,
Greatest when there broke from me
Storm of virgin cruelty.

[*The Queen dances to drum-taps and in the dance lays the head
upon the throne.*

Second Attendant. She is waiting.

First Attendant.   She is waiting for his song.
  The song he has come so many miles to sing.
  She has forgotten that no dead man sings.

Second Attendant [*laughs softly as Head*]. He has begun to laugh.

First Attendant.   No; he has begun to sing.

Second Attendant [*singing as Head*].
I sing a song of Jack and Jill.
Jill had murdered Jack;
The moon shone brightly;
Ran up the hill, and round the hill,
Round the hill and back.
A full moon in March.

Jack had a hollow heart, for Jill
Had hung his heart on high;
The moon shone brightly;
Had hung his heart beyond the hill,
A-twinkle in the sky.
A full moon in March.

[*The Queen in her dance moves away from the head, alluring and
refusing.*

First Attendant [*laughs as Queen*].

Second Attendant. She is laughing. How can she laugh,
  Loving the dead?

First Attendant. She is crazy. That is why she is laughing.

                              [*Laughs again as Queen,*
  [*Queen takes the head and lays it upon the ground. She dances*

before it—a dance of adoration. She takes the head up and
dances with it to drum-taps, which grow quicker and quicker.
As the drum-taps approach their climax, she presses her lips to
the lips of the head. Her body shivers to very rapid drum-taps.
The drum-taps cease. She sinks slowly down, holding the head
to her breast. The Attendants close inner curtain, singing, and
then stand one on either side while the stage curtain descends.

Second Attendant. Why must those holy, haughty feet descend
From emblematic niches, and what hand
Ran that delicate raddle through their white?
My heart is broken, yet must understand.
What do they seek for? Why must they descend?

First Attendant. For desecration and the lover's night.

Second Attendant. I cannot face that emblem of the moon
Nor eyelids that the unmixed heavens dart,
Nor stand upon my feet, so great a fright
Descends upon my savage, sunlit heart.
What can she lack whose emblem is the moon?

First Attendant. But desecration and the lover's night.

Second Attendant. Delight my heart with sound; speak yet again.
But look and look with understanding eyes
Upon the pitchers that they carry; tight
Therein all time's completed treasure is:
What do they lack? O cry it out again.

First Attendant. Their desecration and the lover's night.

THE END

THE KING OF
THE GREAT CLOCK TOWER

1935

TO
NINETTE DE VALOIS

ASKING PARDON FOR COVERING
HER EXPRESSIVE FACE WITH A MASK

THE KING OF THE GREAT CLOCK TOWER

PERSONS IN THE PLAY

First Attendant   The King
Second Attendant   The Queen
              The Stroller

When the stage curtain rises it shows an inner curtain whereon is per-
haps a stencilled pattern of dancers. At the right and left sides of the
proscenium are a drum and gong. The Queen should wear a beautiful
impassive mask; the Stroller a wild half-savage mask. It should cover
the upper part of his face, the lower part being hidden by his red
beard. The Attendants stand by drum and gong; they slowly part the
curtains, singing.

Second Attendant. They dance all day that dance in Tir-nan-oge.
First Attendant. There every lover is a happy rogue;
    And should he speak, it is the speech of birds.
    No thought has he, and therefore has no words,
    No thought because no clock, no clock because
    If I consider deeply, lad and lass,
    Nerve touching nerve upon that happy ground,
    Are bobbins where all time is bound and wound.
Second Attendant. O never may that dismal thread run loose;
First Attendant. For there the hound that Oisin saw pursues
    The hornless deer that runs in such a fright;
    And there the woman clasps an apple tight
    For all the clamour of a famished man.
    They run in foam, and there in foam they ran,
    Nor can they stop to take a breath that still
    Hear in the foam the beating of a bell.
    [When the curtains are parted one sees to left the King and Queen
    upon two thrones, which may be two cubes. There should be two
    cubes upon the opposite side to balance them. The background
    may be a curtain hung in a semicircle, or a semicircle of one-
    foot Craig screens.
    The two Attendants sit down by drum and gong. They remain
    facing the audience at either side of the stage, but a little in
    the shadow.

The King. A year ago you walked into this house,
   A year ago to-night. Though neither I
   Nor any man could tell your family,
   Country or name, I put you on that throne.
   And now before the assembled court, before
   Neighbours, attendants, courtiers, men-at-arms,
   I ask your country, name and family,
   And not for the first time. Why sit you there
   Dumb as an image made of wood or metal,
   A screen between the living and the dead?
   All persons here assembled, and because
   They think that silence unendurable,
   Fix eyes upon you.

> [*There is a pause. The Queen neither speaks nor moves. First
> Attendant strikes the drum three times.*]

                        Captain of the Guard!
   Some traveller strikes a blow upon the gate.
   Open. Admit him.

First Attendant [*speaking as Captain of the Guard, without turning
   his head*]. I admit him, King.

> *The Stroller enters*

The King. What is your name?

The Stroller.   Enough that I am called
   A stroller and a fool, that you are called
   King of the Great Clock Tower.

The King.   What do you want?

The Stroller. A year ago I heard a brawler say
   That you had married with a woman called
   Most beautiful of her sex. I am a poet.
   From that day out I put her in my songs,
   And day by day she grew more beautiful.
   Hard-hearted men that plough the earth and sea
   Sing what I sing, yet I that sang her first
   Have never seen her face.

The King.   Have you no wife,
   Mistress or friend to put into a song?

The Stroller. I had a wife. The image in my head
   Made her appear fat, slow, thick of the limbs,
   In all her movements like a Michaelmas goose.
   I left her, but a night or two ago
   I ate my sausage at a tavern table—
   A stroller and a man of no account
   I dine among the ganders—a gander scoffed,

Said I would drink myself to sleep, or cry
My head among the dishes on the table,
Because of a woman I had never seen.
The King. But what have I to do with it?
The Stroller.   Send for the Queen.
The ganders cannot scoff when I have seen her.
The King. He seems a most audacious brazen man,
   Not caring what he speaks of, nor to whom,
   Nor where he stands.
The Stroller.   But never have I said
   Brazen, audacious, disrespectful words
   Of the image in my head. Summon her in
   That I may look on its original.
The King. She is at my side.
The Stroller.   The Queen of the Great Clock Tower?
The King. The Queen of the Great Clock Tower is at my side.
The Stroller. Neither so red, nor white, nor full in the breast
   As I had thought. What matter for all that
   So long as I proclaim her everywhere
   Most beautiful!
The King.   Go now that you have seen!
The Stroller. Not yet, for on the night the gander gabbed
   I swore that I would see the Queen, and that—
   My God, but I was drunk—the Queen would dance
   And dance to me alone.
The King.   What?
The Stroller.   Dance, and dance
   Till I grow grateful, and grown grateful sing.
The King. Sing out you may, but not from gratitude.
   Guard, flog this man!
The Stroller.   What, flog a sacred man?
The King. A sacred man?
The Stroller.   I ran to the Boyne Water
   And where a sea-mew and the salt sea wind
   Yelled Godhead, on a round green hillock lay;
   Nine days I fasted there—but that's a secret
   Between us three—then Aengus and the Gods
   Appeared, and when I said what I had sworn
   Shouted approval. Then great Aengus spoke—
   O listen, for I speak his very words—
   'On stroke of midnight when the old year dies,
   Upon that stroke, the tolling of that bell,
   The Queen shall kiss your mouth,'—his very words—

Your Queen, my mouth, the Queen shall kiss my mouth.

The King. Come, Captain of the Guard.

First Attendant [speaking as Captain of the Guard]. King, I am here.

The King. This man insults me and insults the Queen.

   Take him and bring me his head.

First Attendant [speaking as Captain of the Guard]. I take him, King.

The Stroller. I go; but this must happen:

                         [Counting on his fingers] First the Queen

   Will dance before me, second I shall sing.

The King. What, sing without a head?

The Stroller.   Grateful I sing,

   Then, grateful in her turn, the Queen will kiss

   My mouth because it sang.

The King.   Stand where you are!

   Stand! All from the beginning has been lies,

   Extravagance and lies. Who is this man?

   Perhaps if you will speak, and speak the truth,

   I may not kill him. What? You will not speak?

   Then take him, Captain of the Guard.

First Attendant [speaking as Captain of the Guard]. I take him.

The King. And bring his head as evidence of his death.

   If he was not your lover in that place

   You come from, if the nothing that he seems,

   A stroller and a fool, a rambling rogue

   That has insulted you, laugh, dance or sing,

   Do something, anything. I care not what

   So that you move—but why those staring eyes?

Second Attendant [singing as Queen in a low voice].

                O, what may come

                Into my womb?

The King. Ah! That is better. Let the voice ring out

   Let everybody hear that song of joy.

Second Attendant [singing as Queen].

                 He longs to kill

                 My body, until

                 That sudden shudder

                 And limbs lie still.

                 O, what may come

                 Into my womb,

                 What caterpillar

                 My beauty consume?

The King. I do not know the meaning of those words

That have a scornful sound.
> [*The King goes to right and returns with the head of the Stroller, and lays it upon the cubical throne to the right nearest audience.*

Sing, Stroller and fool.
Open that mouth, my Queen awaits a song.
> [*The Queen begins to dance*

Dance, turn him into mockery with a dance!
No woman ever had a better thought.
All here applaud that thought. Dance, woman, dance!
Neither so red, nor white, nor full in the breast,
That's what he said! Dance, give him scorn for scorn,
Display your beauty, spread your peacock tail.
> [*The Queen dances, then takes up the severed head and stands in centre of the stage facing audience, the severed head upon her shoulder.*

The King. His eyelids tremble, his lips begin to move.
First Attendant [*singing as Head in a low voice.*]
> Clip and lip and long for more—

The King. O, O, they have begun to sing.
First Attendant [*singing as Head*].

> Clip and lip and long for more,
> Mortal men our abstracts are;
> *What of the hands on the Great Clock face?*
> All those living wretches crave
> Prerogatives of the dead that have
> Sprung heroic from the grave.
> *A moment more and it tolls midnight.*

> Crossed fingers there in pleasure can
> Exceed the nuptial bed of man;
> *What of the hands on the Great Clock face?*
> A nuptial bed exceed all that
> Boys at puberty have thought,
> Or sibyls in a frenzy sought.
> *A moment more and it tolls midnight.*

> What's prophesied? What marvel is
> Where the dead and living kiss?
> *What of the hands on the Great Clock face?*
> Sacred Virgil never sang
> All the marvel there begun,
> But there's a stone upon my tongue.
> *A moment more and it tolls midnight.*

[*When the song has finished, the dance begins again, the Clock strikes. The strokes are represented by blows on a gong struck by Second Attendant. The Queen dances to the sound, and at the last stroke presses her lips to the lips of the head. The King has risen and drawn his sword. The Queen lays the head upon her breast, and fixes her eyes upon him. He appears about to strike, but kneels, laying the sword at her feet. The two Attendants rise singing, and slowly close the inner curtain.*

First Attendant. O, but I saw a solemn sight;
　　　　Said the rambling, shambling travelling-man;
　　　　Castle Dargan's ruin all lit,
　　　　Lovely ladies dancing in it.
Second Attendant. What though they danced! Those days are gone,
　　　　Said the wicked, crooked, hawthorn tree;
　　　　Lovely lady or gallant man
　　　　Are blown cold dust or a bit of bone.
First Attendant. O, what is life but a mouthful of air?
　　　　Said the rambling, shambling travelling-man;
　　　　Yet all the lovely things that were
　　　　Live, for I saw them dancing there.
[*The Queen has come down stage and now stands framed in the half-closed curtains.*
Second Attendant. Nobody knows what may befall,
　　　　Said the wicked, crooked, hawthorn tree.
　　　　I have stood so long by a gap in the wall
　　　　Maybe I shall not die at all.
　　　　　　[*The outer curtain descends*]

ALTERNATIVE SONG FOR THE SEVERED HEAD

　　　　Saddle and ride, I heard a man say,
　　　　Out of Ben Bulben and Knocknarea,
　　　　What says the Clock in the Great Clock Tower?
　　　　All those tragic characters ride
　　　　But turn from Rosses' crawling tide,
　　　　The meet's upon the mountain side.
　　　　A slow low note and an iron bell.

　　　　What brought them there so far from their home,
　　　　Cuchulain that fought night long with the foam,
　　　　What says the Clock in the Great Clock Tower?

Niam that rode on it; lad and lass
That sat so still and played at the chess?
What but heroic wantonness?
A slow low note and an iron bell.

Aleel, his Countess; Hanrahan
That seemed but a wild wenching man;
What says the Clock in the Great Clock Tower?
And all alone comes riding there
The King that could make his people stare,
Because he had feathers instead of hair.
A slow low note and an iron bell.

THE END

THE HERNE'S EGG
1938

THE HERNE'S EGG

PERSONS IN THE PLAY

Congal, *King of Connacht*
Aedh, *King of Tara*
Corney, *Attracta's servant*
Mike, Pat, Malachi, Mathias, Peter, John, *Connacht soldiers*

Attracta, *A Priestess*
Kate, Agnes, Mary, *Friends of Attracta*
A Fool
Soldiers of Tara

SCENE I

Mist and rocks; high up on backcloth a rock, its base hidden in mist; on this rock stands a great herne. All should be suggested, not painted realistically. Many men fighting with swords and shields, but sword and sword, shield and sword, never meet. The men move rhythmically as if in a dance; when swords approach one another cymbals clash; when swords and shields approach drums boom. The battle flows out at one side; two Kings are left fighting in the centre of the stage; the battle returns and flows out at the other side. The two Kings remain, but are now face to face and motionless. They are Congal, King of Connacht, and Aedh, King of Tara.

Congal. How many men have you lost?
Aedh. Some five-and-twenty men.
Congal. No need to ask my losses.
Aedh. Your losses equal mine.
Congal. They always have and must.
Aedh. Skill, strength, arms matched.
Congal. Where is the wound this time?
Aedh. There, left shoulder-blade.
Congal. Here, right shoulder-blade.
Aedh. Yet we have fought all day.
Congal. This is our fiftieth battle.
Aedh. And all were perfect battles.
Congal. Come, sit upon this stone.
 Come and take breath awhile.
Aedh. From daybreak until noon,
 Hopping among these rocks.

Congal. Nothing to eat or drink.
Aedh. A story is running round
  Concerning two rich fleas.
Congal. We hop like fleas, but war
  Has taken all our riches.
Aedh. Rich, and rich, so rich that they
  Retired and bought a dog.
Congal. Finish the tale and say
  What kind of dog they bought.
Aedh. Heaven knows.
Congal.   You must have thought
  What kind of dog they bought
Aedh. Heaven knows.
Congal.   Unless you say,
  I'll up and fight all day.
Aedh. A fat, square, lazy dog,
  No sort of scratching dog.

SCENE II

The same place as in previous scene. Corney enters, leading a Donkey, a donkey on wheels like a child's toy, but life-size.

Corney. A tough, rough mane, a tougher skin,
  Strong legs though somewhat thin,
  A strong body, a level line
  Up to the neck along the spine.
  All good points, and all are spoilt
  By that rapscallion Clareman's eye!
  What if before your present shape
  You could slit purses and break hearts,
  You are a donkey now, a chattel,
  A taker of blows, not a giver of blows.
  No tricks, you're not in County Clare,
  No, not one kick upon the shin.
    [*Congal, Pat, Mike, James, Mathias, Peter, John, enter, in the
    dress and arms of the previous scene but without shields.*
Congal. I have learned of a great hernery
  Among these rocks, and that a woman,
  Prophetess or priestess, named Attracta,
  Owns it—take this donkey and man,
  Look for the creels, pack them with eggs.

Mike. Manners!

Congal.   This man is in the right.
  I will ask Attracta for the eggs
  If you will tell how to summon her.

Corney. A flute lies there upon the rock
  Carved out of a herne's thigh.
  Go pick it up and play the tune
  My mother calls 'The Great Herne's Feather'.
  If she has a mind to come, she will come.

Congal. That's a queer way of summoning.

Corney. This is a holy place and queer;
  But if you do not know that tune,
  Custom permits that I should play it,
  But you must cross my hand with silver.
                    [*Congal gives money, and Corney plays flute.*

Congal. Go pack the donkey creels with eggs.
              [*All go out except Congal and Mike. Attracta enters.*

Attracta. For a thousand or ten thousand years,
  For who can count so many years,
  Some woman has lived among these rocks,
  The Great Herne's bride, or promised bride,
  And when a visitor has played the flute
  Has come or not. What would you ask?

Congal. Tara and I have made a peace;
  Our fiftieth battle fought, there is need
  Of preparation for the next;
  He and all his principal men,
  I and all my principal men,
  Take supper at his principal house
  This night, in his principal city, Tara,
  And we have set our minds upon
  A certain novelty or relish.

Mike. Herne's eggs.

Congal.   This man declares our need;
  A donkey, both creels packed with eggs,
  Somebody that knows the mind of a donkey
  For donkey-boy.

Attracta.   Custom forbids:
  Only the women of these rocks,
  Betrothed or married to the Herne,
  The god or ancestor of hernes,
  Can eat, handle, or look upon those eggs.

Congal. Refused! Must old campaigners lack

The one sole dish that takes their fancy,
My cooks what might have proved their skill,
Because a woman thinks that she
Is promised or married to a bird?

Mike. Mad!

Congal. Mad! This man is right,
But you are not to blame for that.
Women thrown into despair
By the winter of their virginity
Take its abominable snow,
As boys take common snow, and make
An image of god or bird or beast
To feed their sensuality:
Ovid had a literal mind,
And though he sang it neither knew
What lonely lust dragged down the gold
That crept on Danae's lap, nor knew
What rose against the moony feathers
When Leda lay upon the grass.

Attracta. There is no reality but the Great Herne.

Mike. The cure.

Congal. Why, that is easy said;
An old campaigner is the cure
For everything that woman dreams—
Even I myself, had I but time.

Mike. Seven men.

Congal. This man of learning means
That not a weather-stained, war-battered
Old campaigner such as I,—
But seven men packed into a day
Or dawdled out through seven years—
Are needed to melt down the snow
That's fallen among these wintry rocks.

Attracta. There is no happiness but the Great Herne.

Congal. It may be that life is suffering,
But youth that has not yet known pleasure
Has not the right to say so; pick,
Or be picked by seven men,
And we shall talk it out again.

Attracta. Being betrothed to the Great Herne
I know what may be known: I burn
Not in the flesh but in the mind;
Chosen out of all my kind

That I may lie in a blazing bed
And a bird take my maidenhead,
To the unbegotten I return,
All a womb and a funeral urn.
   *[Enter Corney, Pat, James, Mathias, etc., with Donkey. A creel
   packed with eggs is painted upon the side of the Donkey.*
Corney. Think of yourself; think of the songs:
   Bride of the Herne, and the Great Herne's bride,
   Grow terrible: go into a trance.
Attracta. Stop!
Corney.   Bring the god out of your gut;
   Stand there asleep until the rascals
   Wriggle upon his beak like eels.
Attracta. Stop!
Corney.   The country calls them rascals,
   I, sacrilegious rascals that have taken
   Every new-laid egg in the hernery.
Attracta. Stop! When have I permitted you
   To say what I may, or may not do?
   But you and your donkey must obey
   All big men who can say their say.
Congal. And bid him keep a civil tongue.
Attracta. Those eggs are stolen from the god.
   It is but right that you hear said
   A curse so ancient that no man
   Can say who made it, or any thing at all
   But that it was nailed upon a post
   Before a herne had stood on one leg.
Corney. Hernes must stand on one leg when they fish
   In honour of the bird who made it.

                'This they nailed upon a post,
                On the night my leg was lost,'
                Said the old, old herne that had but one leg.

                'He that a herne's egg dare steal
                Shall be changed into a fool,'
                Said the old, old herne that had but one leg.

                'And to end his fool breath
                At a fool's hand meet his death,'
                Said the old, old herne that had but one leg.

I think it was the Great Herne made it,
Pretending that he had but the one leg
To fool us all; but Great Herne or another
It has failed these thousand years.
Congal. That I shall live and die a fool,
  And die upon some battlefield
  At some fool's hand, is but natural,
  And needs no curse to bring it.
Mike.   Pickled!
Congal. He says that I am an old campaigner,
  Robber of sheepfolds and cattle trucks,
  So cursed from morning until midnight
  There is not a quarter of an inch
  To plaster a new curse upon.
Corney.   Luck!
Congal. Adds that your luck begins when you
  Recall that though we took those eggs
  We paid with good advice; and then
  Take to your bosom seven men.
    [*Congal, Mike, Corney, Mathias, James, and Donkey go out.
    Enter timidly three girls, Kate, Agnes, Mary.*
Mary. Have all those fierce men gone?
Attracta. All those fierce men have gone.
Agnes. But they will come again?
Attracta. No, never again.
Kate. We bring three presents.   [*All except Attracta kneel.*
Mary. This is a jug of cream.
Agnes. This is a bowl of butter.
Kate. This is a basket of eggs.
                    [*They lay jug, bowl and basket on the ground.*
Attracta. I know what you would ask.
  Sit round upon these stones.
  Children, why do you fear
  A woman but little older,
  A child yesterday?
  All, when I am married,
  Shall have good husbands. Kate
  Shall marry a black-headed lad.
Agnes. She swore but yesterday
  That she would marry black.
Attracta. But Agnes there shall marry
  A honey-coloured lad.
Agnes. O!

Attracta.   Mary shall be married
 When I myself am married
 To the lad that is in her mind.
Mary. Are you not married yet?
Attracta. No. But it is almost come,
 May come this very night.
Mary. And must he be all feathers?
Agnes. Have a terrible beak?
Kate. Great terrible claws?
Attracta. Whatever shape he choose,
 Though that be terrible,
 Will best express his love.
Agnes. When he comes—will he—
Attracta. Child, ask what you please.
Agnes. Do all that a man does?
Attracta. Strong sinew and soft flesh
 Are foliage round the shaft
 Before the arrowsmith
 Has stripped it, and I pray
 That I, all foliage gone,
 May shoot into my joy—
    [*Sound of a flute, playing 'The Great Herne's Feather*
Mary. Who plays upon that flute?
Agnes. Her god is calling her.
Kate. Look, look, she takes
 An egg out of the basket.
 My white hen laid it,
 My favourite white hen.
Mary. Her eyes grow glassy, she moves
 According to the notes of the flute.
Agnes. Her limbs grow rigid, she seems
 A doll upon a wire.
Mary. Her human life is gone
 And that is why she seems
 A doll upon a wire.
Agnes. You mean that when she looks so
 She is but a puppet?
Mary. How do I know? And yet
 Twice have I seen her so,
 She will move for certain minutes
 As though her god were there
 Thinking how best to move

A doll upon a wire.
Then she will move away
In long leaps as though
He had remembered his skill.
She has still my little egg.
Agnes. Who knows but your little egg
Comes into some mystery?
Kate. Some mystery to make
Love-loneliness more sweet.
Agnes. She has moved. She has moved away.
Kate. Travelling fast asleep
In long loops like a dancer.
Mary. Like a dancer, like a hare.
Agnes. The last time she went away
The moon was full—she returned
Before its side had flattened.
Kate. This time she will not return.
Agnes. Because she is called to her marriage?
Kate. Those leaps may carry her where
No woman has gone, and he
Extinguish sun, moon, star.
No bridal torch can burn
When his black midnight is there.
Agnes. I have heard her claim that they couple
In the blazing heart of the sun.
Kate. But you have heard it wrong!
In blue-black midnight they couple.
Agnes. No, in the sun.
Kate.   Blue-black!
Agnes. In the sun!
Kate.   Blue-black, blue-black!
Mary. All I know is that she
Shall lie there in his bed.
Nor shall it end until
She lies there full of his might,
His thunderbolts in her hand.

SCENE III

*Before the gates of Tara, Congal, Mike, Pat, Peter, James, Mathias,
etc., soldiers of Congal, Corney, and the Donkey.*

Congal. This is Tara; in a moment
  Men must come out of the gate
  With a great basket between them
  And we give up our arms;
  No armed man can enter.
Corney. And here is that great bird
  Over our heads again.
Pat. The Great Herne himself
  And he in a red rage.
Mike. Stones.
Congal.   This man is right.
  Beat him to death with stones.
     [*All go through the motion of picking up and throwing stones.
     There are no stones except in so far as their gestures can suggest
     them.*
Pat. All those stones fell wide.
Corney. He has come down so low
  His legs are sweeping the grass.
Mike. Swords.
Congal.   This man is right.
  Cut him up with swords.
Pat. I have him within my reach.
Congal. No, no, he is here at my side.
Corney. His wing has touched my shoulder.
Congal. We missed him again and he
  Rises again and sinks
  Behind the wall of Tara.
     [*Two men come in carrying a large basket slung between two
     poles. One is whistling. All except Corney, who is unarmed,
     drop their swords and helmets into the basket. Each soldier
     when he takes off his helmet shows that he wears a skull-cap
     of soft cloth.*
Congal. Where have I heard that tune?
Mike. This morning.
Congal.   I know it now,
  The tune of 'The Great Herne's Feather'.
  It puts my teeth on edge.

SCENE IV

Banqueting hall. A throne painted on the backcloth. Enter Congal, alone, drunk, and shouting.

Congal. To arms, to arms! Connacht to arms!
  Insulted and betrayed, betrayed and insulted.
  Who has insulted me? Tara has insulted.
  To arms, to arms! Connacht to arms!
  To arms—but if you have not got any
  Take a table-leg or a candlestick,
  A boot or a stool or any odd thing.
  Who has betrayed me? Tara has betrayed!
  To arms, to arms! Connacht to arms!
    [Goes out to one side. Music, as drum and concertina, suggests
      breaking of wood. Enter, at other side, King of Tara, drunk.
Aedh. Where is that beastly drunken liar
  That says I have insulted him?
          Congal enters with two table-legs
Congal. I say it!
Aedh.   What insult?
Congal.   How dare you ask?
  When I have had a common egg,
  A common hen's egg put before me,
  An egg dropped in the dirty straw
  And crowed for by a cross-bred gangling cock,
  And every other man at the table
  A herne's egg.   *[Throws a table-leg on the floor.*
      There is your weapon. Take it!
  Take it up, defend yourself.
  An egg that some half-witted slattern
  Spat upon and wiped on her apron!
Aedh. A servant put the wrong egg there.
Congal. But at whose orders?
Aedh.   At your own.
  A murderous drunken plot, a plot
  To put a weapon that I do not know
  Into my hands.
Congal.   Take up that weapon.
  If I am as drunken as you say,
  And you as sober as you think,
  A coward and a drunkard are well matched.
    [Aedh takes up table-leg. Connacht and Tara soldiers come in,

they fight. The fight sways to and fro. The weapons, table-legs,
candlesticks, etc., do not touch. Drum-taps represent blows. All
go out fighting. Enter Pat, drunk, with bottle.

Pat. Herne's egg, hen's egg, great difference.
There's insult in that difference.
What do hens eat? Hens live upon mash,
Upon slop, upon kitchen odds and ends.
What do hernes eat? Hernes live on eels,
On things that must always run about.
Man's a high animal and runs about,
But mash is low, O, very low.
Or, to speak like a philosopher,
When a man expects the movable
But gets the immovable, he is insulted.

        Enter Congal, Peter, Malachi, Mathias, etc.

Congal. Tara knew that he was overmatched;
Knew from the start he had no chance;
Died of a broken head; died drunk;
Accused me with his dying breath
Of secretly practising with a table-leg,
Practising at midnight until I
Became a perfect master with the weapon.
But that is all lies.

Pat.   Let all men know
He was a noble character
And I must weep at his funeral.

Congal. He insulted me with a hen's egg,
Said I had practised with a table-leg,
But I have taken kingdom and throne
And that has made all level again
And I can weep at his funeral.
I would not have had him die that way
Or die at all, he should have been immortal.
Our fifty battles had made us friends;
And there are fifty more to come.
New weapons, a new leader will be found
And everything begin again.

Mike. Much bloodier.

Congal.   They had, we had
Forgotten what we fought about,
So fought like gentlemen, but now
Knowing the truth must fight like the beasts.
Maybe the Great Herne's curse has done it.

Why not? Answer me that; why not?
Mike. Horror henceforth.
Congal. This wise man means
We fought so long like gentlemen
That we grew blind.
  [*Attracta enters, walking in her sleep, a herne's egg in her hand.
  She stands near throne and holds egg towards it a moment.*
Mathias. Look! Look!
She offers that egg. Who is to take it?
Congol. She walks with open eyes but in her sleep.
Mathias. I can see it all in a flash,
She found that herne's egg on the table
And left the hen's egg there instead.
James. She brought the hen's egg on purpose
Walking in her wicked sleep.
Congal. And if I take that egg, she wakes,
Completes her task, her circle;
We all complete a task or circle,
Want a woman, then all goes—pff.   [*He goes to take the egg.*
Mike. Not now.
Congal. This wise man says 'not now'.
There must be something to consider first.
James. By changing one egg for another
She has brought bloodshed on us all.
Pat. He was a noble character,
And I must weep at his funeral.
James. I say that she must die, I say;
According to what my mother said,
All that have done what she did must die,
But, in a manner of speaking, pleasantly,
Because legally, certainly not
By beating with a table-leg
As though she were a mere Tara man,
Nor yet by beating with a stone
As though she were the Great Herne himself.
Mike. The Great Herne's bride.
Congal. I had forgotten
That all she does he makes her do,
But he is god and out of reach;
Nor stone can bruise, nor a sword pierce him,
And yet through his betrothed, his bride,
I have the power to make him suffer;
His curse has given me the right,

I am to play the fool and die
At a fool's hands.
Mike.   Seven men.
  [*He begins to count, seeming to strike the table with the table-leg,
     but table and table-leg must not meet, the blow is represented
     by the sound of the drum.*
One, two, three, four,
Five, six, seven men.
Pat. Seven that are present in this room,
Seven that must weep at his funeral.
Congal. This man who struck those seven blows
Means that we seven in the name of the law
Must handle, penetrate, and possess her,
And do her a great good by that action,
Melting out the virgin snow,
And that snow image, the Great Herne;
For nothing less than seven men
Can melt that snow, but when it melts
She may, being free from all obsession,
Live as every woman should.
I am the Court; judgement has been given.
I name the seven: Congal of Tara,
Patrick, Malachi, Mike, John, James,
And that coarse hulk of clay, Mathias.
Mathias. I dare not lay a hand upon that woman.
The people say that she is holy
And carries a great devil in her gut.
Pat. What mischief can a Munster devil
Do to a man that was born in Connacht?
Malachi. I made a promise to my mother.
When we set out on this campaign
To keep from women.
John.   I have a wife that's jealous
If I but look the moon in the face.
James. I am promised to an educated girl.
Her family are most particular,
What would they say—O my God!
Congal. Whoever disobeys the Court
Is an unmannerly, disloyal lout,
And no good citizen.
Pat.   Here is my bottle.
Pass it along, a long, long pull;

Although it's round like a woman carrying,
No unmannerly, disloyal bottle,
An affable, most loyal bottle.   [*All drink.*
Mathias. I first.
Congal.   That's for the Court to say.
A Court of Law is a blessed thing,
Logic, Mathematics, ground in one,
And everything out of balance accursed.
When the Court decides on a decree
Men carry it out with dignity.
Here where I put down my hand
I will put a mark, then all must stand
Over there in a level row.
And all take off their caps and throw.
The nearest cap shall take her first,
The next shall take her next, so on
Till all is in good order done.
I need a mark and so must take
The herne's egg, and let her wake.

> [*He takes egg and lays it upon the ground. Attracta stands mo-
> tionless, looking straight in front of her. She sings. The seven
> standing in a row throw their caps one after another.*

Attracta. When I take a beast to my joyful breast,
   Though beak and claw I must endure,
   Sang the bride of the Herne, and the Great Herne's bride,
   No lesser life, man, bird or beast,
   Can make unblessed what a beast made blessed,
   Can make impure what a beast made pure.

   Where is he gone, where is that other,
   He that shall take my maidenhead?
   Sang the bride of the Herne, and the Great Herne's bride,
   Out of the moon came my pale brother,
   The blue-black midnight is my mother.
   Who will turn down the sheets of the bed?

   When beak and claw their work begin
   Shall horror stir in the roots of my hair?
   Sang the bride of the Herne, and the Great Herne's bride,
   And who lie there in the cold dawn
   When all that terror has come and gone?
   Shall I be the woman lying there?

SCENE V

Before the Gate of Tara. Corney enters with Donkey.

Corney. You thought to go on sleeping though dawn was up,
  Rapscallion of a beast, old highwayman.
  That light in the eastern sky is dawn,
  You cannot deny it; many a time
  You looked upon it following your trade.
  Cheer up, we shall be home before sunset.
                    Attracta comes in
Attracta. I have packed all the uneaten or unbroken eggs
  Into the creels. Help carry them
  And hang them on the donkey's back.
Corney. We could boil them hard and keep them in the larder,
  But Congal has had them all boiled soft.
Attracta. Such eggs are holy. Many pure souls,
  Especially among the country-people,
  Would shudder if herne's eggs were left
  For foul-tongued, bloody-minded men.
                Congal, Malachi, Mike, etc., enter
Congal. A sensible woman; you gather up what's left,
  Your thoughts upon the cupboard and the larder.
  No more a herne's bride—a crazed loony
  Waiting to be trodden by a bird—
  But all woman, all sensible woman.
Mike. Manners.
Congal.   This man who is always right
  Desires that I should add these words,
  The seven that held you in their arms last night
  Wish you good luck.
Attracta.   What do you say?
  My husband came to me in the night.
Congal. Seven men lay with you in the night.
  Go home desiring and desirable,
  And look for a man.
Attracta.   The Herne is my husband.
  I lay beside him, his pure bride.
Congal. Pure in the embrace of seven men?
Mike. She slept.
Congal.   You say that though I thought,

Because I took the egg out of her hand,
That she awoke, she did not wake
Until day broke upon her sleep—
Her sleep and ours—did she wake pure?
Seven men can answer that.

Corney. King though you are, I will not hear
The bride of the Great Herne defamed—
A king, a king but a Mayo man.
A Mayo man's lying tongue can beat
A Clare highwayman's rapscallion eye,
Seven times a liar.

Mike.   Seven men.

Congal. I, Congal, lay with her last night.

Mathias. And I, Mathias.

Mike.   And I.

James.   And I.

Peter. And I.

John.   And I.

Pat.   And I; swear it;
And not a drop of drink since dawn.

Corney. One plain liar, six men bribed to lie.

Attracta. Great Herne, Great Herne, Great Herne,
Your darling is crying out,
Great Herne, declare her pure,
Pure as that beak and claw,
Great Herne, Great Herne, Great Herne,
Let the round heaven declare it.

   [*Silence. Then low thunder growing louder. All except Attracta
   and Congal kneel.*

James. Great Herne, I swear that she is pure;
I never laid a hand upon her.

Mathias. I was a fool to believe myself
When everybody knows that I am a liar.

Pat. Even when it seemed that I covered her
I swear that I knew it was the drink.

Attracta. I lay in the bride-bed,
His thunderbolts in my hand,
But gave them back, for he,
My lover, the Great Herne,
Knows everything that is said
And every man's intent,
And every man's deed; and he

Shall give these seven that say
That they upon me lay
A most memorable punishment.

[*It thunders. All prostrate themselves except Attracta and Congal.
Congal had half knelt, but he has stood up again.*

Attracta. I share his knowledge, and I know
Every punishment decreed.
He will come when you are dead,
Push you down a step or two
Into cat or rat or bat,
Into dog or wolf or goose.
Everybody in his new shape I can see,
But Congal there stands in a cloud
Because his fate is not yet settled.
Speak out, Great Herne, and make it known
That everything I have said is true.

[*Thunder. All now, except Attracta, have prostrated themselves.*

Attracta. What has made you kneel?
Congal.   This man
That's prostrate at my side would say,
Could he say anything at all,
That I am terrified by thunder.
Attracta. Why did you stand up so long?
Congal. I held you in my arms last night,
We seven held you in our arms.
Attracta. You were under the curse, in all
You did, in all you seemed to do.
Congal. If I must die at a fool's hand,
When must I die?
Attracta.   When the moon is full.
Congal. And where?
Attracta.   Upon the holy mountain,
Upon Slieve Fuadh, there we meet again
Just as the moon comes round the hill.
There all the gods must visit me,
Acknowledging my marriage to a god;
One man will I have among the gods.
Congal. I know the place and I will come,
Although it be my death, I will come.
Because I am terrified, I will come.

SCENE VI

A mountain-top, the moon has just risen; the moon of comic tradition, a round smiling face. A cauldron lid, a cooking-pot, and a spit lie together at one side of the stage. The Fool, a man in ragged clothes, enters carrying a large stone; he lays it down at one side and goes out. Congal enters carrying a wine-skin, and stands at the other side of the stage. The Fool re-enters with a second large stone which he places beside the first.

Congal. What is your name, boy?
Fool.   Poor Tom Fool.
    Everybody knows Tom Fool.
Congal. I saw something in the mist,
    There lower down upon the slope,
    I went up close to it and saw
    A donkey, somebody's stray donkey.
    A donkey and a Fool—I don't like it at all.
Fool. I won't be Tom the Fool after to-night.
    I have made a level patch out there,
    Clearing away the stones, and there
    I shall fight a man and kill a man
    And get great glory.
Congal.   Where did you get
    The cauldron lid, the pot and the spit?
Fool. I sat in Widow Rooney's kitchen,
    Somebody said, 'King Congal's on the mountain
    Cursed to die at the hands of a fool'.
    Somebody else said 'Kill him, Tom'.
    And everybody began to laugh
    And said I should kill him at the full moon,
    And that is to-night.
Congal.   I too have heard
    That Congal is to die to-night.
    Take a drink.
Fool.   I took this lid,
    And all the women screamed at me.
    I took the spit, and all screamed worse.
    A shoulder of lamb stood ready for the roasting—
    I put the pot upon my head.
    They did not scream but stood and gaped.
      [Fool arms himself with spit, cauldron, lid and pot, whistling 'The Great Herne's Feather'.

Congal. Hush, that is an unlucky tune!
  And why must you kill Congal, Fool?
  What harm has he done you?
Fool.   None at all.
  But there's a Fool called Johnny from Meath,
  We are great rivals and we hate each other,
  But I can get the pennies if I kill Congal,
  And Johnny nothing.
Congal.   I am King Congal,
  And is not that a thing to laugh at, Fool?
Fool. Very nice, O very nice indeed,
  For I can kill you now, and I
  Am tired of walking.
Congal.   Both need rest.
  Another drink apiece—that is done—
  Lead to the place you have cleared of stones.
Fool. But where is your sword? You have not got a sword.
Congal. I lost it, or I never had it,
  Or threw it at the strange donkey below,
  But that's no matter—I have hands.
        [*They go out at one side. Attracta, Corney and Donkey come in.
        Attracta sings.*
Attracta. When beak and claw their work began
  What horror stirred in the roots of my hair?
  Sang the bride of the Herne, and the Great Herne's bride.
  But who lay there in the cold dawn,
  When all that terror had come and gone?
  Was I the woman lying there?
        [*They go out. Congal and Tom the Fool come. Congal is carrying
        the cauldron lid, pot and spit. He lays them down.*
Congal. I was sent to die at the hands of a Fool.
  There must be another Fool on the mountain.
Fool. That must be Johnny from Meath.
  But that's a thing I could not endure,
  For Johnny would get all the pennies.
Congal. Here, take a drink and have no fear;
  All's plain at last; though I shall die
  I shall not die at a Fool's hand.
  I have thought out a better plan.
  I and the Herne have had three bouts,
  He won the first, I won the second,
  Six men and I possessed his wife.

Fool. I ran after a woman once.
  I had seen two donkeys in a field.
Congal. And did you get her, did you get her, Fool?
Fool. I almost had my hand upon her.
  She screamed, and somebody came and beat me.
  Were you beaten?
Congal.   No, no, Fool.
  But she said that nobody had touched her,
  And after that the thunder said the same,
  Yet I had won that bout, and now
  I know that I shall win the third.
Fool. If Johnny from Meath comes, kill him!
Congal. Maybe I will, maybe I will not.
Fool. You let me off, but don't let him off.
Congal. I could not do you any harm,
  For you and I are friends.
Fool.   Kill Johnny!
Congal. Because you have asked me to, I will do it,
  For you and I are friends.
Fool.   Kill Johnny!
  Kill with the spear, but give it to me
  That I may see if it is sharp enough.   [*Fool takes spit.*
Congal. And is it, Fool?
Fool.   I spent an hour
  Sharpening it upon a stone.
  Could I kill you now?
Congal.   Maybe you could.
Fool. I will get all the pennies for myself.
    [*He wounds Congal. The wounding is symbolised by a movement
      of the spit towards or over Congal's body.*
Congal. It passed out of your mind for a moment
  That we are friends, but that is natural.
Fool [*dropping spit*]. I must see it, I never saw a wound.
Congal. The Herne has got the first blow in;
  A scratch, a scratch, a mere nothing.
  But had it been a little deeper and higher
  It would have gone through the heart, and maybe
  That would have left me better off,
  For the Great Herne may beat me in the end.
  Here I must sit through the full moon,
  And he will send up Fools against me,
  Meandering, roaring, yelling,

Whispering Fools, then chattering Fools,
And after that morose, melancholy,
Sluggish, fat, silent Fools;
And I, moon-crazed, moon-blind,
Fighting and wounded, wounded and fighting.
I never thought of such an end.
Never be a soldier, Tom;
Though it begins well, is this a life?
If this is a man's life, is there any life
But a dog's life?
Fool.   That's it, that's it;
Many a time they have put a dog at me.
Congal. If I should give myself a wound,
Let life run away, I'd win the bout.
He said I must die at the hands of a Fool
And sent you hither. Give me that spit!
I put it in this crevice of the rock,
That I may fall upon the point.
These stones will keep it sticking upright.
                    [*They arrange stones, he puts the spit in.*
Congal [*almost screaming in his excitement*]. Fool! Am I myself a
      Fool?
For if I am a Fool, he wins the bout.
Fool. You are King of Connacht. If you were a Fool
They would have chased you with their dogs.
Congal. I am King Congal of Connacht and of Tara,
That wise, victorious, voluble, unlucky,
Blasphemous, famous, infamous man.
Fool, take this spit when red with blood,
Show it to the people and get all the pennies;
What does it matter what they think?
The Great Herne knows that I have won.
   [*He falls symbolically upon the spit. It does not touch him. Fool
      takes the spit and wine-skin and goes out.*
It seems that I am hard to kill,
But the wound is deep. Are you up there?
Your chosen kitchen spit has killed me,
But killed me at my own will, not yours.
                    Attracta and Corney enter
Attracta. Will the knot hold?
Corney.   There was a look
About the old highwayman's eye of him

That warned me, so I made him fast
To that old stump among the rocks
With a great knot that he can neither
Break, nor pull apart with his teeth.

Congal. Attracta!

Attracta.   I called you to this place,
You came, and now the story is finished.

Congal. You have great powers, even the thunder
Does whatever you bid it do.
Protect me, I have won my bout,
But I am afraid of what the Herne
May do with me when I am dead.
I am afraid that he may put me
Into the shape of a brute beast.

Attracta. I will protect you if, as I think,
Your shape is not yet fixed upon.

Congal. I am slipping now, and you up there
With your long leg and your long beak.
But I have beaten you, Great Herne,
In spite of your kitchen spit—seven men—   [*He dies.*

Attracta. Come lie with me upon the ground,
Come quickly into my arms, come quickly, come
Before his body has had time to cool.

Corney. What? Lie with you?

Attracta.   Lie and beget.
If you are afraid of the Great Herne,
Put that away, for if I do his will,
You are his instrument or himself.

Corney. The thunder has me terrified.

Attracta. I lay with the Great Herne, and he,
Being all a spirit, but begot
His image in the mirror of my spirit,
Being all sufficient to himself
Begot himself; but there's a work
That should be done, and that work needs
No bird's beak nor claw, but a man,
The imperfection of a man.   [*The sound of a donkey braying.*

Corney. The donkey is braying.
He has some wickedness in his mind.

Attracta. Too late, too late, he broke that knot,
And there, down there among the rocks
He couples with another donkey.

That donkey has conceived. I thought that I
Could give a human form to Congal,
But now he must be born a donkey.
Corney. King Congal must be born a donkey!
Attracta. Because we were not quick enough.
Corney. I have heard that a donkey carries its young
Longer than any other beast,
Thirteen months it must carry it.   [*He laughs.*
All that trouble and nothing to show for it,
Nothing but just another donkey.

THE END

PURGATORY
1939

PURGATORY

PERSONS IN THE PLAY

A Boy   An Old Man

Scene.—A ruined house and a bare tree in the background.

Boy. Half-door, hall door,
  Hither and thither day and night,
  Hill or hollow, shouldering this pack,
  Hearing you talk.
Old Man.   Study that house.
  I think about its jokes and stories;
  I try to remember what the butler
  Said to a drunken gamekeeper
  In mid-October, but I cannot.
  If I cannot, none living can.
  Where are the jokes and stories of a house,
  Its threshold gone to patch a pig-sty?
Boy. So you have come this path before?
Old Man. The moonlight falls upon the path,
  The shadow of a cloud upon the house,
  And that's symbolical; study that tree,
  What is it like?
Boy.   A silly old man.
Old Man. It's like—no matter what it's like.
  I saw it a year ago stripped bare as now,
  So I chose a better trade.
  I saw it fifty years ago
  Before the thunderbolt had riven it,
  Green leaves, ripe leaves, leaves thick as butter,
  Fat, greasy life. Stand there and look,
  Because there is somebody in that house.
             [*The Boy puts down pack and stands in the doorway.*
Boy. There's nobody here.

Old Man.   There's somebody there.
Boy. The floor is gone, the windows gone,
   And where there should be roof there's sky,
   And here's a bit of an egg-shell thrown
   Out of a jackdaw's nest.
Old Man.   But there are some
   That do not care what's gone, what's left:
   The souls in Purgatory that come back
   To habitations and familiar spots.
Boy. Your wits are out again.
Old Man.   Re-live
   Their transgressions, and that not once
   But many times; they know at last
   The consequence of those transgressions
   Whether upon others or upon themselves;
   Upon others, others may bring help,
   For when the consequence is at an end
   The dream must end; if upon themselves,
   There is no help but in themselves
   And in the mercy of God.
Boy.   I have had enough!
   Talk to the jackdaws, if talk you must.
Old Man. Stop! Sit there upon that stone.
   That is the house where I was born.
Boy. The big old house that was burnt down?
Old Man. My mother that was your grand-dam owned it,
   This scenery and this countryside,
   Kennel and stable, horse and hound—
   She had a horse at the Curragh, and there met
   My father, a groom in a training stable,
   Looked at him and married him.
   Her mother never spoke to her again,
   And she did right.
Boy.   What's right and wrong?
   My grand-dad got the girl and the money.
Old Man. Looked at him and married him,
   And he squandered everything she had.
   She never knew the worst, because
   She died in giving birth to me,
   But now she knows it all, being dead.
   Great people lived and died in this house;
   Magistrates, colonels, members of Parliament,
   Captains and Governors, and long ago

Men that had fought at Aughrim and the Boyne.
Some that had gone on Government work
To London or to India came home to die,
Or came from London every spring
To look at the may-blossom in the park.
They had loved the trees that he cut down
To pay what he had lost at cards
Or spent on horses, drink and women;
Had loved the house, had loved all
The intricate passages of the house,
But he killed the house; to kill a house
Where great men grew up, married, died,
I here declare a capital offence.

Boy. My God, but you had luck! Grand clothes,
And maybe a grand horse to ride.

Old Man. That he might keep me upon his level
He never sent me to school, but some
Half-loved me for my half of her:
A gamekeeper's wife taught me to read,
A Catholic curate taught me Latin.
There were old books and books made fine
By eighteenth-century French binding, books
Modern and ancient, books by the ton.

Boy. What education have you given me?

Old Man. I gave the education that befits
A bastard that a pedlar got
Upon a tinker's daughter in a ditch.
When I had come to sixteen years old
My father burned down the house when drunk.

Boy. But that is my age, sixteen years old,
At the Puck Fair.

Old Man.   And everything was burnt;
Books, library, all were burnt.

Boy. Is what I have heard upon the road the truth,
That you killed him in the burning house?

Old Man. There's nobody here but our two selves?

Boy. Nobody, Father.

Old Man.   I stuck him with a knife,
That knife that cuts my dinner now,
And after that I left him in the fire.
They dragged him out, somebody saw
The knife-wound but could not be certain

Because the body was all black and charred.
Then some that were his drunken friends
Swore they would put me upon trial,
Spoke of quarrels, a threat I had made.
The gamekeeper gave me some old clothes,
I ran away, worked here and there
Till I became a pedlar on the roads,
No good trade, but good enough
Because I am my father's son,
Because of what I did or may do.
Listen to the hoof-beats! Listen, listen!
Boy. I cannot hear a sound.
Old Man.   Beat! Beat!
This night is the anniversary
Of my mother's wedding night,
Or of the night wherein I was begotten.
My father is riding from the public-house,
A whiskey-bottle under his arm.

                    [*A window is lit showing a young girl.*
Look at the window; she stands there
Listening, the servants are all in bed,
She is alone, he has stayed late
Bragging and drinking in the public-house.
Boy. There's nothing but an empty gap in the wall.
You have made it up. No, you are mad!
You are getting madder every day.
Old Man. It's louder now because he rides
Upon a gravelled avenue
All grass to-day. The hoof-beat stops,
He has gone to the other side of the house,
Gone to the stable, put the horse up.
She has gone down to open the door.
This night she is no better than her man
And does not mind that he is half drunk,
She is mad about him. They mount the stairs,
She brings him into her own chamber.
And that is the marriage-chamber now.
The window is dimly lit again.

Do not let him touch you! It is not **true**
That drunken men cannot beget,
And if he touch he must beget

And you must bear his murderer.
Deaf! Both deaf! If I should throw
A stick or a stone they would not hear;
And that's a proof my wits are out.
But there's a problem: she must live
Through everything in exact detail,
Driven to it by remorse, and yet
Can she renew the sexual act
And find no pleasure in it, and if not,
If pleasure and remorse must both be there,
Which is the greater?
     I lack schooling.
Go fetch Tertullian; he and I
Will ravel all that problem out
Whilst those two lie upon the mattress
Begetting me.
    Come back! Come back!
And so you thought to slip away,
My bag of money between your fingers,
And that I could not talk and see!
You have been rummaging in the pack.
     [The light in the window has faded out.

Boy. You never gave me my right share.
Old Man. And had I given it, young as you are,
 You would have spent it upon drink.
Boy. What if I did? I had a right
 To get it and spend it as I chose.
Old Man. Give me that bag and no more words.
Boy. I will not.
Old Man.   I will break your fingers.
 *[They struggle for the bag. In the struggle it drops, scattering the
 money. The Old Man staggers but does not fall. They stand
 looking at each other. The window is lit up. A man is seen
 pouring whiskey into a glass.*
Boy. What if I killed you? You killed my grand-dad,
 Because you were young and he was old.
 Now I am young and you are old.
Old Man [*staring at window*]. Better-looking, those sixteen years—
Boy. What are you muttering?
Old Man.   Younger—and yet
 She should have known he was not her kind.
Boy. What are you saying? Out with it! [*Old Man points to window.*

My God! The window is lit up
And somebody stands there, although
The floorboards are all burnt away.
Old Man. The window is lit up because my father
Has come to find a glass for his whiskey.
He leans there like some tired beast.
Boy. A dead, living, murdered man!
Old Man. 'Then the bride-sleep fell upon Adam':
Where did I read those words?

                         And yet
There's nothing leaning in the window
But the impression upon my mother's mind;
Being dead she is alone in her remorse.
Boy. A body that was a bundle of old bones
Before I was born. Horrible! Horrible!   [*He covers his eyes.*
Old Man. That beast there would know nothing, being nothing,
If I should kill a man under the window
He would not even turn his head.   [*He stabs the Boy.*
My father and my son on the same jack-knife!
That finishes—there—there—there—
          [*He stabs again and again. The window grows dark.*
'Hush-a-bye baby, thy father's a knight,
Thy mother a lady, lovely and bright.'
No, that is something that I read in a book,
And if I sing it must be to my mother,
And I lack rhyme.
     [*The stage has grown dark except where the tree stands in white
       light.*
                         Study that tree.
It stands there like a purified soul,
All cold, sweet, glistening light.
Dear mother, the window is dark again,
But you are in the light because
I finished all that consequence.
I killed that lad because had he grown up
He would have struck a woman's fancy,
Begot, and passed pollution on.
I am a wretched foul old man
And therefore harmless. When I have stuck
This old jack-knife into a sod
And pulled it out all bright again,
And picked up all the money that he dropped,

I'll to a distant place, and there
Tell my old jokes among new men.
                    [*He cleans the knife and begins to pick up money.*
Hoof-beats! Dear God,
How quickly it returns—beat—beat—!

Her mind cannot hold up that dream.
Twice a murderer and all for nothing,
And she must animate that dead night
Not once but many times!
                    O God,
Release my mother's soul from its dream!
Mankind can do no more. Appease
The misery of the living and the remorse of the dead.

THE END

THE DEATH OF CUCHULAIN

1939

THE DEATH OF CUCHULAIN

PERSONS IN THE PLAY

Cuchulain	An Old Man
Eithne Inguba	A Blind Man
Aoife	A Servant
Emer	A Singer, a Piper, and a Drummer
The Morrigu, *Goddess of War*	

Scene.—A bare stage of any period. A very old man looking like something out of mythology.

Old Man. I have been asked to produce a play called *The Death of Cuchulain*. It is the last of a series of plays which has for theme his life and death. I have been selected because I am out of fashion and out of date like the antiquated romantic stuff the thing is made of. I am so old that I have forgotten the name of my father and mother, unless indeed I am, as I affirm, the son of Talma, and he was so old that his friends and acquaintances still read Virgil and Homer. When they told me that I could have my own way, I wrote certain guiding principles on a bit of newspaper. I wanted an audience of fifty or a hundred, and if there are more, I beg them not to shuffle their feet or talk when the actors are speaking. I am sure that as I am producing a play for people I like, it is not probable, in this vile age, that they will be more in number than those who listened to the first performance of Milton's *Comus*. On the present occasion they must know the old epics and Mr. Yeats' plays about them; such people, however poor, have libraries of their own. If there are more than a hundred I won't be able to escape people who are educating themselves out of the Book Societies and the like, sciolists all, pickpockets and opinionated bitches. Why pickpockets? I will explain that, I will make it all quite clear.

                [Drum and pipe behind the scene, then silence.
That's from the musicians; I asked them to do that if I was getting excited. If you were as old you would find it easy to get excited. Before the night ends you will meet the music. There is a singer, ℨ

piper, and a drummer. I have picked them up here and there about the streets, and I will teach them, if I live, the music of the beggar-man, Homer's music. I promise a dance. I wanted a dance because where there are no words there is less to spoil. Emer must dance, there must be severed heads—I am old, I belong to mythology—severed heads for her to dance before. I had thought to have had those heads carved, but no, if the dancer can dance properly no wood-carving can look as well as a parallelogram of painted wood. But I was at my wit's end to find a good dancer; I could have got such a dancer once, but she has gone; the tragi-comedian dancer, the tragic dancer, upon the same neck love and loathing, life and death, I spit three times. I spit upon the dancers painted by Degas. I spit upon their short bodices, their stiff stays, their toes whereon they spin like peg-tops, above all upon that chambermaid face. They might have looked timeless, Rameses the Great, but not the cham-bermaid, that old maid history. I spit! I spit! I spit!

[*The stage is darkened, the curtain falls. Pipe and drum begin and continue until the curtain rises on a bare stage. Half a minute later Eithne Inguba enters.*

Eithne. Cuchulain! Cuchulain!

Cuchulain enters from back
                              I am Emer's messenger,
I am your wife's messenger, she has bid me say
You must not linger here in sloth, for Maeve
With all those Connacht ruffians at her back
Burns barns and houses up at Emain Macha:
Your house at Muirthemne already burns.
No matter what's the odds, no matter though
Your death may come of it, ride out and fight.
The scene is set and you must out and fight.

Cuchulain. You have told me nothing. I am already armed,
I have sent a messenger to gather men,
And wait for his return. What have you there?

Eithne. I have nothing.

Cuchulain.   There is something in your hand.

Eithne. No.

Cuchulain.   Have you a letter in your hand?

Eithne. I do not know how it got into my hand.
I am straight from Emer. We were in some place.
She spoke. She saw.

Cuchulain.   This letter is from Emer,
It tells a different story. I am not to move
Until to-morrow morning, for, if now,

I must face odds no man can face and live.
To-morrow morning Conall Caernach comes
With a great host.

Eithne. I do not understand.
Who can have put that letter in my hand?

Cuchulain. And there is something more to make it certain
I shall not stir till morning; you are sent
To be my bedfellow, but have no fear,
All that is written, but I much prefer
Your own unwritten words. I am for the fight,
I and my handful are set upon the fight;
We have faced great odds before, a straw decided.

   The Morrigu enters and stands between them

Eithne. I know that somebody or something is there,
Yet nobody that I can see.

Cuchulain.   There is nobody.

Eithne. Who among the gods of the air and upper air
Has a bird's head?

Cuchulain.   Morrigu is headed like a crow.

Eithne [*dazed*]. Morrigu, war goddess, stands between.
Her black wing touched me upon the shoulder, and
All is intelligible.   [*The Morrigu goes out.*
   Maeve put me in a trance.
Though when Cuchulain slept with her as a boy
She seemed as pretty as a bird, she has changed,
She has an eye in the middle of her forehead.

Cuchulain. A woman that has an eye in the middle of her forehead!
A woman that is headed like a crow!
But she that put those words into your mouth
Had nothing monstrous; you put them there yourself;
You need a younger man, a friendlier man,
But, fearing what my violence might do,
Thought out these words to send me to my death,
And were in such excitement you forgot
The letter in your hand.

Eithne.   Now that I wake
I say that Maeve did nothing out of reason;
What mouth could you believe if not my mouth?

Cuchulain. When I went mad at my son's death and drew
My sword against the sea, it was my wife
That brought me back.

Eithne.   Better women than I
Have served you well, but 'twas to me you turned.

Cuchulain. You thought that if you changed I'd kill you for it,
   When everything sublunary must change,
   And if I have not changed that goes to prove
   That I am monstrous.
Eithne.   You're not the man I loved,
   That violent man forgave no treachery.
   If, thinking what you think, you can forgive,
   It is because you are about to die.
Cuchulain. Spoken too loudly and too near the door;
   Speak low if you would speak about my death,
   Or not in that strange voice exulting in it.
   Who knows what ears listen behind the door?
Eithne. Some that would not forgive a traitor, some
   That have the passion necessary to life,
   Some not about to die. When you are gone
   I shall denounce myself to all your cooks,
   Scullions, armourers, bed-makers and messengers,
   Until they hammer me with a ladle, cut me with a knife,
   Impale me upon a spit, put me to death
   By what foul way best please their fancy,
   So that my shade can stand among the shades
   And greet your shade and prove it is no traitor.
Cuchulain. Women have spoken so, plotting a man's death.

                Enter a Servant

Servant. Your great horse is bitted. All wait the word.
Cuchulain. I come to give it, but must ask a question.
   This woman, wild with grief, declares that she
   Out of pure treachery has told me lies
   That should have brought my death. What can I do?
   How can I save her from her own wild words?
Servant. Is her confession true?
Cuchulain.   I make the truth!
   I say she brings a message from my wife.
Servant. What if I make her swallow poppy-juice?
Cuchulain. What herbs seem suitable, but protect her life
   As if it were your own, and should I not return
   Give her to Conall Caernach because the women
   Have called him a good lover.
Eithne.   I might have peace that know
   The Morrigu, the woman like a crow,
   Stands to my defence and cannot lie,
   But that Cuchulain is about to die.
    [*Pipe and drum. The stage grows dark for a moment. When it*

lights up again, it is empty. Cuchulain enters wounded. He tries
to fasten himself to a pillar-stone with his belt. Aoife, an erect
white-haired woman, enters.

Aoife. Am I recognised, Cuchulain?
Cuchulain.   You fought with a sword,
  It seemed that we should kill each other, then
  Your body wearied and I took your sword.
Aoife. But look again, Cuchulain! Look again!
Cuchulain. Your hair is white.
Aoife.   That time was long ago,
  And now it is my time. I have come to kill you.
Cuchulain. Where am I? Why am I here?
Aoife.   You asked their leave,
  When certain that you had six mortal wounds,
  To drink out of the pool.
Cuchulain.   I have put my belt
  About this stone and want to fasten it
  And die upon my feet, but am too weak.
  Fasten this belt.   [*She helps him to do so.*
                  And now I know your name,
  Aoife, the mother of my son. We met
  At the Hawk's Well under the withered trees.
  I killed him upon Baile's Strand, that is why
  Maeve parted ranks that she might let you through.
  You have a right to kill me.
Aoife.   Though I have,
  Her army did not part to let me through.
  The grey of Macha, that great horse of yours
  Killed in the battle, came out of the pool
  As though it were alive, and went three times
  In a great circle round you and that stone,
  Then leaped into the pool; and not a man
  Of all that terrified army dare approach,
  But I approach.
Cuchulain.   Because you have the right.
Aoife. But I am an old woman now, and that
  Your strength may not start up when the time comes
  I wind my veil about this ancient stone
  And fasten you to it.
Cuchulain.   But do not spoil your veil.
  Your veils are beautiful, some with threads of gold.
Aoife. I am too old to care for such things now.
                  [*She has wound the veil about him.*

Cuchulain. There was no reason so to spoil your veil;
  I am weak from loss of blood.
Aoife.   I was afraid,
  But now that I have wound you in the veil
  I am not afraid. But—how did my son fight?
Cuchulain. Age makes more skilful but not better men.
Aoife. I have been told you did not know his name
  And wanted, because he had a look of me,
  To be his friend, but Conchubar forbade it.
Cuchulain. Forbade it and commanded me to fight;
  That very day I had sworn to do his will,
  Yet refused him, and spoke about a look;
  But somebody spoke of witchcraft and I said
  Witchcraft had made the look, and fought and killed him.
  Then I went mad, I fought against the sea.
Aoife. I seemed invulnerable; you took my sword,
  You threw me on the ground and left me there.
  I searched the mountain for your sleeping-place
  And laid my virgin body at your side,
  And yet, because you had left me, hated you,
  And thought that I would kill you in your sleep,
  And yet begot a son that night between
  Two black thorn-trees.
Cuchulain.   I cannot understand.
Aoife. Because about to die!
                   Somebody comes,
  Some countryman, and when he finds you here,
  And none to protect him, will be terrified.
  I will keep out of his sight, for I have things
  That I must ask questions on before I kill you.
    [*She goes. The Blind Man of 'On Baile's Strand' comes in. He
    moves his stick about until he finds the standing stone; he lays
    his stick down, stoops and touches Cuchulain's feet. He feels
    the legs.*
Blind Man. Ah! Ah!
Cuchulain.   I think you are a blind old man.
Blind Man. A blind old beggar-man. What is your name?
Cuchulain. Cuchulain.
Blind Man.   They say that you are weak with wounds.
  I stood between a Fool and the sea at Baile's Strand
  When you went mad. What's bound about your hands
  So that they cannot move? Some womanish stuff.
  I have been fumbling with my stick since dawn

And then heard many voices. I began to beg.
Somebody said that I was in Maeve's tent,
And somebody else, a big man by his voice,
That if I brought Cuchulain's head in a bag
I would be given twelve pennies; I had the bag
To carry what I get at kitchen doors,
Somebody told me how to find the place;
I thought it would have taken till the night,
But this has been my lucky day.
Cuchulain.   Twelve pennies!
Blind Man. I would not promise anything until the woman,
The great Queen Maeve herself, repeated the words.
Cuchulain. Twelve pennies! What better reason for killing a man?
You have a knife, but have you sharpened it?
Blind Man. I keep it sharp because it cuts my food.
    [*He lays bag on ground and begins feeling Cuchulain's body, his
    hands mounting upward.*
Cuchulain. I think that you know everything, Blind Man.
My mother or my nurse said that the blind
Know everything.
Blind Man.   No, but they have good sense.
How could I have got twelve pennies for your head
If I had not good sense?
Cuchulain.   There floats out there
The shape that I shall take when I am dead,
My soul's first shape, a soft feathery shape,
And is not that a strange shape for the soul
Of a great fighting-man?
Blind Man.   Your shoulder is there,
This is your neck. Ah! Ah! Are you ready, Cuchulain!
Cuchulain. I say it is about to sing.   [*The stage darkens.*
Blind Man.   Ah! Ah!
    [*Music of pipe and drum, the curtain falls. The music ceases as
    the curtain rises upon a bare stage. There is nobody upon the
    stage except a woman with a crow's head. She is the Morrigu.
    She stands towards the back. She holds a black parallelogram,
    the size of a man's head. There are six other parallelograms near
    the backcloth.*
The Morrigu. The dead can hear me, and to the dead I speak.
This head is great Cuchulain's, those other six
Gave him six mortal wounds. This man came first;
Youth lingered though the years ran on, that season
A woman loves the best. Maeve's latest lover,

This man, had given him the second wound,
He had possessed her once; these were her sons,
Two valiant men that gave the third and fourth:
These other men were men of no account,
They saw that he was weakening and crept in;
One gave him the sixth wound and one the fifth;
Conall avenged him. I arranged the dance.

> [*Emer enters. The Morrigu places the head of Cuchulain upon
> the ground and goes out. Emer runs in and begins to dance. She
> so moves that she seems to rage against the heads of those that
> had wounded Cuchulain, perhaps makes movements as though
> to strike them, going three times round the circle of the heads.
> She then moves towards the head of Cuchulain; it may, if need
> be, be raised above the others on a pedestal. She moves as if in
> adoration or triumph. She is about to prostrate herself before it,
> perhaps does so, then rises, looking up as if listening; she seems
> to hesitate between the head and what she hears. Then she
> stands motionless. There is silence, and in the silence a few faint
> bird notes.*
>
> *The stage darkens slowly. Then comes loud music, but now it is
> quite different. It is the music of some Irish Fair of our day.
> The stage brightens. Emer and the head are gone. . . . There is
> no one there but the three musicians. They are in ragged street-
> singers' clothes; two of them begin to pipe and drum. They
> cease. The Street-Singer begins to sing.*

Singer.   The harlot sang to the beggar-man.
        I meet them face to face,
        Conall, Cuchulain, Usna's boys,
        All that most ancient race;
        Maeve had three in an hour, they say.
        I adore those clever eyes,
        Those muscular bodies, but can get
        No grip upon their thighs.
        I meet those long pale faces,
        Hear their great horses, then
        Recall what centuries have passed
        Since they were living men.
        That there are still some living
        That do my limbs unclothe,
        But that the flesh my flesh has gripped
        I both adore and loathe.   [*Pipe and drum music.*
        Are those things that men adore and loathe
        Their sole reality?

What stood in the Post Office
With Pearse and Connolly?
What comes out of the mountain
Where men first shed their blood?
Who thought Cuchulain till it seemed
He stood where they had stood?

No body like his body
Has modern woman borne,
But an old man looking on life
Imagines it in scorn.
A statue's there to mark the place,
By Oliver Sheppard done.
So ends the tale that the harlot
Sang to the beggar-man.   [*Music from pipe and drum.*

THE END